Palgrave Studies in the Enlightenment, Romanticism and Cultures of Print
General Editors: **Professor Anne K. Mellor** and **Professor Clifford Siskin**

Palgrave Studies in the Enlightenment, Romanticism and Cultures of Print will feature work that does not fit comfortably within established boundaries – whether between periods or between disciplines. Uniquely, it will combine efforts to engage the power and materiality of print with explorations of gender, race, and class. By attending as well to intersections of literature with the visual arts, medicine, law, and science, the series will enable a large-scale rethinking of the origins of modernity.

Titles include:

Melanie Bigold
WOMEN OF LETTERS, MANUSCRIPT CIRCULATION, AND PRINT AFTERLIVES IN THE EIGHTEENTH CENTURY
Elizabeth Rowe, Catharine Cockburn, and Elizabeth Carter

Ildiko Csengei
SYMPATHY, SENSIBILITY AND THE LITERATURE OF FEELING IN THE EIGHTEENTH CENTURY

Noah Comet
ROMANTIC HELLENISM AND WOMEN WRITERS

Alexander Dick
ROMANTICISM AND THE GOLD STANDARD
Money, Literature, and Economic Debate in Britain 1790–1830

Elizabeth Eger
BLUESTOCKINGS
Women of Reason from Enlightenment to Romanticism

Ina Ferris and Paul Keen (*editors*)
BOOKISH HISTORIES
Books, Literature, and Commercial Modernity, 1700–1900

John Gardner
POETRY AND POPULAR PROTEST
Peterloo, Cato Street and the Queen Caroline Controversy

George C. Grinnell
THE AGE OF HYPOCHONDRIA
Interpreting Romantic Health and Illness

Anthony S. Jarrells
BRITAIN'S BLOODLESS REVOLUTIONS
1688 and the Romantic Reform of Literature

Jacqueline M. Labbe
WRITING ROMANTICISM
Charlotte Smith and William Wordsworth, 1784–1807

Michelle Levy
FAMILY AUTHORSHIP AND ROMANTIC PRINT CULTURE

April London
LITERARY HISTORY WRITING, 1770–1820

Robert Miles
ROMANTIC MISFITS

Tom Mole
BYRON'S ROMANTIC CELEBRITY
Industrial Culture and the Hermeneutic of Intimacy

Robert Morrison and Daniel Sanjiv Roberts (*editors*)
ROMANTICISM AND *BLACKWOOD'S MAGAZINE*
'An Unprecedented Phenomenon'

Catherine Packham
EIGHTEENTH-CENTURY VITALISM
Bodies, Culture, Politics

Nicola Parsons
READING GOSSIP IN EARLY EIGHTEENTH-CENTURY ENGLAND

Jessica Richard
THE ROMANCE OF GAMBLING IN THE EIGHTEENTH-CENTURY BRITISH NOVEL

Andrew Rudd
SYMPATHY AND INDIA IN BRITISH LITERATURE, 1770–1830

Erik Simpson
LITERARY MINSTRELSY, 1770–1830
Minstrels and Improvisers in British, Irish and American Literature

Anne H. Stevens
BRITISH HISTORICAL FICTION BEFORE SCOTT

David Stewart
ROMANTIC MAGAZINES AND METROPOLITAN LITERARY CULTURE

Rebecca Tierney-Hynes
NOVEL MINDS
Philosophers and Romance Readers, 1680–1740

P. Westover
NECROMANTICISM
Travelling to Meet the Dead, 1750–1860

Esther Wohlgemut
ROMANTIC COSMOPOLITANISM

David Worrall
THE POLITICS OF ROMANTIC THEATRICALITY, 1787–1832
The Road to the Stage

Palgrave Studies in the Enlightenment, Romanticism and Cultures of Print
Series Standing Order ISBN 978–1–403–93408–6 hardback
978–1–403–93409–3 paperback
(*outside North America only*)

You can receive future titles in this series as they are published by placing a standing order. Please contact your bookseller or, in case of difficulty, write to us at the address below with your name and address, the title of the series and the ISBN quoted above.

Customer Services Department, Macmillan Distribution Ltd, Houndmills, Basingstoke, Hampshire RG21 6XS, England

---

Romanticism and the Gold Standard

Money, Literature, and Economic Debate in Britain 1790–1830

Alexander Dick
Department of English, University of British Columbia

palgrave
macmillan

First published 2013 by
PALGRAVE MACMILLAN

Palgrave Macmillan in the UK is an imprint of Macmillan Publishers Limited, registered in England, company number 785998, of Houndmills, Basingstoke, Hampshire RG21 6XS.

Palgrave Macmillan in the US is a division of St Martin's Press LLC, 175 Fifth Avenue, New York, NY 10010.

Palgrave Macmillan is the global academic imprint of the above companies and has companies and representatives throughout the world.

Palgrave® and Macmillan® are registered trademarks in the United States, the United Kingdom, Europe and other countries.

ISBN 978–1–137–29291–9

This book is printed on paper suitable for recycling and made from fully managed and sustained forest sources. Logging, pulping and manufacturing processes are expected to conform to the environmental regulations of the country of origin.

A catalogue record for this book is available from the British Library.

A catalog record for this book is available from the Library of Congress.

Typeset by MPS Limited, Chennai, India.

Contents

List of Illustrations

Preface and Acknowledgments

This book is about money and literature. More specifically, it is about British Romantic literature and the economic debates commonly known as the 'bullion controversy' that culminated with the introduction of the gold standard in 1816. The book began as a section of the PhD dissertation I wrote at the University of Western Ontario in the late 1990s. My intent was to publish an article. It was when, as a postdoctoral fellow at the University of Toronto, I started working on the bullion controversy in earnest that I discovered how extensive the field of monetary debate was in the Romantic period. Over the next several years I built the archive of pamphlets, reviews, newspapers, broadsides, and satires, as well as economic treatises, poetry, fiction, and prose that forms the basis for the book. The bulk of the research and almost all of the manuscript were completed at the University of British Columbia as well as at the British Library, the British Museum, and the Bank of England.

When I began, few literary scholars had heard of the suspension of cash payments or the bullion controversy or even the many prominent political economists who participated in it. A colleague once said that he had had two conversations about David Ricardo in his life, both of them with me. Since then, the state of the British economy in the early nineteenth century has been the subject of several important articles, chapters, and books. These have all influenced my thinking about money and literature in different ways. But it seems to me the field has yet to answer satisfactorily its one prevailing question: what exactly is that relation? Many critics have treated it as a homology. Literature and money are both made up of signs and thus each is liable to the same structural, existential, and psychological difficulties as the other. The problem, as I explain in Chapter 1, is that this homology assumes that literature and money, not to mention language and subjectivity, are structurally parallel parts of the same abstract whole, 'commercial society' or even more broadly 'modernity'. Of course, there is no question that modern life is saturated by semiotic stimulants of all kinds: the advertising industry banks on it. Our ability to decode these signs derives from practices of figuration and protocols of genre through which just about anything can be compared to anything else. Undoubtedly such interchangeability resembles the protocols and stimulations of financial exchange. But the sense that these signs and our responses to them are part of one large, abstract experience has a history. My purpose is to look at these homologies and parallels from a new angle by telling a small part of that story, one that was a turning point in the development of both money and literature.

The *full* story, which for obvious reasons I cannot tell, begins long before the period covered by this book. Since the era of wooden tallies and cuneiform tablets, the medium we call money has had one primary function: to transfer wealth. Literature is also a medium, though its function is different: to interpret or express our feelings about the world we live in and our place in it. Literature cannot make you rich (well, not directly anyway), but can tell others what a good thing it is that you are rich or that your neighbor is not. For a very long time, the distribution of both media was restrained by the limitations of available communication technologies and by the adequacy of local traditions and beliefs. Over the course of the seventeenth and eighteenth centuries, as technologies improved and as people looked jealously beyond their localities to the goods and opportunities available elsewhere, both monetary and literary media expanded and diversified. Because the primary vehicle for the expansion of finance was print, the same technology that fostered the increase in literacy, the line between monetary and literary media became increasingly unclear. Records of shipments and lists of stock prices accompanied explanations of financial terms, guides for how apprentices should treat their customers, and moral tirades against the coarse manners of the *nouveau riche* all of which seemed, uncannily, to borrow characters and figures from the others. Europe's almost constant state of war in the eighteenth century not only increased the size of various national debts, including Britain's, at an exponential rate, it also intensified a general skepticism about where that wealth was coming from, prompting investment in rival firms and encouraging forms of communal sentiment and individual self-reliance. Private banks and companies enriched themselves by issuing loans and bills that competed with new government issues, not to mention personal credits and forgeries, and persisting forms of local credit, religious doctrine, and social prestige expressed in a variety of popular literary forms. There were attempts to consolidate the financial system, especially in the wake of several credit crises, and these became occasions for more intense public debate. In Britain, these debates came to a head in the first decades of the nineteenth century. In 1797, after an invasion scare had caused a run on the nation's banks, Parliament suspended cash payments, meaning that holders of banknotes could not redeem them for coins. As it turns out this was a canny thing to do, for the continuation of hostilities against France gave the government a very good excuse to expand its national debt and subsidize agriculture with cheap available bank credit. The gold standard was introduced in 1816 as part of a package of reforms of the coinage system that was a first step in the process of resuming cash payments after the war ended. But those who encouraged reform also believed that gold would stabilize the financial system according to universal scientific principles of production and exchange. They also believed that it would have an important residual effect: to distinguish the proper mechanisms of economic exchange from the advice of practical experts or expressions of over-confidence or dismay in the popular press that made up the bulk of economic argument.

The problem was that neither really worked: financial crises continued to happen; the income gap got larger; forgery remained rampant; and the economic debates that had created the demand for a standard in the first place continued in full force in economic and literary circles. Nevertheless, the idea that Britain had a standard became one of the keystones of nineteenth-century economic, social, and even religious thought. It did so mainly through processes of dissemination. Even as the lively press of the Romantic period promulgated and controverted this new standard – support for gold was by no means universal – the idea that some kind of standard was necessary was more widely accepted. If the standard was not gold, it would still have to have some kind of form, one that would both stand outside the arena of public finance, as gold was also supposed to, but which would not change its value in the market as gold, unfortunately, did. Refined and abstracted in this way, 'Literature' became the medium of standardization. It did so not because it functioned like gold, but precisely because it did not. In its self-conscious concern with the difficulty of not solving all of capitalism's abiding problems, British Romantic literature served as a forum for normalizing that difficulty. And because it had that capacity it could be increasingly removed from the fray of public debate. This is how we came to accept as a fundamental standard that there are no standards. My title is 'Romanticism and the Gold Standard', but my refrain is more radical: 'Romanticism is the standard'.

Might something as diverse and contested as the concept of 'literature' was in the early nineteenth century be relevant to the financial anxieties of the twenty-first? When I started this project, in 2000, the financial world was in the midst of the so-called 'dot.com' bubble, a period when in a wave of technological euphoria, investors bought up countless tiny 'start-up' Internet companies at astronomically inflated prices hoping to discover the next Google. The year 2001 marked the end of this frenzy – as it did the end of so much else. Yet, as I finish the book, in 2012, much of the world is still reeling from the biggest financial collapse in almost a century, one that was caused not by a particular fad, and not entirely by malicious mismanagement (though there is always some of that), but rather by the ordinary course of financial affairs: bank loans, mortgages, insurance, social policy. Through this period of decline and confusion, and in the face of government cutbacks, literary culture has survived; more, it has increasingly asserted its significance *beside* the world of business that it often blames for its and the world's many economic and social problems. How many entrepreneurs sponsor operas that then openly satirize, if not outright malign them to those same entrepreneurs' delight? The national media of many countries (the CBC, the BBC) have two primary broadcast mandates: news and culture. At times this double mandate can leave listeners and viewers with the sometimes puzzling sense that each mandate is out to undermine the other, such as when a stand-up comedian interviews a corporate executive or a banker. And yet, the fact that these mandates co-exist is what makes these media necessary and even, in an odd way, comforting. Academics have encountered some of the same perplexity in recent years. Faculty in the humanities in particular often feel themselves to be under considerable duress owing to the demands of financial accountability. But for the most part the students keep demanding courses that will make them 'better people' even as they expect untold riches through commercial savvy. Ultimately, how and why literary scholars came to be understood as able to meet these two seemingly conflicted demands are perhaps the underlying questions that have motivated my research.

Of course, they are not the only things that have motivated me. I have many people to thank for their support and friendship during the writing of this book. Robert Miles, Christina Lupton, Miranda Burgess, Sandy Tomc, and Adam Frank read substantial portions of the manuscript at various points and their incisive critical judgments helped shape the character and tenor of the argument. Angela Esterhammer and Heather Jackson were instrumental in seeing this project through its earliest stages and I have strongly benefited from their support and friendship since. In Vancouver, I am very fortunate to be part of a dynamic community of literary scholars, especially my immediate colleagues in eighteenth-century and Romantic studies, Nicholas Hudson, Bo Earle, and Scott Mackenzie, as well as Sian Echard, Patricia Badir, Vin Nardizzi, Stephen Buy-Bray, and Deanna Kreisel. I have benefited from the energy and talents of many students and graduate students, especially the two Research Assistants I was fortunate to hire near the beginning of the project, Karen Selesky and Eddy Kent. Among the many Romanticists whose advice and friendship have helped sustain this research are Michelle Levy, Fred Burwick, Jonathan Mulrooney, Jeffrey Cox, Michael Gamer, Paul Younquist, Alan Bewell, Deidre Lynch, Evan Gottlieb, Joel Faflak, Tilottama Rajan, Samuel Baker, Ina Ferris, Fiona Robertson, Gavin Budge, and Phillip Connell. Clifford Siskin and Anne Mellor, the editors of *Palgrave Studies in Enlightenment, Romanticism and the Cultures of Print*, were enormously patient with me. They are models of collaborative goodwill and scholarly acumen. Likewise, Paula Kennedy, Benjamin Doyle, and their colleagues at Palgrave while always professional have been kind, generous, and helpful throughout this long process. From the British Museum, Sheila O'Connell, Assistant Keeper of British Prints Before 1800, and Catherine Eagleton, Curator of Modern Money, guided me through the process of procuring images. Their colleague, Virginia Hewitt, the former Curator of Paper Money first introduced me to the huge and varied collection of bank notes and note designs that was, in some respects, the starting point for this study. Members of staff at the Bank of England Library and Historical Gallery were patient and accommodating. I am enormously thankful to them all.

An early version of the first two parts of Chapter 4 was published as '"The Ghost of Gold": Forgery Trials and the Standard of Value in Shelley's *The Mask of Anarchy*' in *European Romantic Review* 18 (2007): 381–400 (available at www.tandfonline.com). Some portions of Chapter 5 appeared in 'Austen, Sincerity, and the Standard' in Tim Milnes and Kerry Sinanen, eds., *Romanticism, Sincerity, and Authenticity* (Palgrave Macmillan, 2010) and are reproduced here with permission from Palgrave Macmillan. Another section of Chapter 5 appeared as 'Walter Scott and the Financial Crisis of 1825: Fiction, Speculation, and the Standard of Value' in Ian Haywood, ed., *Romanticism, Forgery, and the Credit Crunch* as part of the *Romantic Circles Praxis Series* (2012). I thank the editors of these publications for their feedback and support and for their assistance in arranging permissions.

I owe a further considerable debt to my family. My parents William and Madelyn have been a constant source of encouragement and helpful lively debate. My daughters, Isobel and Jennifer, were born while this book was being written. They are my inspiration. I dedicate the book to my wife Alison Brown, who survived the blood, sweat, and tears, and without whose unrelenting support the book would never have been completed.

1
Realms of Gold

> For a hundred years the system worked, throughout Europe, with an extraordinary success and facilitated the growth of wealth on an unprecedented scale. To save and to invest became at once the duty and the delight of a large class. The savings were seldom drawn on and, accumulating at compound interest, made possible the material triumphs which we now all take for granted. The morals, the politics, the literature, and the religion of the age joined in a grand conspiracy for the promotion of saving. God and Mammon were reconciled. Peace on earth to men of good means. A rich man could, after all, enter the Kingdom of Heaven – if only he saved. A new harmony sounded from the celestial spheres.[1]

Introduction: Romanticism and the gold standard

In June 1816, the British Parliament did something no one had ever done before: it officially introduced a gold standard. Until 1816, 'money' in Britain comprised a massively heterogeneous network of varying exchange practices and social conventions. It existed in a variety of forms: bullion, coins, tokens, bills of exchange, promissory notes, government bills, and banknotes. These were exchangeable in a number of different institutions: goldsmiths, shops, country and metropolitan banks, factories, and agencies. Forgery was a crime and a nuisance, but for many people it was also a way to facilitate commerce where sanctioned practices were inaccessible. Money also had social meanings. In early-modern times, money was conceived metaphorically as blood, food, animals, and birds. Money was life. It could also be death: ill-got riches were wounds; excessive debt was a disease. Francis Bacon once remarked that 'money is dirt' in both senses of the term, land and muck. Money was a means for people to calculate their social worth. It was a way to distinguish the rich from the poor, men and women, husbands and wives. Money could be given as a gift, received as a token of gratitude, held up as a pledge of honor, and hoarded as a form of rebellion. The ability to create money was a sign of ingenuity; destroying it meant power. Money was a means of escape and a mark of bondage, a charm and a curse, a ticket to ride and a prison sentence.[2]

By the middle of the nineteenth century, all that had changed. Most people regarded their bills and coins as means of exchange in a homogeneous system held together by a universal principle: the gold standard. Gold is a durable metal that retains its chemical constitution even at extremely high temperatures. It has thus been revered by many cultures as inherently valuable. But it was not only its physical qualities that made gold precious. Gold was, by tacit consent, the general equivalent for everything, the universal standard of value. Held in reserve, but exchangeable on demand, gold served as the natural limit for credit and debt: the amount of gold held by the banks marked the real boundary beyond which all modes of fiscal speculation could not go. Gold became a symbol of national prudence and individual discipline. God and Mammon were indeed one.[3]

At least, that was the theory. Although it was sometimes touted as such, the gold standard did not herald an age of sound economic reasoning and free markets. Few people even noticed that the legislation had passed, not even the radical press. Under the gold standard, the British financial system was far from a smooth operation. There were banking and stock crises in 1825, 1833, 1837, 1844, and recurrently thereafter.[4] Even when times were good, the nineteenth century witnessed poverty and exploitation on a mass scale that belied the stability the gold standard promised. Governments sidestepped the standard whenever extraneous influences affected its price or drained reserves.[5] Money remained an object of curiosity and of confusion. People held it when they should have spent, and spent it when they should have saved. Some regions adopted the standard, and others did not.[6] The courts were awash in white-collar crime, the prisons full of forgers and confidence men.[7] Though to some it was an article of faith, the gold standard was seldom indisputable.[8]

How did an economic principle that everyone knew did not really work come to play such a central role in British national identity and intellectual culture? John Maynard Keynes, whose sardonic account of the gold standard (the epigraph to this introduction) betrays his skepticism toward 'natural' market stability, had two answers: (1) protectionist trade policies throughout the British Empire made prices, including that of gold, unusually stable throughout most of the nineteenth century;[9] (2) heralded by political economists and the popular press alike as the wellspring of market exchange, the myth that gold was the universal, unchanging standard allowed people to forget their own history. 'When the actual events of a hundred years have not disturbed his illusions,' Keynes wrote, 'the average man regards what has been normal for three generations as a part of the permanent social fabric.' People believed in 'the future permanence of [their] own happy experiences' and 'disregarded the warning of past misfortunes'.[10]

While not a strictly Keynesian study, *Romanticism and the Gold Standard* takes seriously the idea that the logical contradictions, social inequalities, and variable meanings of money were absorbed into the cultural fabric of British society after the introduction of the gold standard in 1816. While the popular view in the nineteenth century was that the gold standard would ensure Britain's long-term economic stability, most politicians, radicals, financers, farmers, writers, readers, and consumers of popular literature and intellectual media were aware of the alienation, division, and disharmony in politics and social life that the gold standard in some ways suppressed and in others fomented. At the time of its introduction, more people distrusted than believed in the gold standard and many sought alternatives within and to the bourgeois marketplace in which they lived and worked. The resulting debates and disagreements entrenched a pervasive and complex idea that a standard was possible. The idea that money has a standard enabled the fluidity and freedom of the market that in other respects it seemed to deny: a society as diverse and divisive as Britain in the nineteenth century *could* be held together by the mediating force of free exchange between individuals, what we in hindsight recognize as the liberal principle of diversity within consensus. The gold standard is thus not a constitutive but a 'regulative ideal', projecting a universal or 'absolute' value encoded in concepts of divinity, genius, and universality and measuring, though not delimiting, the constantly shifting values of British commerce.[11] The standard is a product of practices, regulations, and arguments operating through institutions of exchange and networks of information. These include economic policies, religious beliefs, political debates, and aesthetic productions. The aim of this book is to trace the networks of exchange and information that made up the standard.

By a 'standard', I mean a unit or concept that measures things or ideas relative to each other. A meter is a standard of distance. A pound is a standard of weight. A dollar is a standard of money. None of these exists in nature. Gold is a scarce commodity whose market value is always in flux and whose appeal is by no means universal. In fact, to a great extent the appeal of an object like gold has nothing to do with intrinsic qualities but rather with how it looks on beautiful people or associates with certain ideas of glory or wealth – and these will change depending on who is looking at it. The same could be said for the standards used to grade undergraduate essays, rate movies, determine fashions, or elect politicians. What is interesting about standards is the extent to which people believe in their validity while knowing they are arbitrary. In the West, we take pride in endorsing whatever standards we want, changing them if we wish, and claiming them as uniquely our own.[12] Our laws and institutions ensure that differences are respected, if not celebrated. The modern standard is an example of what the philosopher Charles Taylor calls a 'modern social imaginary', a general belief about the world that has 'no ontological status' but comes to exist through the distinctions and intersections that constitute ordinary life and the various means we invent to appreciate and measure the differences that exist between individuals and cultures.[13]

To clarify this difficult idea, it will be helpful to review briefly the story of the gold standard. It is often said that when Parliament suspended cash payments at the Bank of England in 1797, Britain went off the gold standard. This is not true: there was no gold standard in Britain (or anywhere else) until 1816. In seventeenth- and eighteenth-century political economy the concept of intrinsic value was based on feudal ideals of proprietorship and stewardship. It was represented iconically in monuments, buildings, poems, and coins as the 'King's standard'.[14] In mercantilism, the dominant economic discourse of early modernity, intrinsic value referred to the integrity of the economy as a whole, its consistency and order, corresponding at once to a divine order in the cosmos, to a hierarchical order on earth, and to a healthy circulation in the body.[15] In a word, the standard of value was rhetorical, a 'rule-governed' instrument of civic administration 'whose procedures themselves were delimited by the institutions that organized interaction and domination'.[16] In the terms of this rhetoric, too much money or too much bad money was an aberration to the idea of intrinsic value. However, the actual value of the coinage in Britain (as in the rest of Europe) was determined by proclamation. Governments debased their coinages, substituting pure metals for alloys, almost routinely.[17] Decades of economic expansion, increasing demand,

and dire mismanagement obviated the fact that the system did not operate in practice as it was supposed to in theory.[18]

The response to such practical inconsistencies was a drive to rethink the 'King's standard' in a new form. If moral unity or royal authority could be imagined and encouraged perhaps the system might right itself. Such views did have some practical effects. Writers contemporary with the financial revolution – Locke, Davenant, Petty, Barbon, Rice, and others – understood that the use of cheaper instruments of exchange such as debased coinages and paper money was a necessary, indeed inevitable, consequence of economic expansion: their aim, in campaigning for full-bodied coins (in the case of Locke), land-based fiscal management (Petty), or tight government control (Barbon and Davenant) was to ensure that the system retained a modicum of order in keeping with the broader demands of the state rather than just the local interests of individuals.[19] In 1717, Isaac Newton established a firm price for the guinea, 21 shillings, in an effort to prevent good silver from being melted down and shipped abroad and a plethora of foreign coins from circulating in Britain. But Newton overvalued the guinea and the exodus of silver continued until the small change of the nation was more or less a token economy, paper money became, almost necessarily, practically and legally acceptable as cash, and the country found itself on a *de facto* gold standard.[20] After the South Sea Bubble and the failure of various other schemes, debates periodically resurged about how the government was managing the national finance, how best to control or consolidate it, and how to understand the principles by which it ran.

What is impressive about these debates is the extent to which they assumed that commerce was a fluid and dynamic system that operated, like the human body, through the power of its own circulatory drives and operations.[21] For most merchants, already used to dealing with bills of exchange and other practical modes of transfer and identification, the state's demands for centralization were an annoyance while, ironically, the state itself was coopting these very methods to ensure its own 'liquidity'.[22] By the middle of the eighteenth century, most of the national debt had been consolidated in 'the funds' and it was rare for members of the upper classes not to invest to some extent in government bonds. A series of significant decisions in the 1750s and 60s established the legality of paper money. What critics objected to was not so much the expansion of national wealth but rather the way the credit system was moving the seat of power away from the country and into the city. Yet, even those who distrusted paper credit understood its benefits. A paper system could flourish, writers like Richard Cantillon and David Hume argued, as long as it served a free market of commodities that would circulate around the body of the nation rather than stagnate in the organs of state. Eighteenth-century economics thus conceived of a double standard: on one hand, money, especially coin, embodied traditional virtues of honesty and strength; on the other, as paper, money represents the imaginative foresight and resilience of the new entrepreneurial spirit.

Not until the 1790s did the idea of a completely de-personalized objective standard, one we associate with modern finance, begin to take hold – and even then it was highly contentious. Many in finance and government did not believe it was practicable to impose an arbitrary limit on commercial activity. British finance operated through a balance between credit expansion – loans, informal credit, small city and country banks – and convertibility: at any point, holders of credit could exchange their notes at the Bank of England for gold or silver. A sufficiency of coin necessary to redeem all the notes (and other forms of credit) circulating in the country was neither necessary (as Adam Smith argued, the ideal ratio of paper to gold is about 18 to 1) nor possible. Britain's national debt had already begun to rise at a steady rate through the eighteenth century; the war against France starting in 1793 caused it to increase exponentially. A sudden reduction of credit would devastate an economy largely reliant on credit and notes. So when the British government decided to disallow the exchange of paper and gold at the Bank of England in February 1797, following an invasion scare and a demand for hard cash, it did so not to adopt a new paper money system but rather to extend a paper money system that already existed.

Of course, there was considerable outrage mainly from the opposition, who decried the suspension as a travesty of Britain's so-called 'ancient standard' and from currency traders who had been enriched by the administration's earlier efforts to enhance the nation's gold reserves. The attacks against the suspension renewed in 1809 when, after a decade of relative stability, the price of gold shot up and the country was gripped in a panic over inflation. Seizing an opportunity to criticize the government on fiscal grounds, the opposition called for a committee to investigate the suddenly high price of gold. Two years later the committee reported that the high price of gold had been caused by the Bank of England's untenable expansion of credit; the only way to bring the price of gold and everything else back down was to reinstate convertibility. The government refused, and the recommendations of the Bullion Committee, as it was called, were defeated. In the meantime, the committee's Report inspired a vociferous and wide-ranging debate on economic policy, the 'bullion controversy', that raised questions of how money and credit work, what the standard of value is, and most importantly, who has the right to define it.

The bullion controversy did not lead directly to the gold standard; as the failure of the Bullion Committee's recommendations attests, it was not a popular option. But on May 11, 1812 John Bellingham, a failed businessman who had been falsely imprisoned in Russia, murdered Prime Minister Spencer Perceval, who had been an unrelenting advocate of suspension, in the lobby of the Houses of Parliament. Perceval's successor, Robert Jenkinson, the Second Earl of Liverpool, was more conciliatory. He supported free trade and market commerce, including the gold standard. His father had outlined the theoretical principles of the gold standard in his *Treatise on the Coins of the Realm in a Letter to the King* in 1805, and the Second Earl had himself been Master of the Royal Mint for two years. As Prime Minister, however, Liverpool was pragmatic and cautious, especially on matters relating to agriculture, which were strongly connected to the currency question.[23] The cheap credit extended to farmers for wartime provisioning made them and their bankers prosperous, but the end of hostilities made the resulting inflation of food prices seem superfluous. Bad harvests also pushed the price of domestic corn higher still. Observers began to encourage the import of European corn. To protect the farmers, the government introduced a Corn Law excluding imports unless prices dropped below 80 shillings a quarter. Prices skyrocketed, farmers across the country lost their shirts, and many banks failed. The government abolished the London Bread Assize to defray bakers' losses at the high price of corn and the bakers raised prices accordingly.[24] Now the government faced insurrection from the country and the cities. It suppressed public meetings and suspended *habeas corpus*. Thomas De Quincey would later call the whole affair a 'public embarrassment'.[25]

To appease Whig and radical clamors for economic improvements – and to avoid an election – the Liverpool administration finally legislated the gold standard. It did so as part of a broader Act reforming the silver coin. Using new coining technologies developed by Boulton and Watt, and following the plan outlined in *Coins of the Realm* the silver coins could be produced as tokens while gold coins were issued 'full-bodied' so as not to circulate. On the recommendation of the economist David Ricardo, by that time one of the leading lights in the campaign for the gold standard, the government made gold available to currency traders first as bullion; stamped with an 'R', the bars were christened 'Ricardoes' by the London press. One-pound gold coins, called sovereigns, were issued in limited supplies in 1818, though the suspension of cash payments remained in effect. A committee was finally established in 1819 led by the future Prime Minster, Robert Peel, to plan the resumption. The committee duly announced that cash payments would resume – but this did not actually happen until 1821.

In the wake of these delays, the bullion controversy took on a decidedly speculative cast. For 20 years, disputants had asked who had the right to determine the standard of value. In the wake of the Corn Law crisis, they asked instead what Britain would look like under the new standard. Would it be a largely market-driven society in which the various classes, landed, professional, and working, competed openly for limited resources? Or, with agricultural protection, would Britain return to being the estate-modeled hierarchical culture it had been in the eighteenth century? Or would some new, moral society emerge? Following E. P. Thompson, historians have come to recognize that the agricultural crisis of 1815 and the economic reforms that followed it, including the introduction of the gold standard, represented a fundamental change in British culture.[26] From that point, British history is marked by rivalries and conflicts not between country and city, or land and commerce, but rather between classes of people vying for the privilege of determining not only their place and purpose within a mainly commercial nation but also the precise character of that nation as a whole.

This book examines the debates surrounding the gold standard before and immediately following its introduction in 1816 to argue that they mark the emergence of the modern standard. Rather than examine the gold standard's ascendancy in the Victorian and modern periods (from 1830 to 1970),[27] the book focuses on its formative development, in the late eighteenth and early nineteenth centuries, and particularly the series of contentious debates about currency, money, and the standard of value in order to explain how contentious it was, to show the kinds of alternatives its critics proposed, and to consider how these alternatives were, paradoxically, instrumental to the establishment of the standard. My interest in these debates over currency thus does not lie only with its place in the history of political economy or in the progress of market capitalism. I am primarily interested in the way the controversy about the standard opens up broader questions about the nature of discourse and mediation. This project is at base an archival one, since it is in the archive of economic pamphlets, journalism, broadsides, caricatures, as well as treatises, poems, and novels that the relation between discourse and standardization unfolds. The archive of pamphlets, poetry, fiction, and journals that makes up the controversy is replete with contentious and contradictory reflections on gold, paper, their relationship, and their social and political effects. The archive also includes many figures we associate with literary Romanticism: Coleridge, De Quincey, and Scott contributed directly to the debates in pamphlets, lectures, and essays; Shelley, Keats, Byron, and Austen referred to them in their poems, novels, and letters. A central goal of the book, then, is to reinterpret British Romanticism in this context.

But, conversely, my argument also depends on the idea that 'Romanticism' is not peculiar to the poetry and fiction of the period but rather occurs in many fields, including political economy, philosophy, journalism, theology, and popular politics. These discourses shared a sense that gold could *not* be the one, true, standard of value. Their attempts to institute a standard of any kind were really shorthand for a complicated nexus of intersecting and problematic economic, social, and cultural ideas. My literary claim is that through their interest in these concerns, the Romantics and their contemporaries produced self-conscious and ironic experiments with genre, form, and engagement. But my historical claim is that these productions in turn strongly influenced the theoretical and ideological formation of the nineteenth-century economy. Some of the Romantics' ideas about money were intended as alternatives to the gold standard and others, defenses of it. Irrespective of their polemical position, once these ideas entered the literary marketplace they inspired further reflections on what the role of literature in a modern economy was. As a disposition that embraced unity and division, metaphysical confidence and social anxiety, Romanticism came to supplement the moral deficiencies and logical contradictions of the economy and thus embody a standard that the economy could not sustain. To put the point simply: Romanticism *is* the standard.

Literary history and standardization

It is of course nothing new to say that Romanticism is a contradictory enterprise encompassing both metaphysical speculation and popular protest. It is thus possible to argue that Romanticism was both a product of changes in the economy and opposed to them. On one hand, there does seem to have been a preponderance of discussion about money among English and European writers during the Romantic period; this is no doubt a consequence of the unprecedented growth of global finance during the eighteenth century and of the almost constant state of financial panic during the Napoleonic War. The dates of the suspension, 1797–1821, coincide exactly with the period between Wordsworth and Coleridge's first collaborations and the death of Keats. Just as the suspension of cash payments which took Britain 'off gold' signals the advent of a ghostly, insidious, and fragile currency, so Romanticism in its depiction of ghosts, conspiracy, and fragility crystallized its problems and dangers. On the other hand, the Romantics were not exactly friends of commerce. From Wordsworth's dismayed reaction to popular culture in the Preface to *Lyrical Ballads* to Shelley's curt announcement in the *Defense* that 'Poetry, and the principle of Self, of which money is the visible incarnation, are the God and Mammon of the world', to the anti-utilitarianism of Dickens, Arnold, and Ruskin, the idea that literary values of individual conscience and fellow-feeling could provide a moral compass, a standard for commerce is a mainstay of literary humanism to this day. The Romantics expressed reservations about market finance and political economy in books and papers that were bought and sold in that same market, and in systems of representation liable to the same indirection and mistrust as paper money. Money was as much a source of moral anxiety as it was of intellectual stimulation. The Romantics were by no means unique in these concerns. Many political economists shared them, including those who supported and theorized the gold standard.

Nevertheless, monetary questions have until very recently warranted little more than a few footnotes in the mainstream of British Romantic studies. This neglect implies two broad assumptions: either there has always been a standard or there never will be one. In criticism, these assumptions usually, and somewhat paradoxically, overlapped. The New Critics and their followers read the Romantics as architects of a distinctively ironic mode of self-reflection, manifest in dialectical experiments with literary form and opposed to Enlightenment reason. But the New Critics also insisted that a writer's commitment to figuration, irony, and indirection 'implies a principle of organic relationship' between form and context that is itself reflective of tensions and ambiguities in the world.[28] Deconstructionist critics, skeptical of the New Critics' optimistic investment in reality, assumed that the figurative dynamics of literary works reflected a crisis of representation inherent in both language and money.[29] Meanwhile, cultural materialists entrenched the idea that Romantic writers on both sides of the political spectrum were suspicious of bourgeois commerce and political economy. Tories like Coleridge and Austen, they claimed, thought that trade was ruining the country and the traditional hierarchical values that had once controlled it, while radicals like William Cobbett and Percy Shelley despised the 'new aristocracy' of bankers, accountants, and their 'feelosofy' for empowering their own interests and for alienating people and communities from one another. Naturally, these writers would have expressed their belief in the 'real value' of land, gold, and domestic harmony through their complex experiments with linguistic and literary irony. Another irony is that in foregrounding this naturalism, New Critics, deconstructionists, and cultural materialists all assumed the standard form of commercial exchange.

By contrast, the crises attending Britain's paper credit system have been the subject of extensive commentary in eighteenth-century studies, and particularly on the novel. This is largely due to the influence of J. G. A. Pocock. In the 1970s and 80s, Pocock postulated the idea that eighteenth-century thinkers strongly advocated the ideals of civic virtue, civil society, and property-ownership, ideals which they inherited from an earlier republican tradition of Machiavelli, Montesquieu, and Harrington, because they felt threatened by the speculative habits of the new 'men of credit', their comfort with fluctuating prices and entrepreneurial risk, and the perpetual but largely untenable future that their accounts and stock sheets promised.[30] Responding to Pocock in the 1990s, critics such as Sandra Sherman, James Thompson, Catherine Gallagher, Liz Bellamy, and Deidre Lynch[31] argued convincingly that narrative fiction crystallized anxieties about the speculative character and effects of finance, but it could also, they claimed, model various strategies for regulating and calming those anxieties, especially among women writers whose marginal relation to the economies of patronage and monopoly publishing meant that they were far more reliant on the open market than their male contemporaries. In Lynch's account, Francis Burney and Jane Austen invented reflective characters whose 'indescribability, exceptionality, and polyvalence' presented to their readers fantastic versions of their own presumed 'deep' selfhood beyond the flat, systematic circulation of values in commercial society.[32]

More recently, the argument that literature cultivates 'deep' subjectivity from within flat, circulating media (money and print) has been reframed in accounts of the development the disciplines of political economy and literature. In *Genres of the Credit Economy: Mediating Value in Eighteenth- and Nineteenth-Century Britain*, Mary Poovey underscores the importance of 'disciplinary differentiation' that produced distinct yet competing models of value during the first half of the nineteenth century: the 'economic' and the 'romantic'. During the eighteenth century, she argues, the line between 'fact' and 'fiction' in eighteenth-century writing was far from distinct: economic and literary writers borrowed tropes and forms from each other. Poovey then traces the division of the disciplines through the questions of value made evident by the growth of the financial system and its attendant crises. What she calls 'the economic establishment' became narrower, more professional, more objective, and more scientific.[33] Literature became more self-reflexive and 'arcane', plagued by struggles and contentions that, now 'elaborated in twentieth-century graduate schools', have no value at all.[34] There are exceptions to these distinctions. Currency radicals, most notably William Cobbett, used popular literary devices to inspire their audiences to resist the new economic regime and imagine a communal society. Nineteenth-century realist fiction could 'gesture' or allude to conflicts and controversies (such as the suspension of cash payments or the collapse of a London bank) that lay outside its plot dynamics, but would only be interpreted in its metaphorical and symbolic connotations. The resulting 'undecidability' between reference and meaning allowed authors to enhance their readers' familiarity with events while 'augmenting the pleasure of reading'.[35]

Poovey's concession to the novel makes clear that to treat literary and political economy either as utterly distinct, even oppositional disciplines or as belonging to one and the same cultural disposition is to overlook the nuances of the two fields' continuous entanglement. Yet, to treat that entanglement as simply the mark of a period's literary character is to neglect the fact that such entanglements were also prevalent in its political economy. To be sure, a certain *laissez-faire* capitalist mentality was prevalent in the political economy of the Romantic period, but it was by no means predominant. The contributors to the bullion controversy – including economists, journalists, satirists, poets, and novelists – had distinct and idiosyncratic ideas of what the standard of value was and how money was supposed to work. The controversy brought to a head questions about whether a general character or standard culture was even possible.

This is the predicament that James Chandler identifies in *England in 1819* as the 'Romanticism' that persists in modern critical theory and historicist criticism. For Chandler, history explains the significance of an object or event by 'situating' it within the particular circumstances of its original context. To do this, the historian must know as much about the situation as will lend itself to the interpretation of the object. The historian thus assembles an array of types – key images, events, authors, and personalities – that define the situation. This is not simply a spatial arrangement: the arrangements of types in any given era also make peoples and cultures of different times comparable. These comparisons comprise a network of 'radical contemporaneity' exemplified by the historical novel, cultivated in institutions like galleries and museums, and promulgated in departments of History and English. But this sets up a curious tautology: objects of study come to represent the situation that is supposed to explain them. Thus, in Chandler's analysis, the more elements of commercial society are used to explain the characters in Scott's novels, the more they come to embody a particular idea of commercial society.[36] Chandler's solution to this conundrum is for critics to embrace the contingency of any claim about the past and thus to signal their own break from empirical presumptuousness. Chandler admits that such a move is profoundly 'Romantic' in orientation for the way that it foregrounds imaginative speculation over and above rational contextualization.

Chandler's hypothesis also points to an imaginative and self-reflexive streak in political economy. Most economists thought of their field as a 'science' and tried to be as objective as possible about their subject. But the debate about the standard of value was built on some astonishingly difficult and foundational questions: who has the right to say what the standard of value is? What are the proper roles of expertise and intellectualism? How might money solve the problem of social inequality? What kind of nation (and Empire) should Britain be? In raising these questions, economists and their critics had no choice but to be speculative, and those speculations in turn helped establish their credibility. But many of those political economists' deep distrust of speculation, their preference for 'real' rather than 'fictitious' values, also compelled them to question or at any rate hedge their own bets. The Romantics were not, then, speculative or subjective in opposition to an entirely objective (and thus deluded) field of economics: on the contrary, political economists and Romantics alike imagined futures and the dispositions needed to survive them. It is in the way that these fields engaged each other that the modern standard came to exist.

In making such a claim, I am operating within (and indebted to) several fields of study at once and it is from their interstices that the story I am telling about standardization will emerge. The argument that the literature of a given era can tell us something about its monetary and commercial systems – and vice versa – is a mainstay of the 'new economic' criticism. The primary assumptions of these fields include: (1) money and language, both systems of signs, are structurally similar or 'homologous'; (2) the same problems of representation and alienation affecting language are evident in money; (3) literature's and especially Romanticism's investment in sincerity, authenticity, nature, and individuality was a reaction against the malaise apparently caused by these homologous representational systems.[37] This homology actually has a long pedigree: instances of it can be traced to the eighteenth century, to the early-modern period, and to medieval and classical philosophy. It is premised on the idea that the primary function of both money and literature is representation. My argument is that this premise has a history, the history of standardization. If there is a parallel to be made between money and language it should therefore be seen in this historical light.

To an extent, my purpose is to bring the history of standardization to economic criticism. Linguistic historians use the term 'standard language' or, in English linguistics, 'Received Standard English' to describe the ideal modes of speech, diction, syntax, grammar, and punctuation prescribed by grammarians in the eighteenth century and then adopted as the 'correct' modes of writing and communicating by scientists, educators, and poets in the nineteenth.[38] Throughout this process, regional dialects, cultural variations, and technical jargon showed a remarkable tenacity. On one hand, they were judged by linguists to be substandard forms and should be avoided in general and official communication. On the other, linguistic variability was adopted by some literatures – but only insofar as it reflected differences of class and style from an imagined norm of conduct and expression. The classification of language into 'standard' and substandard forms signals the 'linguistic masterplot of purification'.[39] Recently, philologists have begun to re-evaluate this masterplot not only to trace the persistence and vitality of 'non-standard' verbal forms but also to develop a broader theory of language, genre, and rhetoric built on the premise that every linguistic utterance combines conventional generic features with local modifications. Language is not a universal entity.

A similar turn toward the historical variability of monetary forms and meanings in social life has taken place in the field of monetary history. Economic historians have largely regarded deviations from the capitalist theory of money as a neutral sign of value as at best anomalous and at worst contemptible. The view of the value of money is, as Hume first proposed, 'neutral': its function is merely to represent in a convenient form the 'real value' of commodities in exchange. In the 1980s and 1990s, several criticisms of this home truth emerged from within the discipline of economics. Deirdre McCloskey famously inaugurated the study of economic rhetoric with her charge that principles of like rational choice predominating in the discipline are products of a rigid commitment to certain underlying assumptions about communicative standards, reflecting, in turn, political rubrics of 'normal' behavior and identity. Steven Horwitz similarly urged that economic theory has been hamstrung to archetypes of linguistic representation that overlook the 'communicative function' of money. In Horwitz's 'hermeneutical' approach, 'money prices communicate preferences and tastes, as well as signal profit opportunities ... while at the same time maintaining and stable liberal order'.[40] But like early historians of the standard language, and often citing modernist thinkers such as Ferdinand de Saussure, Hans-Georg Gadamer, and Georg Simmel, as well as free-market thinkers like Milton Friedman and Friedrich Hayek, this newer strand of monetary theory uses the presumably universalizing function of language writ-large to confirm the universality of systematic market relations.

By contrast, recent historians of money are interested in the way money facilitates forms of exchange and expression between people and communities. As well as within prescribed systems of social order, valid forms of exchange occur as a means of local organization often in opposition to larger social orthodoxies. Just as recent histories of language understand verbal expression, adaptation, and revision to be inseparable from the life of a text or of a person – both being entities that exist in and through time and social relations – so recent histories of money see the values expressed in monetary forms and modes of exchange as constitutive of the identities of the people and communities who use them. Sociologists such as Geoffrey Ingham and Viviana Zelizer, and historians like Craig Muldrew, Geoffrey Clark, Margot Finn, and Deborah Valenze, argue that money changes its meaning and function depending on how it circulates through society. Muldrew, for instance, sees fluid, horizontal forms of credit exchange co-existing in local markets with more rigidly hierarchical value systems more familiar in histories of feudal and early-modern estates. Finn shows that supposedly archaic credit systems based on hierarchical notions of honor and privilege persisted in the journals, court reports, and literature of the nineteenth and early twentieth century. Focusing on the other end of the social ladder, Valenze has documented the way the English poor, and especially women, used abstract formulations of price to situate themselves within and resist social and religious hierarchies.[41]

Another area to influence this study is Romantic print culture. Rapid changes in the technology and economy of publishing made books cheaper, and changes in the law of copyright meant that massive amounts of information and new sources of literary pleasure were accessible to many more people than had been possible before.[42] The demand for reading material also enabled more people to become writers and printers themselves, which in turn prompted the use of print as a vehicle for popular protest. The printing press was a vehicle of radical protest 'with unerring consistency' throughout the periods of civic unrest and European conflict that straddled the French Revolution.[43] In the wake of such diversification, print became an object of censorship and legislation: controlling the people meant controlling information. But eighteenth-century politicians also used print to expand their influence by, for instance, producing census data, excise records, and legislative reports.[44] The demand for regulation gave rise to new educational institutions, such as the modern university, forums for intellectual debate, such as critical reviews, and venues of promotion, such as literary magazines. By organizing the diversity of knowledge, information, and opinion made possible by the press into disciplines and faculties, the new pedagogical institutions produced new systems of abstract thought, new genres of literary communication, and new modes of intellectual work.[45] Literature standardized during the early nineteenth century by enshrining a 'high culture' around which the larger field of writing might be classified and measured.

Yet, the regulative impulse was also adumbrated by a sense – born of a combination of empirical honesty and ambitious scope – that the institutions being set up to discipline and standardize knowledge would never *quite* be able to accomplish that task. The work of knowledge, that is, would never be complete and would always be developing alongside the field of writing that it sought to rationalize. This does not mean, however, that an absolute faith in the standard was transformed into absolute relativism. On the contrary: the contention over the standard, including Romantic contributions to it, helped inspire a sense that standards were necessary even if they were more fluid than they had been in the past. This is what Charles Taylor in his writings on secularism and multiculturalism identifies as the 'measure' of individual consciousness in the face of mutability and variation.[46] Of course, such realizations extend beyond the monetary realm. For instance, the control of Britain's increasingly diverse and divided population was as much a motive for economic policy reform as the difficulties of finance and debt. But these policies, like their monetary counterparts, had to acknowledge the value of diversity in order to justify their reforms, and this motive was as critical to the development of literary Romanticism as to political economy.[47]

The other field to influence my account of the standard is affect theory. Operating at the conjunction of several fields – critical theory, the history of language, cognitive science, and psychology – the study of affects starts from the idea that bodies communicate through processes of social contact that both resist and adapt to received norms of communication.[48] To think about money and the gold standard by way of affect might seem counterintuitive: we tend to think of emotions as fundamentally irrational or, at any rate, embodied as opposed to highly rational and abstract systems like money and credit. But as already discussed, the history of money is replete with instances of the way symbolic and communicative forms of exchange, some related intimately to the body, sexuality, and nature, resist generalization and regulation. With such resonances in mind, several scholars have already adapted affect theory to make sense of the sometimes fraught and vexed relations at stake in monetary exchange and the way these relations are re-interpreted in literature. Andrea Henderson has examined the way forms of subjectivity and its attendant feelings (pain, pleasure) were through the Romantic period rationalized and, in many instances, incorporated into standard norms of bodily and sexual behavior.[49] Ian Baucom argues that while eighteenth-century fiction was one of the 'discursive forms' that 'enabled the rise of financial capitalism', he draws an important distinction between the 'theoretical realism' of bank ledgers and account books, which used widely in the Atlantic slave trade turned human beings into property, and the 'melancholy realism' of literature, art, and much political economy, that emphasized the uncanny yet critical inhumaneness of the very commercial system it helped to formulate.[50] Robert Mitchell's study of 'state finance' and 'sympathy' demonstrates that especially at moments of financial crises, political economists and poets offered alternative modes of affective communication as alternatives to the dehumanizing effects of finance capitalism, alternatives that were as self-consciously 'speculative' as finance but far less alienating. Mitchell traces the role that anxiety, fear, and other emotions played in catalyzing much of the financial writing of the eighteenth century, including Scottish political economy, abolitionist literature, and Romantic poetry. Mitchell and Baucom propose that as well as disrupting standard models of social and subjective behavior, affect produces alternative systems of containment and self-regulation that produce and oppose economic policy.[51]

But even as these scholars note the influence of affect on the formation of generalized economic systems ('commercial society'), they also insist on positioning Romanticism beyond or beside it, repeating the Romantic-historicist trap of the type diagnosed by Chandler. Indeed, implicit in all of these analyses of Romanticism's commercial context is the idea that the literature of the period was responding to, even if it was not opposing, the massive general systematic entity called 'commercial society' that its historical moment had produced. I argue the reverse: the Romantics helped invent 'commercial society' by incorporating notions of value, affect, and genre into a new idea of a standard that would measure a field of varying and often independent discourses that existed alongside and around it. In this capacity, Romanticism operated in conjunction with a good deal of political economy. Over the course of the next four chapters, I delineate the transformation of two affective registers common to the economic and literary writing of the Romantic period and instrumental to the formulation of the standard. These are *confidence* and *embarrassment*. Confidence is an emotion or disposition that establishes trust between individuals and the state. Confidence grounds networks of social relations like credit, but it also underlies the regulative mechanisms that policy-makers and theorists developed to control those networks. Paradoxically, then, confidence operates through a fluid dynamic of speculation but cannot acknowledge the risks and dangers that this dynamic entails. In an attempt to overcome this paradox, political economists and literary writers experimented with another affective register that exposed and embraced the perplexities of economic exchange: embarrassment.

Confidence and embarrassment

In his 1802 *Enquiry into the Paper Credit of Great Britain*, considered by many to be the most important statement on the subject between Smith and Ricardo, Henry Thornton defined credit as 'that confidence that subsists among commercial men in respect to their commercial affairs'.[52] Confidence, Thornton went on, 'disposes them to lend money to each other' and 'to sell and deliver goods in consideration of an equivalent promised to be given at a subsequent period'.[53] In Thornton's reckoning, confidence is what enables people to participate in commerce. It is not an abstract or regulative concept, but an ethical practice that generates 'equivalent' values. In making confidence the definition of credit, Thornton was following Sir James Steuart, the contemporary and sometime rival of Adam Smith, whose *Principles of Political Economy* made money, credit, and banking far more instrumental to commerce than Smith and his followers did.[54] Indeed, Thornton went one step further than Steuart. Confidence is the condition by which commerce can take place at all; 'if there be commerce,' Thornton writes, 'a certain degree of commercial credit must also subsist ... in a society in which law and the sense of moral duty are weak there will, of course, be little confidence or credit, and there will also be little commerce'.[55]

The problem, though, is that if money only has value because of the trust between bankers and their agents, it cannot necessarily be trusted: think of all the tricksters who inhabit eighteenth- and nineteenth-century literature, culminating in Herman Melville's 'confidence man'. This is why Thornton himself argued for a gold standard. There had to be some visible, symbolic means to assure the public that their trust in money was worthy. In his *Dictionary*, Samuel Johnson defines confidence first as 'trust' and second as 'rashness', a distinction that implies the term's duplicity.[56] The trouble with confidence is that it is at once the source of commercial power and the potential means of its undoing: it breeds insecurity, doubt, even criminality.

The solution to the problem of confidence was the invention of a new disposition, one that would enable the economy to standardize and acknowledge its internal inconsistencies and irregularities. This was embarrassment. Like confidence, embarrassment was, in the eighteenth century, a financial term, meaning an excess of and thus an inability to pay debts. Characters in eighteenth-century novels are constantly hounded by their 'embarrassments' most of which have to do with owing money. The earliest uses of the term as an equivalent to guilt or shame do not occur until the 1820s, though there is obviously a moral injunction attached to the indebtedness that the term was previously used to connote. The root of the English word embarrass is the French *embras* which literally means to hinder or stop. In this sense then, to be unable to pay your debts, to be embarrassed, is the hindrance that, in Thornton's terms, prevents commerce from taking place. Yet to feel that embarrassment and atone for it is the key to establishing the confidence that makes commerce function in the first place. Johnson defined embarrassment simply as 'perplexity': I think that definition is apt.

According to the American sociologist Erving Goffman, whose essays and books on the 'presentation of self' have strongly influenced my approach, embarrassment is unlike shame or guilt in that it is a social and socially cohesive affect rather than a personal and disruptive one.[57] To be embarrassed by an action means acknowledging an infraction of social decorum ('oh dear, I spilled milk all over your carpet') and inviting, even expecting, general agreement that the infraction will *not* have long-term disruptive consequences ('that's quite all right; it's easily cleaned; let's all clean it up'). In general, embarrassment is something we would all like to avoid, but in its signs and markers – a blush, a sense of confusion, a stammered apology – embarrassment also has a social purpose. Being embarrassed means acknowledging ethical infractions but at the same time leaving room for strategies of social cohesion that will, if not overlook, then recoup those infractions. Everyone in the eighteenth century was in debt, and nations excessively so; they still are. It is the ability to express and thus to control debt, or embarrassment, that keeps the modern national economy afloat.

Embarrassment as I am using the term resembles in some respects the idea of shame outlined by the American psychologist Silvan Tomkins. Like disgust and contempt, shame is in Tomkins' reckoning, a 'positive' affect because it enables the subject to distinguish self from environment. Yet, Tomkins also notes extensively that the distinction between inside and outside is rarely in full effect. To distance oneself from the source of shame, one must first experience it. 'Only a scene that offers you enjoyment or engages your interest can make you blush.'[58] No affect, in Tomkins' view, can be self-contained; each rubs against other affects more pleasurable or painful than it. Like embarrassment, then, shame manifests the sometimes stultifying perplexity of human interaction: its visible effects (the blush), however, also open it into the social network where its confusions are not disentangled or corrected but reformulated as understanding or forgiveness. As Robert Mitchell claims, affect manifests itself as 'dissonance, interference, and static', but it also provides opportunities for further reflection and from that 'the emergence of something new'.[59] For Mitchell, the moments of intensity and connection that constitute the literary encounter with the challenges of finance capitalism produce new and sometimes oppositional systems of thought such as Shelley's 'shadows of futurity'. My sense is that such moments of connection comprise scenes of embarrassment in which the flow of finance is recalibrated, by way of legislation, popular pressure, intellectual debate, or ideology critique.

It is in its capacity both to express the breakdown of trust and to perform the necessary social recalibration that embarrassment comes to function as a mechanism of standardization both against and alongside confidence. To clarify this point, I want to review a recent debate between the philosopher Martha Nussbaum and two prominent literary critics on the question of how affect relates to value; I will then move on to trace how the economist David Ricardo had already engaged that debate in the Romantic period. In *Upheavals of Thought*, Nussbaum argues that emotions correlate the relations between individual subjects and a world that seems contingent and unreasonable. Emotions, she argues, are 'forms of evaluative judgment that ascribe to certain things and persons outside a person's own control' that thus become of 'great importance for the person's own flourishing'.[60] They constitute a 'way of seeing' or interpretations of objects, people, or ideas in the world. In turn they embody 'beliefs' about the 'value' of an object or event. Nussbaum's chief example is her delayed reaction to the news of her mother's death: removed from the scene of death by the demands of a busy schedule, Nussbaum relates, she only began to feel the sadness of her loss when she had an opportunity to reflect on it and then, in succession, felt anger at the untimeliness of her mother's death and remorse over the choices that removed her from her family circle before finally confronting the fact of her mother's absence. What Nussbaum puts forward as the key to ethical feeling is a mediating point, a 'value' that manifests itself by way of the link between object and subject, in this case, mother and daughter. That value is not in itself an object, but the rational consequence of a belief in the importance of the other to the 'flourishing' of the one – in a word, confidence. Nussbaum traces this conception of emotion not only to Aristotle and the Stoics but also to Hume and Smith who sought in their theories of sentiment to ascribe to the passions a rational intentionality and thus correlate the existential fact of individuality with the social necessity of human commerce.[61]

A number of literary critics object to Nussbaum's stoical commitment to the rationality of emotion. Charles Altieri, for instance, asserts contra Nussbaum that 'many of the values we project and enjoy are very difficult to correlate with the forms of generalization that reason requires if it is to take public responsibility for its judgments', arguing instead that what matters about feelings is 'the resistance they give to the terms belief provides'.[62] Instead of general standards or beliefs, Altieri puts affective expression at the center of a process of agreement: 'it may be rational to admit or need to depend on expressive processes for appreciating and negotiation of our difference'.[63] Similarly, Thomas Pfau contends in *Romantic Moods* that Nussbaum's confident, intentional view of emotions leaves out experiences – his examples are paranoia, trauma, and melancholy – that do not fit into normative categories of morality. In contrast to Nussbaum's emotions, Pfau offers 'mood' as a 'holistic, nonintentional, perspicacity' which 'stages the confrontation of subjectivity with historical forces that the subject can neither anticipate nor transcend'.[64] For Pfau, moreover, the aesthetic expression of emotion registers an underlying social dynamic: even the most disturbing emotions form networks of association and rhetorics of self-consciousness that counter the autonomous rationality presumed in modern thought.[65] Immersed in Kantian aesthetics, Altieri and Pfau favor a responsive, non-utilitarian view of art in contrast to Nussbaum's functionalism. But what is crucial for me about their accounts of the relation between affect and aesthetics, accounts that I correlate to Goffman's notion of embarrassment, is the way they stress the functionality of expressive art, the way it turns the apparent irreducibility of affective crisis into new networks of sociality.

Sociologists have also made a case for the reflexivity that Pfau and Altieri stress is the impetus for aesthetic affects. In *The Consequences of Modernity*, Anthony Giddens distinguishes between the way pre-modern people reflect on their lives through 'the reinterpretation and clarification of tradition', by which even the most literate merely reinstate the conventions of the past in their present, with the way modern forms of reflection constitute the 'routinization of daily life [that] has no intrinsic connections with the past at all'.[66] In modernity, Giddens argues, the iconic or totemic standards that imaged traditional social norms give way to constant reappraisal. 'The reflexivity of modern social life,' he writes,

> consists in the fact that social practices are constantly examined and reformed in the light of incoming information about those very practices, thus constitutively altering their character ... All forms of social life are partly constituted by actors' knowledge of them. Knowing 'how to go on' in Wittgenstein's sense is intrinsic to the conventions which are drawn upon and reproduced by human activity. In all cultures, social practices are routinely altered in the light of ongoing discoveries which feed into them. But only in the era of modernity is the revision of convention radicalized to apply (in principle) to all aspects of human life, including technological intervention into the material world. It is often said that modernity is marked by an appetite for the new, but this is not perhaps completely accurate. What is characteristic of modernity is not an embracing of the new for its own sake, but the presumption of wholesale reflexivity – which of course includes reflection upon the nature of reflection itself.[67]

What is distinctive about this new order of reflexivity is that all the conventions and traditions – standards if you will – are open to change. Even concepts tested in laboratory or academic conditions cannot 'remain separated from the activities and events to which they related'.[68] Giddens' other example here is telling: 'The lay individual cannot necessarily provide formal definitions of terms like "capital" or "investment," but everyone who, say, uses a savings account in a bank demonstrates an implicit and practical mastery of those notions. Concepts such as these, and the theories and empirical information linked to them, are not merely handy devices whereby agents are somehow more clearly able to understand their behaviour ... They actively constitute what that behaviour is and inform the reasons for which it is undertaken.'[69] Whereas holders of coins and banknotes would at one time have relied on their recognition of traditional authority figures embossed on them in order to trust their value, or trusted credit that they had established with their immediate friends and neighbors, in the modern world people trust banks because the sheer volume of controversy and debate about banking that people face every day make its basic institutions and conventions familiar, even integral to their subjective lives. Giddens' focus on reflection brings into focus many of the issues discussed by critics from Raymond Williams on about the changes in the 'structures of feeling' that accompanied the general move from the country to the city, a shift that, to use Giddens' term, 'disembedded' individuals from the customs of village life which had circumscribed them for centuries.

To underscore how the tension between confidence and embarrassment that I have been outlining here makes itself felt in Romantic period economics I want to turn to one of its most important figures, David Ricardo. Ricardo has come down to us as the most rationalistic and forthrightly materialistic economist of his generation, and there are good reasons for this. A friend and protégé of Jeremy Bentham and James Mill, Ricardo is widely seen as a flag-bearer for nineteenth-century utilitarianism. He was a staunch advocate of the labor theory of value and of the gold standard. He held adamantly to Say's Law that continual supply will always create requisite demands, human appetite being 'insatiable'. People work not because it is beneficial to do so, but because it is the only means to sustain themselves relative to their station in life. The struggle for resources between classes plays out in the market, which Ricardo was one of the first to conceive as inevitably, if crushingly, competitive. Any interference in that market by the state – levying taxes, inflating the debt, or suspending convertibility – stops the market from operating as it ordinarily and naturally would. Scholars have found traces of Enlightenment psychology in Ricardo's work.[70] But he downplayed sympathy to the processes of distribution and valuation. Ricardo's political economy envisions 'rational economic man without the capacity for mutual sympathy – or any other moral or affective capacities'.[71]

But while a moral sense may be unnecessary in Ricardo's estimation, other senses, like intelligence, patience, and foresight, not to mention desire, lust, and greed have important parts in economic development.

Ricardo understood (in a way that Adam Smith did not) that values *change* with respect to variable conditions and improvements. Art and culture, which Smith classified either 'unproductive' or as a means to overcome the fatigue and drudgery of work, plays a more provocative role in Ricardo's thought as key instances of the way values are affected by time. In a famous passage in the *Principles of Political Economy and Taxation,* Ricardo observed that the value of some exceptional commodities, such as 'rare statues and pictures, scarce books and coins, [and] wines of a peculiar quality' comes not from labor but from 'scarcity alone' and 'varies with the varying wealth and inclinations of those who are desirous to possess them'.[72] Although such rarities 'form a very small part of the commodities daily exchanged in the market', nevertheless, for Ricardo, they are at the same time exemplary of the dynamic nature of value more broadly conceived. Neither the scarcity nor the utility nor the cost of any commodity measured in terms of labor is ever really reflected by market values. As Ricardo wrote in a late letter, 'there is not in nature any correct measure of value, nor can any ingenuity suggest one ... what constitutes a correct measure for some things is a reason why it cannot be a correct one for others'.[73] As a landowner and Member of Parliament, Ricardo became increasingly aware of the deleterious effects of market forces on all sectors of society and of the difficulties Parliament faced in trying to alleviate them. To the end, though, he was convinced that the best way for government to benefit society was to limit its involvement in the economy.

The polarities of materialism and dynamism, or what Ricardo later called 'absolute value' and 'exchangeable value', provided a solution to the conceptual and discursive difficulties encountered in the bullion controversy. On one hand, Ricardo was convinced that a standard existed in 'absolute' terms as the value of labor used to produce any commodity relative to the difficulty and cost of its production. On the other hand, although Ricardo believed that the gold standard was necessary to restrain the self-interest of bankers, he did not agree with the Smithian moral and aesthetic principles on which this idea of the standard was based. Instead, Ricardo argued that the standard of value was a universal average of market activity, something that bankers and politicians could not control but had to respect. This standard did not 'tend' to the value of labor; rather, it exerted considerable pressure on labor, compelling it to adjust to market forces and making value a dynamic paradox of universal (absolute) and temporary (exchangeable) forces.

Ricardo clarified this paradox in a very distinctive way. For the third edition of his *Principles of Political Economy and Taxation*, published in

1821, Ricardo added a short section called 'On an Invariable Measure of Value' to the seminal first chapter, 'On Value'. Ricardo insisted that political economy must assume 'as near an approximation to a standard measure of value as can be theoretically conceived' for the sake of calculation and argument.[74] It is by this approximation that political economists will be able to stop their endless wrangling over paper and gold so that they can concentrate on what really matters. If, he says, we simply stop agonizing over the contradictions and inconsistencies that we observe in the economy, and simply recognize that such contradictions are inevitable then the whole thing will run much smoother:

> If, then, I may *suppose myself* to be possessed of a standard so nearly approaching to an invariable one, the advantage is, that I shall be enabled to speak of the variations of other things, without embarrassing myself on every occasion with the consideration of the possible alteration in the value of the medium in which price and value are estimated ... although I fully allow that money made of gold is subject to most of the variations of other things, I shall suppose it to be invariable, and therefore all alterations in price to be occasioned by some alteration in the value of the commodity of which I may be speaking.[75]

The importance of this rhetorical leap should not be underestimated. It invites its readers to stop thinking about the paradox of representation and 'suspend their disbelief' (as Coleridge said in the *Biographia Literaria* which appeared in the same year as Ricardo's *Principles*) in the existence of the standard. It is precisely by suspending embarrassing questions like where the value of the standard comes from or how such a fiction could have any bearing on reality that Ricardo can build his market system.

But while Ricardo tried to avoid embarrassment, others were embarrassed on his behalf. Indeed, it is the prevalence of the sense that social and affective disruption can lead to the formation of new standards in both political economy and aesthetics since the Romantic period that has continually brought these disciplines together even as many of their practitioners have sought to keep them apart. Giddens' theory of modernity emphasizes the constitutive role of dissent and disagreement in the processes of cultural formation; it is this understanding of dissent that I also see operating in the affect theory of Altieri and Pfau. Underlying this interplay is Walter Benjamin's materialist aesthetics. The history of the modern subject as Benjamin conceived it is replete with fissures and corruptions that even in the most idealistic conception would always undermine its internal unity, even in the negative sense implied by Kantian indifference. For Benjamin, the solution to this problem was the revaluation of the aesthetic, not as a sign for intrinsic value or social cohesion – a kind of aesthetic gold standard – but rather as the point of access for a relentless critique of universals, a critique that could only be fulfilled *through* rather than *against* the propagation of capitalism and its technologies of circulation and exchange.[76] But there is an even earlier touchstone for this dialectic: the ambiguous tonality and self-reflexive skepticism of Romantic poetry – what Keats called its 'mawkishness' – exacerbates the perplexing tensions between privacy and publicity, moral judgment and aesthetic pleasure that make up the poetic experience.[77] To conclude this introduction, I will use Keats to show how the literary manifestation of 'embarrassment' can be used to understand its complex interrelations with monetary and economic thought.

Realms of gold

My study of how the embarrassment of literary Romanticism helped to inculcate the new standard in Britain during the nineteenth century will proceed through a series of cases in a more or less progressive narrative about how the Romantics engaged with monetary issues across the period from 1790 to 1830. Throughout, I will be examining the intersections between Romantic writing and political economy of various forms and genres, secular and Christian, conservative and radical. In each case, however, I will consider this intersection by way of questions and issues that have been for the most part overlooked by economic critics. Thus, in Chapter 2 I examine the bullion controversy as a 'media event' to see how the concern with who has the right to say what money is, practical experts or philosophical intellectuals, affected the monetary issues at stake in it. In Chapter 3, I argue that Coleridge's engagement with Christian political economy in both its radical and conservative valences instilled a new and highly ambiguous understanding of the relation between belief, authority, and debt that in turn strongly influenced cultural criticism. The last two chapters concern poetry and the novel respectively. Chapter 4 shows how Shelley transformed radical critiques of the government's mishandling of monetary forgery in the restriction period into a poetics of 'imitation'. Chapter 5 looks at the way Austen and Scott took up the question of cultural and national difference that was brewing within the monetary controversies.

In all of these cases, I stress the extent to which the debates *failed* to produce a viable alternative to the gold standard as such, but, at the same time, the writers' consciousness of that failure, their awareness of the limitations and inequalities implicit in gold standardization, and the embarrassed forms and genres that resulted from those realizations, helped to produce the modern standard.

Before embarking on these cases, and to illustrate how the interplay between confidence and embarrassment, economics and literature, will function in the remainder of this study, I want to trace the career of a phrase that encapsulates its broader concerns: 'realms of gold'. The phrase is usually associated with John Keats, who used it in the opening line of his sonnet 'On First Looking into Chapman's Homer'. But it did not originate with him. It was coined by Alexander Pope in his *Epistle to Bathurst* subtitled 'On the Uses of Riches':

> The crown of Poland, venal twice and age,
> To just three millions stinted modest Gage.
> But nobler scenes Maria's dreams unfold
> Hereditary realms, and worlds of gold.
> Congenial souls! whose life one av'rice joins,
> And one fate buries in th' Asturian mines.[78]

As Pope explains in his note to the passage, its subject is Joseph Gage, the 'Grandee of Spain', who with his wife Lady Mary tried to buy the crown of Poland from the proceeds of their investments in John Law's Mississippi fiasco. Indeed, the entire epistle is made up primarily of vignettes illustrating how *not* to use money. As an alternative, Pope presents the Man of Ross, a gentleman farmer who lives off a relatively paltry 500 pounds a year, employing tenants, giving to charity, and founding a hospital. Pope's contrary depictions of the Man of Ross and John Gage do not amount to a simple contrast between feudal and bourgeois values. Gage is not 'venal' because he is bourgeois but because he believes that he can achieve high social standing with 'gold' rather than validate his natural standing through good works. In Pope's formulation, Gage's gold 'imps' that 'Blessed paper credit! last and best supply / That lends Corruption lighter wings to fly!'[79] The Man of Ross is by contrast an emblem of virtue and responsibility.

Pope's characterization of the Man of Ross demonstrates the extent to which early-modern standards of value – property, authority, Christianity (by way of charity) – persisted into the eighteenth century by way, as Pocock shows at length, of the civic republicanism of Machiavelli and

Harrington. But Pope also brings these standards together to underscore not simply their viability but also their variability. The 'Epistle to Bathurst' thus marks an early instance of the argument that standards can be both multiple and authoritative, a disposition that we have come to identify as taste. As formulated by the Earl of Shaftesbury and Francis Hutcheson, the standard of taste was supposed to be a bulwark against the rational individualism of Hobbes and the nominalism of Locke. We learn, they claimed, to understand the value of objects in the world not through possession and consensus but rather through appreciation and disinterestedness. The model for this kind of socialized perception is art, which requires that we relinquish individual prejudices or feelings and embrace the universal principles of harmony, balance, and grace. Extending this aesthetic sensibility to morals and politics, we see the needs of society outweighing the demands of individuals. Whatever investments we make in accordance with this general need, therefore, will always be good. As Terry Eagleton remarks, 'to aestheticize morality and society in this way is in one sense the mark of a serene confidence'.[80]

The problem with the standard of taste is that it always risks collapsing over into the realms of individual satiety that by its own judgment it considers distasteful: the overexertion of authority, for instance, or the greed of the connoisseur. This is always a risk, moreover, because it is through our individual perceptions of the world that we come to appreciate the general good – and the link between these is not always clear. Pope's *Rape of the Lock* for instance is an argument against luxury disguised as a 'linguistically luxurious text'.[81] As a result of this self-transgressive tendency, the standard of taste was at the mercy of the individualisms, rational or consumerist, that in its socio-ethical disposition it sought to control. The point, in Shaftesbury, Hutcheson, and others is to cultivate forms in which social equanimity or 'common sense' can be objectified. Yet even within its own aesthetic formula those forms could become the basis for their own undoing. It was Burke who resolved this problem through his distinction between the beautiful and the sublime. Beauty, for Burke, is a 'social quality' that represents relation and restraint. The sublime, by contrast, embodies 'enterprise, rivalry, and individuation ... the anti-social condition of all sociality'.[82] As Peter de Bolla showed in his analysis of the debates surrounding the national debt and the Seven Years War, the distinction between social need and individual desire remained a palpable dialectic in the economic sphere that its aesthetic reformulation could not ultimately synthesize.[83]

In other respects, though, the tension between social ethics and aesthetic pleasure was a Gordian knot waiting to be cut. William Hogarth based his aesthetics – one that influenced Fielding and Sterne – not on a presumed common sense but precisely on an individualized affection.[84] Taste, these writers showed, could be as variable and contingent as the objects it contemplated. Desire, not sympathy, drives the engine of taste. In his *Essays*, Hume positioned 'On the Standard of Taste', in which he underscored both the political necessity of such a standard of social parity and its empirical impossibility, just prior to the essays on money, interest, and public credit. In 'On Public Credit', Hume tried to insist that 'stock-jobbers' should not be permitted to have any say in monetary policy; such offhanded bias would seem to confirm Hume's confidence in intellectual civility over expert practice. Yet, as 'On the Standard of Taste' had already proved, there is no way to guarantee intellectual authority through political station – and so the later remark comes to betray its own indeterminacy.[85]

The paradigm case for the way the standard of taste undermines its own social restrictiveness is the treatment of money in Smith's *Wealth of Nations*. Smith, whose *Theory of Moral Sentiments* is in many respects the most important argument for the importance of taste in legal and social affairs, actually offers two quite distinct, even conflicting theories of money that stretched the 'confidence' of taste to an untenable extent. The first, in Book I, Chapter 4, 'Of the Origin and Use of Money', cribbed from Francis Hutcheson's *System of Moral Philosophy*, uses classical history and legal arguments to suggest that the value of money lies not only in the scarcity and utility of precious metals but, more importantly, in the 'virtue' of those governments that have been able to keep the inherent value that results from the scarcity pure.[86] This historical aesthetics was given pride of place by Dugald Stewart in his lectures on political economy at the University of Edinburgh and then disseminated throughout England by his students Francis Horner, Henry Brougham, James Mackintosh, and James Mill in several articles in the *Edinburgh Review*. Smith's second chapter on money, in Book II, Chapter 2, 'Of Money Considered as a particular Branch of the general Stock of the Society', is a much more technical description of the way money circulates in relation to other forms of capital and can, potentially, fail them. It is here that Smith warns that an extensive paper money system was only so many 'wagons in air' borne by 'Daedalian wings'.[87] Smith argued here that the most effective way of regulating paper credit is not to associate it with unadulterated coin, but to limit it to small communities in which the various borrowers and lenders are already known to each other and to terms of short, manageable durations: the so-called 'Real Bills Doctrine'. Smith's nuanced, but practical defense of paper credit was appropriated by the opponents of the *Edinburgh Review*, financial experts and Bank of England Directors, to give some credence to their actions during the suspension of cash payments. In his 1790 eulogy, Stewart noted that Smith had been well aware that his 'liberal principles' of sociability and free trade 'in different counties and at different times' were in 'danger' of 'rash application' and that it was the purpose of government to ensure that such applications did not go too far.[88] The state is thus tasked with restoring the standard of taste. But who is watching the state?

This problem is also evident in the close relationship between finance and the press. The first newspapers to come to prominence in London were the stock papers, marine lists, and price currents such as John Houghton's *Collection for Improvement of Husbandry and Trade* (1693), John Castaing's *Course of the Exchange* (1697), John Freke's *The Price of the Several Stocks* (1714), and later *Lloyd's List* (1733).[89] These were essentially numerical tables of current prices in the London markets and on the Royal Exchange, together with the names of ships coming into and leaving the London docks. By the 1720s, the price currents had combined with the newssheets, military announcements, political reportage, and royal gossip, to become fully fledged newspapers and magazines, though in some cases more than half of their pages were taken up with advertising. For the most part, the combination of news, stock prices, advertising, and opinion was meant to encourage and expand commerce. Even as they printed the latest stock and currency prices, miscellanies like *The Gentleman's Magazine* described the fashions of the 'better sort' to reinforce hierarchical divisions within society. Business dictionaries and handbooks such as Malachy Posthlewayt's *Universal Dictionary of Trade and Commerce* (1755) and *Britain's Commercial Interest Explained and Improved* (1757) taught merchants to conceive of themselves as a coherent social group and to interact with representatives of other classes, cultures, and countries.[90] These publications drew on religious teachings and 'proverbial' wisdom about money, banking, marriage, and social conduct to imagine the virtuous merchant: they also encouraged confidence *in merchants themselves* that would ensure the equanimity and patience needed to balance the self-interest of commercial desire and allow them some entry into the polite sectors of British society. The same publications made it possible for those above and below the commercial sector to understand how it worked and thus cultivated a demand for the benefits of commerce in general. In the meantime, the association between paper credit and weak or perverse femininity, already understood since Addison, had become a cultural commonplace.[91]

It was in this context that the meaning of Pope's ironic phrase 'realms and worlds of gold' was reversed. In the early 1800s, the *European Magazine and London Review*, which billed itself as a source for history, literature, fashion, and the arts, was fond of misquoting Pope's 'Visionary worlds and realms of gold' in its triumphant accounts of Columbus' voyages and the pleasure house of the Spanish Count Gondemar.[92] Relying on the circulation and distribution of the very luxury objects it was celebrating, the editors would have been rather silly to take as critical or moralistic a line as Pope. More likely, both the writers being reviewed and the reviewers themselves were advertising the 'best' of all the objects on display. Indeed, the *European Magazine* eschewed the political and moral contexts altogether, to the point that the phrase 'realms of gold' becomes another convenient circulating commodity. That indifference marks a turning point in the history of value. In removing Pope's line from the discourse of taste and situating it within the popular discourse of fashion, the magazine implies an entirely different kind of standard, one responsive to the flux of the market rather than to the appreciation of discerning intellectuals.

By the time Keats came to the phrase 'realms of gold', then, the line between the general good and individual desire was far from strong. Taste was at the mercy of the very processes it was supposed to regulate. Pope's distinction between commerce and taste had become utterly confused, perplexed, in a word, embarrassed. Keats' sonnet, then, represents an attempt to transform this embarrassment into the basis for a new kind of standard. Here it is in full:

> Much have I travell'd in the realms of gold,
> And many goodly states and kingdoms seen
> Round many western islands have I been
> Which bards in fealty to Apollo hold.
> Oft of one wide expanse had I been told
> That deep-brow'd Homer ruled as his demesne
> Yet did I never breathe its pure serene
> Till I heard Chapman speak out loud and bold:
> Then felt I like some watcher of the skies
> When a new planet swims into his ken;
> Or like stout Cortez when with eagle eyes
> He stared at the Pacific – and all his men

> Look'd at each other with a wild surmise –
> Silent, upon a peak in Darien.[93]

As published in the December 1, 1816 issue of Leigh Hunt's radical weekly *The Examiner*, the sonnet first appeared in an article puffing (though not uncritically) the 'new poets' sandwiched between a satirical description of the Directors of the Royal Academy on a fishing junket to Hampton Court and an account of a meeting of concerned gentlemen to rescue one Lord Cochrane from debtor's prison. The Royal Mint was preparing to issue its first full-value one-pound coins in more than 150 years. Political economists were touting the return to the 'ancient standard' though as the newspapers of the time suggest, the public appetite for the reforms was relatively small. Given the nature of the writing alongside which the poem first appeared, it is plausible to read it is as an attempt to discover a new kind of standard. Rather than commercial confidence, the sonnet seems to embrace an epic spirit, rooted in classical virtue and producing feelings of admiration and openness.

But a careful reading of the sonnet shows that the economic concerns it seems to reject actually persist. By 'looking into' Chapman's translation of Homer – a *book* – Keats points to the fact that it is not a cohesive idea, but rather an object, a configuration of words, pages, and bindings.[94] Looking into Chapman entails not only literary immersion but also critical evaluation. The unity that the sonnet promises in the figure of the original 'great poet' Homer is compromised by historical 'mistakes' (Balboa found the Pacific, not Cortez), by translation (Chapman, not Homer), and by social fragmentation (it is Cortez' men, not the great man himself, who has the final, wondering reaction). Whatever sublime experience the poem tries to convey is also mitigated by its excessive figuration. The feeling of wonder that comes from reading Chapman's Homer is only 'like' that of the 'watcher of the sky'; the simile entails that aesthetic appreciation is *not* the same kind of feeling as an assured empirical knowledge but rather something we take on trust. The concluding reference to 'Darien', which may have reminded readers of the disastrous expedition of the Scottish government to found a colony there in the late 1690s, points to the history and failure of global colonization.[95]

We might conclude that Keats' sonnet reflects the relativity of value under capitalism. Nothing can be trusted. Unity is an illusion. The only truth is that there are no truths. We have no permanent standard just as Keats had no Greek. The caustic remarks that Hunt makes in the articles surrounding the poem about the spendthrift habits of the nation's supposed leaders imply a similarly desperate conclusion.

But Keats' poem *does* offer a standard by which these contradictory claims might be conceived on a single scale. Chapman's Homer signifies neither gold nor paper and the poem cannot signal a firm commitment to an economic position in defense of either or both; rather poetic form itself crystallizes the reconciliation of these various positions and media within a single evaluative frame. Much as the advocates of the gold standard did with their claim that gold was the 'ancient standard of the realm', so Keats' poem offers a fantastic origin for itself in the classical and Renaissance pasts. But the point of the poem is that this origin is a fantasy that has been produced by translations, readings, and interpretations. Such transformations might offer a way to conceptualize a value beyond the fluid, transient values of the market yet still offer a way to participate in that market. The sublimity that the poem is famous for projecting is thus an effect of a formal capacity in literary writing to make contradiction a positive value.

Keats' sonnet both stands outside of commerce, as the sublime relic of a confident, classical standard and as the embarrassing conduit for the reestablishment of a standard within commerce. It would thus be wrong to say that in using the phrase 'realms of gold' in 'On First Looking into Chapman's Homer' Keats was simply reviving Pope's critique of commerce. Keats was no fan of Pope or Augustan poetics; as Charles Cowden Clarke notes in his *Recollections of Writers*, it was to overcome their familiarity with Pope's translation, which they knew only 'scrappily', that he and Keats turned to Chapman in the first place.[96] Such a turn suggests an attempt on the young Romantics' part to reach beyond the practical, Virgilian inflections of the Augustans and imagine something more radical and contradictory: Greek epic packaged in the Elizabethan and Italian mold of the sonnet. This repackaging in no way entails the possibility that Pope's moral distinction might not still be circulating or, indeed, that the irony of the *European Magazine* using it to advertise luxury goods might not catch some enlightened reader's eye. Keats says, quite forthrightly, that he is a traveler in the 'realms of gold', which suggests that he is a global tourist or at least a reader of the *European Magazine* in which the expansion could be experienced vicariously. To feel different ('then felt I ...') after 'looking into' Chapman's Homer prompts a comparison between Homer and the realms of gold that hinges on a discrepancy in their value: some make us feel, some do not, some objects are ancient and universal, some are present and contingent. In this way, Keats' poem offers a standard (Homer) that it also reveals to be the product of a collecting and comparative impulse.

It is on this point that Keats' sonnet intersects with Ricardo's *Principles*. Ricardo's claim was that the standard is something that people assume in order for this necessary competition to continue rather than something in which they must believe in order to make it stop. The standard is part of economic practice. It is 'tacit knowledge' of a highly specialized kind and people should simply stop thinking about it. The vicissitudes of money are simply too confusing, too embarrassing to be addressed every time someone uses it. The value of money was, in the language of later nineteenth-century economics, marginalized. Whatever oppositional or regulative forces were implicated in the monetary system would become part of the fabric of the culture at large where it would not necessarily disrupt the economy. The reception history of 'On First Looking into Chapman's Homer' shows exactly the same tendency. The original setting of the poem in a radical newspaper devoted in many instances to the ongoing debates about paper credit, national debt, and the various media used to interpret them – such as in the essays that surrounded the poem in the December 1, 1816 issue – was entirely forgotten almost as soon as it appeared. While Keats' sonnets were not as widely known as the poems from the *Lamia* volume before the 1840s (when his reputation rose rapidly in Europe and America), 'On First Looking into Chapman's Homer' was anthologized repeatedly through the 1820s and was consistently touted by Keats' early readers as the undisputed best of his sonnets and obviously the work of a natural, spontaneous genius. The circumstances surrounding Keats' death in 1821 had already made him into something of a *cause célèbre*; the archetypal poor, sick, misunderstood bohemian, as exemplified by Shelley's *Adonais*, and the panegyrics over his sonnet suggest a further attempt to promote Keats' avant-garde credentials.[97] Once it appeared in *Palgrave's Golden Treasury* in 1861, with notes by none other than Alfred Lord Tennyson, the poem entered the cultural zeitgeist of English readers not as a reaction to current, economic affairs, as it had appeared in *The Examiner*, but rather as an example of the distinctive power of literature to challenge, even contradict, the conventional assumptions about the moral benefits of material facts, philosophical certitude, or industrial strength that were so prevalent in Victorian economy and culture. In celebrating Keats the poet as the very opposite of the man of business, in distinguishing poetry clearly from the realms of gold, and in anthologizing 'On First Looking into Chapman's Homer' as a supreme instance of English poetry, Keats' fans, readers, and editors reversed Keats' own argument; rather than conceive many positions and perspectives at once, the sonnet became a standard determining the relative value of them all.

My claims in this book are that Ricardo, Keats, and many others besides contributed in various and often overlapping ways to a conversation about money and that this conversation helped to formulate a new idea of the standard of value. To the extent that it engaged the various arguments for and against gold, paper, and other standards that constituted the bullion debates, economic writers and professional financiers debated the direction of the standard until the only possible recourse was to stop debating, to, as Ricardo put it, avoid the embarrassment of not having a standard. As the example of Keats shows, Romantic literature documents the way that embarrassment persisted in intellectual, economic, and literary practices. Once the debate was over and Romanticism itself had been standardized into anthologies and disciplines, its reflective tendencies were absorbed into British culture.

2
The Bullion Controversy

THE STANDARD
What must we for a standard own,
By which the price of things are known?
'Twas thought, time past, by men of sense,
'Twas Guineas, Shillings, Pounds, and Pence;
The Bank has said, and says so still,
'Tis nothing but a Paper Bill;
'Tis in *Sir Francis Burdett's* head,
The Standard is a Loaf of Bread,
While *Adam Smith* did always say
It was the Labour of a Day.[1]

The 'bullion controversy' was a pamphlet debate about money, banking, and the standard of value prompted by the publication of the *Report of the Select Committee on Bullion*, better known as the *Bullion Report*, in June 1810 and lasting until the recommendations of that report were defeated in the House of Commons in May 1812.[2] As the opening of *The Bullion Debate: A Serio-Comic Poem* (quoted above), published in 1811 by the Birmingham agricultural surveyor William Pitt, tells us, the bullion controversy involved an array of participants representing many theoretical and ideological perspectives.[3] At least 800 pamphlets on the subject were published between 1797 and 1821, more than 100 between 1809 and 1812. Extend these dates to between 1790 and 1840 and the number is well over 1,000. Including articles, reviews, letters, speeches, and poems doubles it again to 2,000. Participants included bankers, accountants, merchants, lawyers, politicians, academics, and farmers. Some supported the suspension, others saw it as a catastrophe or had middling views. Many of their questions and concerns were practical in nature. Did a rise in the price of gold mean that money was 'depreciated'? Did increases in banknotes cause inflation? But they also asked larger questions. How is the economy affected by war? How are paper and gold related? Is value determined by labor or desire? What about land? What is money anyway?

Even before the debate really got under way, commentators were disparaging the bullion controversy as a confusing mess. Already in 1808, in his *Letters from England,* Robert Southey remarked that 'upon the policy or impolicy of continuing ... paper money after the immediate emergency had ceased, volumes and volumes have been written'.[4] The sense of impatience that the debate was generating was compounded by the fact that, in Southey's estimation, the paper notes were inconvenient and far too liable to forgery. Writing in *Blackwood's Edinburgh Magazine* in 1824, the conservative critic and philosopher John Wilson recalled with derision the way the bullion controversy had 'inundated the country with treatises innumerable, and most of which [questions] are still undecided'.[5] Political economists meanwhile rewrote the history of their discipline as if nothing but intrinsic value had ever mattered. The bullion controversy was provoked, they said, by wartime anxiety, bankers' self-interest, and public ignorance. Monetary theory that did not confirm the principles of aggregate production, market freedom, and intrinsic value were not just erroneous, but irrelevant. J. R. McCulloch's 1857 *Collection of Scarce and Valuable Tracts on Paper Money and Banking* featured several pamphlets from the bullion controversy, but only those that endorsed a gold standard. Journals like *Blackwood's* and the *Quarterly Review,* neither of which had endorsed the gold standard when it was introduced were by the 1840s its stalwart champions. After World War I, the *Bullion Report* was published without the dissenting opinions of those interviewed by the committee.[6]

Little more was said on the subject until in his 1965 book *Development of the British Monetary Orthodoxy 1797–1875,* Frank Whitson Fetter examined the arguments for and against standardization, in pamphlets and journals, both rational and ludicrous. Fetter regarded the nineteenth century's 'faith' in the gold standard as 'a puzzle'.[7] Why did so many intelligent people, committed to 'enlightenment' and skeptical of idolatry place so much confidence in a shiny metal? Fetter attributed this faith to four causes: (1) English prices were relatively stable after 1825 so there was little popular acclaim against monetary policy; (2) the effects of various credit crises were felt primarily by the finance community; (3) the simplicity of the gold standard was easily marketed by the government; (4) none of its critics could marshal a coherent argument against it.[8] But these reasons were for the most part after the fact. The gold standard evolved through the 'interplay of forces' with 'no simple causation'; it was the 'product of a combination of analysis, economic and political climate of opinion, and the influence of personality'.[9] Fetter resisted the idea that the bullion controversy was in any sense 'clearly defined ... over a single economic issue' and instead read it as a genealogy of theoretical opinions and responses regarding various political 'crosscurrents' and constantly changing social circumstances: war, agricultural distress, political agitation, and regional difference.[10] A Keynesian, Fetter urged that monetary policy could not be understood apart from these factors.[11]

But what is consistent in the bullion controversy is an abiding concern with matters of style, clarity, and patience. Vitriol constantly threatened to overturn agreement, but it also provoked self-consciousness about how the debate was being carried out. This consciousness makes the bullion controversy not just an economic debate but also a media event. By a media event, I mean a conjunction of differing perspectives around a phenomenon or idea. Media events do not produce consensus; their purpose is to generate dispute. Samuel Weber notes that in a media event, 'things, people, and places come to pass' (as in Hume's theater of the mind);[12] it is only when frames or forms are placed around these events that they come to make general sense, though that sense is usually trumped by the irreconcilable perspectives of those involved. For William Warner, writing about early criticisms of the novel, a media event 'eludes comprehension' in any definitively structural or intentional sense; it cannot be said either to represent a cultural milieu or to instigate cultural change. Yet, in Warner's view, a media event can register 'symptoms of change working within [its] avid consumers' and thus be regarded as 'something that carries genuine effects into culture'.[13] These effects are most keenly felt when the interplay between the participants becomes the subject of discussion and speculation.

In thinking about the bullion controversy in this way, I want to be clear that I am not implying a homology between financial media (banknotes, coins) and 'the media' of intellectual debate (pamphlets, reviews). Media circulate in relation to each other and so reflections on any media impact our observations of others.[14] The bullion controversy exemplifies this process. While I am interested in how ideas about money changed as they found their way through media (pamphlets, reports, reviews) of economic discussion, I am also interested in the way these changes exacerbated the ideological differences between the various participants. Beginning with early debates leading up to the suspension of cash payments in the 1790s and extending to the moment the recommendations of the *Bullion Report* were rejected by Parliament, my account of the bullion controversy will stress the way disputes about money between experts, radicals, politicians, and intellectuals for the most part *failed* to produce a confident view of what money is and instead sprouted a distinctive 'media consciousness' about that failure.[15] During the 1790s and immediately following the publication of the *Bullion Report*, this media consciousness came primarily from financial experts whose perspectives challenged the elegant confidence of Enlightenment philosophy and economics. For that very reason, these expert opinions were the subject of considerable criticism. The prime movers of this critique were the *Edinburgh*, *Quarterly*, and *Monthly Reviews* whose reviewers abjured the experts for their lack of principle, clarity, and style. In turn, however, the *Edinburgh Review* came under fire from experts for failing to comprehend the technicalities of monetary exchange. What eventually emerged from these exchanges was a confidence that a true understanding of the standard would appear, tinged with a sense of doubt and embarrassment about whether it ever could.

Experts and intellectuals in the 1790s

The roots of the bullion controversy lie in the marked increase in British financial activity through the 1780s and 1790s. But these controversies also need to be set against the transformations in the British economy and with it the British Empire during the latter half of the eighteenth century. It may have been clear to everyone in 1760 that 'Britain ruled the waves'.[16] By 1780 it was just as clear the 'empire of the seas', that had operated largely through a balance of interests and trade networks, was starting to unravel. Corruption among East India agents and recalcitrance among the Indian princes not to mention the American colonists were requiring a firmer political hand and a broader global outlook than the mainly local and pragmatic procedures of previous decades.[17] Meanwhile, however, Britain found itself, not altogether unwittingly, at the center of a new financial regime. In 1783, the English Navy took control of Holland's overseas trade routes. The money that had flowed through Amsterdam since the seventeenth century now went through London. To maintain and protect its trade routes, the government took on massive debts, adapting the cycle of militarism and reform begun in the Seven Years War. During periods of conflict, the government increased indirect, consumer taxes, using patriotism as its primary incentive, and then, during periods of peace it offered a variety of reduction schemes such as the sinking fund. This gave the government extra credibility to escalate the debts again when a new war started.[18] To defray liability, the government distributed these debts to city bankers and financiers who in turn issued their own loans and printed their own bills. While Britain consolidated its economic power, it also diversified its financial and commercial activity. This gave new influence to experts in the financial sector.

Experts – bankers, accountants, and financiers – were a complicating but motivating force in the bullion controversy. Historians of Britain's intellectual scene in the late eighteenth and early nineteenth centuries, otherwise known as 'the Romantic public sphere', stress the way that presence of radicals and women fragmented the original idea of the public sphere as a zone of rational, equal debate among private, independent citizens.[19] But scholars have overlooked the important role played by experts in the expansion of that sphere. The reason for this is that highly specialized interests of experts, in science, or law, or finance, lie beyond the political and social reforms about which most of the literature of the period was concerned. But participants in such debates also rely on expert information to maintain their presumed equality. 'If experts are the source of the public's knowledge', notes the science historian Stephen Turner, 'and this knowledge is not essentially superior to unaided public opinion, not genuinely expert, the "public" itself is presently not merely less competent than the experts but is more or less under the cultural or intellectual control of the experts', leading to feelings of 'ambivalence'.[20]

But, Turner argues, the tendency to lump all experts into one 'culture' misses the fact that not all experts are the same. A biochemist, a general physician, a massage therapist, a political pundit, and a health department bureaucrat have different kinds of expertise and thus different relationships to the public and the state, some influential and some dependent. The public sphere, Turner concludes, can examine the lines of expert communication that constitute the state and its legal apparatuses. In *Rethinking Expertise*, Harry Collins and Robert Evans outline a 'periodic table of expertise', comprising different practices from across a spectrum of knowledge from specialized research to political debate. On one extreme is 'non-specialist ubiquitous knowledge' which includes everything from language acquisition to 'beer-mat knowledge' to public understanding and 'folk wisdom'.[21] On the other is specialist or tacit knowledge, including in particular 'contributory knowledge', the close, technical expertise which 'enables those who have acquired to it contribute to the domain to which the expertise pertains'.[22] Between these two lies the frequently overlooked domain of 'interactional expertise'. 'The idea of interactional expertise', they write, 'implies that complete fluency in the language of a specialist domain can be acquired in the *absence* of full blown immersion in the form of life' in which contributory knowledge is usually acquired.[23] It is in this interactive zone that conflicts between experts, the state, and the press arise.

The main forum for interactive expertise during the bullion controversy was the pamphlet. Longer than essays and reviews but shorter than treatises, pamphlets were stand-alone publications focused on a single specific topic or goal, directed at a close circle of like-minded readers, and generally disparaging of all opposition, real and potential. With roots in the propaganda wars of the English Revolution, the pamphlet became the crucial medium of political conviction in the eighteenth century.[24] They were coverless and much cheaper than books, usually selling for one or two shillings, giving them a wide audience. But they did have title pages, epigrams, prefaces, introductions, and other trappings of larger and more exclusive publications. They could thus be serious and philosophical without being expensive or inaccessible. The economic pamphlet was a slightly different entity. Its appeal was technical rather than emotional or ideological. But the effect was the same. On one hand, authors brought precise, technical, and practical experience to bear on ongoing discussions among equals; on the other hand, they tried to elevate their profiles beyond professional practice by engaging in the sphere of public policy and political debate. Respondents questioned whether practical experience was sufficient to explain anything as complex and heterogeneous as money to a largely inexpert public and, accordingly, whether the ephemeral nature of the pamphlet was the right venue for such discussions. But such dissent frequently appeared in *other* pamphlets with just as much technical jargon, the resulting controversies broadening the audience even more. The controversies provoked by these exchanges also served to elevate the social and political prestige of men of business; this explains why leading publishers like Murray, Longman, and Debrett sold the pamphlets through many editions.

The first skirmish of the bullion controversy came during the periodic financial crises of the 1790s as bankers, currencies traders, insurance brokers, and radical dissenters debated the question of who was responsible for the nation's financial drain after the declaration of war against France in 1793. Following a sudden run on specie, the Pitt administration urged the Bank of England to issue new credit and possibly suspend cash payments. The Bank Directors refused, saying that as a private company, it was not responsible for sustaining the nation's war effort in this way. The crisis was averted when Nathan Rothschild procured a large shipment of gold into the nation's coffers. In the wake of this success, Pitt changed tactics and began a period of vigorous investment in overseas currency trading. In September 1795, Walter Boyd of Benfield, Boyd, and Company agreed to make the government a substantial loan to make up losses that the British had incurred in the war. The loan was estimated at between 18 and 30 million pounds; at a discount just under 5%, Boyd earned about a million. He converted some of the funds into bullion but he transferred most of the loan into Bills of Exchange and sent them to the West Indies and Holland where they were converted into coin, bullion, and commodities. The government agreed to reimburse the loan through a Hamburg bank. Though clearly motivated by profit, the loan was also taken as a sign of Boyd's allegiance to a state he knew to be more powerful than himself and, given the wartime economy, worthy of his dedication. In the third and last of his *Letters on Regicide Peace*, Edmund Burke used the example of Boyd's loan as a sign of Britain's faith in government.[25]

To opposition critics the real goal of the loan was to enrich the government and its city cronies. 'Were an opinion to be formed', wrote the insurance agent William Morgan, 'of the national prosperity from a few instances of overgrown merchants and capitalists in the principal towns, we might perhaps be led to conclude, that at no former time had it ever attained its present height. But this is a very wretched delusion. The commerce, like the agriculture of the country, is continually engrossed into fewer hands, and we are hastening into that state which knows only of two class of men – the very rich and the very poor.'[26] Morgan conceived of the national debt as a single entity in which the central government speculates and gambles with the taxes of farmers and merchants whose own 'employment' has no such centralizing tendency. Genuine confidence, in Morgan's view, is tied to communities and individuals. As a founder of the modern insurance industry, Morgan was no stranger to the profitability of speculation, and there is some irony in his complaint about its dangers. His point was to prevent this profit from becoming restricted to the national powers at the expense of local businessmen and their agents.

Another response to Boyd's loan came from a familiar Romantic source. In the second issue of his journal *The Watchman*, published on March 9, 1796, Coleridge featured an essay on Boyd and the government entitled 'The Loan'. How is it, he asked, that such corrupt dealings are not known to the public? One answer is 'the legal disadvantages which attend the task of *reporting* the speeches' in Parliament. The press' limited access enabled the government to claim rather casually that the contract between the administration and Boyd was completely normal. Bankers and government officials knew what money was and how it worked. As companionable experts, they represented the nation's creditable wealth. 'Mr. Pitt saw the necessity of a respectable support from the wealthier Citizens of London, with a "*force* and *precision*," which left him no doubt of the justice of the claim of Messrs. Boyd and Party. It was "*founded in the nature of things!*"'[27] Through the force of party-political rhetoric, Pitt could turn his corruption into an object. Much of Coleridge's prose of the 1790s is dedicated to exposing such vacuous claims to objectivity.

The most strenuous attack on the loan came from Thomas Paine. Though not widely known as an economic thinker, Paine came from a mercantile family and trained as a customs official. During the American Revolution, he helped found the Bank of North America as a way to pay and feed General Washington's troops after the Battle of Valley Forge. In 1787, when Western Pennsylvania farmers and merchants complained of its high interest rates and Eastern bias, Paine defended the Bank, arguing that it was only as solvent as its local customers allowed and that monopoly control would eventually destroy it.[28] Ten years later, Paine used the same argument to predict that English finance would indeed collapse because it was too centralized in the hands of the state. Published first in Paris in the summer of 1796, *The Decline and Fall of the English System of Finance* went through fourteen printings in its first year and was translated into several European languages.[29] Paine's argument is that the national debt has increased steadily since the end of the seventeenth century and with the continuation of war against France would collapse under the weight of its own excessive debts. With its titular allusion to Edward Gibbon's *Decline and Fall of the Roman Empire*, the pamphlet presents itself as a radical exposé of a fraudulent house of cards.

Paine's strategy was to be as consistent and simple as possible. 'Nothing', the pamphlet begins, 'is more certain than death, and nothing more uncertain than the time of dying; yet we can always fix a period beyond which man cannot live ... If then any other subject, such for instance, as a system of finance, exhibits in its progress a series of symptoms indicated decay, its final dissolution is certain, and the period of it can be calculated from the symptoms it exhibits.'[30] The size of the national debt correlates to Britain's military expansionism: every time that Britain has gone to war since the founding of the Bank of England, the national debt has increased by a factor of 1.5. Financial speculation is connected to violence, bloodlust, and ignorance; thus exposed, the entire distinction between theoretical information and physical suffering breaks down, bringing, in Paine's eyes, the financial system with it. 'Every English stock-jobber and minister boasts of the credit of England. Its credit, say they, is greater than that of any country in Europe. There is a good reason for this; for there is not another country in Europe that could be made the dupe of such a delusion. The English funding system will remain a monument of wonder, not so much on account of the extent to which it has been carried, as of the folly of believing in it.'[31] Paine's point is that all money follows the same general principles: although the government hides its centralizing tendencies behind the cover of local businesses, the real fact is that the entire system has become a single all-encompassing delusion: 'Let financers diversify systems of credit as they will, it is nevertheless true, that every system of credit is a system of paper money.'[32]

This was a mistake and Paine's critics jumped on it. By claiming that paper credit was a 'system' administered by the Bank of England, Paine had overlooked its complexity and expediency. In his *Letter to Thomas Paine*, the London banker Daniel Wakefield caricatured Paine as a 'man of theory' whose 'shrewdness and plausibility' makes a simplistic mathematical formula seem like a historical inevitability. Wakefield understood (and supported with figures and tables) the 'numerous and essential facts, by a fair discussion of which, [Paine's] arguments would be refuted, the fallacy of [his] conclusions demonstrated, and [his] boastful theory totally overthrown'.[33] But Wakefield also used his specialized knowledge of the inner-workings of finance to advance the idea that it really did add up to a solvent Bank and a national treasure, which Paine's calumny and ignorance jeopardized. Were Paine's 'malignity against [his] country and its prosperity ... too powerful to be restrained, it would have enabled [him] with more speciousness, and perhaps success, to have endeavoured to undermine the well-grounded confidence reposed on the faith and credit of the British government'.[34] Knowing what Paine does not, that the Bank of England is indeed solvent (and having the data to prove it), Wakefield 'lamented [Paine's] want of candour' and 'rejoiced for my country'. Wakefield's feelings of self-assurance on discovering the errors of Paine's pamphlet become the ground for a renewed confidence; that Paine had to spread lies about the fragility of paper credit is proof that the credit system is indeed strong. 'It appeared to me favourably ominous for the credit of Britain, that her enemies were driven to the necessity of employing engines of falsehood in their attacks.'[35]

Other critics argued that the government's recourse to specific investment opportunities to fund the war signaled its trust in prudent banking and expert knowledge. Ultimately, they said, Paine's intent was not to refute the solvency of the Bank of England but rather to undermine the confidence of the nation. Paine's 'impotence of words and unfounded assertions would excite derision', wrote George Chalmers 'if the malevolence of his purpose did not incur abhorrence. In this arduous hour, it becomes every good subject to endeavour to expose to public detestation the designs of an incendiary, whose sole aim is to goad and plunge society into despondency and anarchy.'[36] For Joseph Smith, the persuasiveness of Paine's logic is enough to undermine confidence in public finance and the state:

> Mr. Paine has not omitted to point out a mode by which he apprehends it may be easy to destroy the credit of the Bank, and with it the government itself. Such are his avowed designs! They are large and comprehensive; but are they not equally cruel and malignant? Not merely to the proprietors of the Bank, and the persons who administer the British Government, but to every man, woman, and child in the nation. Who is able to calculate the dreadful consequences, were the people to become the dupes of such pernicious ingenuity! What Briton, or rather what human being, who is not utterly destitute of the feelings of humanity, can forbear to shudder at a proposition so extensively calamitous![37]

To know how the Bank really works, then, is to protect and preserve it. With such charges, Paine's critics could assert the synchronicity of patriotism and expertise.

The attacks on Paine gave the administration cover to reorient its fiscal policies away from the risks of currency trade and toward central banking. When the run occurred, in February 1797, the government quickly urged the Bank to suspend cash payments on the very grounds outlined by Wakefield and others: credit would sustain confidence and thus the nation in a time of war. Whig Members of Parliament urged that the suspension of cash payments was 'an act of rapine on the public creditor'.[38] They were apoplectic at the possibility that the Bank Restriction Act would enable the government to increase the national debt without any public recourse or political discretion. Charles James Fox urged that like any private banker, the Bank of England must be held to account: an inconvertible currency controlled by the Bank is 'fraudulent'.[39] Pitt replied that the government had to suspend cash payments because of the demands on the Bank of England from the countryside. Only new credit would ensure confidence. Without this trust, 'we should necessarily be left without any resource to which our commerce, our manufactures, or our spirit of national enterprise could look for support, vigour, and extension'.[40]

The suspension inspired vociferous satire. One well-known epigram quipped, 'of Pitt and England / Men say without vapour / That he found it of gold/ And left it of paper'.[41] James Gillray published several satirical prints on the Bank crisis. In 'Political Ravishment', he depicted a lascivious William Pitt seducing an affronted 'Old Lady of Threadneedle Street' (Illustration 2.1). In 'Midas Transmuting All into Paper', a bloated Prime Minister spews paper money from his fat mouth while wearing a vest of gold (Illustration 2.2). Both point to the popular view that the Bank restriction was an attempt by government to co-opt the fragile credit of the Bank while hoarding the precious medals for its military adventures. In the caption of the latter print, Gillray had scratched out 'gold' and substituted it with the word 'paper'. Yet Gillray's politics

Illustration 2.1 James Gillray, 'Political Ravishment or The Old Lady of Threadneedle Street', 1797. © The Trustees of the British Museum. Used with Permission

Illustration 2.2 James Gillray, 'MIDAS Transmuting all into Paper', 1797. © The Trustees of the British Museum. Used with Permission

were ambiguous. In 'Political Ravishment' the victimization of the Bank implies that the viewer's sympathy is drawn to it, even though it/she is hardly a sympathetic figure. In 'Midas' Whig politicians cower in the coat tails of the Tory Pitt while, in the background, dark warships loom, and it is unclear whether these are invading French or adventuring British.[42] *The Guinea Note: A Poem*, by the Scottish agriculturalist and Jacobite Alexander Campbell, calling himself 'Timothy Twig', offered highly equivocal 'help' to bankers in a time of great consternation. 'Persecution is at all times hard to be endured', the narrator comments in the 'Proem'; 'the more so, when there remains but small hope of relief to the sufferer. I own that at present, Bankers, of all others, seem peculiarly to claim the consideration of every denomination of people, and, under that impression, the Poet hath made his essay to help them a bit.'[43] The poem is a denunciation of nationalized bank paper: 'curse the GUINEA NOTE! Say I, / Its very semblance blights my eye!'[44] The poem also features series of difficult and contradictory notes – including a long rejoinder against Paine – suggesting that while opposition to paper money itself is hardly a workable solution, the abandonment of paper credit altogether would be a disaster. The poem concludes that the best way to regulate paper credit is with a network of spies watching over bankers and reminding people of the untrustworthiness of their investments.

Another critic was the government's former agent, Walter Boyd. The shift in policy away from currency trading after the suspension of cash payments was a serious blow to his fortune. By 1797 he was bankrupt and imprisoned in France, where he remained until 1814. Still, between 1799 and 1801 Boyd managed to publish a series of attacks on the suspension that are now widely regarded as foundations of gold standard economics. Rather than accuse the Bank of England of outright fraud, as Paine had done, Boyd criticized the bankers and the government for ignoring the real foundations of international finance. In his first *Letter to the Right Honourable William Pitt*, he argued that with the demand to suspend cash payments the Bank of England had reneged on its 'obligation' to convert notes into specie on demand.[45] Convertibility sustains the 'natural exchange in metals between Britain and the Continent', and the suspension of cash payments resulted from bankers' refusal to acknowledge the need for 'natural measures' of value. Central bankers, in Boyd's account, distort the natural flow of money by offering attractive loans at reduced rates, knowing that they will make 'a much tidier profit out of the whole arrangement'.[46] Backing these claims with charts correlating Bank of England notes, the national debt, and general prices, Boyd offered a precise, expert argument for the stabilizing power of convertibility.

But Boyd's reputation preceded him. The anonymous author of *Brief Observations on a Late Letter Addressed to the Right Hon. William Pitt* called Boyd the spokesman for a 'race of calculators and financial theorists' whose anxieties about the solvency of the Bank of England reflected a dangerous disregard for the authority of property and an equally mischievous sympathy for the French Revolution.[47] Boyd's most strenuous opponent was Sir Francis Baring. Baring represented a class of 'gentlemanly capitalists', who oversaw the financial administration of the growing Empire. His family had founded one of London's most successful private banks and subsequently moved into the ranks of the landed gentry.[48] Against Boyd's claims for mercantile prudence, Baring stressed the centrality of the Bank of England to Britain's social order. Baring defended the Bank on the grounds that the intelligence and circumspection of its Directors provides the chief means of regulating a paper currency, a currency that must extend as far as the demand for it will go.[49] Against Boyd's Newtonian claim that an excess issue of paper notes 'has a tendency to depreciate that money or paper, is a principle universal recognized ... as invariable an operation as the laws of gravitation', Baring offered an image of the Bank of England centering a beautiful cosmic system:

> It has hitherto been beyond the power of human research to ascertain correctly the causes and mode in which this immense machine moves; and yet the fact is beyond a doubt. We may consider, with wonder and astonishment, the small space which the sun appears to fill in the firmament, while we know and feel that every part of our globe benefits by the vivifying effects of its rays. The Bank of England is, to the Agriculture, Commerce, and Finance of Great Britain, its sun: and the circulation of fifteen millions and a half of its paper is the basis on which its convenience, property, and safety have hitherto rested.[50]

Boyd and Baring represent the polarities in an emerging contention within the banking community between centralized, domestic investment and international currency trading, what economic historians call 'bullionism' and 'anti-bullionism'. But the metaphors used by Boyd and Baring also show that what was at stake in these contentions was not just a contest between gold and paper, but interacting pictures of the entire financial world, based in an understanding of principles felt for the most part unconsciously by experts working independently of national institutions.

As opposition to the Bank of England became more pointed, the symbolic image of the Bank became stronger. Its defenders were able to capitalize on the anger and anxiety that the extension of the national debt seemed to be provoking to promote the necessity of a governing institution, the Bank of England, and a class of experts to run it. By the same token, the more technical the debate became, the harder it was for the public to comprehend it. This was not for want of trying: several reviewers tried to encompass the burgeoning monetary controversies as part of their discussions of current political events. After summarizing Boyd's and Baring's pamphlets as well as those by the Cambridge Unitarian William Frend, and the banker Thomas Surr in its 'Retrospect of Domestic Literature – Theology and Morals', *The Monthly Magazine* reflected that it could not 'enter into the controversy' but could only 'recommend to those who interest themselves in such subjects, an attentive perusal of the pamphlets of these gentlemen'.[51] *The New Annual Register* favored Frend, but noted that he could have brought 'the question within moderate bounds, if our acute and ingenious author had not admitted other causes which, although he deemed them inferior will predominate in certain minds according to their peculiar habit of thinking'.[52] The problem with expert writing, the *Register* implies, is that it is too idiosyncratic; in reviewing many different opinions, the reviews fail to discern general principles.[53] Faced with myriad opinions about how to manage the financial system, the annuals and monthlies reached their limit. Their confusion is made palpable by the fact that they classified the financial disputes under the rather benign heading of 'domestic literature'. But it was this generalization that, in later decades, led reviewers to define a broader, intellectual mode of financial knowledge.

Motley compositions: authority and expertise in the bullion controversy

Contrary to Whig apprehensions, the first decade of the nineteenth century did not see a complete fiscal breakdown in Britain. When the Bank Restriction Act was passed, a group of London merchants published a letter in *The Times* in which they declared their willingness to respect Bank of England notes. The Treaty of Amiens in 1802, which saw a temporary halt in hostilities in the war against France, gave some hope that the government would restore convertibility. This hope manifested itself theoretically in the 1805 publication of *A Treatise on the Coins of the Realm, in a Letter to the King*, by the Earl of Liverpool, Charles Jenkinson, father of the future Prime Minister. Returning the economic conversation to its first principles, Jenkinson made a strong case that the Bank should retain a large supply of unused full-value coins, the purpose of which was to harness and limit the circulation of tokens and banknotes. Jenkinson also made clear many of the inconveniences attending the wide use of bank paper precipitated by the suspension of cash payments.[54] By and large, the situation had stabilized: most people were prepared to live with the 'mixed' arrangement of bank paper, worn silver, and foreign coin.[55]

In the midst of this relative calm, the price of gold rose suddenly and Francis Horner, a founding editor of the *Edinburgh Review* but by 1809 a fledgling Whig MP, called a committee to investigate.[56] Its *Report of the Select Committee on the High Price of Bullion* castigated the Governor and Directors of the Bank of England for lacking even a basic understanding of political economy, declared that the high price of bullion had been caused by an irresponsibly excessive issue of Bank of England notes in the wake of the 1797 suspension of cash payments, and recommended that the government return the currency to full convertibility within two years.[57] But, the *Bullion Report*, as it came to be called, was in Horner's words 'very clumsily and prolixly drawn', a 'motley composition'.[58] Apart from Horner, Henry Thornton was also on the Bullion Committee, along with the Tory economist William Huskisson and, in his last outings, the playwright Richard Brinsley Sheridan. While the actual report was a mere 60 pages long, extensive interviews with financial experts and bankers amounted to almost 300. The central conclusion of the report – that the gold standard is both part of Britain's legal and economic heritage and the best possible way to assure the nation's economic strength on the world stage by enabling its merchants to act with confidence – contains two quite divergent positions: collective legal precedent and individual economic opportunity. While the committee conceded that the restriction of cash payments had been necessary in a time of war, and the majority of their interviewees had stated categorically that the high price of bullion was the direct result of its being shipped abroad to pay British troops, the committee also downplayed the pressures of the war on domestic exchange. Such inconsistencies undermined the consensus that Thornton, Horner, and Huskisson had hoped to achieve.

The *Bullion Report* was immediately controversial. To Nicholas Vansittart, Chancellor of the Exchequer, the report was nothing but a series of incomprehensible abstractions that had either fundamentally misunderstood or outright ignored the advice and information the committee received from the many experts and policy-makers they interviewed; in its zeal to make these abstractions law, the committee had failed to take into account the practicalities of commerce and the vicissitudes of war. Vansittart castigated the committee for 'intemperance and insolence, of false pretensions, and vanity, of error, of absurdity'.[59] Other respondents scoffed at the committee's lack of expertise. Conversely, several pamphleteers foregrounded their own technical knowledge of the 'facts' surrounding depreciation, their familiarity with the numerical data, and the practical rules of banking and currency exchange. Many of their pamphlets featured tables and charts on the course of exchange or the size of the national debt or the price of gold.

The pamphleteers' purpose, clearly, was not only to assure the general public of the Bank's economic solvency or of paper money's moral legitimacy – both were understood – but rather to convince them that the country's finances were already in capable, expert hands. But in so doing, the writers also risked alienating their public audience. To soften the blow, as it were, the pamphleteers couched their technical data in a rhetoric of familiarity, as if to allow their readers into an ongoing conversation and make them feel both knowledgeable and comfortable. Many authors declared that they had written letters to friends and colleagues within the financial community out of a need to share concerns and anxieties and then published later because the information contained in it was deemed to be publicly useful. Other pamphleteers were more deliberate and adventurous. In his *Observations on Money*, James Cruikshank used an assortment of stock phrases and connective clauses to ensure that his audience was following his complex, detailed, and at times technical prose.[60] On the title page of *An Examination of the Report of the Bullion Committee* Simon Cock declared that he was a 'Commercial Agent in Liverpool'. In his prefatory 'Advertisement' he insisted that his only motive in commenting on the Report was 'rather as a man of business than as an author'. Cock's pamphlet has many charts and figures through which he refuted 'the details in which the Evidence (in my judgment) is defective'. But his summation could hardly be called a rational or practical alternative to the evidence he has scrutinized. Instead, it parrots the three conclusions of the *Bullion Report* merely by inserting a capitalized 'NOT' in each.[61]

Most of the pamphlets deferred, though seldom uncritically, to the broader philosophical knowledge of established and authoritative writers on the subject as a way to connect their close technical understanding of a part of it to the larger field of monetary economics as a whole. Adam Smith and John Locke, who had advocated for a metallic standard, were the two most common authorities cited. Yet these citations could be contradictory. Most pamphleteers cited them to defend the *Bullion Report*'s claim for the necessity of convertibility as the only natural means of currency regulation. In the first of two pamphlets entitled *The Defense of Banknotes*, John Grenfill cited both Locke and Smith to argue that the actual standard metal of currency exchange for these thinkers was silver, not gold. Cock referred admiringly to Locke's *Considerations of the Lowering of Interest* as a way to defend its own claims for the basis of monetary value in trade rather than in intrinsic value.

By contrast, in *Commerce As It Was, Is, and Ought to Be*, John Inglis put a series of quotations from Adam Smith, John Locke, and the *Bullion Report* on the left-hand page and used the right or recto side to insert his own commentaries. A part of Sir James Steuart's *Principles of Political Economy*, in which the already paper-heavy Scottish banking system was both defended and simplified, was edited and republished in pamphlet form in 1810 and 1812, though the purpose of the publication was to warn its readers of the dangers of 'excessive issue'.[62]

The problem that experts faced was how to explain their practical knowledge of financial affairs and criticisms of the *Bullion Report* without either betraying their self-interest or confusing their readers. To address this, they insisted on the difference between the vaguely radical presumptions of the Bullion Committee and the national importance of the Bank. But this strategy also backfired. On September 20, 1810, one of the Directors, Randall Jackson, delivered a speech at the Bank attacking the Bullion Committee for infringing on the bankers' time and expertise and for questioning their honor and prestige: 'When the character of any individual or body of men is publicly attacked', he said,

> it becomes a duty to take the first opportunity of vindicating that character; and although I am as unwilling as any man to step out of the line of my professional pursuits yet I feel too strongly how much I owe to this institution, in the interest of the public, and to my own interest, to overlook animadversions contained in the Report to which I have alluded. That Report appears to me to contain in effect very serious charges against the validity of our stock, and our public stock. I wish it to be understood that I do not mean to speak disrespectfully of the Committee, nor to attribute their Report to the influence of party motives; but I must observe that that Report is clearly and avowedly inconsistent with the evidence taken before that Committee. That inconsistency is indeed so glaring and so material, that I could not wish for any more complete vindication of this institution than the universal publicity of that evidence. The fallacies contained in the Report are of such a nature that it is in my mind of considerable consequence to guard against or remove as soon as possible the impression they are calculated to produce.[63]

The next day, Jackson's speech was published verbatim in the *Daily Chronicle* and it immediately became a subject of scorn and ridicule in political and intellectual circles. William Cobbett, whose series of attacks on the Bank of England in the *Political Register* would eventually become the most widely read document in the period, devoted an entire letter to reprinting the *Chronicle*'s version of the speech in full – no further comment was necessary. David Ricardo, then just embarking on his writing career, ridiculed it in a letter to the *Chronicle*: 'I was doomed to listen to an unmeaning attack on what was called the party spirit which dictated the Report, and to a repetition of the worst of the erroneous opinions which were delivered in evidence to the Committee, and which the Report itself so ably refuted.'[64]

Another response to Jackson came in Huskisson's *The Question Concerning the Depreciation of Our Currency Stated and Examined*, one of the most widely discussed in the controversy. Huskisson called Jackson the 'learned advocate' for those whose 'pens are employed to propagate most false and dangerous theories'.[65] But Huskisson was in an odd position: as the leading Tory member of the Bullion Committee, he represented the 'Canningite' faction of Tories who endorsed financial and economic reform. But he was still a member of the governing party. This meant that he had to prove, on the strength of his own mixed position, that support for the recommendations of the *Bullion Report* did not entail anti-ministerial or anti-British sentiments. To do this, Huskisson borrowed Steuart's and Thornton's distinction between 'circulating credit', the medium of commercial confidence, and 'paper money', a mere 'promise' based on 'authority' and issued by monopoly institutions.[66] On this foundation, Huskisson could turn a series of contradictory statements about the general entity 'money' into a dialectical system. 'It is', Huskisson wrote, 'the essence of money to possess intrinsic value' and that money was thus to be considered different in kind from 'circulating credit' which has no value as capital. The market value of gold is determined partly by the rate of exchange and partly by the credit activity of traders. Yet the value of gold coins is only what it is 'publically proclaimed' or 'accurately ascertained' to be: its 'intrinsic value' is based on authority. What Huskisson seems to have stood for, then, was not so much the commodity value of gold as the iconic value of coins and, with them, the state. Indeed, he preferred debasement as a remedy to the reduced availability of gold over the depreciation of paper credit. Packaged in a series of scientific maxims about the standardizing and regulative power of commodities, he could appear to sanction both state power and the free market at the same time.[67]

The responses to Huskisson were even more vociferous than the response to the *Bullion Report*. Several writers spoke to Huskisson's apparent 'betrayal' of the interests of country landowners that the report's commitment to gold – and thus international commerce – entailed.[68]

Others argued again that increase in the price of gold had occurred as a result of its continued demand on the continent. The unnecessary limitation on domestic credit would thus, in the words of John Hill, 'involve the country in extreme distress and embarrassment ... the issue [of bank paper] is the only circumstance which has prevented the scarcity of precious metals from being sooner and more severely felt, and from producing a ruinous embarrassment in the trading and pecuniary concerns of the nation'.[69] Among Huskisson's outspoken adversaries was Sir John Sinclair, the Scottish man of letters, patron of philosophy and the arts, and compiler of the statistical account of Scotland, published in 20 volumes between 1791 and 1799. In 1797, as a defender of the rights of local communities to conduct their own economic affairs, he had been an outspoken opponent of the restriction; in 1810, as Chairman of the Board of Agriculture, Sinclair supported the Bank, publishing a series of pamphlets urging that since commerce and especially agricultural commerce operates primarily on credit, there is no reason for the restriction ever to stop. Sinclair was deeply aware of the need to connect with an interested, but inexpert audience. His first pamphlet, *Political Maxims Regarding Coin and Paper Currency*, consists of a list of key terms and definitions, resembling Huskisson's. In another, he replied directly to Huskisson, point by point. Another was a speech he delivered in Parliament. He also used a number of different publishers. Still all of Sinclair's reviews were also decidedly patriotic and relied heavily on the notion that respect for state institutions like Parliament and the Bank of England was as natural as respect for aristocratic peers.[70] 'There are some points so closely connected with the safety and existence of a great Country, that they ought not to be rashly tampered with, nor brought under discussion, without the most urgent necessity. I particularly allude to its established Religion and to its established Government; and after these, in point of importance, I consider the species of Currency which is found to be the best suited to the circumstances of a Nation.'[71] Sinclair's pamphlets exemplify the paradox of confidence. While on one hand, Sinclair was warning against the 'rash' or over-confident tampering with the standard that, he suggests, the *Bullion Report* was recommending, he was also urging his readers to respect paper credit in the same way that they respect the authority of the state.

Sinclair's pamphlets prompted more responses, most of them defending Huskisson: 'Your observations do not meet Mr. Huskisson's reasoning in any point whatever', wrote William Kingsman, 'I perceive you flapping on in the lower regions of air, while the person you are remarking on is totally out of your sight.'[72] Sinclair seems to have read

Adam Smith, Kingsman charged, but completely missed his point. 'If you have ... suppressed his reasoning, it is a pity, as the public may be led to look for the omission by an inquiry, at the Bank, how much bank stock you hold in your own possession.'[73] Huskisson himself responded to Sinclair's pamphlets in a series of articles in *The Quarterly Review*, co-written with George Canning and George Ellis. Interestingly, they did not use the review to correct Sinclair's misconceptions. Indeed, they entirely overlooked the elder statesman's proposal to correlate the amount of paper money in circulation against records of agrarian production and instead repudiated his self-aggrandizing style, right down to the arrangement of titles, subtitles, apologia, and dedications.[74] In their review of Huskisson's own pamphlet, Ellis praised his reluctance to take a firm stand on the question of the standard: 'that which we regard as the peculiar and more valuable characteristic of this work', Ellis wrote,

> is the caution with which the writer has avoided every topic which could lead to a pretext for party animosity, on a subject in which every political party must have the same common interest. This is the true test of sincerity; it is that by which all impartial men will judge; and we feel confident that when this important question shall be referred to the decision of the legislature, it will be decided on its own merits only; and that where safety of the whole community is at stake, every minor interest will be disregarded.[75]

The state, it seems, knows better. This is hardly a surprising conclusion for a conservative publication like *The Quarterly*. Yet, it is not simply on its own authority that the state will decide the bullion question (as Sinclair assumed) but rather on the basis of its 'sincere' and 'impartial' respect for the authority of scientific facts. The implication is that the solution to problem of the standard cannot be found merely through the force or conviction of a maxim or declaration. It can only be arrived at through the patient deliberation on facts and 'merits'. This was a crucial position for *The Quarterly* to take: it enabled the question of standard to be deferred to the broader field of public debate – including, most importantly, the reviews.

The most prolific reviewer of bullion tracts in this period was Joseph Lowe. Not much is known about him. Having attended both St. Andrews and Edinburgh Universities, Lowe was well-versed in Scottish economic thought. But unlike Horner and Huskisson, who were lawyers, Lowe became a businessman, first in Holland then in London. He wrote articles for *Lloyd's Evening Post*, still the most important stock current in circulation, as well as pamphlets on the economic state of the nation and the Empire. Though he also contributed to the *Edinburgh Review*, most of his work as a reviewer appeared in the *Monthly Review*, the oldest if not the most respected review journal in the field.[76] In this venue, Lowe wrote more on the bullion controversy than any other reviewer of the period; he reviewed the *Bullion Report*, Huskisson's *Depreciation* and several responses to it, and many less noteworthy contributions. He also produced, in the course of a review of Davis Giddy's *A Plain Statement of the Bullion Question*, an extensive theoretical essay on the interrelation between bullion shortages, foreign exchange, and the progress of the war. Lowe was particularly sensitive to matters of rhetoric and style and the presumption of authority that they can inspire. He was skeptical of any writer who showed signs of excess 'wit'[77] or 'confidence and vehemence' and encouraged them to 'take pains in collecting information and digesting it'.[78] He approved Husskison's 'definitions' and 'first principles' and praised 'the clear and convincing character of his mode of illustration'.[79] Lowe also appreciated 'brevity'. Reviewing William Blake's *Observations on the Principles which Regulate the Course of Exchange* (and with which he generally agreed), Lowe observed that

> like other writers on the subject of money, Mr. Blake seems to be strongly impressed with a sense of the ignorance that has hitherto prevailed concerning it, and has therefore chosen to give his illustrations at great length. We cannot help thinking that he has carried this point rather too far; and that in common with the most eminent authors on political economy he has not been duly sensible that brevity is compatible with perspicuity, and how much less forbidding that study may be rendered by careful condensation.[80]

By contrast, Robert Mushet's heavily redacted 'series of elaborate calculations' was 'valuable' but not 'attractive'.[81] Lowe was poignantly conscious of 'the proneness of practical men to find the solution of a general embarrassment, in the particular circumstances which pass under their personal observation' leading them to miss the general principles inherent in economic processes.[82]

But for Lowe, brevity and clarity did not entail that writers dedicate themselves exclusively to theoretical principle at the expense of practical knowledge. It is because of their attention to the vicissitudes of monetary practice as well as to the need for theoretical consistency that Lowe praised Huskisson and Blake. Lowe was not favorably impressed with the *Bullion Report* for the same reason; the Committee's dedication to Smithian principles had led them to overlook the practical evidence that was put before them and rush into hasty and ill-timed recommendations:

> The Committee, or at least the members whom rumour states to have taken a lead in framing the Report, were evidently better acquainted with the principles than with the practice of trade; and they do not appear to have been aware of the necessity of supplying this deficiency, by a rigid scrutiny of the documents contained in their appendix. The allotment of four months to the object of their appointment seemed perhaps to them, as it doubtless did to the public, an ample allowance of time; yet, such is the peculiar intricacy of this subject, and so numerous are the considerations which require comparison and analysis, that twice that period would not be more than sufficient for the attainment of digested and satisfactory conclusions.[83]

Lowe's sense of patience here is telling. Had the Committee waited to publish their findings, the controversy and many of the intricacies for which they were blamed might have been avoided altogether. But that remains only a possibility.

In a letter to the *London Times*, 'Civis' was no less critical of the Bullion Committee's haste. Reading the *Bullion Report*, he wrote

> will hardly leave a doubt on the mind of any unbiased person, that the Committee have, on some material points of the question, formed their opinion much too hastily; that they have set up some principles with too little consideration of the exceptions to which they were liable; that they have passed too superficially over some important facts and documents, which stand in the way of their conclusions; and that they have treated with too little attention, or rather, with too much contempt, the opinion of those 'merchants of extensive deftness and intelligence', whom, for the sake, they say, of their *opinions*, they thought it right to call before them.[84]

Time is the key to resolving the bullion question. Only once all requisite information has been assembled and discussed will a proper, authoritative theory emerge. Civis' point is that this had in fact already happened: the pages and pages of interviews that appeared as the report's massive appendix contained precisely the kinds of information that the Committee needed to devise more comprehensive proposals and the expert authority of the interviewees guaranteed the benefits of that information. The Committee's haste prevented them from appreciating the nuanced views before them. Yet, it also enabled the report's many respondents and defenders to publish and circulate their 'expert opinions'. Even though their recommendations were rejected and widely attacked, the Bullion Committee's brash confidence generated the media event that would familiarize and thus standardize economic discourse.

Currency and style in the *Edinburgh Review*

If the newspapers and journals of the period were the key to resolving the bullion controversy, or at least standardizing its discourse, then the *Edinburgh Review* might easily be assumed to have been a main instrument of that process. The *Edinburgh* was the leading quarterly of the period, its circulation upwards of 14,000 by 1810. Educated in the lecture halls and academic clubs of Edinburgh University and Courts of Session, its founding editors, Francis Horner, Sydney Smith, Francis Jeffrey, and Henry Brougham saw themselves as standard-bearers for Adam Smith's vision of a commercial society regulated by political respect, intellectual judgment, and aesthetic taste.[85] While articles on a variety of economic, literary, and political topics were frequent and varied – many of them important contributions to their respective fields in their own right – more pages were given over to the question of money in the journal's first decades than any other: about 40 articles in 25 years. As Jon Klancher has suggested, the *Edinburgh*'s key rhetorical tool was what he calls 'general signs' – money is his example – that 'turn nearly any subject into an intellectual surveyor's map' and 'deprives objects, ideas, or ideologies of their apparent distinctiveness'.[86] Through this general view, the *Edinburgh* advanced a consensus of consistency, stability, and universality that bridged the disciplines. Horner brought these presumptions to London and they grounded the recommendations of the Bullion Committee. Though the Committee failed to change policy in its wake the *Edinburgh*'s advocacy of the gold standard, first by Horner and subsequently by J. R. McCulloch, was at least partly responsible for its ascendancy.

The extent to which the *Edinburgh*'s strategy of selective generality worked has, however, been challenged by some recent interpretations. Jerome Christensen has seen in the *Edinburgh*'s early concern with conspiracy and sectarianism a shadowy image of the *Review* itself – as a conspiratorial, sectarian, and cultish publication – that its editors desperately sought to avoid but which its critics routinely exposed. Mark Shoenfield and Ian Duncan have noted how rival publications such as the *Quarterly Review* and *Blackwood's Edinburgh Magazine* used the *Edinburgh*'s commercial bias and Whiggish sympathies to undercut its cultural authority with a public that was equally invested in notions of property, tradition, and hierarchy.[87] These concerns are also evident in the *Edinburgh* itself; its 'general signs', especially money, were compromised from the start by the journal's own confidence. But it was not strictly in its rivalry with Tory publications (like the *Quarterly* and eventually *Blackwood's*) that the *Edinburgh*'s seemingly ubiquitous hold on economic ideas weakens. Even before the *Quarterly* first appeared (in 1809), the *Edinburgh*'s intellectual authority had already been compromised by its unsuccessful attempts to beat financial experts at their own game. It was only by turning financial expertise *itself* into a ground for economic authority that the *Edinburgh* could plausibly assert the link between market value and intellectual truth.

The first target of the *Edinburgh*'s economic program was Thornton's *Inquiry into the Nature and Effects of the Paper Credit of Great Britain*.[88] Thornton was a prominent member of the London banking establishment, and a leader of the evangelical Clapham sect that also included William Wilberforce and Hannah More. Personally ambitious and outwardly successful, he was also self-conscious and socially awkward, at once insistently punctual and hopelessly loquacious.[89] *Paper Credit* is an ambitious and contradictory work. Thornton tried to make his technical knowledge clear to a wide non-technical readership. His title deliberately echoed Smith's *Enquiry into the Nature and Causes of the Wealth of Nations* and Steuart's *Inquiry into the Principles of Political Economy*. Thornton was clearly invoking the generic protocols of the *Inquiry*, packaging his views as a systematic set of observations on familiar phenomena. He also cites Smith extensively. But while the early chapters begin with general definitions (of money, credit, and confidence), they become increasingly longer and more confusing as the particular details of monetary circulation and distribution pile up.

As already discussed, Thornton defined 'credit' as the 'confidence' that merchants have in each other, the 'patience' they need to wait out returns on loans. Paper is the most convenient way of signifying that confidence.[90] Nevertheless, the credit system must have checks to regulate its distribution. Echoing Baring, Thornton claimed that these checks are the responsibility of bankers who issue notes and set rates of interest. But bankers are liable to the same temptations as ordinary merchants in stretching confidence too far and issuing too much money. A central bank, like the Bank of England, should limit the amount of credit it extends to local bankers. Thornton also asserted that the value of money ultimately lay in precious metals: 'gold coin is to be viewed chiefly as a standard by which all bills and paper money should have their value regulated as exactly as possible ... the main, indeed, the only point is to take all reasonable care that money shall in fact serve as that standard', but under that condition of 'care' it can hardly be said to embody a truly free market.[91] The fact that the suspension of cash payments in 1797 did not provoke massive inflation proves that a sufficient banking system could sustain confidence when precious metals are not available.[92]

It was to the question of the competence of expert bankers like Thornton that Horner turned in his review of *Paper Credit*, the last and longest article in the first issue of the *Edinburgh Review*. Horner appreciated Thornton's effort to mediate market and banking principles as Smith (whom Horner had studied extensively) had done before him. But Horner was concerned that Thornton's practical expertise compelled him to overlook philosophical foundations. Invoking Smith, Horner reframed Thornton's 'system of banks' into a 'subdivision of labour, which extends itself over an opulent and industrious country'.[93] Also like Smith, Horner relied on a general notion of rational perspicuity, not just the patience of bankers and merchants, to form the basis for financial competence.

> Bankers possess, from their situation, very superior means of *distinguishing* the careful trader from the improvident. The bill transactions of the neighbourhood pass under their *inspection*; and by this *information* they are enabled to *measure out confidence* very nearly in a *just proportion*. In fact, it is considered as a regular branch of their professional experience, that they should *appreciate* the credit of the various traders within their district of circulation; and this sort of *practical sagacity* they are understood to *cultivate* with great assiduity.[94]

Because their motive is profit, bankers overlook the public interest that is always on the minds of philosophers. To avoid this selfish tendency, the Bank of England 'retains another check of a highly important nature, over the banks of the country. The issue of its own notes is restricted, in ordinary times, by the obligation to convert them into specie.' Such an obligation ensures that any 'local rise in prices' of which an independent banker might take advantage 'will be produced within the district of that country paper, but prices in London will remain as before' and thus not threaten the general equilibrium of the nation as a whole.[95] If the obligation to convert notes into specie is removed then the Bank has a responsibility to limit its notes *as if* convertibility were still in place. Professional bankers need a gold standard, either in the form of free convertibility or the virtual equivalent because they are temperamentally incapable of holding those standards on their own.

Horner also appealed to rhetorical principles – precision, subordination, clarity – to mount his critique of Thornton: 'the work indicates, throughout, an author unpracticed in composition ... he rarely attains precision and distinctness of expression'; 'Most of the prolixity, and some of the obscurity, which oppress the reader in its present shape, would have been avoided, if the temporary topics, which formed his original object, had been sunk into a subordinate digression'; 'nothing can be more unsatisfactory and cumbrous, than the illustrations by which he labours to expound this very fallacious position'.[96] This critique has important economic corollaries. By producing the data in which the 'speculative inquirer' might 'confide', the English practitioner contributes to the broader production of public confidence. When, as in the case of Thornton, the English author does not have sufficient rhetorical skill and thus 'little management in the disposition of his materials', he will be 'frequently ... embarrassed in the explanation of arguments' and thus incapable of putting the public at ease.[97] By contrast, in his review of *Thoughts on the Restriction of Payments at Banks of England and Ireland*, by Lord Peter King, a Whig Irish peer and descendant of John Locke, Horner makes a special point of suggesting that the 'uniform effect' of managing money with a gold standard 'may be perceived' because 'the evidence by which it is proved, and the reasonings by which it is explained, [are] very ably and perspicuously described'.[98] Horner praises King for his 'calmness' and 'clearness'; 'the author is liberal and accurate', 'the pamphlet a model for similar publications'; 'It is by innumerable repetitions of this sort, that an impression may at length be made, even on vulgar understandings, in favour of an enlightened policy; and the assent of the multitude habituated to the results of the genuine philosophy, whose high aim is to emancipate mankind from practical error, and to ameliorate their political condition.'[99] In lauding King's style, Horner was not simply cultivating agreement with the pamphlet's Whig politics or free-market principles. He was establishing a connection between the viability of the gold standard and the rhetorical principles of the *Edinburgh Review*.

Horner could not resist the idea that the difference between Thornton's specialized approach and his own broader, philosophical mode was a matter of national difference. 'In England', Horner writes, 'which is the native-country of political economy, the works, contributed by professional men, form a large deposit of authenticated facts.

For these we are primarily indebted to that diffused literature, which multiplies the demand for varied information, and has already liberalized the practitioners in almost every walk of industry.'[100] Publications of this kind were 'suggested by such occasional events, in the fluctuation of our commercial prosperity, as rouse a general interest, and direct the curiosity of the public to that quarter of the great machine, in which the derangement is supposed to have taken place'. That the 'South Sea scheme' and the 'embarrassments' of the 1695 coinage crisis did not lead to permanent reforms in the banking and monetary systems prove that English professionals were too invested in their own profit to see general stakes clearly. They did not participate in the debates over money and value at the time 'and that curious system, by the operation of which the use of precious coin is now almost superseded, had remained in a great measure unknown to all but the bankers and traders of London, until the suspension of cash payments at the Bank of England produced that copious information, which, in various forms, has been communicated to the public'. By contrast to the specialist knowledge of financial experts the 'habits' of 'the speculative inquirer are incompatible with a personal knowledge of detail'. Accordingly, Horner argues, 'it is necessary that the labour of accumulating the particular facts, should be separated from the more liberal task of generalizing these into principles; and that they, who are qualified to combine larger views, should be furnished, by the minute accuracy of others, with descriptions in which they may confide'.[101]

The problem that Horner diagnosed in his early reviews was the tendency of experts to cultivate exclusive fields of understanding from which intellectuals (like himself) and the public (whom he served) presumably had no access. Experts forget that they are part of a republic of letters and threaten it with irrelevance. To combat this tendency, Horner uses the Enlightenment critique of rhetorical excess against not only the financial technocrats' style but also their professional practice. Unlike a merchant, whose speculations are naturally tempered by the costs of trade and production, a banker 'manages an important part of trade, at an expense far inferior to what the merchants themselves must have incurred, had they continued to conduct it separately by their own clerks'.[102] The tendency is for bankers to cultivate a false distinction between monetary signs from 'real' economic activity:

> The *ingenuity* of these money-dealers, in sparing the circulating medium, is aptly illustrated by a custom which prevails among the city bankers. Each of them sends a clerk, at an appointed hour in

> the afternoon, to a room provided for their use. Each clerk there exchanges the drafts on other bankers received at his own house, for the drafts on his own house received at the houses of other bankers. The balances of the several bankers are transferred from one to another, *in a manner which it is unnecessary to explain in detail*, and the several balances are finally wound up by each clerk into one balance. The difference between the whole sum which each banker has to pay to all other city bankers, and the whole sum which he has to receive from all other city bankers, is, therefore, all that is discharged in bank notes or money; a difference, evidently, much less in its amount than that to which the several differences would be equal.[103]

Horner emphasizes the cultish appearance of financial transactions by purposefully ignoring the real details of its operation.[104]

In the process, Horner reconsidered the central role of the Bank of England, which Thornton had argued was during the restriction crisis a matter of expediency. 'If', Horner wrote, 'the Bank of England must now be considered as a national establishment, not merely influencing, by the superior magnitude of its capital, the state of commercial circulation, but guiding its movements according to views of public policy, an important revolution has taken place since the first erection of that corporation as a banking establishment.'[105] Whereas the legal power over money previously and 'immediately' held by the crown is in the hands of an institution that in its very nature 'blends' interests and powers. However, the 'organization of this establishment, possessed of such means to control the operations of commerce, as well as to facilitate the advance of financial supplies, may, into our political constitution already so complicated, introduce a new principle of action, the effect of which cannot be clearly discerned. Perhaps an unbounded field will be opened for the extension of ministerial influence. Perhaps an unexpected control may be gained to the people, over the views and measures of the executive.'[106]

Horner's was the template for later reviews by Henry Brougham, James Mackintosh, Sydney Smith, and James Mill. In a review of Thomas Smith's *Theory of Money and Exchange* Mill lamented the 'vague and confused ideas' about money that 'almost necessarily infect our mode of thinking with regard to the whole science' and the 'melancholy abundance' of pamphlets and theories purporting to explain the field but whose minute differences and distinction, exploded by the heated rhetoric of 'positions and refutations', make the field 'in the highest degree perplexed, obscure, and defective', one in which nothing but 'ignorance prevails'.[107] For Mill, the subject requires answers to general questions ('What is Money?') and a 'definition in the ancient form'.[108] Smith claimed that there is no standard of value except the 'artificial' or 'imaginary' standard that accountants adopt in order to render their calculations equivalent; Mill thought this was 'absurd'. The English pound is not a technical convenience but a general idea derived from the weight of a standard bushel of corn. In true Enlightenment fashion, Mill distinguishes between 'going to market', which he regards as the real economy, and 'accounting' which he figures as purely nominal. Against Smith's notion that cultures all over the world use whatever objects are at hand as their currency (African cowries is his example), Mill charges that even the most 'primitive' peoples will endeavor to measure the relative value of commodities by means of objects with more generally acceptable utility. He then recounts the standard history of coinage from barter to commodity money to fiat exchange, all based on the principle of relative use.

In 1812, Smith published a reply: *The Bullion Question Impartially Discussed in an Address to the Editors of the* Edinburgh Review. Defending the idea of the 'artificial standard' he outlined in *A Theory of Money and Exchange*, Smith compared the standard to lines of longitude: its utility derives from the way it helps set a position within the commercial system rather than from the way it refers to some idea of another supposedly 'useful' commodity. Understanding money means situating oneself within the flow of exchange and thus comprehending its internal vicissitudes rather than adapting definitions and associations from outside it. But Smith also assessed the rhetorical differences between the intellectual authority assumed by the *Edinburgh Review* and his own brand of financial expertise. 'Of all men', he wrote, 'a reviewer is the person who ought to observe, most studiously, a rigid neutrality, and to keep himself free from all political bias. Indeed, I conceive that the moment he joins a political party he forfeits all claim to the character of a candid and impartial judge.'[109] Judgment, in Smith's view, is tied to one's precise understanding of the subject at hand and not a matter of status or taste. 'You have yourselves', he writes, 'somewhere described the office and functions of a reviewer, and among other things have mentioned the particular advantages to be derived from his labours in this country, where all have now the ambition for at least the appearance of learning; as by the intervention of a review an acquaintance with modern productions, sufficient to enable a man to talk of them, may be acquired by man who have no opportunity of procuring the originals or time to peruse them.' Yet, because their knowledge is based on acquaintance and not on any deep contributions to a field, the reviews will be irrelevant to the real issues at hand:

> if instead of a criticism on the new productions, your review be filled with original essays on the same subjects, this advantage will be lost, and the reader who takes up the work will be disappointed, and may throw it away in disgust. I do not mean here to insinuate any thing against the merits of your essays, or to say that the man who did read them would, in general, really feel himself disappointed:– very far from it: I am convinced that there are very few subjects on which an essay from the pen of the Editors of the *Edinburgh Review* would not give both entertainment and instruction – But, although this be the case, yet the reader must feel disappointed, because he expected something else ... Instead of being able to repeat what such a man has said on such a subject, the reader will only have it in his power to relate what the Edinburgh reviewers think on that subject.[110]

In spite of their pretensions to 'real' knowledge, the *Edinburgh* reviewers are mere purveyors of entertainment. Mill had contrasted Smith's 'artificial' standard with Berkeley's and Steuart's versions of the same idea that Mill insists do have genuine referents in the value of land and in the anticipation of employment. Smith admitted that he has not read Sir James Steuart, or Adam Smith, or Bishop Berkeley (though he intimated a willingness to do so). In the meantime, his own literal sensibility actually gets the better of Mill: he quotes in his pamphlet at length from the philosophers and can find no mention of the ideas Mill proposes.

At stake in Smith's criticisms is a distinction between 'facts', which Smith argues are the accumulated impartial truths that the accounting community develops through its expert conversations with itself, and 'opinions' which he subscribes to the *Edinburgh Review*. For Smith, it is precisely the speculative nature of Mill's conjectural history that undermines its confidence in the gold standard. 'How an article can at one time, be equal to itself and at another unequal; how its variations can be measured by a thing, which *invariably* represents a *certain* proportion of itself are propositions which I cannot conceive nor understand.'[111] Smith's 'artificial' standard represents a different order of speculation, one based not on philosophical authority, but on the accumulation of financial data, coursing through the commercial world and compelling investors and accountants alike to anticipate, observe, and theorize new facts and relations as they emerge.

By 1812, the *Edinburgh Review* had become less sure of its Enlightenment values and style. Indeed, between 1811 and 1817, when Horner died and the more rigidly philosophical McCulloch became its chief economic commentator, the *Review* was less a venue for the propagation of Smithian principles than it was for the circulation of conflicting economic opinion. Nowhere is this more apparent than in the debate between David Ricardo and Thomas Malthus over the relative importance of production and consumption in the determination of exchange value inaugurated by Malthus' comments on Ricardo's contribution to the bullion controversy, *The High Price of Bullion*, in an omnibus review of monetary pamphlets. Money is meaningful only to the extent that it is useful, Ricardo argued. It has no social meaning otherwise. Precious metals are intrinsically useful for trade because everyone accepts them in exchange for goods. And bullion is useful as a standard because its value tends to stay stable over time, even though its market price varies in the short term. Banks supply temporary money for local transactions when metals are needed elsewhere. Indeed, they also encourage trade. 'The establishment of the bank and the consequent issue of its notes', Ricardo wrote, 'operate as an inducement to the exportation either of bullion or of coin, and are beneficial only in as far as that object may be accomplished. The bank substitutes a currency of no value for one most costly, and enables us to turn the precious metals (which, though a very necessary part of our capital, yield no revenue) into a capital which will yield one.'[112] Ricardo thus reinterpreted Smith's metaphor of the 'highway in the air' which many commentators used as a warning of paper credit's fragility to clarify the benefits of banknotes. 'Smith compares the advantages attending the establishment of a bank to those which would be obtained by converting our highways into pastures and corn-fields, and procuring a road through the air. The highways, like the coin, are highly useful, but neither yields any revenue.'[113]

Before he was a political economist, Ricardo had been a successful city broker, one of the founders of the London Stock Exchange. The curt, uncompromising character of his early monetary writing reflects this success. He had great faith in what he called 'the ordinary course of things'.[114] Unless notes were convertible into metal, there would be no natural outlet for the value of capital earned in trade. Access to commodities keeps the channels of trade open; suspending that access will close them. 'The exportation of the specie may at all times be safely left to the discretion of individuals; it will not be exported more than any other commodity, unless its exportation should be advantageous to the country.'[115] Those trading in precious metals are actually stabilizing the economy because they maintain the flow of specie abroad. Ricardo accepted that this is a potential cause of anxiety. 'Some people might be alarmed at the specie leaving the country, and might consider that as a disadvantageous trade which required us to part with it; indeed the law so considers it by its enactments against the exportation of specie; but', he goes on, 'a very little reflection will convince us that it is our choice, and not our necessity, that sends it abroad; and that it is highly beneficial to us to exchange that commodity which is superfluous, for others which may be made productive'.[116]

The cause of fiscal embarrassment, Ricardo concluded, is government interference. Unnatural restrictions like the suspension of cash payments or the military blockade make trading gold more difficult and market corrections to take more time. But the inducement to trade is so strong that the trade goes on regardless:

> Were it possible to carry the law against melting or exporting of coin into strict execution, at the same time that the exportation of gold bullion was freely allowed, no advantage could accrue from it, but great injury must arise to those who might have to pay, possibly, two ounces or more of coined gold for one of uncoined gold. This would be a real depreciation of our currency, raising the prices of all other commodities in the same proportion as it increased that of gold bullion. The owner of money would in this case suffer an injury equal to what a proprietor of corn would suffer, were a law to be passed prohibiting him from selling his corn for more than half its market value. The law against the exportation of the coin has this tendency, but is so easily evaded, that gold in bullion has always been nearly of the same value as gold in coin.[117]

There is in this argument more than a hint of dark, surreptitious goings-on. But Ricardo's point was that illegal exports speak to a fundamental human urge that the authorities cannot appreciate. Knowing that a black market in metals is actually the 'real' market hidden within attempted government control is a source not of panic but of pride. In the last sentence of the essay, Ricardo sought to quell the 'alarm' that people were feeling at the idea of bullion leaving the country. 'I am well aware', he wrote, 'that I have not added to the stock of information with which the public has been enlightened by many writers on the same important subject. I have no such ambition. My aim has been to introduce calm and dispassionate enquiry into a question of great importance to the state' – and then he added on a patriotic note – 'the neglect of which may be attended with consequences which every friend of his country would deplore'.[118]

Impressed with Ricardo's conviction, Francis Horner asked him to review the *Bullion Report* for the *Edinburgh*. Ricardo refused: his practical style, he said, was not up to the demands of the *Edinburgh*'s philosophical rigor. Horner turned to Malthus. In some respects, he was a natural choice. Malthus was already well known as the author of the *Essay on the Principles of Population*, in which he had accused radical optimists like Godwin and Condorcet of claiming that given time and universal freedom, human beings would become self-sufficient, even immortal. Overpopulation prevents such a wonderful but hopelessly idealistic future from ever arriving. Yet, in the second edition of the *Essay*, Malthus argued that a healthy respect for 'moral restraint' (by which he meant delayed marriage) would work just as effectively.[119] Like Ricardo and Horner, Malthus had an optimistic respect for the relation between self-reliance and social equanimity. Like Huskisson, Ricardo, Blake, and Lowe, Malthus endorsed the natural utility of precious metals and understood the principles of foreign trade. But Malthus was less sure that restoring convertibility would stabilize prices and restore confidence. Contributing a compendium of the *Bullion Report* and related pamphlets, including Ricardo's and Huskisson's, Malthus was able to confirm the basics of the *Edinburgh*'s bullionist stand overall while at the same time offering criticisms of and corrections to specific claims. Along with many of the report's critics, Malthus agreed 'with what has been often urged, both in print and in conversation, that the Bullion Committee ought to have attended more to the opinions of able and experienced merchants and men of business whom they examined. It was their duty to get as large and correct a body of facts as possible ... it was also their duty to hear the *opinions* of all those who were examined, in order that they might see the subject in different lights in which it would naturally present itself to different understandings, and under different circumstances', though he was careful to state that the members of the Bullion Committee were 'much better able to come to just conclusion, than anybody of the practical merchants that could be chosen' and that the Bank Directors were responsible for maintaining the value of the currency.[120]

On the question of demand more generally, Malthus was circumspect. Huskisson and Ricardo had asserted, with the *Bullion Report*, that the main cause of the rise in the price of bullion was the unchecked increase in the quantity of banknotes issued by the Bank of England. Malthus disagreed: there was no question that a redundancy existed, but it was not the cause of the rise in bullion price. The 'payments necessary to be made, for the supply of past or present wants' is the cause of the outflow of precious metals.[121] Given 'mercantile difficulties and great purchases', influencing the supply and demand of commodities, it was imprudent in Malthus' view to limit discussion only to currency.

> It is unquestionably true, as stated by Mr. Ricardo, that no nation will pay a debt in the precious metals, if it can do it cheaper by commodities; but the prices of commodities are liable to great depressions from a glut in the market; whereas the precious metals, on account of their having been constituted, by the universal consent of society, the general medium of exchange, and instrument of commerce, will pay a debt of the largest amount at its nominal estimation, according to the quantity of bullion contained in the respective currencies of the countries in question ... whatever variations between the quantity of currency and the commodities may be stated to take place subsequent to the commencement of these transactions, it cannot be for a moment doubted, that the cause of them is to be found in the wants and desires of one of the two nations, and not in any original redundancy or deficiency of currency in either of them.[122]

In Ricardo's account, money is only a vehicle for the continual investment in the production of commodities, the supply of which will always be met by commensurate demand. But demand will not necessarily meet supply, resulting in a 'glut' of commodities and a fall in prices, which will in turn reduce profits and wages.

This difference of opinion about supply and demand would inspire Ricardo and Malthus to enter into a long correspondence. Malthus' broader view of the currency question was influenced by his observations of the 'difficulties' attending market behavior rather than only its principles; Ricardo, though conceding some of Malthus' arguments, never abandoned his belief in the natural equanimity of free markets. Eventually, this concern with the importance of consumer demand and especially its effects on agriculture would alienate Malthus from the *Edinburgh Review* circle. But what is important about Malthus' comments on Ricardo's *High Price of Bullion* is that, like Thomas Smith's attack, they point to certain perplexities within the *Review*'s sheen of philosophical confidence; indeed, Malthus makes this perplexity apparent from within the pages of the *Review* itself. Alongside the bullion controversy proper, in which those perplexities had been palpable, the *Edinburgh Review*'s failure to fully comprehend the vicissitudes and embarrassments of monetary debate in its era signals the demise of the Enlightenment status quo.

It is not surprising, then, that in an 1813 review of Madame de Stael's *De La Littérature*, Francis Jeffrey would bemoan the end of the Enlightenment project of uniting the empirical sciences under the umbrella of a virtual standard of reason and taste. Like de Stael, Jeffrey admired the idea of progress, but he was critical of her belief in the perfectibility of humanity, echoing Malthus' critique of Godwin and Condorcet from 15 years before. But Jeffrey was mainly concerned in the review with the proliferation of 'invention and ingenuity' and the 'expansion of commerce'. The expansion of commerce precipitated the increased consumption of poetry and the 'transitory and passive impressions' they inspire, in contrast to the 'virtuous' disciplines, of philosophy and history, leading to 'boredom and idleness' among aristocrats and proletarianization of the rural 'lower orders'.[123] The ironies of Jeffrey's lament have been noted before: the *Edinburgh Review* itself depends upon the demand for quick instruction. That irony is compounded by the *Edinburgh*'s leading role in the campaign to reform the currency, and political economy with it. But the real irony is that Jeffrey was right. The proliferation of print had damaged the Enlightenment mission by saturating the very field of economic debate with so many views and opinions. Not until his reviews of Scott would Jeffrey begin to revive the old standard, and then it existed squarely in the past. In 1813, it was still an open question.

In the meantime, there were other proposals for making the financial system more rational and unified. Joseph Hume, 'the People's MP', sought to put the coinage onto a decimal system enabling people of all ranks to calculate prices and investments.[124] David Ricardo returned to the monetary fray with his *Proposal for an Economical and Secure Currency* to argue that government should set the standard with bullion instead of gold, allowing it to find its natural market price before, as coin, it begins to affect the price of other commodities.[125] Underlying the plan is the utilitarian idea, derived from Bentham and Mill, that people will survive temporary crises through their own aptitude and perseverance: government policies like the suspension of cash payments are not really necessary even if, in moments of panic, they seem to be. Ricardo's proposal met with widespread agreement, not least from the government who used it as the basis for their return to convertibility, and by J. R. McCulloch who, in his review of Ricardo's *Proposal* in the *Edinburgh*

Review, blamed the farmers for the credit crisis and argued that anything less than full convertibility was un-British.[126]

But neither Ricardo's plan nor McCulloch's interpretation of it met with universal assent. Against Ricardo's plan, Thomas Smith agued that since merchants rely on variable prices to make a profit, convertibility would eventually slow commerce until it was depriving the country of a currency at all.[127] In the October 1818 issue of *Blackwood's*, John Gibson Lockhart wrote a positive review of Ricardo's *Principles*. But he followed it with a blistering attack on McCulloch's claim that Ricardo had proven that the various classes of society exist in a state of perpetual antagonism. 'If political economists chuse to depart from the common use of language', Lockhart wrote, to label the relations between classes 'a perpetual opposition of interests, and, consequently, a state of perpetual hostility, let them have the consistency to call it a *general* opposition of interests; and let the rest of mankind admit that, if in one sense they be mutual enemies, in a more comprehensive view of the matter, they are mutual friends and cannot do without one another'.[128] Lockhart then compared the benefits of landed property and inherited wealth against the cut-throat competitiveness of the Ricardian marketplace:

> A rich man, like a watering-pan in the hands of Providence, serves to diffuse more generally and usefully the means of subsistence while the envious absurdity of the human heart grudges even existence to that which feeds it! As if the flesh of our bodies should rise, in unhallowed insurrection, against the heart. All would be watering-pans, all would be hearts; but this is not the order of nature nor of Providence, which must ultimately prevail. After derangement shall be succeeded by derangement, and revolution to revolution – after having exhausted all the forms of madness of misery, of murder, and of blood, it is only by returning to the order and subordination of nature, that wretched and weary mortals can escape from anarchy and despotism, and expect to find, if not happiness, at least safety and repose.[129]

This is a paternalist argument in which the landlord extends the means of subsistence to those he deems worthy and in the interest of his own public standing. But the diction of this passage also points to a moral claim that once the competitive marketplace collapses, a 'natural' hierarchical order will return.

By the mid-1820s, then, even as McCulloch was espousing the scripture of Ricardian principles in his lectures and reviews, classical political economy, especially on matters of currency, remained in hot competition with other economic ideologies. And while few commentators, and even fewer readers were as sure of the intricacies of finance as the experts Ricardo and Smith, most nevertheless understood the underlying political implications of both Lockhart's and McCulloch's reviews: the end of the war would shift the balance of power. Establishing a new standard required that the increasingly divergent interests of the professional, landed, and working classes be reconciled. The bullion controversy thus entered a new speculative phase. The concern with expertise would persist, but it would be accompanied by social concerns: agriculture and the condition of the people who lived on it, industry and the condition of people who worked within it. What would Britain look like under a new standard? Given the complications of belief, imitation, and regulation that the new gold standard seemed to present, was a consistent standard possible at all? It was these questions that galvanized the Romantic response to the bullion controversy.

3
The Idea of Paper Money

'Great have been the advantages to this country by commerce' Coleridge declared in his 1819 *Lectures on the History of Philosophy*: 'Next to the Church it has been the great source of information (and art and science ...) but most assuredly the main support of freedom, nay, the very cause of freedom as actual and as practicable throughout the country, and of that general diffusion of knowledge which, if we have fewer wells now, fewer reservoirs, makes us have a hundred more frequent brooks which may be shallow but yet go bubbling and chattering and conveying fertility where they go.' In some ways this is a surprising thing for Coleridge to have said. We are used to thinking that his mature phase was conservative, even reactionary. Though not necessarily opposed to commerce, he was at least resistant to its democratic potential. But Coleridge clearly believed that a liberal economy benefited the nation by making the exchange of goods and information faster and easier. This liberal economy was also a standardized economy: 'I feel that you may pass from one end of England to the other and scarcely know you are twenty miles from London, from the general uniformity of language, habit, and information. I feel that by the confidence made necessary between man and man, it has given a physical strength to the country perfectly new and unknown in any periods of the history of the world.'[1]

Haunting Coleridge's confidence was his unease with its proliferation. The target here was the 'shallow' and 'fertile' popular press. Thus the opening phrase of this passage, 'Next to the Church', is crucial. It implies that confidence must be subordinate, even obligated to a rival standardizing force: the Christian establishment. In his later work, from *The Statesman's Manual* to *On the Constitution of Church and State*, Coleridge delineated a 'national church' or 'clerisy' a conglomerate or company of intellectuals, funded by the landed aristocracy, paid for through taxes, and charged with the 'cultivation' of the national conscience to guide the economic and political progress made possible by the modernizing impulse of 'civilization'. At the center of this process of cultivation is the idea which he defined as 'that conception of a thing, which is not abstracted from any particular state, form, or mode, in which the thing may happen to exist at this or at that time; nor yet generalized from any number or succession of such forms or modes; but which is given by the knowledge of its ultimate aim'.[2] Coleridge may well have been thinking about the gold standard. As he wrote in an 1819 letter, he believed that the standard of value did not exist either as a material entity or as moral dogma but rather was 'ideal'; the general lack of appreciation for the standard's inherent complexity, Coleridge urged, is the product of the 'want of insight' into the standard's prophetic form.[3] With the idea, Coleridge mediated the network of supply and demand, credit and debt, and freedom and responsibility that were being debated in economic pamphlets, newspapers, and sermons into a comprehensible form that did not compromise the complexity of the debate.

Coleridge is an important figure in story of the standard. Coleridge reformulated the relation between commerce and Christianity, liberty and subordination that already existed in economic discourse. His idea of paper money roughly parallels the 'liberal Tory' consensus that was emerging in political, economic, and theological discourse after the war and that included the gold standard.[4] But this consensus could not overcome the hardships and inequalities of the economy. Coleridge's idealism does not even imply a unity – religious or otherwise – but on the contrary, a conjunction of elements that are seldom equal and rarely distinguishable.[5] This idealism, which is also an embarrassment, became a crucial trope in monetary writing after Coleridge. Writers as different as William Hazlitt, Thomas de Quincey, and F. D. Maurice combined Coleridge's metaphysics and Ricardian materialism to delineate a standard that was neither strictly commercial nor wholly theological. In stressing that thought is 'labour' these commentators conceived a dialectic that was not only crucial to the disposition of literary scholarship, but grounded the modern idea of the standard.

Corn, cash, and Christianity

If we limit the history of political economy to the Scots, to writers like David Hume and Adam Smith or Francis Horner and Henry

Brougham, then of course it will take on a decidedly secular cast.[6] By contrast, religion informed English political economy well into the nineteenth century. The dominant economic ideology of the early modern period, Mercantilism, was based largely on the doctrine of divine infallibility embodied in the authority of the state.[7] In 1767, Robert Lowth, Bishop of Oxford and later London and, at one time, Oxford Professor of Poetry, preached: 'Government in general is the ordinance of God ... it is the duty of every individual to acquiesce to that form of government under which Providence has placed him.'[8] Farmers and traders alike were expected to model themselves on the principle of authority; whatever surplus money they made also belonged to God. Much of the 'conservative ideology' of writers like Swift, Fielding, Johnson, and Burke came from the conflict they felt between the Anglican concept of obligation and the misuse of that trust by the state. Most people's understanding of how money worked came from sermons and proverbs. These also stressed the authority of the state, even in the face of the individual freedoms and sinful luxuries that money at the same time seemed to provide. Popular eighteenth-century economics depended upon a general knowledge of scripture: the injunctions of sermons, utterly conventional though most of them were, were understood to be relaying authoritative truth. Poetry and political economy, likewise, could portray the workings of an empirical and, often, immoral world and still appeal and even embody in its classical allusions or rational form, the authority of the Divine.

Economic developments and their accompanying controversies and debates in the eighteenth and nineteenth centuries eroded this scriptural authority.[9] But while there was some push back from conservative clerics and philosophers, over the course of the century, Christian economics gradually came to replace its reliance on textual authority with standards of reason and feeling, a new mode of religious confidence located in the mind of the individual believer. Though the views expressed by Christian economists (including those whom we would otherwise think of as secular) differed, sometimes in radical ways, they shared a paradoxical distrust of textual authority and faith in the power of textual production. Through the circulation of these texts, the principle of the gold standard, a principle that denied the authority of monetary text in its governmental form as paper credit, achieved widespread acceptance.

Consider in this regard Joseph Priestley. During the 1760s, Priestley delivered a series of lectures on political economy at Warrington

Academy. Published by Joseph Johnson in 1788, the *Lectures on History and General Policy* outline a theory of value based on a Unitarian understanding of mutual benefits deriving from individual confidence. Priestley had little time for the hierarchical standards, sanctioned by divine authority and embodied in agricultural property, as advocated by conservative churchmen and Augustan essayists. 'Agriculture', Priestley opines 'is yet far from being brought to the perfection of which it is capable; and nothing but the strongest inducements from commerce, or absolute necessity, the mother of inventions, will enable us to judge of what perfection it is capable.'[10] Money enters Priestley's political economy as part of a critique of mercantile colonialism, in particular the outrageous expense of maintaining the American colonies and the slave trade. Money represents price, and there can be no price until there is an exchange economy. State money created through debasement, restrictions on interest, or the manipulation of trade balances is harmful to this economy. In Priestley's estimation, there is nothing wrong with paper credit as long as it circulates according to its intent. The 'danger arises from persons promising, in the form of a bill or note, more than they may be able to pay at the time promised. And while a man's credit, or that of a bank, is good, their promissory notes will circulate exactly like cash, without any thing being represented by them.'[11]

Such views were familiar to his audience, the sons and daughters of middle-class merchants and traders.[12] Like Adam Smith, Priestley did not encourage his readers to disrespect government, but they did not owe any obligation or debt to it or its 'promises'. All promising, as urged by David Hume and by Priestley's fellow Unitarian Richard Price, is liable to false expectations: what is promised will not necessarily be true. In order to be valid, Price argues, a promise must be empirically 'true' even in a future in which the conditions of 'truth' might change.[13] Price was no stranger to finance. He had been an adviser to the young Pitt during the 1780s. And he was one of the pioneers of life insurance, penning several pamphlets on the establishment of mutual assurance schemes for naval widows.[14] Yet he insisted that the form of speculation served the greater good and not for individual gain. In his sermons, Price urged his followers to abandon the pursuit of money because it was 'attended with inward anguish, with the curse of heaven, and inconceivable future danger'.[15] Money works, he and Priestley contend, only if it does not cause embarrassment.

Unitarianism marked an 'important transition stage', as Charles Taylor describes, 'on the "long march" of the order of mutual benefit into our social imaginary'.[16] To recall, Taylor understands by a social imaginary the standards of various fields, societies, and cultures that make up the multifarious differences of modernity. He distinguishes this condition from the mutuality of ancient and early modern societies, in which the standards of life were understood to be universal and authoritative, promulgated by institutions and texts. The Cambridge divine William Paley took the next step in the long march. Although he preached social obligation in the manner of Lowth, he also argued that authority must always also conform to the greater good. In his 1785 *Principles of Moral and Political Philosophy*, Paley argued with Locke that the true standard of value was labor and that all forms of authority were obliged to it for their maintenance rather than the other way around.[17] Our sense of moral obligation is not to be directed at the state as the representative of divinity or even at scripture as the word of God but rather toward the general utility of our actions. Respect for authority could be entirely in keeping with utility because order and restraint were necessary to a thriving commercial state. Since the suffering of some could act as a model for the benevolence of others, complete social equality was neither possible nor strictly desirable. Respect for the Bible as divine utterance and as proverbial authority is commensurate with empirical truth, as long as the utterance or authority is morally beneficial.

After Paley, utilitarians associated economic reason with Christian belief, though they felt no sense of duty toward the Established Church. The authority of Anglican preaching might be politically or morally suspect, but it also provided a paradigm for popular dissemination. Governments speak in terms of authority and speculation: the press speaks and circulates truth. Especially in a satirical mode, utilitarian writing used Christian teaching as a template for its critique of textual authority. Jeremy Bentham's 1817 *Plan of Parliamentary Reform, in the Form of a Catechism* in which he satirically castigated the union of aristocrats and bureaucrats in government for their obvious self-interest and flimsy reasoning galvanized the radical cause against the government's fiscal policy.[18] The first edition of the *Plan* was a best-seller. And when Bentham's publishers refused to print a second edition, Thomas Wooler brought out an abridged version along with Bentham's acknowledgment to him in his radical weekly, *The Black Dwarf*. Bentham's arguments against the 'interests' of parliamentarians and bankers catalyzed radicals to believe that the solution to the financial crisis was their own advocacy and its medium, the free press. In August 1818 Bentham received two letters from 'Imlac', who was also one of Wooler's correspondents, praising *Parliamentary Reform* as a 'revelation' and requesting Bentham's approval for a more extended treatment of the link between paper credit and parliamentary corruption. 'My whole publication', Imlac announced, 'will be an octavo, principally on the finance and paper system. – a system which, if many years longer persevered in, will, I am quite confident, produce an explosion, the fatal consequences of which few have the most distant conception, because few have ever reflected on them. I believe it is near at hand, and am also convinced the corruption of the House of Commons is the cause; and the only remedy, or means of averting the impending danger, annual election of representatives of a most extended suffrage – in short, the ascendancy of the people.'[19] Part of Imlac's plan was that writers and critics like himself and Bentham should expose the injustice of the government monopoly on credit, though he was wary of what might happen should that system fail. 'The press', Imlac suggests, 'and cheap publications are a new and extraordinary engine, and its quiet but rapid orientation must produce *some* effect. God only knows what it will be. I confess I am alarmed. I dread lest violence should attempt to remedy those evils, which the coolest judgment and moderation can alone remove.'[20] What was needed was a forum of understanding, a new public sphere that might rebuild the credit of the nation.

But Paley also influenced a very different group of Anglican evangelicals. Their theology was built around the idea of atonement: the suffering of Christ redeems the harsh and tedious life of the sinners He ultimately saves.[21] Evangelicals stressed the discontinuity between an earthly experience governed by desire, sin, and doubt and the divine grace that would reward perseverance. One of their leaders, Henry Thornton, argued that a credit economy relies on a circulating medium and on a cycle of credits and debts, though these work best if they are held to refer to some secure and universal standard, the permanence of which is as much a matter of trust or faith as it is of quantifiable reserves. The existence of this reserve is a product of Divine will; accordingly, any extension of credit beyond its limit is as much a debt to Christ (who had already fulfilled the bargain) as it is a credit to the state. Saving is not a sign of mortal goodness but rather a testament of personal suffering for the sake of future salvation. Thornton's friend and neighbor William Wilberforce was even more adamant that religion should play an active role in the formation of economic and legal policy: the soul of the individual was governed by a sense of conscience that, however painful, would nevertheless move him to appreciate the significance of restraint, obedience, and thoughtfulness apart from whatever selfish advantages he could accrue. Rather than see economics and religion as analogous disciplines, evangelicals understood them as mutually dependent elements of a typological world-view.[22]

Though not openly evangelical himself, Malthus was an important ally in the evangelical cause. Already in his reviews of the bullion controversy, Malthus had warned that an economy committed to supply and not conscious of the vicissitudes of demand was liable to gluts that would only add to the difficulties caused by under-consumption. Like Ricardo he refuted Adam Smith's easy conflation of labor value and utility, as if such a union of moral and material ideas were plain common sense. But he disagreed with his friend that the alternative to this conflation was to turn labor into a metaphysical or moral principle. In Malthus' view, first established in the *Essay on Population* and developed largely in conversation with Ricardo, work was something people had to do to purchase the commodities they needed to sustain themselves, but just because there were more commodities to be had did not automatically mean that people would work harder. On the contrary, people stop working if commodities come easier to them. If underemployment or lethargy cause demand to slow, then production slows with it. The problem is not that supply fails to meet correlate demands, but that people might not be inclined to work hard enough to meet their own demands. Overproduction would lead to general indolence.

Malthus' view of human motivation was not strictly economic, but cultural.[23] Economic activity was mediated, positively or negatively, by situations, contexts, and beliefs. It was for this reason that the dangers inherent in market economies, such as under-consumption or overpopulation could be ameliorated by 'moral virtues' as advocated by education and the Church. Malthus' orientation toward economic culture, however, also entailed a somewhat begrudging commitment to the symbolic and social value of the country. The idea that the agricultural sector had to be protected *at the expense* of commerce or manufacturing was highly dangerous. This does not mean that commerce should cease or that entrepreneurs should be in any sense degraded or repressed. As Malthus noted in his 1814 pamphlet *On the Corn Laws*, commercial people 'infuse fresh life and activity into all classes of the state, afford opportunities for the inferior orders to rise by personal merit and exertion, and stimulate the higher orders to depend for distinction upon other grounds than mere rank and riches. They excite invention, encourage science, and the useful arts, spread intelligence and spirit, inspire a taste for conveniences and comforts among the labouring classes; and, above all, give a new and happier structure to society, by increasing the proportion of the middle classes, that body on which the liberty, public spirit, and good government of every country must mainly depend.'[24] *Suddenly* redirecting domestic markets to manufactured goods by allowing importations of corn and retracting credit risked a sudden collapse in a sector that, at the end of the day, still employed a huge segment of the population. Malthus argued for a patient approach to the 'advantages and disadvantages' of both sides of the debate.

Malthus' approach to agriculture conveyed the sense that society had to be divided between those who worked and those who thought. And thought, too, had to be split between immediate or practical questions and more far-reaching, even spiritual issues. Two writers who brought this strand of Malthusianism to bear on the currency debate were Edward Copleston and Thomas Chalmers. Before becoming Bishop of Llandalf in 1827, Copleston was Bursar of Oriel College, Oxford and the tutor of Robert Peel who chaired the committee on the projected resumption of cash payments in 1819.[25] His *Letter to Peel on the Pernicious Effects of a Variable Standard of Value especially as it relates to the Condition of the Lower Orders and on the Poor Laws* (1819) was the most widely read pamphlet to appear around the deliberations of Peel's committee.[26] Like Malthus and Chalmers, Copleston accepted that government should from time to time interfere in the economy, such as during periods of sudden inflation, but such practical endeavors should not take the place of general cycles of success and failure, trial and reward, which are determined by God. The real basis for understanding the economy is the realization that work, including intellectual work, is the necessary lot of human beings. Copleston's most important contribution to the debate was his exposure of the 'money illusion', the idea that people pay too much attention to the nominal value of money (what they think it can buy) rather than to its real value (what it is actually worth). When the 'end' of economic debate 'is accomplished for a time, and the truth is perceived and acknowledged, how soon is the attention exhausted, and the mind returns with pleasure to that state of slovenly repose in which we are too apt to indulge, unless when excited by considerations of interest and duty ... Dexterity in practice is by no means a criterion of well-grounded knowledge.'[27] It is 'practical men' who neglect the larger principles of political economy. Because financers and policy-makers are easily swept up by their concern with market prices and monetary circulation, they mistake the market for the real economy of which it is only part.

To combat what he called the 'quixotic enthusiasm' of policy-makers, journalists, and financial experts, Copleston insisted that intellectuals should attend to 'real' values, which, like Ricardo, he argued derive from the cost of producing scarce but desirable commodities. Appreciating this real value could not, however, be assumed: it must be continually reflected on so that the moral values that spring from such reflections – the dignity of labor, the necessity of social unity – are not overlooked. In 'State of the Currency', a *Quarterly* review of a proposal for reducing the national debt published in 1822, Copleston urged that no 'one' cause could be found for the difficulties attending currency reform: 'it is now pretty generally felt, that our embarrassments arise from a combination of causes' including both supply and demand, the mutual responsibilities of banks and government, the rights of the public and private individuals.[28] 'It is impossible in theory', Copleston thus concluded, 'to prescribe a limit to these operations' including the fixing of a standard in any particular medium or unit of account.[29] But although that standard is set and known, it does not end the difficulties that the market economy entails. Our understanding of what the standard is, how it works, what it does, depends upon our willingness to probe the difficulties that attend its function and circulation.

Chalmers too was an academic and a divine. Unlike Copleston, however, Chalmers was also an influential preacher and, by the early 1830s, a significant figure in church and political circles. But Chalmers was an economist long before he was a minister. Chalmers' 1808 treatise, *Natural Resources,* written when he was only 23, is a work of astute economic analysis anticipating the method if not the conclusions of Ricardo. Inspired in large part by Malthus, whose *Essay* he had read as a teenager, Chalmers made a case for both the inevitable distinction between the various economic classes, concluding that a redundant working class would necessarily be useful in the military, and also finding an outlet for a necessary and useful system of taxation. Both nationalistic and militaristic, Chalmers' early work is typical of wartime economic polemic; it was, however, a complete failure, barely reviewed and not republished.[30]

Following this failure and a spiritual conversion, Chalmers became Minister of Tron Church in Glasgow, one of Scotland's poorest neighborhoods, and then Professor of Divinity at the University of Edinburgh. His economic writing in these years, notably his *Christian and Civic Economy of Large Towns,* is committed to the central significance of the establishment church to a mixed urban society. Still a devoted Malthusian, Chalmers insisted that government should not interfere in commercial activity: bankruptcy, he insisted, was as much a stimulant to moral reformation as misery and war were to population reform.

Yet, there must still be moral guardians to 'deliver lessons ... raising the whole tone of [the listener's] mind and infusing ... the elements of duty' necessary for personal reformation.[31] The Church would provide mutual benefits at times of increasing economic individuation. By the 1830s the evangelical thesis had become widespread, and divines could speak assuredly of 'the standard of the cross' as easily as they could of the gold standard.[32]

Though Coleridge's open dislike for Malthus probably would have disinclined Chalmers and Copleston to take him altogether seriously, Chalmers' defense of establishment is nevertheless close to Coleridge's argument for the 'National Church'. Like Coleridge, Chalmers urged that religion could instill in people the confidence required to survive a free, commercial economy. The church embodies the true standard to its parish. Coleridge also understood and, indeed, exemplified the sheer emotional and economic difficulty that evangelicals took to be the earthly proof of an ideal standard in God's will. In this respect, Coleridge is a bridge between Christian economics and the literary discourse of the later nineteenth century, in which the difficulty of comprehending the standard in any singular or even divine form was the starting point for the comprehension of a new sense of cultural difference. To arrive at this point, Coleridge had to challenge the premise behind the singular standard that economists, radicals, and even some preachers promulgated. Coleridge's main target in this mission was not Chalmers or any other divine, but the journalist, satirist, and political pit-bull William Cobbett.

Coleridge, Cobbett, and 'The Bullion Controversy'

'Coleridge is in town', Charles Lamb wrote to William Hazlitt in November 1810; 'He is writing, or going to write, in the *Courier* against Cobbett, and in favour of paper money.'[33] From the moment the Bullion Committee was formed in 1809, Cobbett (then incarcerated at Newgate) attacked their deliberations and the debates that followed in a series of letters published in his weekly *Political Register*. In 1813, Cobbett collected the letters into a single volume entitled *Paper v. Gold*; they were subsequently republished, with updates, additions, and new titles almost yearly until the late 1830s. As his punning title suggests, Cobbett did not endorse the gold standard. All state credit was in his estimation fraudulent; the only true money was that which passed between people, reflecting, like his own 'paper', the real value of common knowledge and material wealth. Even in their packaged form, the letters retain the immediacy and anger of their original occasional setting. And this is exactly the unsettling effect Cobbett sought. For Cobbett, the function of the press was to expose the deceit and corruption within the political and financial systems and replace them with a vision of national unity. For Coleridge, whose writings 'against Cobbett and in favour of paper money' appeared in his own journal *The Friend* and then in the conservative daily, *The Courier*, the complexity of the debates surrounding the suspension was the key to understanding them. Money does not signify the value of things, Coleridge argued. It is the conduit by which things manifest their value within an organic system of evolving positions and purposes. Reducing money to a general sign, material object, or social unity negates its primary existence as a complex, fluid medium best interpreted by an intellectual elite. To defend paper money, as Lamb and Hazlitt knew, was to argue against democratic politics.

But Lamb's remark also points to a curious, Escher-esque irony: Coleridge defended paper money in newspaper articles attacking Cobbett's newspaper attacking paper money. In fact, Coleridge and Cobbett shared many views on money. They agreed that the solution to the crisis lay in land, the value of which Cobbett linked to the sturdy practicality of local village farmers and Coleridge associated with institutions that large property owners supported, especially the Church of England. Both disliked Malthus, though in other respects their economic views are also similar to his. Where their views really diverged was on the role of print journalism. Coleridge regarded journalism as an unhealthy, even 'narcotic' profession and newspaper writing, especially Cobbett's, as uninformed, unreliable, slippery, and sly – all too easily manipulated by political institutions and self-interest. But Coleridge was also 'intoxicated' by the *frisson* of newspaper writing and the promise of an immediate and wide readership. He saw it as an opportunity to develop his philosophy in accessible public venues and he was hardly averse to making his political affiliations clear especially when, in the case of *The Watchman* and *The Friend*, *The Morning Post* and *The Courier*, readers assumed partisanship.[34]

Although Coleridge and Cobbett were on opposite sides of the bullion controversy, comparing their respective views on it can tell us a good deal about how writers outside its immediate fray helped to transform its intractability as a 'media event' into models of standardization. Since the seventeenth century, newspapers comprised the synthetic operations that were coming to define modern notions of standardization: in bringing many positions together, newspapers and journals could imply a common standard without having to say what it was, thus hiding their partisanship with the guise of equanimity. In the highly charged political atmosphere of the Romantic period, open partisanship was more often the climatic norm than the stormy exception. Cobbett was a master manipulator of this partisan discourse. The letters frequently convert social distrust and comic irreverence into a highly charged sense of popular unity. What alarmed establishment writers was not Cobbett's antagonism to political economy (in fact, they were sympathetic), but the democratic potential of his rhetoric. Armed with such distrust of governing institutions, the public, it was feared, would have a reason to unite.

Inspired by Paine's *Decline and Fall of the English System of Finance*, but clearly influenced by the many radical satires of the ministry's fiscal policies in the 1790s, including Coleridge's *Watchman*, Cobbett channeled his deep frustration with his own disenfranchisement into sustained attacks on the bullion controversy. Throughout *Paper v. Gold* Cobbett maintains a constant sense of disaffection with the outrageous calumnies of the Tory press while making any number of outrageous charges of his own, exemplifying what Kevin Gilmartin calls Cobbett's 'bricolage ... a capacity to accommodate contradiction'.[35] Cobbett was very good at making 'the system' of political economy feel like an all-consuming and incontestable force but 'if Cobbett sometimes drew on the sense of impersonal determination that was emerging in economic and sociological analysis, he was ruthlessly critical of any effort to use the disappearance of agency as an excuse for existing conditions, or, worse yet, as a pretext for transcendental explanation'.[36] All economic policies had, in Cobbett's view, a foundation in individual motives – most of them entirely self-serving. Yet those motives were routinely justified as simply part of the way things were. In many cases, he simply let the various proponents of currency reform hang themselves. Many speeches were printed verbatim (from parliamentary and newspaper reports, a genre Cobbett himself had helped to found), Randall Jackson's arrogant upbraiding of the Bank of England's detractors being only the most startling.

Cobbett believed that once his readers understood that the fragmented world he described for them was the product of the collusive and oppressive dogmas perpetuated by an elite establishment they would put their trust in new forms of social cohesion.[37] But Cobbett was also nostalgic for an old country order of local obligation and exchange. The gentleman farmers he addresses in *Paper v. Gold* have, he says, a more fundamental understanding of what is being lost in the new finance economy than many of their urban fellows. In the introduction to the collected edition, Cobbett remarks that 'the great and general misery' attendant on the paper-money system was caused not only by the suspension of cash payments, but also by efforts to restrict the resulting bank issues by its opponents. The people have been duped not by one side of the debate or the other but by the collusion of bankers and parliamentarians, who project a 'feeling of confidence' about their notes to distract the people from unjust wars and heavy taxation.[38] His solution was to trace the theory of money back to its 'origins' and to see in this history the way bank charters and credits have been misappropriated and abused by those in power. The purpose of the letters was to expose this collusion, an effort that depended upon a free press. In other words, while he was nominally in favor of the convertibility of paper into gold, the real standard of value is the free exchange of substantiated beliefs.

Underlying such convictions was a loose utilitarian theology. Cobbett famously contended that the best use of the church was not 'preaching' but rather the housing of the poor. In the 1820s, though, Cobbett published a series of *Monthly Sermons* that were meant to instill in the lower classes a sense of confidence in their own virtue and restraint but also to demonstrate that sense of virtue to the middle-class readers as well. In keeping with his democratic politics, Cobbett could be decidedly tolerant. In his *History of the Protestant Reformation*, published in 1826 in the wake of the burgeoning Catholic Emancipation movement, Cobbett decried the founding of the Church of England not to endorse Roman doctrine but rather to malign a bureaucratic establishment whose origins lay in the fragmentation of a general medieval order. Cobbett's hope was that in recognizing that establishment for what it was – the cause of social inequality – the people would embrace their own freedom.[39]

Cobbett tied this political unity to national, religious, and even racial purity. In letter 9 of *Paper v. Gold*, Cobbett wrote a long diatribe on the funeral of Alexander Goldsmidt. A Jewish financier and one of the richest men in London, Goldsmidt shot himself in 1809 when his investments faltered in the wake of the sudden increase in the value of gold. Cobbett began the letter by saying that people have to combine practice with principle. He then quoted the newspapers to show how they puffed Goldsmidt as a 'pillar of the city', repeating with some dismay the claims that report of his death would affect stock prices as much as a war or other catastrophe. Is it true? Cobbett asked. If so, then how can we place so much trust in a system of 'puffs' so risky that it compels people to shoot themselves? This lead Cobbett to contrast the circulation of fraudulent 'paper' – implying a parallel between stocks and news in the process – with his own sense of the 'facts':

> Now, Gentlemen, this is quite enough to enable you to judge of the real character of GOLDSMIDT, who is so extolled by our courtly newswriters, who have, doubtless, their reasons for what they do; you will from these facts alone, facts which cannot be denied, be able to judge, whether this man is deserving of the character, which, with so much industry, is given him; whether he was that kind, benevolent, disinterested, generous, and noble-minded man, which he has been represented to be; or, whether with all his outward show of liberality and generosity, he was as to his essential practices, still a money-loving, a money-massing Jew, and nothing more; and if any additional proof of this were wanting, what need we but the simple fact of his having killed himself, *because he was losing a part of his immense wealth*; a truly Jew-like motive for the commission of an act – at which all human nature shudders? Gentlemen, how much more to be respected and to be pitied are hundreds and thousands of your industrious and honest neighbours, who had their *all* snatched from them in a moment, and who, after a life of labour and of abstinence, saw themselves deprived of the means of buying a dinner; and that, too, observe, without any fault of theirs; without any greedy speculation; any desire on their part to gain by over-reaching their neighbours, or to possess any thing which was not the fair fruit of their labour?[40]

Cobbett affirmed a parallel between financial speculation and celebrity that he also wanted to distinguish from facts, opinions, and quotations. But Cobbett's anti-Semitism points to the ugly side of this realism, its racial exclusivity.[41]

It was on the matter of simplicity that Coleridge wrote against Cobbett. In the introductory essays of *The Friend*, for instance, Coleridge made clear that there will be no easy transition between comment and comprehension. The journal was to be devoted to 'the communication of such delight as rewards the march of TRUTH', but that truth is by no means a *fait accompli*.[42] 'In the establishment of principles and fundamental doctrines, I must of necessity require the attention of my reader to become my fellow-labourer.'[43] Attention and thought cannot produce a dogmatic confidence. Instead, what Coleridge called 'legitimate reasoning' can only be accomplished by a 'successive few' readers who appreciate that hard effort will not necessarily produce a singular or simple point of view. A free press, Coleridge insisted, will open the British public sphere to the damaging effects of 'foreign', influences that presume the simple and indistinctive movement of concepts from one discipline to another. Only a difficult, allusive, and 'connected' style will produce real value by manifesting and maintaining the contingencies of social and national differences. The authority that grounds moral as well as economic standards of value cannot come from a single source; so, Coleridge insisted, they cannot be universal.[44]

The sense of connectedness was the basis for Coleridge's defense of the national debt in 'On Vulgar Errors Respecting Taxes and Taxation', published in the November 9, 1809 edition of *The Friend*.[45] For Coleridge, taxes are part of an evolving network of already existing debts. Legislated by government but freely given by citizens, taxes manifest the mutual trust of individuals and states. Crucially, this trust is never fully realizable. Its effectiveness is contingent largely on the abilities of those in charge. 'Taxes', he wrote, 'often are injurious to a country; at no time, however, from their amount merely, but from the time or injudicious mode in which they are raised'.[46] To compensate for this contingency, the tax system can never co-opt all individual income. The criteria of secure taxation are not isolated amounts paid into it but rather the benefits accrued from the surplus resulting from state sponsorship: 'Whether a System of Taxation is injurious or beneficial on the whole is to be known, not by the amount of the sum taken from each individual, but by that which remains behind.'[47] Because the momentum of capital accumulation is geared toward surplus production, the redistribution of that surplus through the state becomes the means by which the economy achieves stability. In times of war or hardship, taxation erodes this remainder, and it becomes the responsibility of the state to supply it: this is the origin of the national debt. The debt is a manifestation not of state power, but of the state's sacrifice to the operation of commerce. It motivates individual action beyond grudging obligation and toward confidence:

> What made the stoppage of the national Bank the conversation of a day without causing one irregular throb, or the stagnation of the commercial current in the minutest vessel? I answer without hesitation, that the cause and mother principle of this unexampled confidence, of this *system* of credit, which is as much stronger than mere positive possessions, as the soul of man is than his body, or as the force of a mighty mass in free motion, than the pressure of its separate component parts would be in a state of rest – the main cause of this, I say, has been our NATIONAL DEBT.[48]

Coleridge looked back to the medical and scientific metaphors for monetary circulation popular in the eighteenth century. But whereas Locke and others had used such metaphors to show how monetary systems might transcend a debt economy, Coleridge argued that the debt itself, which motivates taxation, is the engine of state finance.

Coleridge channeled his theory of taxation into the series of six editorials entitled 'The Bullion Controversy' he published in *The Courier*, published by Coleridge's friend, Daniel Stuart, in 1811 and 1812.[49] He rehearsed well-worn anti-bullionist truisms about the fundamental difference between gold, which is a commodity, and money, which is merely a means of exchange: 'As soon as a commodity becomes money, it ceases to be a commodity; even as a bag of guineas sold by its weight at Paris or Pekin loses the nature, as well as the name, of money.' He also repeated the anti-bullionist maxim that there is no evidence to support the claim that the high price of bullion is a consequence of restriction:

> if this be true, the effect must have begun at some certain time after the establishment of the cause, and from that time must have regularly, however gradually, increased. Is this the fact? No! It is notorious that for years together, in spite of this Restriction, the Exchange was in favour of this country. The Bullion market has risen and fallen, turned for us and against us much in the same way it used to do before the Bill passed. The theory then is demonstrably false.[50]

Coleridge pilloried the gold standard advocates Francis Horner, Lord Peter King, and William Cobbett as 'Crow King, Jo King, and No King' and under the counter-persona 'Thynne King' trounced the whole idea of depreciation:

> If I went into any shop in London to pay the tradesman a bill of seventeen shillings, and offered him a one-pound note; and if he said, 'I must have two shillings more: the note, I take for fifteen shillings.' – This I should call a depreciation of Bank-paper. But instead of this, the tradesman takes my one-pound, gives me three shillings in change, thanks me, and requests the favour of my future custom. Can you deny this to be the fact? No; they reply, – this we all know. Well then, since there is no difference in point of facts, wherein lies the dispute?[51]

Safe in the ideological arms of the conservative *Courier*, Coleridge was candid in his political allegiances. He bemoaned the 'pernicious trick, of some Journalists, who, however difficult, however complex a subject may be, however it may have divided the opinions of the wisest and best informed men, still address the mass of their readers on it, as if it were '"as plain as a pike-staff"'.[52] By contrast, Nicholas Vansittart's speech against the *Bullion Report* 'contains more original views, and fuller hints for the true *philosophy* of the question than any thing we have yet read on this eagerly controverted subject'.[53]

Underlying these witticisms, however, was Coleridge's hope that readers of *The Courier* would also be inclined to think past common sense and toward a more nuanced appreciation for the complexity of the monetary system. The chief mistake radical 'demagogues' made in denouncing paper money and the taxation system it serves lay in the belief that every payment made to the state incurred a proportionate debt owed to the individual payee. This is a false analogy. If an individual defaults on a debt, Coleridge agreed, he should go to prison. But the state is different. It is in no one's interest that the state becomes bankrupt, which is what would happen if all its debts were called in. The state can never pay itself back since it is its own creditor. In lending money to the state in the form of taxes each individual is in fact crediting every other. 'Who are the nation's creditors? The answer is every Man to every Man.'[54] To make this purpose clear Coleridge promised 'a rapid, yet we trust, plain and satisfactory history of money, taken in its most general sense, as whatever has value among men according to what it *represents* rather than what it *is*'. This was not to deny that money has a value, even a positive or intrinsic value: 'The high expedience that some part of this representative medium should possess an intrinsic, and universally acknowledged, value, in order to be a common measure of the rest, is admitted, but yet forms a distinct and subordinate question. Among nations at all civilized, the latter, thought general, is not universal, or in an *absolute* sense necessary; the former is strictly both universal and necessary.' Appreciating the viability of this standard will come, Coleridge hints, from a 'sketch in the form of history' which 'will contain in itself both the elementary laws, which govern the movements of the circulating medium, and the disturbing forces which result either from a collision of the laws themselves, or from the complexity of the agents'.[55] But when it came time to tell that history, Coleridge related an anecdote about the barter system still being used in the American South. In a kind of negative prophecy, the system as it exists stands for principles that cannot be articulated.

Reducing such difficulties to a simple ideological formula as Cobbett was doing meant that money could be ascribed the status of a referent.

But this, in Coleridge's estimation, would deny it the status of a moral act. And this, rather than referential power, is what makes money viable as a medium of social cohesion. The difficulty is that monetary exchange will on its own not produce consistent returns since individualities and localities will not necessarily be attuned to the same demands. More than fluctuations in the price of gold, the monetary system is liable to 'the *disturbing forces* of men's hopes and fears which vary as their dispositions and degrees of information vary'. Indeed, Coleridge sometimes feared that these forces would hinder the process of reflection he hoped might reinstate the standard. In a contemporary notebook entry, Coleridge wrote: 'Money – Paper money – Peace – War – How comes it that all men in all companies are talking of the depreciation &c &c – & yet that a discourse on Trans substantiation would not be a more withering Scirocco than the attempt to explain philosophically the true cure & cause [of] that which interests all so vehemently.'[56] How Christian thought might do this was the subject of his Lay Sermons.

The symbolic economy of the Lay Sermons

Christian economics was very much in line with the liberal tenor of political economy especially on matters of individual liberty and commercial freedom. Coleridge too was annoyed by brazenly political attempts to curtail this independence. He didn't even like the Corn Laws.[57] In 1814, living in Calne in southwest England, Coleridge delivered a 'butchery sort of speech of an hour long to a very ragged but not very butchery audience' decrying the Corn Laws and defending the public's right to a fair market price. The speech was evidently received well: 'Loud were the Huzzas! If it depended on the Inhabitants at large, I believe they would send me up to Parliament.'[58] His notes on Johann Gottlieb Fichte's *Handelsstaat,* which argued for a closed, national economy, shows that he had no 'confidence in a *philosopher* who has displayed such glaring Ignorance in the principles of State-organization of human Nature as it exists, nay even as it essentially *is* and of course ought to be'.[59]

But Coleridge also differed with the Christian economists, as he did explicitly with Cobbett on how commercial liberty could thrive under the auspices of a strong state and a Church establishment. My contention, to recall, is that Coleridge's argument against the grain of political, radical, and Christian economies helped to transform a defunct trust in biblical scripture into a new kind of standard signified by literature. The key texts in this transformation were the two Lay Sermons. Delivered as fears of revolt in the face of the agricultural crisis and the campaign to instate the gold standard were at their peak, the *Statesman's Manual*, 'addressed to the higher classes of society', argued that the Bible represents a better legislative guide than political economy, while *Blessed Are They Who Sow Beside Waters*, better known as the second Lay Sermon, was aimed primarily at the commercial classes, and urged respect for the property rights that would ensure that proper legislation was possible.[60] The onus of the *Statesman's Manual*, like that of Coleridge's journalism, was to distinguish from simple solutions, which Coleridge described as 'enthusiasm' or 'superstition', a subtler appreciation for the economy's fundamental complexity.

The Statesman's Manual opens with Coleridge attacking the 'jealous priesthood' that would withhold the Bible from general study. The priests of common sense, Coleridge urged, presume either that they know better or that everyone already knows what the Bible says. By contrast, Coleridge insisted that the tensions and debates between readers are fundamental to the Bible's longevity and significance. It is not a definitive theory but a meeting point between doctrinal perspectives. That dissenting zeitgeist derives not from the scarcity or restrictiveness of religious knowledge but rather from the bounty of divine creation. In other words, Coleridge conceived of God as a 'donor' whose charity signals a commitment to humanity. God's benevolence, Coleridge noted, has been hitherto thought of as a reason to restrict access to religious understanding. 'The very excellence of the Giver has been made a reason for withholding the gift; nay the transcendent value of the gift itself assigned as the motive of its detention.'[61] Coleridge countered this by suggesting that the Bible is an open text, waiting for the faithful to interpret and understand it. That understanding, however, requires a form of confidence or trust on the part of the nation's leaders in the lessons the Bible holds. 'In common with your worldly inferiors, you will indeed have directed your *main* attention to the promises and information conveyed in the records of the evangelists and apostles: promises that need only a lively trust in them, on our own part, to be the means as well as the pledges of our *eternal* welfare!'[62] The key to that trust is the realization that our debt to God will never be repaid. This realization leads, in turn, to a renewed sense of purpose that the vicissitudes of war and unemployment have shattered, a reformation in the comprehension of social and moral obligations. In Christian economics, profit cannot be reserved for moral or political ends, since that would deny individual freedom. But freely given charity and philanthropy are signs of faith and good conscience. Coleridge made the additional claim that this surplus, like all existence, depends upon a primary Divine investment. Acts of goodness become a mortgage on this supreme gift. Surplus value, while free, is also always already owed.

The second Lay Sermon, addressed to the 'Middle and Higher Ranks of Society', made the difficulty of such offerings even more apparent. Its chief argument was that the 'Commercial Spirit' in Britain needs to be 'counteracted' by Christianity.[63] Yet, in this case Coleridge was struggling not only against the inclination of a landed aristocracy toward political rather than religious solutions but also against a middle class who, after wartime inflation had enabled many of them to become rich, found themselves ill-equipped to handle the fallout from a sudden economic downturn. Surprisingly, Coleridge blamed the suddenness of the crisis on

> the twin paramount causes, the Paper Currency and the National Debt ... Retrace the progress of things from 1792 to 1813, when the tide was at its height, and then, as far as its rapidity will permit, the ebb from its first turn to the dead low-water mark of the last quarter. Then see whether the remainder may not be generalized under the following heads. Fluctuations in the wages of labor, alternate privation and excess (not in all at the same time, but successively in each) consequent improvidence, and over all discontent and a system of factious confederacy.[64]

Coleridge's solutions to this confusion were to distinguish Agriculture from Commerce and connect the former with spiritual growth. Agriculture, Coleridge urges, has 'positive ends ... 1. to make the means of subsistence more easy to each individual 2. To secure to each of its members THE HOPE of bettering his own condition or that of his children 3. The development of those faculties which are essential to his Humanity, i.e. to his rational and moral Being'.[65] Sustained by the national debt, 'the Spirit of Commerce is itself capable of being at once counteracted and enlightened by the Spirit of the State, to the advantage of both'.[66]

Yet, as he had done in the *Statesman's Manual*, Coleridge made the 'spirit of the state', a kind of symbolic consciousness of national unity, a decidedly conditional affair. The people needed 'a public and parliamentary declaration of the moral and religious grounds that had determined the Legislature to act'. But this had to be conjoined to

> a humble confidence in the blessing of God on the measure; and of their hopes that this sacrifice to principle as being more exemplary

> from the present pressure on the Revenue of the State, would be the more effective in restoring confidence between man and man – I am deeply convinced, that more sterling and visible benefits would be derived from this one solemn proof and pledge of moral fortitude and national faith, than from retrenchments to a tenfold greater amount. Still more, if our Legislators should pledge themselves at the same time, that they would hereafter take council for the gradual removal of counteraction of all similar encouragements and temptations to Vice and Folly, that had alas! been tolerated hitherto, as the easiest way of supplying the exchequer. And truly the financial motives would be strong indeed, if the Revenue Laws in question were but half as productive of money to the State as they are of guilt and wretchedness to the people.[67]

Such a call for reform insisted on a proclamation of principles rather than their realization. Principles are the 'pledge' that the government owes back to God – and to the people to whom God also works in trust. And money is the embodiment of this trust.

Coleridge believed that the best way of ensuring this standard was to protect the revenues of land, allowing the aristocracy to fulfill their traditional role; 'as the specific ends of Agriculture are the maintenance, strength, and security of the state', Coleridge noted in the second lay sermon, 'so ... must its *ultimate* ends be the same as those of the State'.[68] Overhauling the financial system according to market principles on the assumption that the value of land is a form of capital ignores the purpose of aristocracy. 'All reform or Innovation, not won from the free Agent by the presentation of juster Views and nobler interests, and that does not leave the merit of having effected it sacred to the individual proprietor, it were folly to propose, and worse than folly to accept. Madmen only would dream of digging or blowing up the foundation of a House in order to employ the materials in repairing the walls.' Coleridge's trust in nobility was distinctive not simply for its combination of commerce and property – that was common – freeing the aristocracy, but for the occasion that this combination gave to the people to think critically about the way various systems of belief could be channeled.[69] Britain could thus renew its faith in 'national property' by diverting tax revenues away from the agricultural sector, enabling landowners to invest in local improvement and religious education. This would entail that the upper ranks attend to their own moral responsibilities as the guardians of 'nationality' and the middle ranks understand the importance of those responsibilities to their own being.

But it also required the middle ranks to support and, through taxation, leave the upper classes to their independent moral responsibilities.

Arguments like Chalmers' for the Established Church and Cobbett's for Anglo-Christian purity were thus insufficient, because they did not acknowledge the contradiction between liberty and hierarchy that Coleridge saw was essential to economic order. Simple claims are hardly unusual, Coleridge notes: 'It seems a paradox only to the unthinking, and it is a fact that none but the unread in history, will deny, that in periods of popular tumult and innovation the more abstract a notion is, the more readily has it been found to combine, the closer has appeared its affinity, with the feelings of a people and with all their immediate impulses to action.'[70] The clamor after abstractions is understandable: 'The human understanding *musing* on many things snatches at truth, but is frustrated and disheartened by the fluctuating nature of its objects; its conclusions therefore are timid and uncertain, and it hath no way of giving permanence to things but by reducing them.'[71] The answer to this uncertainty could not be a mere statement of confidence, since that would deny the fact of the complexity of experience and the emotions that make it clear. The answer was not abstraction (supply, demand, paper, gold) but relation or, as Coleridge put it, the 'act of faith' that 'is scarcely less than identical with its own being' in 'the *possibility* – of every position, to which there exists any correspondence'. This 'copula' is 'the spiritual substratum of the whole complex body of truths' regarding our relation with and existence in divinity.[72] The basis for Coleridge's standard, then, is not identity but, on the contrary, interpretation, the active decision to say what something is. The principle behind exchange value is metaphor, the ascription of meaning in other, relative terms. A value is not a statement of truth or authority that scripture harnesses a free economy, but rather a metaphorical expression of a relational order freely acknowledged. Thus 'the prerogative of the Bible', irreducible to any doctrine or superstition, is that we must *believe* and that such belief is manifest in surplus investments; 'this is the privilege of its believing students. With them the principle of knowledge is likewise a spring and principle of action. And as it is the only *certain* knowledge, so are the actions that flow with it the only ones on which a secure reliance can be placed.'[73]

Trust is the connecting point between Coleridge's economics and his theory of the symbol. It is well known that the word symbol derives from the Greek *symbolon*, meaning a 'gathering' or collection. In the middle ages, a 'symbol' was a broken coin or token that, when brought together with its match, could be used as a means of identification or passport, often during communion. The underlying principle was that the whole value generated by this unity was greater than the sum of its parts: it manifested the unity of the community under God. Symbolic money does not mean state money in its immaterial or fiduciary form, but rather as money created for the purpose of sustaining the whole economy rather than facilitating trade. This is the sense of symbolic money used by George Berkeley in *The Querist* where he proposed that the function of state credit is to fund public works (such as roads and monuments) that will in turn stimulate other economic activity.[74]

Coleridge borrowed Berkeley's argument for symbolic money in 'On Vulgar Errors' against arguments that wartime taxation is a needless drain on the nation's wealth and responding to an article that appeared 'in a provincial paper of a recent date' complaining that the millions of pounds used to fund Britain's continental expeditions could have been used domestically to build towns, or 'give 100l. to 2,000 poor families in every county in England and Wales'.[75] Such benevolence on the part of the state is noble, but ultimately fallacious. By funding the war effort, the government provides opportunities for other branches of the economy to work and grow. 'Which is better? To give money to the idle, the houses to those who do not ask for them, and towns to counties which have already perhaps too many? Or to afford opportunities to the industrious to earn their bread, and to the enterprising to better their circumstances, and perhaps found new families of independent proprietors?' Expenditures by the state to the wealthy will ultimately create employment among the lower orders. In this case, then, money is not a drain on national well-being, but a stimulant of its industry, which Coleridge refers to as a 'symbol': 'the only mode, not absolutely absurd, of considering the subject would be, not by the calculation of the *money* expended, but of the *labour* of which money is a symbol'.[76] 'It is the National Debt', likewise, 'which by the rapid nominal rise in the value of things, has made it impossible for any considerable number of men to retain their own former comforts without joining in the common industry' including 'all the symbols of the rank in which [they were] born'.[77]

Accordingly, 'a fuller and fairer symbol of Taxation, both in its possible good and evil effects, is to be found' not in the conventional metaphor of circulating blood, well used by Hume, Paine, and other Enlightenment thinkers, but rather 'in the evaporation of waters from the surface of the planet. The sun may draw up the moisture from the river, the morass, and the ocean, to be given back in genial showers to the garden, the pasture, and the corn-field; but it may likewise force away the moisture from the field of tillage, to drop it on the stagnant pool, the saturated swamp, or the unprofitable sand-waste.' Better than the human body, 'The gardens in the south of Europe supply, perhaps, a not less apt illustration of a system of Finance judiciously conducted, where the tanks or reservoirs would represent the capital of a nation, and the hundred rills hourly varying their channels and directions under the gardener's spade, give a pleasing image of the dispersion of that capital through the whole population, by the joint effect of Taxation and Trade.' And this analogy led Coleridge to another between the state and commerce: 'For Taxation itself is a part of Commerce, and the Government may be fairly considered as a great manufacturing house carrying on in different places, by means of its partners and overseers, the trades of the ship-builder, the clothier, the iron-founder, &c.'[78] With this shift from bodily to agricultural to manufacturing metaphors, Coleridge corrected the economics by interlocking and refracting its referents.

There is, of course, something highly imaginative, even illusory, about Coleridge's symbol.[79] And there is something decidedly metonymic about Coleridge's famous definition of the symbol in the *Statesman's Manual* as 'characterized by a translucence of the Special in the Individual, or of the General in the Especial, or of the Universal in the General'.[80] The symbol is always about to appear; it never refers to something else. In thus figuring the symbol as a prolepsis Coleridge was thinking of the symbol not as a presence but only as a potential realization of present action, of a conscious decision to establish a relation in the face of its acknowledged contingency. This contrasts with his understanding of allegory as a historical genre. 'The histories and political economy of the present and preceding century partake in the general contagion of its mechanic philosophy, and are the *product* of an unenlivened generalizing Understanding.'[81] Whereas allegory is merely the '*counterfeit* product of the mechanical understanding', the symbol is the imagined and thus enacted fulfillment of God's gift, returned in hope if not in kind. This is what Coleridge means when he says that 'the Scriptures, are the living *educts* of the Imagination'. The Bible provides a 'reconciling and mediatory power, which incorporating the Reason in Images of the Sense, and organizing (as it were) the flux of the Senses by the permanence and self-circling energies of the Reason, gives birth to a system of symbols, harmonious in themselves, and consubstantial with the truths, of which they are the *conductors*'. It is in this sense that, Coleridge concludes, 'the Sacred Book is worthily entitled the WORD OF GOD'.[82]

In the Lay Sermons, Coleridge revived the argument for textual authority that had been lost in economic discourse in a new and more dialectical form. Coleridge knew that on its own such an unequal system would be unpalatable; hence the investment in the Church establishment that, as the moral guardian of all, was also the moral object of the economy's fundamental disequilibrium. Thus, for Coleridge, the ambivalence of economic freedom – that it is not free at all – becomes an opportunity for a new understanding of what exactly that freedom consists in. Indeed, that understanding grounded Coleridge's writing after 1816, from *The Biographia Literaria* to *Aids to Reflection* and *The Logic*. We exist, Coleridge urged, both in the shadow of a divine unity and as free agents. The difficulty of reconciling these positions is the task of the program of hermeneutics that Coleridge sought to delineate. The clerisy, Coleridge's influential version of the public intellectual class, comprising faculties of philosophers and divines drawn from the younger sons of the landed gentry and paid for with church tithes, were to interpret God's gift and thus push the waters of commerce through the channels of protected agricultural revenue to perform their social good. This was, in short, the 'idea' of the constitution that at the end of his career Coleridge imagined as the educational legacy of the bullion controversy. And, although *The Statesman's Manual* may well have been read by fewer scholars than actual statesmen, Coleridge's idea, perhaps ironically, helped to establish the standard as a cultural as well as economic principle.

The standard and the idea

On the flyleaf of John Taylor's 1830 *Essay on Money*, Coleridge wrote this:

> I believed myself to stand alone an unsupported Paradoxist but nevertheless compelled to admit, that this fact, that not the least difficulty exists in any part of the Kingdom of raising money on reasonable Security, is a fair presumption against its deficiency. The Evil it seems to me, is very contrary of that supposed in the Writer's Answer – Every year produces a new troupe of Rich Men so that the Capitalists, like the Lemmings or Norwegian Mountain-Rats, exhausting the materials on which the Capital can be employed, turn against each other – and the ominous Work of Underselling, Cheap shops, &c &c commences. – Observe, however, that this does not in the least weaken my conviction as to the illegitimacy of bullion money – i.e. the confusion of

> representant and represented. The perfection of Money is ideality – or where the Medium, the circulating Word, is in itself, like the Air of which the Word materially consists, below any calculable value. The hitherto unsolved problem, the desideratum ingens, of the SOCIAL STA[T]E is an unforgeable Medium. This attained, Paper would approach the perfection of the Idea.[83]

Taylor will be familiar as half of Taylor and Hessey, the firm that published, among other works, Keats' *Lamia* volume and Coleridge's *Aids to Reflection* before folding in the market crash of 1825, after which he and his brother James became monetary reformers. The Taylors were adamant that the most secure monetary system was an inconvertible standard regulated strictly by law which they called 'symbolic money'. They also insisted that this purely legal standard must be a commodity, because it is only by being bought, sold, and owned that it can be said to have any value at all and because it is only by being constantly exchanged that the commodity will achieve its 'natural price'.[84] In contrast, Coleridge claimed that the value of money was not tied to any commodity. By believing that value lies in material things (like gold), or by transferring confidence from the meaning of money to the things it buys, people divest money of this cohesive power. By regarding money as an object exchangeable for other objects, individuals open themselves to forgery and other forms of double-dealing. Money will become, as Coleridge says, the 'perfection of the Idea' when its users give themselves up to the 'Air of which the Word materially consists', the circulation of value.

The remark on the idea of paper money cited above appears in a marginal note on the flyleaf of one copy of a single relatively unknown pamphlet published many years *after* the contentions with which it is concerned were largely settled. A minor point perhaps, but given the argument I have been making about the relation between monetary value and monetary debate it does have bearing. As Heather Jackson has shown us in her studies of reading and note-taking habits in the Romantic era, 'readers had been deliberately trained to mark and annotate books' and thus understood that 'books do not grow, but are made; that they are constructed from separate parts that can be dismantled and used again somewhere else'.[85] In relation to the book business, marginal notes might be understood as discrete acts of individualization within an economy that, thanks to the perennial debates over copyright, was forever establishing new and more truculent standards of permanent truth and intrinsic value. Coleridge clearly did not believe in such a standard, as both his fastidious marginalizing and his constant revisions to his own poems indicate, though he *did* believe both in authorial copyright and in the permanence and universality of certain sacred ideas. As Coleridge said, ideas are tied directly to the media ('state, form, or mode') in which they circulate, and it is only as media that ideas have value at all.[86]

In assuming this, Coleridge left himself open to precisely the kind of dissent that he encouraged in his journalism. These criticisms were particularly acute in 1816. The publication of *Christabel* inspired an obstreperous debate in the reviews between *The Times* and *The Courier*, which championed the poem's invocation of poetic mysteries, and William Hazlitt in *The Examiner* who found in its mystical aesthetics an excuse for the mystification of aristocratic rule. This debate was the background for Hazlitt's 'review' of *The Statesman's Manual*, which appeared several days before the sermon was published and, on the basis of an advertisement in the *Times* accused Coleridge of spouting philosophical nonsense and Tory propaganda: 'His imagination thus becomes metaphysical, his metaphysics fantastical, his wit heavy; his arguments light, his poetry prose, his prose poetry, his politics turned – but not to account.'[87] Hazlitt's review was a more democratically appealing blend of plain speech and social concern, and he extended that rhetorical poise to the reviews of the Lay Sermons that followed. Hazlitt's trust in Enlightenment principles of public opinion, honest work, and material value exacerbated the difference between his own investment in economic fact and Coleridge's seeming trust in metaphysics and spirituality. Even the idea of a lay sermon, Hazlitt noted, 'puts us in mind of Mahomet's coffin, suspended between heaven and earth, or of the flying islands of Laputa which hovered over the head of Gulliver'.[88] Coleridge was, for Hazlitt, a phenomenon of pure media, indeed a media event unto himself. He is an 'original mode of composition – as long as he does not put to paper, the first sentence cannot contradict the second ... His are all maiden ideas; immaculate conceptions.'[89] Coleridge's style, Hazlitt went on, 'is the "Secret Tattle" of the press. Each several work exists only in the imagination of the author, and is quite inaccessible to the reader ... Let the experiment be tried and if on committing the manuscript to the press, the author is caught in the fact of a single intelligible passage, we will be answerable for Mr. Coleridge's loss of character.'[90]

Hazlitt wrote about British monetary policy and economic debate in much the same terms as he attacked Coleridge. In an essay on 'The Speeches of Brougham and Western' concerning the agricultural distresses, and published just prior to his exposé of the *Statesman's*

Manual, Hazlitt fumed: 'all that has been said or written upon [money] is a palpable delusion – an attempt to speak out and say nothing'.[91] To Hazlitt, the shipment of money used to pay troops in 1797 – the cause of the suspension crisis – was 'a real bona fide waste of the means, wealth, labour, produce, or resources of the country'. But the underlying problem, he went on, is the 'unproductive labour' of government policy-making itself, the term here equating government spending with the human cost of militarization:

> That money laid out in war is thrown away is self-evident from this single circumstance, that government never refund. The reason is, because they never do any thing with their money that produces money again. They are the worst bankers in the world. The Exchequer is a true Sinking Fund. If you lend money to a farmer, a manufacturer, a merchant, he employs it in getting something done, for which others will pay, because it is useful ... But money sunk in a war brings in no returns – except of killed and wounded.

He then cited Coleridge's essay on taxation in the *Friend* as an example of the 'partly willful and partly shallow sophistry' that gets spoken around the issue of taxation.

While Hazlitt's attacks on Coleridge and British monetary policy similarly exemplify his utter loathing for Tory propaganda, other pieces show a decidedly Coleridgean influence. Indeed, while Hazlitt may have despised Coleridge's political confidence, he shared his existential embarrassment. In his early *Essay on the Principles of Human Action*, Hazlitt refuted Enlightenment and utilitarian arguments that 'self-interest' should be the foundation for morality. A sense of self could only be assembled through the records of past deeds and present sensations whereas a sympathetic understanding of others, the basis for any ethical system, could only come about through an imaginary 'interest' or 'investment' in their potential goodness toward us. By defining the imagination in this way, Hazlitt involved his ethics in a series of contradictions. On one hand, the basis for individual actions toward another is his 'disinterested' appreciation for the other's well-being and this disinterest 'is always absolutely independent of, uninfluenced by the feelings of the being for *whom he acts*, whether this be himself, or another'. On the other hand, that disinterest can only be motivated by vague reflections on the future. 'When we say that future objects act upon the mind by means of the imagination, it is not meant that such objects exercise a real power over the imagination, but merely that it is by means of this faculty that we can foresee the probable or necessary consequences of things, and are interested in them.'[92] In Hazlitt's view, there can be no confidence of the intentional kind because there is nothing to feel confident about except the 'disinterested' sense of future well-being inspired by our feelings or sensations.[93]

Like Coleridge, Hazlitt offered an ethics for a world without standards. Indeed, when he says in the *Essay* that the self cannot calculate 'like debits and credits' the obligations he owes to the other, Hazlitt seems to be imagining the kind of universal indebtedness at stake in Coleridge's Lay Sermons. This embarrassment is especially powerful in his 1827 essay 'On the Want of Money'. The subject of the essay is constantly on the lookout for his creditors, actual and potential, and for ways to avoid them, 'what excuse to make to the servants, what answer to send to the tradespeople; whether to laugh it off, or be grave, or angry, or indifferent; in short to know how to parry off an evil which you cannot help'.[94] In characteristic style, and in keeping with the contradictions of his philosophy of apparent disinterestedness, Hazlitt blends feelings of anxiety with the pains of hunger: 'Humiliating Contemplations! Miserable uncertainty! ... without one's breakfast, one has not the resolution to do anything!'[95] At one point, a shilling coin is discovered in a coat pocket, and the writer descends to breakfast with a self-satisfied joy that is so forced as to betray its underlying helplessness. In this and other essays, Hazlitt conceived his demoralization at the hands of desire as a 'commitment to intersubjectivity'. Disinterestedness implies a negation of selfhood, but also a record or model of the person in that negative state. Hazlitt's Coleridgean embarrassment becomes its own standard.

Thomas De Quincey was also influenced by his reading of and acquaintance with Coleridge even if that influence sometimes manifested itself as frustration with Coleridge's overbearing verbosity and pretension.[96] De Quincey understood that the world was a different place from the one it had been in the eighteenth century and that 'simple' solutions, like the labor theory of value, could not reflect its complexities. Yet, as with both Coleridge and Hazlitt, difficulty became for De Quincey the only possible alternative to this stalled sense of principle. This preference for difficulty, an embrace of what De Quincey calls the 'master-key for unlocking' our 'past embarrassments', is especially apparent in his writings on the bullion question.[97] Early in 1819, De Quincey published in the *Westmoreland Gazette* a series of 'Papers of the Bank of England' in which he dismissed the widespread belief that excess issues had caused the price of banknotes to fall and the value of gold to rise. In the first of these, De Quincey wrote obliquely 'there is no such thing among coins as a *standard of value*. Whosoever uses the expression as denoting any thing real – demonstrates his ignorance of the very foundations of political economy.'[98] Though addressed to Peel's 1819 committee and responding to Copleston, the subject of the papers that follow is the question over the disparity between banknotes and bullion as debated in 1810–11. Like Coleridge's bullion controversy editorials, De Quincey's papers offered a broadly historical picture of the monetary system to distinguish it from the narrower views of the financial experts. But unlike Coleridge, De Quincey actually reviewed the history, in painstaking detail. The papers are indeed a sprawling, fragmented argument, complete with charts and tables, and a lengthy digression on the national debts of England and France from the sixteenth century to 1811. For all of its complexity, though, De Quincey's aim as stated in the conclusion was simple. He proved that the price of gold did rise in the summer of 1809. But he also proved that this rise did not cause a fall in the value of paper:

> the Bank of England is of all the national Banks which exist in Europe the only Bank whose issues are revolving issues; that consequently in the circulation of her notes action and reaction are constantly equal; that, if a hundred pounds too much were thrown out from the Bank into circulation, then a hundred pounds more than usual must by necessity be thrown back from the circulation in the Bank; and finally, by inevitable consequence, that, – if the Bank, if the merchants of London, if the Lords and Commons of England, if the crown, should all combine their efforts, – they could not, under the present constitution of the Bank, keep out in circulation one single pound note beyond the amount necessary for the national uses.[99]

By 1819, this was a fairly commonplace view: a constant circulation of credits and debts sustains the Bank, not its reserves of bullion. This is not to say that the value of these debts is constant; they are not in themselves the standard, any more than gold, the value of which has always been fluid. But what De Quincey imagines here is a cycle of exchanges that, under the command of his own scholastic argument, produced not coherent but dynamic comprehensiveness.

It was not Coleridge, however, but Ricardo who seems to have been De Quincey's preferred model of intellectual rigor and economic clarity. We are all familiar with Ricardo's famous appearance as the 'man of capital' at the conclusion of *Suspiris de Profundis* – a man at the center of a beautiful machine, making subtle changes in its brilliant order at the touch of his fingers. The sublimity of this image, though, is an effect of the way De Quincey *reads* Ricardo. Ricardo's style is significant precisely because it is most clear when it appears most obscure. Ricardo's obscurity was a consequence of the fact that he developed firm principles for knowledge that is, by and large, tacit. We do not see what Ricardo shows us – just as in Hazlitt's essay we do not know that the shilling is in our coat pocket – but we do know that the by-ways and alleys that make up finance's fantastic urban architecture are there. The only times people pay attention to this knowledge are in moments of panic or when they are confronted with money questions in specialized terms. Ricardo converts that panic into intellectual fuel, which in turn drives his readers' desire to know how the economic actually works into the realization that they barely know what its language means. 'The obscurity, where any exists in Ricardo, is rather permitted than caused by his style of exposition: in part it adheres to the subject, and in part it grows out of the lax colloquial application which most men have allowed to the words, *value*, *labour*, and *rent*; so that, when they find these words used with a stern fidelity to one sole definition, they are confounded. Pulled up sharply by the curb-chain of Ricardo, they begin to fret, plunge, and grow irritated.'[100] Reading Ricardo entails being taken out of one's ordinarily complacent reliance of a tacit, vicarious understanding of economic truths and seeing the precariousness of daily life. Ricardo's principles thus meet with a response akin to the sublime in De Quincey's aesthetics: a fretful anxiety that occurs not in confrontation with overwhelming power, but rather, as in the murder essay, with the comprehension of meaning within the mundane.

The general misunderstanding of Ricardo's style was a function of the fact that, as De Quincey says, Ricardo always wrote for a specialized audience: 'it was the *clerus*, and not the *populus* whom Ricardo addressed'.[101] It is here that De Quincey betrayed Coleridgean sympathies. Ricardo requires, De Quincey then suggests, a hermeneutics, a theory of interpretation, what he calls at the end of the essay, a 'commentary'. As Margaret Russett has pointed out, 'commentary' signals in De Quincey the action taken by the critic to create his subject, in De Quincey's case Romanticism (in his writings on Wordsworth) and political economy.[102] As a result of this commentary, De Quincey mystified Ricardo's economics, transforming it from a practical defense of free trade and stock-jobbing, into the transcendental force out of which economic understanding, and from it economic stability, emerges. Ricardo's *Principles*, in contrast to the Smith's 'system' 'was a work *de pincipiis*, a searching inquiry into principles, or first beginnings, as the gold rings from which all the rest is suspended'.[103]

Connecting De Quincey's account of the bullion controversy and his valorization of Ricardo to Coleridge's views on money was their common understanding that debt regulates the standardized economy rather than an economic standard restraining debt. Most commentators on De Quincey's political economy agree that its governing principle is a 'psychology of desire': it is our demand for pleasure that drives economic production and not the other way around.[104] In fact, though, De Quincey's later writings on value, most notably his *Logic of Political Economy* published in 1845, suggest that desire is always the consequence of a debt that has its ultimate origin in the gift of life – as the prostitute Ann gives up hers to the suffering student De Quincey in the *Confessions*. Our desires can never be fulfilled because there is always another debt to pay. From this embarrassment comes the reflexive consciousness that makes the standard possible. There is something holding the social state together – Ricardo knows it, so does De Quincey – but it exists only as a kind of sublime product of continual drive and disappointment.

De Quincey was not the only commentator to combine Coleridgean metaphysics with Ricardian materialism. After his death, Coleridge's name became widely synonymous with lethargy and addiction. But he also influenced Victorian social and economic thought. His children, who edited and reissued many of his philosophical works, were partly responsible for this revival. Rather than see him as a critic of political economy or, worse, as a deranged metaphysician, the younger Coleridges depicted him as an exemplar of the Christian intellectual, struggling, even laboring, as evangelicals like Copleston recommended, to understand the truths of nature so that we mere mortals would not have to. Beginning with Henry Nelson Coleridge's edition of the *Table Talk* (first published in 1835 with repeated editions until the 1880s), Coleridge became the paragon of the intellectual laborer. 'Coleridge's mind', Henry Nelson recalls in his preface, 'was too deep, subtle, and peculiar to be fathomed by a morning visitor'.[105] And although he was from time to time 'mastered by' his own intellectual genius, it was his struggle to achieve 'a universal Christian philosophy' for a modern age that made him great: 'desultory as his labours, fragmentary as his productions at present may seem, to the cursory observer – my undoubting belief is, that in the end it will be found that Coleridge did, in his vocation, the day's work of a giant'.[106]

Sara Coleridge's 1850 edition of *Essay On My Own Times* is notable for its effort to render all of her father's journalistic writings, including the important essays on taxation and the bullion controversy, into a comprehensive philosophical whole. Her inclusion of selections from *The Watchman* had the potential to disrupt this image, requiring Coleridge to excise significant portions of the early writings in the name of political consistency. At the same time, in her lengthy introduction to the edition, Sara used the progress from the *Watchman* to the *Courier* and beyond to argue that her father's career exemplifies the 'growth' of all writers toward the fulfillment of a system, the 'immaturity' of which is inevitably tainted by youthful exuberance.[107] In 1852, the publisher Edward Moxon issued an edition of Coleridge's *Lay Sermons*, edited and annotated by the poet and philosopher's son, Derwent. In his preface, Derwent Coleridge described the sermons as having 'somewhat of an occasional character, with an express reference to a particular conjunction of affairs, not without an appearance, though an appearance only, of political bias, and with considerable warmth of language, they conciliated no prepossessions, and were calculated to serve no party purpose. Above all, they were found to require a fixity of attention in the perusal, and an amount of patient afterthought, which it would be unreasonable to expect from the many, and which is not easy to obtain, for any deeper process of self-knowledge, even from a few.'[108] The chief characteristic of the sermons is their difficulty, which also, Coleridge writes, entails a range of subjects and varied tones and positions suitable to the complex issues they describe.

Another group with Coleridgean predilections was the Cambridge Apostles Julius Hare, F. D. Maurice, John Sterling, and, after they left for London, Richard Chenevix Trench, Henry Hallam, and Alfred Tennyson. Not really a distinct movement with a clear doctrinal vision, the Cambridge scholars were a loose collective whose members experimented with various religious affiliations and schools of thought. By the late 1820s, Hare and Maurice had become devotees of a strenuously intellectual form of liberal Anglicanism that abandoned both the mechanical simplicity of the radical Unitarians and the evangelical emphasis on sin and atonement and embraced instead a Coleridgean idea of 'the Central Unity ... of the living being'. In a letter to Derwent Coleridge, published as the dedication to the second of *The Kingdom of Christ; or, Hints to a Quaker* (1842), Maurice expressed his sympathy for Coleridge's reformist view 'that he who first entertains a reverence for inward Truth, and then acquires a reverence for outward Signs, begins in the spirit, and is made perfect in the flesh'.[109] These signs, Maurice went on, are 'signs of the existence of that universal body' and are 'indispensable in a higher sense ... they are the voice in which God speaks to his creatures, the very witness that their fellowship with each other rests on their fellowship with Him, and both upon the mystery of Being; the very means of which we are meant to rise to the enjoyment of the highest blessings which He has bestowed upon us'. Manifested in 'the idea of a CHURCH UNIVERSAL', Maurice's 'higher' signs are Coleridgean symbols, reflections of a divine providence which to interpret is a duty.[110]

As well as an avowed admiration for Shelley and the Lake Poets, the Apostles shared a firm loathing for Benthamite utilitarianism. This did not, however, mean that they were antagonistic to political economy per se or to the cause of social liberty. Both Maurice and Sterling entertained revolutionary sympathies in the late 1820s – supporting Catholic Emancipation for instance – which, as Carlyle noted, seemed to contradict the taste for 'transcendental moonshine' that they imbibed from Coleridge.[111] In fact, precisely this combination of humanistic idealism and social libertarianism characterizes the Apostles' creed. Sterling for instance wrote at length that the certain knowledge necessary for social reform and economic improvement was only accessible through an 'inward strength' attainable in Christian faith.[112] Riding a wave of Shelleyan fervor, Hallam and Trench (with support from Tennyson and Maurice), proselytized the poet's liberalism, combining it with Wordsworthian and Coleridgean 'spirit' into a kind of Romantic *gemeinschaft*, to fellow railway passengers in Scotland and to Spanish refugees. In 1836, Maurice put himself forward for the Drummond Chair in Political Economy at Oxford on the ground that there was no one else qualified for the position. Maurice wrote to Hare that he would try to do due diligence in the post 'to save us from being a nation of money getters' and he received a groundswell of support from several Tractarians who had been utterly dissatisfied with the apparently anti-Christian views of the Drummond Chair's previous occupiers and who, it seemed, were attempting to place the study of economics firmly within the rubric of High Church moralism.[113] Maurice was finally turned down for the post (in favor of the more liberal Herman Merivale) because of his disestablishment views on infant baptism. Instead, he assumed the more companionable post of the Professor of English Literature and History at King's College, which had been established in 1828 as an Anglican counter to University College's utilitarian leanings.

The main venue for the Apostles was *The Athenaeum*, founded by Sterling and Maurice in 1828. In its very first issues, Maurice put a Laker stamp on the weekly by publishing a series of articles on 'Contemporary Authors' in which they praised Coleridge, Wordsworth, and Southey, as well as Shelley, Edgeworth, and Moore and excoriated the likes of Brougham, Mill, and Mackintosh.[114] Maurice and Sterling championed the difficulty and complexity of the Lake Poets and held Shelley's poetry to be an embodiment of the same spirit especially because it seemed thereby to contradict its own politics. But the *Athenaeum* was also a crucial vehicle for the Apostles' economic views. Acknowledging the need for 'steam-engines and commercial competition', Maurice stressed that the public must also be aware of the 'stifling atmosphere of cotton-mills' and 'the flood of debasement and misery which rolls along out streets, and overflows our prisons'.[115] All of the Apostles chafed at the idea of the Reformed Parliament and believed, as Coleridge had taught, that the state should be controlled by an elite propertied class, taught and guided by an intellectual clerisy. Yet, Maurice was also an admirer of Jean-Baptiste Say's *Practical Politics*, noting that the subtlety of his theory was a testament to the complexity of the economy itself, a complexity that must be understood in relation to both a mixed society and to divine purpose. The November 29, 1829 issue opened with a 'Conversation on Political Economy' modeled on the semi-fictional works of Jane Marcet, in which two parliamentarians debate the extent to which the labor of dressing mutton chops should be recompensed or treated as a 'pleasure' in itself. It was precisely the kind of 'speculative' reasoning on offer in Parliament and in the press that Maurice and Sterling objected to. In short, what the Apostles sought to convey was an ideal standard of value, one rooted in the spiritual mystique of high literary culture.

In their own ways, Hazlitt, De Quincey, and Maurice transformed Coleridge's critique of Christian economics into the ground for a new, quasi-secular variant, a kind of writing that combined realistic accounts of the hardships of daily and historical experience with an awareness of scientific, economic, and theological principles, a genre that today we might call critical theory or, in its broadest sense, 'literature'. It is no wonder, I think, that Victorian writers like Dickens and Eliot could bring Romantic aesthetic ideals and practical political economy together in their novels because, as I have argued, that combination was already present in Romantic economics itself. But it is in its relation to Christian economics that Coleridge's articulation of a literary standard – the symbol, the 'idea of paper money' – comes to have its most resilience. If Romanticism persists today as a 'post-secular' phenomenon, it does so not in the service of a Chalmerian establishment but rather as the realization of the fundamental disunity of economic life. This realization is born of frustration and understanding rather than artistic naiveté. But it became the hallmark of a new, complex idea of standardization.

4
Monetary Forgery and Romantic Poetics

Forging banknotes was a capital crime in Britain in the eighteenth and nineteenth centuries. Only during the Romantic period, however, was the death penalty routinely enforced. In 1796, no one in Britain was hanged for forgery. By 1818, 313 people had been sent to the gallows. A further 512 were transported to Botany Bay for passing forged notes. Considering that more than a thousand people were arrested for forgery, the conviction rate was very high. But it pales in comparison to the 300,000 forged notes the Bank of England received between 1797 and 1834. The circumstances surrounding the high incidence of banknote forgery in the period were equally unsettling. Following the suspension of cash payments, the bank issued – for the first time – one- and two-pound notes. They were poorly designed and easy to forge. To deter forgers, the Bank pursued a vigilant campaign of prosecution. This put it in a strange situation legally. The Bank was protecting the currency, but its own policies were behind the high incidence of forgery in the first place. The crisis finally came in December 1818 when two juries, acting against the advice of the judges, acquitted because they could not tell the difference between forged notes and the Bank's. The acquittals led to reforms that curtailed juries' ability to act with such discretion.[1] Nevertheless, the statutes relating to forgery were not significantly altered until 1829 and even then forgery remained a capital offense.

Not surprisingly, monetary forgery was a controversial issue in the Romantic period. It was a crucial bone of contention to those politicians and economists who believed that the government's failure to implement the gold standard that already existed in law had severe social as well as financial consequences. In response, the Bank of England as well as other commercial and philanthropic organizations mounted campaigns to produce an 'inimitable note' that would adequately represent the intrinsic value of 'real' currency in a way that existing note issues clearly could not. In turn, radical commentators used the ease with which Bank of England notes could be forged as evidence of state corruption and thus the impetus for a gold standard. Even those journalists, like William Cobbett, William Hone, and Thomas Wooler, who did not endorse standardization, pilloried the Bank and the government for prosecuting holders of notes that the Bank itself had 'forged'.

Percy Shelley also mentioned gold and forgery a number of times in his poems and the social inequality and political divisions underlying the forgery problem is a prominent topic in his post-Waterloo writings. Critics are familiar, of course, with Shelley's distaste for political economy, its relentless 'calculations' of self-interest and its neglect thereby of broader political, philosophical, and ethical concerns: the unreliability of language, the purpose of pleasure, the nature of emotion and its relevance to social understanding. But, as I have already suggested, these concerns were actually fundamental to the economic discourse of the restriction period in all its conservative, radical, expert, and journalistic permutations. What made Shelley different from the journalists was his insistence that poetry might contribute to these debates in a direct way. Indeed, what Shelley called 'the poetic spirit' – a unifying force that exists through and in the mutual respect of individuals and both known and disseminated by the nation's intellectual elite – is in many respects another way of conceiving of confidence; Shelley's poetics represents in this perspective a fairly straightforward call for a universal standard of value.

But Shelley also embraced a contradiction that, while not inimical to political economy, was nevertheless a distraction to be avoided. On one hand, Shelley's spirit manifests the supreme knowledge of absolute, universal value; on the other, spirit is at the mercy of history and thus to the genres and forms of understanding that must be exchanged or imitated in order to adapt to it. In disseminating the absolute values that will prevent forgery, we participate in a kind of forgery ourselves. Shelley himself believed that this knowledge was precisely what made poetic understanding more truthful than economics, especially since it was only in the complex vectors of poetic form that it could be made apparent. After Shelley, this contradiction became the basis for a new mode of late Romantic poetics, one that in its engagement with economic debates and its experiments with self-conscious modes of poetic failure and collapse, reformulates Shelleyan confidence into a new dynamic of aesthetic embarrassment.

Radical reform and the 'inimitable' note

Forgery had always been a pressing concern among government economists and financial experts. Coining and clipping were already regarded as forms of treason and even minor offenses against the coin of the realm were prosecuted with utmost diligence.[2] Banknote and other forms of paper money forgery were less common, and, for bankers and other finance professionals, no less aggravating. Paper money was not legal tender so forging it could not be considered a crime against the state, only against property. Not until the William Hales case of 1729, in which several members of Parliament, wealthy financiers, and aristocrats were implicated, was forging private bills a capital crime.[3] Like Hales, accused counterfeiters tended to be young aristocrats forced by excessive debt to sustain their fashionable lifestyles by criminal means. They were defended as men of good families led astray by a corrupt financial system.

Paper-money forgery also had an affinity with social prestige and literary accomplishment. If all writing is essentially fictional, if certain forms of plagiarism are not just acceptable but in fact encouraged by the standards of taste and education of the day, how could forgery be considered a crime? The Reverend William Dodd, the last man in England to be hanged for forgery before the suspension of cash payments published in his own name a much admired sermon, much of which was written for him by Samuel Johnson.[4] A former Church of England Minister and private tutor, Dodd was already notorious for having bribed the Lord Chancellor to secure a living. In 1776, he forged a bond worth 4,200 pounds in the name of a former pupil, the Earl of Chesterfield, but he was discovered when a bank clerk requested a clean copy of the note and the Earl responded that he had never seen it before. Dodd confessed to the crime, was tried at the old Bailey, and was sentenced to death. Although 23,000 people signed a petition demanding a reprieve, Dodd was executed at Tyburn on June 22, 1777. Johnson knew Dodd as a gentleman, if a somewhat simple-minded and selfish one.

The sermon is not an authentic vindication of Dodd's innocence: it is rather a classic example of the death-row confessional. It features, moreover, an encomium against the rash sense of self-worth that had brought Dodd to forgery in the first place. 'Being distinguished and elated by the confidence of mankind, I had too much confidence in myself; and thinking my integrity what others thought it, established in sincerity and fortified by religion, I did not consider the dangers of vanity, nor suspect the deceitfulness of my own heart.'[5] The sermon then redirects confidence away from the financial realm to the spiritual, in which confidence had originated. '*Faith* is a full and undoubting confidence in the declarations made by God in the holy Scriptures; a sincere reception of the doctrines taught by our blessed Saviour, with a firm assurance that he died to take away the sins of the world, and that we have, each of us, a part in the boundless benefits of the universal Sacrifice.'[6] We are all indebted to Jesus for the remission of sin; faith is an expression of our trust in divine credit or benefit. In writing this sermon and not acknowledging it, Johnson made plain the transferability and legitimacy of scriptural forms. 'Dodd got it from me to pass as his own', Boswell records Johnson saying; 'while that could do him any good, there was an *implied promise* that I should not own it. To own it, therefore, would have been telling a lie, with the addition of breach of promise, which was worse than simply telling a lie to make it be believed it was Dodd's. Besides, Sir, I did not *directly* tell a lie: I left the matter uncertain.'[7] Johnson assumed that as long as Dodd believed that the sermon was his, Johnson was obliged not to reveal his authorship. In revealing himself, Johnson would have been lying and breaking his oath, which are two crimes rather than one. The casuistry is palpable here, and Johnson knew it. The point is that in matters of honor or assumed obligation, the line between truth and lying is decidedly blurred. Indeed, Dodd's conversion in the face of his crimes is a testament to the power of embarrassment as a means of literary acclaim. His five-book poem on duty and sacrifice, *Thoughts in Prison*, was published eleven times, most editions featuring letters (including one by Johnson) defending Dodd as a victim of a hypocritical legal system.[8]

Thomas Chatterton, as well as inventing spurious identity in the figure of the medieval poet Thomas Rowley, was on at least one occasion accused of forging a banknote. But he was lauded as an iconic genius by, among others, Wordsworth and Coleridge. In the mid-nineteenth century, forgery and the figure of the forger became archetypes for both the repulsive criminal fringes of society and the criminality that lurks behind the decorum of the law. This was especially true in the literature because, after all, a forger is himself a kind of artist with a peculiar genius for imitation. In much Victorian writing, an art forger is often also a monetary forger, as indeed was the case of the celebrated portraitist and sometime journalist, Thomas Wainwright, who was transported to Tasmania for forging a number of Bills of Exchange in the name of his wife and sister-in-law, whom he also later confessed to have murdered.[9] But although forgers like Wainwright were often held to represent a corrupt, criminal underworld, they were also regarded, especially by other writers, as paragons of a powerful artistic mystique that only a 'great' liar could maintain.[10]

But the huge numbers of people being sent to the gallows for making Bank of England notes was something altogether different. When cash payments were suspended in 1797, the Bank's introduction of small one- and two-pound notes put considerable pressure on its printers. Before the suspension, three men printed 2,000 notes per day. By 1800, the rate was 15,000. They were irregular and inconsistent. Some notes had three signatures; others one. Counterfeiting was easier than ever before. Even the bankers were hard-pressed to tell real notes from false ones. Of the 31,000 counterfeit notes that appeared at the Bank of England in 1817, all but 839 were one- and two-pound notes. The initial response to this predicament was the traditional one: relentless criminal prosecution. But this was no longer a matter of pillorying misguided aristocrats. It was a massive and expensive undertaking. The number of forged notes that appeared at the Bank far exceeded the number of forgers the courts were able to prosecute. Among the accused were Bank employees embroiled in elaborate money laundering schemes. Countless letters were received from convicts protesting the horrible conditions, asking that their wives and children be allowed to join them, pleading for lesser charges, or promising to expose other counterfeiters. The Bank's solicitors, Freshfield and Kaye, were kept extremely busy. Though the campaign was intended to protect the Bank and its holdings, the prosecutions cost a great deal of money.[11]

It would be wrong to conclude that the Bank's Directors were entirely malicious. During 1818 and 1819, the forgery question took up more time in Directors' meetings than did any other matter.[12] One proposal entertained by both the government and the Bank was the 'inimitable note'. The Society for the Encouragement of Arts, Manufactures, and Commerce (the same society that sponsored *Annals of Fine Arts* in which Keats' 'Ode on a Grecian Urn' first appeared) formed a committee to review inimitable note designs. The committee reviewed a number of impressive designs, some involving as many as six or seven different fonts, color prints, complex imagery, and highly intricate textures.[13] But when the designs were submitted to J. H. Harper, the Bank's engraver, and his staff they were able to reproduce the notes by hand with such precision that the engravers and engineers could not tell the difference.[14] One of the engravers, Thomas Ranson, was arrested for passing a presumably forged five-pound note; he was later acquitted when two Bank clerks confirmed that his note was genuine.[15] The new designs proved too expensive even for the Bank of England and it retained its basic, easily forged note design. Not until stereographic plating was invented in 1836 would a steam-powered press be able to produce notes faster, cheaper, and more efficiently than copper plating and hand signing.

For most commentators improving the banknotes was simply not enough. Few in the Whig or radical community disagreed that prosecution was necessary in cases of serious and malevolent fraud. The Bank's unwillingness to make a distinction between such cases and those in which honest mistakes were caused by irregularities in its notes was considered by many observers to be morally outrageous if not downright criminal. In his review of the *Returns of Prosecutions and Convictions for Forging Notes of the Bank of England from 1783 to 1813* published in the *Edinburgh Review* in 1818, Henry Brougham described the forgery prosecutions as a 'moral revolution'.[16] In the fifty years prior to the suspension, Brougham recalled, only forty-six people were convicted of forgery; 'even this number was sufficient at the time to excite the disapprobation of wise, and the indignation of good men, against laws which inflicted death on such a crime as forgery, and offered human sacrifices to the Moloch of Paper Credit'.[17] Brougham did not blame the bankers and government outright. The 'whole crime' Brougham wrote, 'is in truth imputable to the small notes'. Only by making banknotes convertible into coin and removing small notes from circulation will British paper credit be 'restored to its original character, and *once more* rendered secure against the evils of excessive issue'.[18] Brougham's nostalgia is telling: British coins never had such security. But the forgery crisis provided an excellent opportunity to expound the idea that they did.

The most pressure came from the radical press. An anonymous pamphlet, *Rotten Rag Manufactory!!!*, subtitled *The Threadneedle-Street Catechism; or Bank Bubble Exposed*, devoted four of its eight pages to railing against the Bank's use of the courts as a way to protect its already engrossed and enfeebled financial system. Like Brougham, it contended that the forgery crisis had been caused by 'the common and cheap manner in which ... notes are executed; by which any engraver's apprentice may easily imitate them; thus holding out temptations to weak and wicked persons' and recommended that the only way to secure the currency against forgery was either for the bank to recall all small notes and issue instead 'tokens, issued under the mint price' or, at least, for merchants to be allowed to stick examples of forgeries in their shop-windows to show people what they looked like.[19] Unfortunately, the pamphlet goes on, Bank clerks had taken to 'collaring' any merchant sticking up forged notes in their windows on the charge of holding a forged note.[20]

The radical newspaperman Thomas Wooler devoted a number of issues of *The Black Dwarf* between December 1818 and May 1819 to the forgery question. The prosecution campaign, he declared, proved the bankers' greed and malevolence: 'the Bank can diminish the offence, whenever it pleases, by issuing notes not quite so easy of imitation. But those notes would cost them more, perhaps a half-penny a piece: and though they pay for them with paper, they cannot afford to give so much as a half penny for a note worth twenty-shillings, or twenty, or a hundred pounds, just as they may please to stamp one or the other number upon the promise to pay.'[21] The bankers were behaving like a bully in the schoolyard, who tempts innocent children into committing petty crimes and then arresting them when they commit them. Wooler accused the bankers of hiring their own inspectors (which was true), obscuring facts with declamatory rhetoric and legal procedure, and even paying forgers to keep the number of executions up. He accused the government, in the person of Lord Sidmouth the Home Secretary, of murdering innocent men, women, and children through the indiscriminate use of the death penalty in property crimes, what was then known as the 'bloody code'. Throughout, he appealed to legal ideals of 'clear evidence' and natural justice. In essence, Wooler wanted to privatize the financial system; as far as he was concerned 'private contracts' between merchants already required 'truth and honesty', a standard of moral conduct, to ensure the validity of their credit. The bloody code of legal statutes had to be replaced, in Wooler's mind, by a 'natural' code of private contracts. The legal historian Phillip Handler suggests that the *Black Dwarf* was largely responsible for inspiring the 1818 forgery acquittals. Most of the jurors were retailers and small merchants whose financial dealings were based primarily in coin or personal credit. They had little time for banks or the national debt. The Bank threatened to sue Wooler for libel but relented on the advice of legal council.[22]

Apart from Wooler, the most prominent critic of the government's mishandling of the forgery file was William Hone. Hone was a compulsive satirist and the Ministry's most dogged adversary. In 1817, he published a series of satires of government policy using familiar elements of the Anglican prayer book as his base texts: *The Late John Wilkes's Catechism, The Political Litany,* and *The Sinecurist's Litany.* In the first of these, the extension of banknotes is treated as an incidence of administrative double-dealing equivalent to the sureties and pensions distributed to Ministry allies or the legal forms required for social assistance:

Q. Why was the Test of Bribery ordained?
A. For the continual support of the Minister's influence, and the feeding of us, his needy creatures and sycophants.
Q. What is the outward part or sign in the Test of Bribery?
A. Bank notes, which the Minister hath commanded to be offered by his dependants.
Q. Why then are beggars submitted to this Test, when by reason of their poverty they are not able to go through the necessary forms?
A. Because they promise them by their Sureties; which promise, when they come to lucrative offices, they themselves are bound to perform.
Q. What is the inward part, or thing signified?
A. The industry and wealth of the People, which are verily and indeed taken and had by Pensioners and Sinecurists, in their Corruption.
Q. What are the benefits whereof you are partakers thereby?
A. The weakening and impoverishing the People, through the loss of their Liberty and Property, while our wealth becomes enormous, and our pride intolerable.[23]

In an early draft, Hone had written 'Bank Notes and Guineas', though he removed the coins, likely because to suggest that both paper money and coins were fraudulent would confuse readers who associated commodity money with real value.[24]

In April of 1817, the Attorney General, Sir William Garrow brought an injunction against Hone for these prints. In December Hone was tried separately for each text in three different courts. The charge in all cases was libel, though the Ministry sought to discredit Hone by calling his pamphlets blasphemy. The underlying problem, the prosecutors made clear, was that Hone's parodies were destabilizing the public comprehension of 'sacred truths'. But what, Hone replied, was that truth? It was merely a 'shadow': it could not be substantiated in any real or material sense. Spirit was a matter of individual feeling, a fact that the government routinely relied on to persuade the public to regard its own injunctions – including its fraudulent paper money system – as real values. Hone's defense rested on the idea that the response to a print was a matter of personal experience: some readers would laugh and some would be shaken. There was no way to predict the moral rectitude of any particular reader. The point of political satire, Hone claimed, was not to attack 'sacred truths' but to expose government hypocrisy. Far from undermining the legitimacy of the catechism or the creed, Hone's parodies took them as the standard against which to measure government fraud.[25]

The most famous satire of the forgery debate is George Cruikshank's illustration, Bank Restriction Note, printed by Hone (Illustration 4.1). It features hanging figures, a rope for a pound sign, Britannia eating her children, a ship bound for Botany Bay, a signature by Jack Ketch, the hangman, and an ironic injunction that it is 'not to be imitated'. In his 1875 memoir, Cruikshank recalled walking down Ludgate Hill one day in December 1818 where he 'saw several human beings hanging on the gibbet opposite Newgate Prison, and to my horror, two of these were women, and, upon enquiring what these woman had been hung for, was informed that it was for passing forged one pound notes. The fact that a poor woman could be put to death for such a minor offense had a great effect upon me.'[26] The Bank Restriction Note was one of his most popular prints. Sold for one shilling, it went through several editions and was printed in other radical papers including Hunt's *Examiner* where it would have been seen by Keats and Shelley. Sales of the Bank Restriction Note netted Cruikshank 700 pounds. Ironically, his attack on the Bank of England made him a good deal of money.

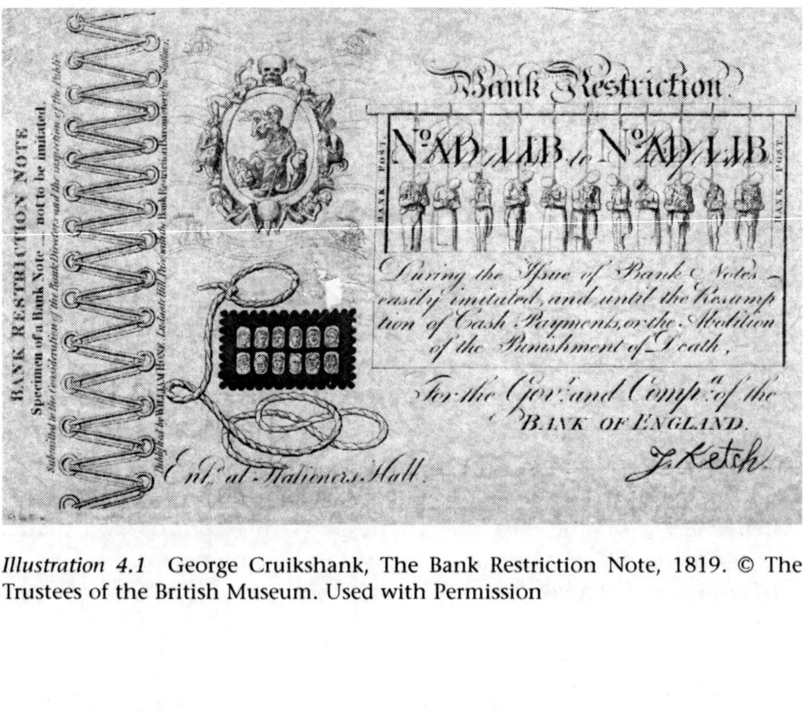

Illustration 4.1 George Cruikshank, The Bank Restriction Note, 1819. © The Trustees of the British Museum. Used with Permission

Like all parodies, Cruikshank and Hone's Bank Restriction Note depends upon the same logic of imitation as paper money itself: its value lies in the extent to which it is an extension or magnification of a material entity (the 'bloody code') which it at the same time seeks to replace with another (the real value of free commercial exchange). Since the value of paper credit is a matter of private agreement between individuals to respect a certain contract, the legal injunction against counterfeiting is completely arbitrary. It would be wrong therefore to regard these satires as critiques of money per se. They looked back to writers like Daniel Defoe and Thomas Paine who, far from objecting to free market principles had supported banking and paper credit in limited forms. The radical response to the forgery crisis was motivated by shock, but it also revived old humanistic models of the economic system built on communal respect, domestic harmony, and natural justice. Wooler, Hone, and Cruikshank saw themselves as defenders of the public sphere, not just constitutionally but also economically free. But their defense must imagine that sphere in an almost impossibly idealistic way.

This idealism becomes clearer still in Abraham Franklin's Bank Restriction Barometer (Illustration 4.2). Modeled on similar thermometers measuring the relative values of 'sin' and 'grace' – a commonplace of eighteenth-century print culture – the Bank Restriction Barometer is, as the subtitle indicates, a 'scale of the effects on society of the Bank Note System and Payments in Gold'. Like earlier religious scales, on which Franklin's satire is based, the thermometer followed sequential narratives of widespread economic and social catastrophe (on the lower end) and 'national prosperity promoted' (on the upper). Once Bank of England and country notes were extended and the circulating medium enlarged, rents increased, and the 'temptation to forge Bank of England notes increased and facilitated' leading to new and harsher laws against it. On the upper end, with 'The Gold Currency restored' and the issue reduced, 'rents and prices fall', everyone buys what they need and 'The Forgery of Notes is at an end'. While the lower narrative simplifies the processes that led to the executions, the upper narrative idealizes the effects of resumption. It is telling that the two female figures depicted at each end of the thermometer are versions, the one glorious, the other lamentational of Britannia depicted on Bank of England notes. Franklin's Britannia is an idealized image of national confidence overcoming the embarrassments of public debt and political disgrace. A similar rhetoric of simplification is evident in the religious thermometer: the lower temperatures follow the sinners

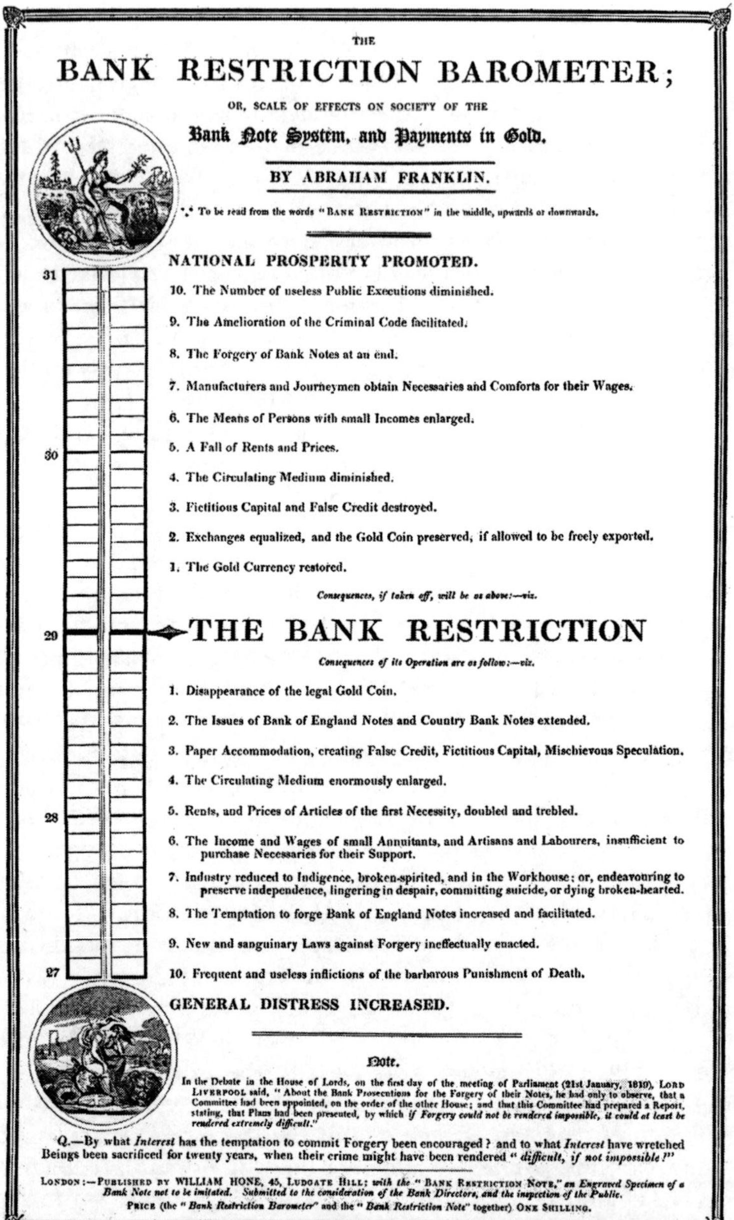

THE

BANK RESTRICTION BAROMETER;

OR, SCALE OF EFFECTS ON SOCIETY OF THE

Bank Note System, and Payments in Gold.

BY ABRAHAM FRANKLIN.

*** To be read from the words "BANK RESTRICTION" in the middle, upwards or downwards.

NATIONAL PROSPERITY PROMOTED.

10. The Number of useless Public Executions diminished.
9. The Amelioration of the Criminal Code facilitated.
8. The Forgery of Bank Notes at an end.
7. Manufacturers and Journeymen obtain Necessaries and Comforts for their Wages.
6. The Means of Persons with small Incomes enlarged.
5. A Fall of Rents and Prices.
4. The Circulating Medium diminished.
3. Fictitious Capital and False Credit destroyed.
2. Exchanges equalized, and the Gold Coin preserved, if allowed to be freely exported.
1. The Gold Currency restored.

Consequences, if taken off, will be as above:—viz.

THE BANK RESTRICTION

Consequences of its Operation are as follow:—viz.

1. Disappearance of the legal Gold Coin.
2. The Issues of Bank of England Notes and Country Bank Notes extended.
3. Paper Accommodation, creating False Credit, Fictitious Capital, Mischievous Speculation.
4. The Circulating Medium enormously enlarged.
5. Rents, and Prices of Articles of the first Necessity, doubled and trebled.
6. The Income and Wages of small Annuitants, and Artisans and Labourers, insufficient to purchase Necessaries for their Support.
7. Industry reduced to Indigence, broken-spirited, and in the Workhouse; or, endeavouring to preserve independence, lingering in despair, committing suicide, or dying broken-hearted.
8. The Temptation to forge Bank of England Notes increased and facilitated.
9. New and sanguinary Laws against Forgery ineffectually enacted.
10. Frequent and useless inflictions of the barbarous Punishment of Death.

GENERAL DISTRESS INCREASED.

Note.

In the Debate in the House of Lords, on the first day of the meeting of Parliament (21st January, 1819), LORD LIVERPOOL said, "About the Bank Prosecutions for the Forgery of their Notes, he had only to observe, that a Committee had been appointed, on the order of the other House; and that this Committee had prepared a Report, stating, that Plans had been presented, by which *if Forgery could not be rendered impossible, it could at least be rendered extremely difficult.*"

Q.—By what *Interest* has the temptation to commit Forgery been encouraged? and to what *Interest* have wretched Beings been sacrificed for twenty years, when their crime might have been rendered "*difficult, if not impossible!*"

LONDON:—PUBLISHED BY WILLIAM HONE, 45, LUDGATE HILL; *with the* "BANK RESTRICTION NOTE," *an Engraved Specimen of a Bank Note not to be imitated. Submitted to the consideration of the Bank Directors, and the inspection of the Public.*

PRICE (the "*Bank Restriction Barometer*" and the "*Bank Restriction Note*" together) ONE SHILLING.

Illustration 4.2 Abraham Franklin, Bank Restriction Barometer, 1819. © The Trustees of the British Museum. Used with Permission

course to hell, while the upper lead not just to personal redemption but also to 'glory' in heaven and a willing acceptance of death. Embracing the moral aim of these prints, in other words, entails not just the destruction of the status quo but the 'death' of the ambiguous embarrassments of life.[27]

Leigh Hunt's radical weekly newspaper *The Examiner* also put considerable pressure on the government to make economic reforms. Hunt was fond of criticizing the fraudulence of the paper credit system, not because credit in itself was bad but because the credit system that was being legislated by the Bank and Parliament was (a) too exclusive and (b) part of an illegal war. Hunt commented on the bullion controversy and on such matters as taxation, the sinking fund, and the national debt as part of his campaign against the war with France. 'The interruption of the supply of bullion, the Bank issues', he wrote in 1810, 'and the prophetic demand of foreign merchants for our specie and nothing else but our specie, no doubt are the very active causes of the depreciation and ruin of paper-money; but the *final* cause is to be found in our wars, that is to say, in entering into enormous expenses, both for ourselves and *our allies, which we never retrieve*'. Hunt then struck home the political hypocrisy at stake in the credit crisis: 'Paper credit, which was first invented to conceal the wants of the State, has been kept up for the same purpose; paper does not truly represent riches; it conceals the defalcation and the bad application of them, and its credit has at last grown too thin not to be seen through.'[28] Hunt regarded banknotes as a false solution – like quack medicine or newspaper bulletins – to general problems of social alienation and government corruption. And, temperamentally, he was committed to the idea that personal exchange – friendship, fellow feeling – was the best solution to this condition.

Hunt's reformist impulses extended to the campaigns to prevent forgery. As early as 1813, Hunt was printing letters from correspondents on the dangers of forgery, the malignancy of the prosecutions, and the inconvenience of the Bank's pathetic solutions.[29] On February 8, 1818, *The Examiner* reported 'that unless some plan be adopted to render the task of forgery much more difficult than it is at present, the retail dealers, and indeed all persons who are in the frequent habit of receiving payments in notes, will be constantly in a state of suffering'. Hunt criticized the Bank's current efforts to prevent forgery by prosecution. 'Transportation and hanging without mercy, it seems equally manifest, will not correct the evil.' The Bank must understand how easy it is to forge notes 'with the aid of ingenious machinery and skillful engravers', yet they make only half-hearted attempts to create an inimitable note. But the real problem is that the bankers have no feeling for the consequences of their prosecutions:

> Some good people, we find, still express their wonder how it is possible that 'respectable gentlemen' can go on sleeping comfortably in their beds, knowing as they do that numberless unhappy wretches are constantly suffering the utmost penalty of the laws, for doing that which a little trouble and a little expense would render as impossible work. But these worthy souls should by the times have discovered – what others have long seen – that public bodies have generally no more feeling than the Portland stone of which their edifices are composed; – that interest, pecuniary interest, is the great lever by which they are moved; – that the claims of generosity and humanity are not among their rules and regulations.[30]

Although Hunt did not think much of banknotes generally, he did believe that finding an inimitable note would provide some solace to the social ills produced by the forgery trials and that artists, engravers, and printers might discover that solution. In February 1819, he published a letter from 'An Artist' complaining that while the members of the committee to investigate forgery might be able to judge 'Chemical and Mechanical inventions', in 'the general opinion of Artists ... the Board does not possess such qualifications as would induce them to put any confidence in their judgment or to turn their minds to the object in view'.[31] Meanwhile, it was reported, engravers and other artists had submitted more than 200 designs at considerable expense. When the designs were submitted, however, several of the committee were in the country and, after an extension, decided not to entertain the artists' proposals after all, refusing at the same time to remunerate their expenses. It is obvious where Hunt's sympathies lay, 'with the pulse of genius beat[ing] high in the feverish hope of success', and not with the Bank of England.[32]

Captivated by the power of their medium, radicals asserted a standard of common interests. But this assertion also repeated a tactical move that economist since Adam Smith had made, including, it should be noted, those representing the Bank of England: distinguishing proper representation (money, art) from false (forgery), that in which the public could be confident and that in which it most assuredly was not. Money has value because it circulates among people who can read it and agree to its value. It is a matter of the naturally uniform taste of a growing class of enlightened readers. For radicals, public credit is an imitation of this, invented by the state to defraud the citizenry and supported by irrational and prejudicial laws sustaining its fraudulent legitimacy. Only real credit, the debts incurred between people for people, had any legitimacy as the basis for a system of exchange. But that standard would thus need to be beyond the market in which its value would be relative. At stake in Wooler's, Hone's, and Hunt's radical satires of paper money and the forgery trials was a standard that would only emerge once the tribulations of politics and world were overcome. It was this temporalized sense of a standard 'to come' emerging, perhaps paradoxically, from a world of representations and imitations, that Shelley crystallized in his poetry.

'The ghost of gold': Shelley's economy of imitation

Ever since Kenneth Neil Cameron published 'Shelley, Cobbett, and the National Debt' in 1943, critics have for the most part agreed that Shelley was a bullionist; he believed with Hume, Cobbett, and Ricardo that gold is the only true currency and that all forms of government interference in the European gold market are tantamount to fraud.[33] In *A Philosophical View of Reform*, the second part of which contains his most sustained attack on the paper money system, Shelley pointed out that 'the government itself abuses the trust reposed in it to debase the coin in order that it may derive advantage from the unlimited multiplication of the mark entitling the holder to command the labour and property of others' but that the system of paper money is a 'far subtler and more complicated contrivance of misrule' than the debasement of coin.[34] As early as *Queen Mab*, Shelley had pledged his allegiance to a labor theory of value. 'There is no real wealth but the labour of man. Were the mountains of gold and the valleys of silver, the world would not be one grain of corn the richer; no one comfort would be added to the human race.'[35]

Shelley also knew about the forgery trials. In a letter to Thomas Love Peacock, written from Naples in January 1819 he quipped: 'Your news about the Banknote trials is excellent good. Do I not recognize in it the influence of Cobbett?'[36] Shelley borrowed much of what he wrote about the forgery crisis from the *Examiner* and the *Black Dwarf*. He sympathized with Wooler over the government and the Bank Directors' egregious mishandling of the forgery question. In *Swellfoot the Tyrant*, for instance, Shelley's satire of the Queen Caroline Affair, Mammon, the Arch-Priest of Famine disinherits his son Chrysaor for championing 'unadulturate coin', bequeaths his entire estate to his daughter, Banknotina, and then marries her off 'to the gallows'.[37] *The Cenci* contains many references to finance and forgery that resemble the kind of comments found in the radical satires.[38] The opening satirical section of *The Mask of Anarchy* is in much the same vein. Lord Sidmouth is 'Fraud', one of the Four Horsemen of the Apocalypse who, led by the skeletal figure of Anarchy, descend upon the cheering victims. Anarchy's declaration 'I AM GOD AND KING AND LAW!' clearly alludes to Wooler's caricature of the Regent usurping the court's power to decide false and true notes.[39]

But these comments do not quite tally with other remarks Shelley made about money and credit. In an 1811 letter to Elizabeth Hitchener, for instance, he exclaimed 'Money ... I covet it. – What you! You a miser, you desire gold, you a slave to the most contemptible of ambitions! No. I am not; but I still desire money, and I desire it because I think I know the use of it. It commands labour, it gives leisure, and to give leisure to those who will employ it in the forwarding of truth is the noblest present an individual can make to the whole.'[40] Gold is clearly not the answer here, and money, it seems, has to power to inspire and encourage poetry and 'truth'. Shelley loaned a good deal of money to his friends, notably Leigh Hunt and William Godwin, and his letters contain many references to creditors and bankers with whom he negotiated credit. In November 1819, Shelley admitted to his friends John and Maria Gisbourne that, although the financial system would likely collapse if there was a 'popular revolution', still 'the existing government, atrocious as it is, is the surest party to which a public creditor can attach himself'.[41]

One way to interpret this ambivalence is to consider it in line with Shelley's complex sense of irony. For Terence Hoagwood, Shelley's poetics, like the theory of money he outlines in the *View*, is a 'skeptical demystification' of the money form that demonstrates in literary form the alienating effects of money even as the poetry critiques them.[42] Jeffrey Cox contends that Shelley's poetics substitutes the system of representation that he finds so problematic in the financial world with a different form of understanding based on love and respect, though this alternative system only comes into view through a difficult process of critical self-consciousness.[43] Jerrold Hogle interprets Shelley's theory of the sign in terms of social class. During the eighteenth century, minor aristocrats (like Shelley's grandfather) forced, by a steady rise in the standard of living, to sell their indentured estates saw their traditional status cheapened by its availability in the market. To replace this lack, the once-landed classes 'turned inward' to ideals of self-motivation and empowerment that were at one time tied to aristocratic privilege. Or they identified with the working class whose claim over the economic value of their labor was also jeopardized by the expanding marketplace.[44] Either way, the attempt to discover a confident sense of identity was at least partly undermined by a nagging sense of alienation. Such anxieties were emblematic of a transition in the concept of credit through the eighteenth and nineteenth centuries from a sign of social obligation and respect between classes to a more limited sign of purchasing power borrowed from financial institutions that transcended old class stratifications.[45] As a first step toward resolving the crises, Shelley exposed the contradictions within the financial system by translating them into his self-consciously figurative verse. He did this, Hogle insists, 'in the hope of discovering the most fruitful kinds of "profit" that could be gained by most people (and poets) when they faced the process of working with and through signs that both promised and denied them the permanent possession of their fullest selves'.[46] Anxieties about monetary representation became a source of poetic expression.

The poem in which Shelley came closest to the radicals' critique was *The Mask of Anarchy*. It was inspired by the 'massacre' of unarmed protesters at a rally for Henry 'Orator' Hunt on August 16, 1819 at St. Peter's Field, Manchester, the Peterloo Massacre. The first half is a satirical portrayal of a number of prominent members of the Cabinet, portrayed as the Four Horsemen of the Apocalypse, Murder, Fraud, Hypocrisy, and Anarchy, slaughtering innocent men, women, and children. In the midst of this massacre, Shelley imagines the appearance of the maid of hope, who lies down under the hellish cavalry and causes their immediate destruction. A voice, usually known as the Spirit of the Earth, explains to the people the causes of their oppression and exhorts them to declare themselves free citizens. Shelley weaves several references to money and finance into this story. Anarchy, Shelley relates, 'bowed and grinned' to the crowd 'As well as if his education / Had cost ten millions to the nation' – a deliberate allusion to the National Debt – and then 'sent his slaves before / To seize upon the Bank and Tower'.[47] The reference to forgery comes as the Spirit of the Earth identifies the people's slavery:

> 'Tis to let the Ghost of Gold
> Take from Toil a thousandfold
> More than e'er its substance could
> In the tyrannies of old.

Paper Coin – that forgery
Of the title-deeds which ye
Hold to something of the worth
Of the inheritance of the Earth.[48]

Shelley's concern here is clearly with the illegitimacy of finance and the exploitation of the working class. Yet, as Steven Jones argues, the ironic use of the term 'inheritance' suggests that the exploitation of labor rests on legal authority not economic principles.[49]

But Shelley went further than the radical satirists in articulating *how* a standard of value might be secured for a genuinely free market system. In the second section of the poem, the Spirit of the Earth's long oration, Shelley turns from an attack on the illegitimate legal authority that had enslaved the people with the 'Ghost of Gold' to outline a different kind of law based on a complex array of abstract ideals: freedom, domesticity, self-knowledge. Much of this section of the speech is laced with economic metaphors that only an audience well-versed in political economy would have understood in their fullest significance. Freedom is 'bread / And a comely table spread ... clothes and fire and food'.[50] Freedom signifies the home, and the home in turn is a microcosm of the network of production, exchange, and reflection that drives the market as a totality. '[I]n countries that are free / Such starvation cannot be'[51] may well be an allusion to Malthus' population principle, which Shelley found utterly reprehensible. Yet, for 'the rich', Shelley says, freedom is 'a check'.[52] The word 'check' was used by Malthus, Ricardo, and others to define the natural limits on demand and production that correct the effects of overpopulation or depreciation. For the political economists, the check is the gold standard. Tied to the permanent value of gold, the free market is both productive and restrictive, a source of credit and a means of restraint. Shelley thus seems to agree with both radical journalists and liberal economists that legislative interference in finance inhibits personal and political freedom.

Rather than document the trials as Wooler had done, Shelley dramatizes the forgery trials to interpret them from a critical distance.[53] Shelley is not so much engaging the legal battle for the standard as he is theorizing the legal problem of what the standard of value actually is. The Four Horsemen play the prosecution and the Spirit of the Earth, the attorney for the defense. The 'great assembly' of the people represent the jury – and indeed, the same class of people that acquitted the banknote forgers in December, 1818 were also those who gathered at St. Peter's Field eight months later. The accused is freedom, or more specifically, the liberal economy. At stake in the trial, as in the forgery trials themselves, is the question of who and what the law stands for. 'What are thou, Freedom?' Shelley's defense lawyer asks:

Thou art Justice – ne'er for gold
May the righteous laws be sold
As laws are in England – thou
Shield'st alike the high and low.

Thou art Wisdom – Freemen never
Dream that God will damn for ever
All who think those things untrue
Of which Priests make such ado.

Thou art Peace – never by thee
Would blood and treasure wasted be
As tyrants wasted them, when all
Leagued to quench thy flame in Gaul.[54]

The last of these stanzas clearly alludes to the suspension of cash payments that had allowed the British government to send its treasure abroad to fight the (for Shelley, illegal) war against Revolutionary France. It is not forgery that is the problem, but the imbalance in power between those who control the money supply and those who use it. Just as the priests control religion, and therefore thought, so the government and the banks hoard and sell the money that properly belongs to the people. The solution is to release the economy from its institutional ground rendering it an autonomous and self-fulfilling process of social, domestic, and sexual exchange.

But what is to stop this autonomous system from falling into relativism and competition? What, in other words, is its standard of value? Shelley's freedom is an abstraction. It therefore fits into the same category of abstraction as 'inheritance' and 'spirit' and is related to the idea of the standard. The other point about freedom is that it is transferable: it is the universal equivalent of all the other abstractions that, for Shelley (justice, peace) make up the happy life. Freedom is thus not money itself or even credit, for these are just the means to asserting individual power in exchange. Instead, freedom makes itself known as a kind of economic sublime that can only be understood intellectually as the result of a process of self-reflection:

Thou art Love – the rich have kist
Thy feet, and like him following Christ,

Give their substance to the free
And through the rough world follow thee

Or turn their wealth to arms, and make
War for thy beloved sake
On wealth, and war, and fraud – whence they
Drew the power which is their prey

Science, Poetry, and Thought
Are thy lamps; they make the lot
Of the dwellers in a cot
So serene, they curse it not.[55]

Whereas the crowd had formerly been dupes of the 'frauds' of government-sanctioned forgery, they now recognize freedom through the 'lamp' of knowledge: science, thought, and, most importantly, poetry. Knowledge also turns the soldiers into disciples of self-sacrifice, though those soldiers are still depicted as 'mak[ing] War / on wealth and war and fraud'.[56] The poem disapproves of this violent reaction for it merely continues the aimless and, in the context of the poem, enslaved cycle of banknotes, forgery, and prosecution pursued by the government: 'when ye complain / with a murmur weak and vain /...Then it is to feel revenge / Fiercely thirsting to exchange / Blood for blood'.[57] But the poem also reinterprets such defensive action as the starting point for a new kind of legal consciousness. It assumes, that is, a level of critical understanding beyond description and exhortation. When Shelley has the Spirit of the Earth call the people to become 'a Great Assembly', a collective whom the Spirit urges so that they can proclaim 'with measured words that ye / Are, as God has made ye, free',[58] he associates the freedom that he has been trying to define throughout the poem with a collective identity. In proclaiming themselves to be autonomous from one another – free agents in the economic system – the people register that they are free from the constraints of a legal apparatus and malevolent oligarchy. But knowing that they are independent and *at the same time* inter-dependent, the people can actually become a true collective.

Near the end of his unpublished pamphlet 'A Philosophical View of Reform' Shelley not only replayed the action of *The Mask* but also capitalizes on its financial metaphors. Having been enlightened by the hitherto unacknowledged legislators of the world to stand firm against oppression, and coming together as a Great Assembly, the passive resisters in the field would, Shelley insisted, have staved off their attackers. In the mercenary system established by the state, the soldier obeys his orders against his own discretion. He 'becomes confused, and massacres those who fly from him by the instinct of his *trade*'.[59] Among these confused feelings, the soldier 'applauds himself by reflecting that these base and dishonorable motives will gain him *credit* among his comrades and his officers who are animated by the same'.[60] However, Shelley went on, 'if he should observe neither resistance nor flight he would be reduced to impotence and indecision ... This unexpected reception would probably throw him back upon a recollection of *the true nature* of the *measures* of which he was made the instrument, and the enemy might be converted into the ally.'[61] Now that they understand 'the true nature' of violence, the soldiers have a sense of the regulative ideal or 'measure' of human conduct. As in the *Mask of Anarchy*, collective consciousness is a sign to be interpreted by the attacking soldiers who become aware of the horrifying implications of their violence.

Most of the discussions of Shelley's arguments about money in the 'View' tend to concentrate only on the second part in which, echoing Cobbett, he retells the financial history of Britain since the founding of the Bank of England as a series of catastrophic dupes and frauds. But Shelley also places this history in a larger context. 'Our present business', he wrote in a bracketed passage (immediately following the direction to consult Cobbett) 'is not with the history of commerce but with [its] consequences. I would awaken from a consideration that the present miseries of our country are nothing necessarily inherent in the stage of civilization at which we have arrived, foresight and hope.'[62] How is this awakening to take place? In the first part of the 'View', Shelley had already provided an account of the rise of European commerce similar to those in other economic treatises including Smith's *Wealth of Nations*. In that earlier stage, which coincides with the Elizabethan period, Shelley finds hope in the works of the 'poets and philosophers', the famous 'unacknowledged legislators' whose schemes and inventions had helped to improve and, indeed, commercialize agriculture. 'The mechanical sciences attained to a degree of perfection which ... it had been accounted madness to have prophesied in a preceding age.'[63] With these advances, the philosophers secured the people's confidence that 'new theories' would produce lasting benefits for 'future ages'.[64]

But the reason why the legislators are unacknowledged is because their business is with the future: 'They are the priests of an unapprehended inspiration, the mirrors of gigantic shadows which futurity casts upon the present.'[65] Although the 'machine' that this 'modern society' became 'is perpetually wearing away or breaking to pieces the wheels of which it is composed', hope has been redeemed in the 'labours of the political philosophers' who established 'the principle of Utility as the substance, and liberty and equality as the forms according to which the concerns of human life ought to be administered'.[66] The exhortations of *The Mask*, its invocation of hope and democratic reform, and its condemnation of the unjust legal system, especially with regard to economic self-sufficiency, point to a comprehensiveness that requires a mechanism of trust. This is the part played by literature in Shelley's economic system. It does not simply represent the standard of value: it *is* the standard. While Shelley did not necessarily advocate a gold standard or a moral standard, he did acknowledge the need for standards in the political administration of the people and their networks of communication and understanding, including money. In this respect, Shelley's poetry helped to entrench the idea of the standard that would, though the nineteenth century, dominate monetary policy and economics – in spite of the fact that Shelley himself might have found that suggestion abhorrent.

Shelley's 1819 works show a desire to revive a standard of popular confidence through the medium of philosophical poetry in the face of 'the new aristocracy' of professional plagiarists, both monetary and literary. *The Mask of Anarchy* and the 'View' express that desire as a kind of call-to-arms though both of them also make clear the sheer difficulty of such an effort. But they do not in themselves embody the standard that Shelley hoped would arise; they merely reflect its shadowy possibility. The 1820 volume *Prometheus Unbound and other Poems* was Shelley's answer to his own call: a poetry that might *be* a standard. Many critics have commented on the difficulty and irony of Shelley's verse drama and attendant lyrics in the 1820 volume: Shelley nowhere declares poetry actually to embody or be the standard without at the same time, metaphorically or directly, showing that it is not. Instead, like the symbols that Shelley insisted at the end of the *Mask of Anarchy* should arise in the wake of popular uprising and political revolt, the standards that the 1820 poems invoke are *potential* standards of political unity that can only arise through a collective effort of sympathetic identification. Yet Shelley also distinguished in the 1820 volume between those readers who will truly understand the standard and those who will merely be caught up either in the reform movement or the mass destruction that will come in its wake. Shelley's solution to the problem of the standard in *Prometheus Unbound* is not the end of difficulty.

This difficulty was related to the forgery question. In the 'Author's Preface' to *Prometheus Unbound*, Shelley makes a surprisingly clear argument for the intellectual authority underlying this new poetic standard by way of a reply both to the anticipated charge that he is merely 'imitating' Aeschylus and to the real charge (in *Blackwood's*, the *Quarterly Review*, and elsewhere) that his poems are merely hackneyed revisions of Godwin's *Political Justice* and Hunt's *Examiner*. Shelley retorted with a rather defensive statement of the restrictedness of his audience. Rather than outline didactic truisms, his 'purpose has hitherto been to familiarize the highly refined imagination of the more select classes of poetical readers with beautiful idealisms of moral excellence'.[67] But with what, exactly, were these readers identifying? 'It is impossible that any one', Shelley noted, 'who inhabits the same age with such writers as those who stand in the foremost ranks of our own, can conscientiously assure himself that his language and tone of thought may not have been modified by the study of the productions of those extraordinary intellects'. Most poets owe 'not the spirit of their genius, but the forms in which it has manifested itself' to 'the peculiarity of the moral and intellectual condition of the minds among which they have been produced'. As a result, 'a number of writers possess the form, whilst they want the spirit of those whom, it is alleged, they imitate'. Anyone can copy another poet's rhetoric or style. But real imaginative genius involves an active, sympathetic engagement with the distinctive 'spirit' of the particular time of the poet, his true standard.[68]

The idea that poetic spirit is a kind of debt works in two ways. On one hand, Shelley admitted (and thus anticipated his critics) that the forms and devices that make up a poem are always adapted from somewhere else. 'Poetry is a mimetic art. It creates, but it creates by combination and representation.'[69] Poetic authorship, in this account, is part of a continuum of production and response.

> One great poet is a masterpiece of Nature which another not only ought to study but must study. He might as wisely and as easily determine that his mind should no longer be the mirror of all that is lovely in the visible universe as exclude from his contemplation the beautiful which exists in the writings of a great contemporary. The pretence of doing it would be a presumption in any but the greatest; the effect, even in him, would be strained, unnatural and ineffectual.[70]

Yet, on the other hand, the poet also has 'internal powers' that 'modify the nature of others', and 'such external influences as excite and sustain these powers; he is not one, but both'.[71] What these powers are, Shelley did not make entirely clear. 'Every man's mind is modified by all the objects of Nature and art; by every word and every suggestion which he ever admitted to act upon his consciousness; it is the mirror upon which all forms are reflected and in which they compose one form. Poets, not otherwise than philosophers, painters, sculptors and musicians, are, in one sense, the creators, and, in another, the creations, of their age.'[72] Shelley's mimesis was not based on the simple representation of phenomenal truth but rather on the circulation of universal ideals available to those with the power to recognize them. Poetry, that is, is the product of a 'spirit of its time' felt by poets. Within the sphere of this influence, the question of whether a poem is or is not an imitation is simply irrelevant. 'If this similarity be the result of imitation, I am willing to confess that I have imitated.'[73] Strongly resembling Coleridge's symbolic economy, Shelley's poetic 'spirit' is restrictive *and* open-ended, free precisely because it has no public existence. The difference between Shelley's mature poetics and the political economy of his day, then, has to do with his development of private consciousness, as the site of standardization as opposed to public institutions.

Shelley's willingness to accept the exclusivity of his poetic program might be seen to ratify in an aesthetic register the gentlemanly exceptionalism evident in, for instance, Johnson's defense of Dodd or the privileges of 'honour' claimed by the artist Benjamin Robert Haydon in his diaries.[74] As gentlemen, that is, these men were exempt from the standard of calculation that demanded they repay their debts, even when they fully acknowledged that they had them. But there is also more to Shelley's appreciation for the tension between imitated form and poetic spirit than just class bravura or ideological conviction. As 'creations of their age', Shelley's poets are liable to the force of sympathetic feeling that sustains the impulse to exchange. This is the central claim of Shelley's preface to *The Cenci*: knowing full well that Beatrice and her family are products of their own time, nevertheless, such critical distance only serves to heighten his audience's sense of itself 'through its sympathies and antipathies ... in proportion to the possession of which knowledge every human being is wise, just, sincere, tolerant and kind'.[75] Forgiveness, Shelley goes on, and thus relative understanding is something Beatrice could not understand, which is what makes her tragedy 'monstrous'.[76] What develops from this combination of feelings – sympathies and antipathies – is not so much an echo of Dodd's exceptionalism but rather of his guilt and remorse.

Prometheus Unbound was Shelley's ultimate statement of this combination of standardization and relativity. If *Prometheus Unbound* seems remote from the economic controversies that Shelley was engaging in, that is partly because its engagement with political questions occurs at such a high metaphorical pitch. The play is a vision of two competing realities, one governed by rules, laws, and institutions (symbolized by Jupiter and the curse) the other governed by the standard of love and poetry (as embodied in Asia) that the world cannot yet comprehend. In a sense, the play reflects the choice that Shelley and his circle felt that they had to make – but could not – between political action and poetic reflection. But having Prometheus repeat the curse – yet another form of repetition or imitation – Shelley seems to have it both ways. Reform will happen not through the violent destruction of the world order, but rather through its revision in literary form, a form that will also provide a point of access to the new world and its new standards.

Within this scheme, Asia has neither a role nor any action other than to inspire the revolution that *Prometheus Unbound* documents. She is at once the prime motivation for social action and entirely removed from it, public while private, material though completely abstract. The main action of the play is the transformation of Prometheus' desire for revenge first into self-pity and then into love which results in Jupiter's fall under the weight of his own tyranny (a scene that echoes the radical pamphlets that Shelley was reading while in Italy) and the coming of a reform he knew he could not challenge. The crucial moments in the play occur with Asia's lyric prophecies. Asia in effect speaks or utters the new reality that she portends. Her words drive the history of the play toward its crisis: 'This is the season, this the day, the hour ... How like death-worms the wingless moments crawl! / The point of one white star is quivering still / Deeping the orange light of widening morn / Beyond the purple mountains.'[77] After he is freed, Prometheus calls her 'light of life / shadow of beauty unbeheld'.[78] Asia is the sun of the world to come, the portent or prophecy, the shadow of futurity that must be interpreted by the (male) poet Prometheus. Immediately on his release, Prometheus and the nymphs retreat into the cave that the Earth has prepared for them. In the meantime, first the Spirit of the Earth and then the Spirit of the Hour narrate the change that occurs in the world with Jupiter's release. In these instances, 'music' plays the same role as Asia herself; it announces the change that no one can stop.[79]

Shelley used a similarly prophetic image of the standard in the 'Ode to Liberty'. One of his most openly radical poems, the poem nevertheless demonstrates how elements of one system can sediment into new, even with opposite trajectories:

> Tomb of Arminius! render up thy dead
> Till, like a standard from a watch-tower's staff,

His soul may stream over the tyrant's head;
Thy victory shall be his epitaph,
Wild Bacchanal of truth's mysterious wine,
King-deluded Germany,
His dead spirit lives in thee.
Why do we fear or hope? thou art already free!
And thou, lost Paradise of this divine
And glorious world! thou flowery wilderness!
Thou island of eternity! thou shrine
Where Desolation, clothed with loveliness,
Worships the thing thou wert! O Italy,
Gather thy blood into thy heart; repress
The beasts who make their dens thy sacred palaces.[80]

Though it recalls the old 'King's Standard', Arminius' standard is not really a visible trope. Instead, it is part of a simile describing both a prophecy and a ghost. Liquid images refer to the familiar metaphor of blood as the 'channels of circulation' used to describe the financial system. But this is all directly to Shelley's point. His poetry does not revive an ancient standard; it points to the possibility of social change. Nevertheless, this possibility is dialectically confounded by the liquid value of the paper in its reader's hands.[81]

Shelley's attempts in *Prometheus Unbound* to redefine poetry as both spirit and form, as both universal and exclusive, came at a time when the question of what poetry – still far and away the most widely published form in the literary market – was actually *for* was very much at issue. John Gibson's Lockhart's attacks on the 'Cockney School' (including Shelley and Keats) in *Blackwood's* were based largely on the idea that their 'suburban' taste flies in the face of the true standards of epic gentility that had been promulgated through the eighteenth century. William Lisle Bowles, whose claims that Pope should not be read because he was 'immoral' inspired raucous attacks from Byron (among others), systemized his argument for poetry's fundamentally didactic purpose in his 1819 tract, *The Invariable Principles of Poetry*.[82] But it was not simply the morals of poets that were at stake. Most arguments against poetry were made on the basis of the greater sincerity and utility of facts and figures over the fanciful imagination. Many borrowed from the attacks on paper money that were still in 1821 railing against the evils of financial speculation, party cabals, and false idols. Thomas Love Peacock's remark in 'The Four Ages of Poetry' that ancient poets were keepers of 'secret histories' brings to mind Horner's 1802 remarks on the cabalism of bankers and Thomas Wooler's attacks on the forgery trials of 1818.[83] As Stephanie Kuduk Weiner has recently argued, these utilitarian attacks against modern poetry were met by several 'republican' responses, including, she argues, Shelley's, that insisted poetry had the same unifying and mobilizing power as a democratic press and free correspondence.[84] Poetry inspired working men and women by appealing to their imaginations, to their sense of what might be. 'We want knowledge', Richard Carlile urged, 'no hypothesis, no speculation, no poetic fictions, no lies, no religion'.[85]

After the *Prometheus Unbound* volume was published in 1820, Shelley continued to experiment with a highly charged metaphorical style in works such as *Epipsychidion* and *Adonais* and, of course, 'A Defence of Poetry'. Shelley's aim was to redefine poetry as an exclusive genre, one whose rules are not simply internal to itself but also known only to those with the proper genius to appreciate their value. This is not to agree with the critical commonplace that the 'Defence' is an anti-economic essay, irrespective of such frequently quoted statements as 'Poetry, and the principle of self, of which money is the visible incarnation are the God and Mammon of the world.'[86] Still, Shelley retained in the 'Defence' a belief in economic liberty that he gleaned from Godwin, Bentham, and Hunt and which he had used previously as the basis for his theory of value. In 'The Four Ages of Poetry', the essay that inspired the 'Defence', Peacock had his tongue only partly in his cheek when he wrote that 'poetry ... like all other trades, takes its rise in the demand for the commodity, and flourishes in proportion to the extent of the market'.[87] This was a sentiment that Shelley had himself acknowledged and it is the reason why, much to Shelley's chagrin, his populist works, particularly *Queen Mab*, continued to sell on the literary black market.[88]

As surely as *The Mask of Anarchy* and the 'Philosophical View' before it, the 'Defence' offered an argument for poetry's particular function not as the object of consumer demand but as the source of a universal value. Adapted, reformed, and promulgated by the world's 'unacknowledged legislators', this standard was the true measure of all others, even though the forces of 'reason' and 'calculation' had replaced that measure with their own oppressive and delusive formulae. Poetry represents a value that conditions all others but which cannot in itself be known. 'All high poetry is infinite; it is as the first atom and the inmost naked beauty of the meaning never exposed. A great Poem is a fountain forever overflowing with the waters of wisdom and delight, and after one person and one age has exhausted all its divine effluence which their peculiar relations enable them to share, another and yet another succeeds, and new relations are ever developed, the source of an unforeseen and an unconceived delight.'[89] Shelley clearly and forcefully understood the role that literature – relentlessly critical, relentlessly difficult, and relentlessly self-effacing at once – might play in a time of mass culture and media saturation. Yet, the irony is that although Shelley wanted this and other definitions of poetry to stand in opposition to money, the definition itself – here at least – sounds uncannily like Coleridge's depiction of the national debt in *The Statesman's Manual*. In imitating Coleridge, or at any rate his metaphor, even unconsciously, Shelley puts himself into the sphere of circulating representation that he wants poetry to transcend. Given such ironies, the interesting thing about Shelley's idea that poetry could be a standard of value is just how hard it was to sustain. And indeed, as much as Shelley might have wanted to reproduce Plato's Republic in post-Waterloo England, the country and, I think, many of his fellow poets were not ready to be philosopher-kings.

The poetics of embarrassment

During the 1820s, Shelley's idea of a poetic standard waned. This was partly a result of the ideological (if not economic) success of the gold standard after the resumption of cash payments. But there was also a strong feeling of exhaustion among those who, like Shelley, had tried to reform the political system through its financial scandals by way of the gold standard, only to see the financial system strengthen in the wake of those very reforms. Shelley's effort to make poetry into a standard of value, especially one that was both politically efficacious and also unknowable, was met with the charge that it was mere imitation – precisely the argument that Shelley had made against the 'forgery' of paper coin and the delusive standards being circulated as an untenable status quo. Reviewing Shelley's *Posthumous Poems* William Hazlitt castigated Shelley's seeming 'originality' in more or less the same terms as he had Coleridge: 'Mr. Shelley's style is to poetry what astrology is to natural science – a passionate dream, a confused embodying of vague abstractions – a fever of the soul, thirsting and craving after what it cannot, indulging its love of power and novelty at the expense of truth and nature ... Poetry, we grant, creates a world of its own; but it creates it out of existing materials. Mr. Shelley is the maker of his own poetry – out of nothing.'[90] In an anonymous review in *Blackwood's*, George Croly compared Shelley unfavorably to the Della Cruscan circle of Robert Merry and Mary Robinson who, in the 1780s and 1790s, had made florid diction, nonsensical metaphors, and high sentiment into a fashion statement.[91] While recognizing the political potential of both his satirical and his metaphysical works, Shelley's followers nevertheless conceded that poetry could not *replace* standards of gentility, morality, and utility without risking a collapse into consumerist trifle. As a result, poetry starts to raise the perplexing question of its own value.

Compare, for instance, Keats' poetics with Shelley's. Robert Kaufman has drawn our attention to a more widespread tendency among critics (dating back to Henry Hallam's 1833 essay on the 'fleshy school') to identify Keats and Shelley together as joint laborers in the later Romantic project of poetic reform. But Kaufman carefully distinguishes between what he calls Shelley's 'prophetic and disseminative negationalism' and Keats' 'constructivism ... his insistence on concretization, fullness, and formal rigor'.[92] The most telling statement of this difference is Keats' 1819 letter to Shelley on *The Cenci* in which the younger poet told the radical to restrain his magnanimity, 'serve Mammon', and 'load every rift of your subject with ore'.[93] As Jeffrey Cox explains, Keats' letter also clarifies the differences in Shelley's and Keats' attitudes toward money:[94] Shelley was overtly opposed, at least intellectually, to the national debt and supportive of radical campaigns like Cobbett's and Hunt's to replace it with a system of moral sincerity and communal love while Keats was more aware of the need to please a consumer public and thus of the commensurate need for poets to curtail their political ambitions or, at any rate, to conceal them within the tight figural arena of genre and form, as gold is hidden in ore.

Keats' letter to Shelley ends a transition that might be said to signal a broader turn from confidence to embarrassment not only in Keats' poetics but also in English poetry generally. Before 1819, Keats flirted with the idea, drawn from Shelley and, more directly, Leigh Hunt, that poetry itself might provide an alternative standard to gold. The centerpiece of Book I of *Endymion* is a catalogue of different forms of human exchange that Keats famously called in a letter to his then publisher John Taylor, a 'pleasure thermometer'. In published form, the lines introducing the pleasure thermometer have a decidedly Huntian ring: 'Wherein lies happiness? In that which becks / Our ready minds to fellowship divine, / A fellowship with essence; till we shine. / Full alchemized, and free of space.'[95] To Taylor, Keats explained that the pleasure thermometer was intended to demonstrate his claim for the 'truth of the Imagination' or of 'Speculation'.[96] The standard of this measurement is fellowship, the 'true' alchemy as opposed to the dream-alchemy of the economists whose 'gold' and 'silver' are invoked repeatedly in the poem as the trappings of a commodity culture in contrast to the truth of poetry. Recalling the spiritual thermometers that had also influenced Abraham Franklin's and William Hone's Bank Restriction Barometer, Endymion's thermometer measures different modes of human exchange beginning with romance and the figure of Orpheus and then ascending to comradeship, friendship, and love. In an earlier draft, Keats opened the passage with a clearer economic subtext: 'Wherein lies happiness? In that which becks / Our ready minds to blending pleasurables / And that delight is the most treasurable / That makes the richest Alchymy.' 'Treasurable' suggests a complex combination of Cockney communitarianism and material wealth – the very problem that Hunt was trying to solve. But Keats wanted to make a clearer distinction between alchemy and love, and so he dropped the 'treasure' metaphor here and in the rest of the poem.

The poems composed during the spring and summer of 1819, when Keats' finances, friendships, and health were at their lowest ebb, reflect this dispositional turn.[97] With their lush, almost fragrant, imagery, the 1819 Odes and Romances parade their status not as measures of social exchange but as objects of consumer desire. Formally, the three romances that open the *Lamia* volume, 'Lamia', 'Isabella', and 'The Eve of St. Agnes' are reproductions of respectively, Keats' own luxurious couplet form – by way of Hunt and more distantly Pope – Byron's ottava rima, and the Spenserian stanza. Each of these poems registers the collapse of the romantic ideal that Keats had sought to vivify in *Endymion*, 'Lamia' being almost a satire of the earlier poem and 'Isabella' and 'The Eve' relentlessly turning the promised escape from ritual to beauty into parodic grotesque.[98] The ode stanza heightens this luxuriousness by extending the Spenserian to ten lines and bringing it closer to its generic source, the sonnet. The poem in which this self-conscious formal experimentation comes to the fore is 'Ode on a Grecian Urn'. Not only is this a poem *about* art – one that puts the old notion of *ut picture poesis* under heightened scrutiny – but also it consistently denies its own viability as an act of representation. Modern critics have found sources for every image in 'Ode on a Grecian Urn', but the underlying result of this historical investiture is the realization that the poem flaunts its own reproducibility.[99] The urn itself, which refers to no existing urn, both idealizes and undermines the whole possibility of artistic reproduction. This does not mean that the poem is merely a consumer object, like a Wedgwood imitation. Nor does it mean, as Cox suggests via Benjamin, that Keats was seeking to restore by a process of critical implication the 'aura' of art.[100] Rather, the poem's formal excessiveness – of reference and of celebration – more closely resembles Benjamin's later argument about film: in compelling its audience to see in close detail the reproducibility of all of its images, film provides a conduit for the critical assessment of reproduction itself in precisely the way that original or 'auratic' art cannot.[101] To be 'teased out of thought', then, means breaking the link between attraction and rationalization; thus, the poem compels us to question whatever confidence we might have that the poem refers to some thing, even a sense or feeling. With its constant questionings and disconnected, almost satirical expressivity ('More happy love! More happy happy love!'), the poem offers itself as an object of constant critical reassessment, the result of which is not a standard per se, but a realization of its impossibility.

There is an economic context for the Ode's embarrassments. First published in *Annals of Fine Arts*, the 'trade journal' as Cox calls it of the Society for the Encouragement of Arts, Manufactures, and Commerce, 'Grecian Urn' is deeply engaged with ongoing debates about the criterion of originality in the valuation of art.[102] Against Joshua Reynolds and the Royal Academy, whom the editors of *Fine Arts* charged with instructing hacks and splashers to merely recreate the great moments of British and classical history, the Society sought to lay artistic production on enlightened 'scientific principles', its Royal Institution to be modeled on the Scottish universities with their distinct disciplinary professoriate, and its students to combine their learning in paintings that embrace the standards of both classical idealism and historical truth.[103] In the context of this mandate, Keats' repudiation of particularity and accuracy on one hand, and of aesthetic unity on the other posits an aesthetics that reflects the mission of the Society and at the same time demonstrates its internal contradictions. But the other important context for Keats' relationship with the Society is its involvement in the campaign to resolve the forgery problem. As discussed above, the Society reviewed many submissions for an inimitable note; some of the designs have a decidedly Keatsian air: Thomas Ranson's figure of Britannia from a five-pound note is perhaps the best example of this. But the complexity of this and other, more mechanical designs is tied up with the very problem that the campaign was trying to address: how to make an unreproducible reproduction, an inimitable imitation?

In light of such questions, the final poem of Keats' 1820 collection, *Hyperion*, might be read as an allegory of economic, even class, distinctions, with Hyperion and the Titans representing an old aristocratic order and Apollo the new spirit of capitalist reason. But the poem also makes these allegories problematic. Keats twins in Hyperion and Apollo the different connotations of gold. Hyperion's realm is 'a palace bright / bastioned with pyramids of glowing gold / And touched with shade of bronzed obelisks'.[104] Egyptian, dark – though also light – the line hints at the 'ancient standard of the realm' envisioned by political economists: the dark interiorized power that represents both luxury and military might: 'when he would taste the spicy wreaths / Of incense, breathed aloft from sacred hills, / Instead of sweets, his ample palate took / Savour of poisonous brass and metal sick.'[105] Hyperion is the Titan of the sun (as Apollo is the god) and so he becomes a beacon to the fallen army, glowing like 'hieroglyphics old' that are interpreted by 'sages and keen-eyed astrologers' as the 'labouring thought ... now lost' but which will be reclaimed again as the futurity of a historical consciousness.[106] With Apollo, Keats seems to be asserting the counter-standard of Shelleyan poetics. As the poet himself admits, though, the transition to Book III weakens the verse from the Miltonic register of the first two and toward luxuriance. If Hyperion's sun-gold represents the ancient standard, Apollo's gold is only implied by poetry: he is 'the gold theme' who 'didst find a lyre all golden by the side'.[107] The implication is that Apollo's gold is not gold as such, but rather a standard of poetic truth and potentially social reform that is at the same time a mystery. As Mnemosyne says, she 'can read / A wondrous lesson in thy silent face'.[108]

In the end, though, Keats had to 'abject' Apollo if only to stop from falling back into the 'mawkish' pose of the Huntian poet that Keats had already left behind in *Endymion*.[109] *The Fall of Hyperion* thus signals a different mode of self-reflexivity about the impossibility of the poetic standard that was already evident in the debates over forgery, that is, about the diffusion of value into relativity. K. K. Ruthven began the critical discussion that many critics have taken up about Keats and finance by remarking that the kind of poem *Hyperion* was turning out to be, as well as Keats' ultimate decision to abandon them altogether were at heart monetary, when toward the end of 1819, Keats' found himself in what he perceived to be insurmountable financial straits.[110] But the *Fall* also shows us the continuity of Keats' thoughts about the relation between economic standards and poetic form. Deliberately and immediately, the poem rejects the old property standard by way of the decaying feast, the 'refuse of a meal / By angel tasted, or our mother Eve' recalling the end of *Paradise Lost*. In the figure of the poet/dreamer, Keats puts a hopelessly self-conscious observer at the poem's center:

> I look'd around upon the carved sides
> Of an old sanctuary with roof august,

Builded so high, it seem'd that filmed clouds
Might spread beneath, as o'er the stars of heaven;
So old the place was, I remember'd none
The like upon the earth: what I had seen
Of grey cathedrals, buttress'd walls, rent towers,
The superannuations of sunk realms,
Or Nature's rocks toil'd hard in waves and winds,
Seem'd but the faulture of decrepit things
To that eternal domed monument.
Upon the marble at my feet there lay
Store of strange vessels and large draperies,
Which needs had been of dyed asbestos wove,
Or in that place the moth could not corrupt,
So white the linen, so, in some, distinct
Ran imageries from a sombre loom.
All in a mingled heap confus'd there lay
Robes, golden tongs, censer and chafing dish,
Girdles, and chains, and holy jewelries.[111]

Recalling Spenser's description of the Cave of Mammon, Ruthven thought that this passage was meant to give the impression of 'a sacred bank'. However, the passage is important not simply because it invokes, once again, the loss of 'Golden Age ideals for those of an age of gold' but because in this new age, such comparisons are impossible to calculate.[112] In trying to measure the sanctuary's age, the poet discusses its height and in trying to determine its size, the poet insists upon its great (eternal) age. The 'distinct' images on the linen tapestries are 'mingled' and 'confused' at the poet's feet. The dreamer's inability to measure according to recognizable standards makes a space for poetic or aesthetic appreciation – not according to the classical standards of beauty and clarity, but rather according to new standards of experience and disarray.

It is possible to read Keats' poem as a further experiment in the idea of a poetic standard based not on its challenge to political economy but as a reflection of a wholly different pedagogical mode, an aesthetic education that requires its own fragmentation in order to justify its utterly ironic deconstruction of all normative modes of rationality and progress. But reading the poem as an experiment in deferral, in mystery, even in cultural critique assumes precisely the kind of advanced network of relative values that came into being with advanced capitalism. To show, self-consciously, that neither poetry nor economics, neither love nor labor can manifest the standard of value is also to assert that if there is a standard of value, a 'thermometer' of understanding, that it lies *elsewhere* than in poetry because, being mere speculation itself, poetry cannot measure other speculative activities.

Other poets writing directly on banking and paper money, including Byron, Moore, and Peacock, employed layers of dialectical interplay to confound distinctions between real value and pervasive imitation. 'What can any body say', Byron wrote in his journal in January, 1821, 'save what Solomon said long before us? After all, it is but passing from one counter to another, from the bookseller's to the other tradesman's – grocer or pastry-cook. For my part, I have met with most poetry upon trunks; so that I am apt to consider the trunk-maker as the sexton of authorship.'[113] Rather than encourage trust in a philosopher-king or unacknowledged legislator as an alternative to financial fraud, the poets used satire and parody to undermine the pretensions not only of political economy but also of poetry itself. In these works, imitation and adaptation – the literary modalities that flaunt their status as 'forgeries' – became the means of undermining the institutional foundation of all 'authentic value', much as Cobbett had hoped to do by flooding the Bank of England with forged banknotes. In the process, however, and also like Cobbett, the Romantic satirists continued to insist that a standard was possible even if it was neither a material object nor socially self-evident. The result is a kind of satiric embarrassment, a perplexed reaction to the incapacity of poetry to overcome the new commercial order that, in turn, becomes the basis for a new kind of reflective poetics.

One of the most famous instances of this reaction are the opening stanzas of canto 12 of *Don Juan*. Byron begins with his poet anguishing over turning 35 and comparing 'barbarous ... middle age ... when we hover between fool and sage, / And don't know justly what we would be at' to 'a printed page, / Black letter upon foolscap', a signature that we recognize as ours but cannot experience other than as the work of something else.[114] Reflecting on age leads him to reflect on the 'illusion' of love being 'o'er' and from love to 'money, that most pure imagination'.[115] In making that comparison, Byron brings up the debate between paper and gold:

> Love or lust makes man sick, and wine much sicker;
> Ambition rends, and gaming gains a loss;
> But making money, slowly first, then quicker,
> And adding still a little through each cross
> (Which *will* come over things), beats love or liquor,

The gamester's counter, or the statesman's *dross*.
O Gold! I still prefer thee unto paper,
Which makes bank credit like a bank of *vapour*.[116]

Gold is more real than paper credit, love, wine, or gambling. But even gold is not permanent enough to escape the tide of ever-shifting values. The next six stanzas are a paean to international banking. 'Who keep the world, both old and new, in pain / Or pleasure? Who make politics run glibber all? / The shade of Buonaparte's noble daring? – / Jew Rothschild, and his fellow-Christian, Baring'.[117] The 'miser' who hoards his gold is 'your only poet' for he possesses that for which others only hope, but the miser is merely 'the intellectual lord of all' whom the fool abuses for not having the temerity to actually use his money.[118] It is only the stamp, then, that both authorizes the money as secure and allows it to circulate through the world. In this respect, money is not like love at all, Byron asserts, but rather like marriage, the legal form of sexual relation rather than real sex.

But even here, the poet is on uneven ground. Marriage hardly prevents adultery and Chancery is full of cases of divorce (such as Byron's own in stanza 18). Similarly, political economists are pilloried for sexual hypocrisy. Malthus, for instance, cannot help but do 'the thing 'gainst which he writes'.[119] Like them, however, the poet promises to be 'serious', but this leads to the return of the writing–money analogy:

I'm serious – so are all men upon paper;
And why should I not form my speculation,
And hold up to the sun my little taper?
Mankind just now seems wrapt in meditation
On constitutions and steam-boats of vapour;
While sages write against all procreation,
Unless a man can calculate his means
Of feeding brats the moment his wife weans.[120]

Like the value of paper money that everyone distrusts, the poet's 'speculations' on marriage and sexuality are little more than tapers in the daylight, enlightening that which is already obvious to most people in practical terms. 'Cash rules the grove, and fells it too besides; / Without cash, camps were thin, and courts were none; / Without cash, Malthus tells you, "take no brides"'.[121] Just as human beings survive through sex though they may harangue against it, so modern people live by credit, though they may seriously, as the narrator says, 'prefer gold'. Byron's world literally is a world without sovereigns. Everything is exchangeable for everything else. There is no need for poetry to discover a standard of value. The standardized monetary economy has already arrived and there is no place from which Byron can stand to articulate a counter claim. Byron's poem is not a critique of the paper money system but an acknowledgment of its all-pervasiveness. Although the narrator makes remarks about political economists, there is no effort to engage with their theories, just as there is no effort to question the legitimacy of the international gold trade. If Byron is satirizing anything, it is the tendency of people of his time and class to rely heavily on credit at the same time as they quote Whig political economy and espouse responsible bullionist views.

Less than a month after completing canto 12 of *Don Juan*, Byron composed *The Age of Bronze* intending it for the third number of *The Liberal*, the paper he had been publishing from Italy with Shelley and Hunt. The poem is a cynical romp through post-war Europe, bemoaning the downfall of Napoleon and the end of heroism. The final stanzas concern economic matters, though the narrator is sheepishly reluctant to speak 'of imposts or of debts' any more than he is to mention 'reform' which in the early 1820s was an ill-favored concept.[122] Byron then accuses the Tory landowners of pursuing the war against Bonaparte against their own interest. 'He was your great Triptolemus; his vices / Destroy'd but realms, and still maintain'd your prices; / He amplified to every lord's content / The grand agrarian alchymy, high rent.'[123] That Byron equates the high price of corn with alchemy prompts a link between inflation and illusion, a typical radical tactic. He then charges that the war had been fought for 'high-market patriots' who used it as an excuse to keep up their rents.[124] There is no heroic marshaling of aristocratic genius here. In the next stanza, Byron describes a credit system still awash in stocks and credit, its wealth coming not from 'ore' but rather from the machinations of bankers, who, as he had done in *Don Juan*, Byron stereotypes as Jewish money-lenders.

If the poem was ever meant to inspire reform or revive poetry, the effort was half-hearted. Byron did not publish this poem in *The Liberal* – Hunt, his family, and the journal were starting to annoy him – but sent it instead to Leigh's brother John who published it in an octavo edition. Thomas Wooler, who wrote the only review of the poem to appear at this time, complained that it was not radical enough. But Byron was not really interested in founding a new British republic. Although the poem laments the degradation of the aristocracy into what he calls the '*landed self-interest*', it certainly never celebrates the bourgeoisie.[125]

Byron's problem with the new England was not that it was operating under a 'fictitious system': Byron had absolutely no trouble with credit per se, even at this time, as his loans to Hunt (against his better judgment he believed) and Mary Shelley testify. His problem simply was that the wrong people governed the country: economists, accountants, and Jews; not Pitts, Napoleons, or Nelsons. Hence the repeated allusions to classical heroes indicate a wish not for gold, but rather for a golden age. In the final stanzas, Byron turns to the fate of the muse, whom he depicts first as Josephine tendering her emperor on St. Helena, and then as a sheltered English bourgeois wife. The final stanza sees the muse herself laughing as Scottish merchants overrun England.

Like *Don Juan*, but more explicitly so, *The Age of Bronze* demonstrates the way Byron opposes the condition of Britain as he sees it with 'the aristocratic symbolic economy expenditure' that Jerome Christensen identifies as the poet's charisma. Christiansen also makes clear, however, that this strength is to a great extent an imitation of an order that Byron nostalgically imagines to have existed in the Augustan period and before.[126] Byron understood perhaps better than anyone else in the period how much poetic value depended on prestige and celebrity.[127] Satire is a tool Byron uses to deflect his readers from their absorption in the economy he describes. But it cannot and will not achieve anything like Shelleyan confidence, which is itself a kind of imitative nostalgia. In a dialectical inversion of Shelley's futurity, Byron imagines the very recent British past exactly as it is (appropriately enough for a poem published in a radical newspaper) such that his own 'strength' also appears utterly flaccid.

Byron's friend and biographer, the Irish poet Thomas Moore, also wrote a number of poems on the bullion question, on the national debt, and financial speculation during the mid-1820s. Most of them first appeared in the *Times of London* alongside reports on the nation's financial affairs. Far from critical attacks on the government, the banks, or the public, the little satires were popular enough that Moore republished them as *Odes on Cash, Corn, and Catholics* in 1828. Like Byron's, Moore's satirical verses do not really offer viable alternatives. Instead, they simply parody the complexities of finance as if to admit that it cannot comprehend them. This indefiniteness is furthered by Moore's choice of genre: comic dialogues (in which there is no winner) and comic song. In 'Dialogue between a Sovereign and a One-Pound Note', for instance, Moore also compares the bullion problem to marriage. The sovereign accuses his 'wife', a banknote (they had been married by 'Parson Van', meaning Vansittart, the Chancellor in 1816), of 'ranging' with silver and producing 'lots of young sixpences' while it seems that she 'can never live together' with the sovereign, one-pound coin. From the point of view of the bullionists, it is the paper money that produces 'false' wealth in the form, here, of token silver coins, while the gold coin sees himself as burning the home fires. The note, in turn, accuses the coin of 'roam[ing]': 'One cannot look askance, / But whip! you're off to France.' It is the gold that travels on the open money market 'leaving nothing but old rags at home'. The reason she 'flirts' with silver is because she has been 'disown'd by [her] natural protector' (gold). Here Moore is restating the complaints of the bullionist and anti-bullionist factions against one another's policies. And yet, the poem ends without taking a position one way or another:

> The Sovereign, smiling on her,
> Now swore, upon his honour,
> To be henceforth domestic and loyal;
> But, within an hour or two,
> Why – I sold him to a Jew,
> And he's now at No. 10, Palais Royal.[128]

The speaker's candor about financial improprieties reinforces the cynicism of the whole poem. Anti-Semitism gives away conservatism. The point here, though, is not that gold is better than paper or vice versa, but rather that the standard of value if there is one does not lie within the purview of the speaker but *out there* in a market over which it has little or no influence.

The best-known satire on paper money from the period is Thomas Love Peacock's *Paper Money Lyrics*, conceived during the financial crisis of 1825–6, though not published until 1837. Sometimes called the first modern financial crisis, the crash of December 1825 came about not because of exogenous circumstances, like war, but through the normal course of financial circulation and diversification. After resumption, the market in precious metals boomed. Investors flocked to new mining companies that were exploring newly discovered veins in South America that had themselves been opened by newly independent nations there. These endeavors required capital, and so the growth of new investment agencies, stock companies, and country banks matched that of the mining sector. By 1824, Britain was in the grip of speculation mania. Though there were confidence men who made up elaborate fictions about the fortunes to be had servicing the new mines, most investors acted in good faith, many on the advice of bankers and lawyers who were happily riding the swell themselves. It might be said that the country was gripped not by speculation but by imitation, everyone following the good fortune of everyone else. The major banks, including the Bank of England, encouraged these practices by issuing extensive loans to prospective investors. But they were also sending their reserves overseas and this led to concerns about shortages at home. When word came at the end of 1825 that the South American mining boom had produced a glut of imports and services with little means to pay, the market took a sudden downturn. Many bankers, including Henry Thornton's son, were ruined and implored the government to suspend cash payments again. This time around, they refused; the gold standard was in place and the bankers would simply have to be confident that fortunes would change. In the meantime, however, the government took the opportunity to centralize the financial system even further by extending the gold standard to Scotland and allowing the Bank of England to open branches in place of ruined country banks. On one hand, mass imitation, bordering in some cases on recklessness, had driven a diversified speculative boom. But this confidence was not replaced by a new 'real', but rather by an enforced confidence in the centralizing capacities of the government and the Bank. Other industries were transformed in a similar way. The traditional publishing houses, like Taylor, Murray, and Constable were overwhelmed by their own investment in expensive editions and were replaced in the wake of the crash by Thomas Tegg and Charles Knight who collected remaindered editions and sold them at below market prices. The turn from triple-decker novels to cheaper 'standard' editions like Bentley's and serialized fiction can also be attributed to the mass commercialization that followed the 1825 crisis.[129]

In *Paper Money Lyrics*, Peacock was not seeking to overturn or replace this curiously paradoxical state of affairs, though his lyrics are 'radical' in the sense that like Wooler's newspapers and Shelley's poems they link banking and paper money to a regime of hypocrisy and falsehood that they hope will soon disappear. 'The Country Banks are breaking / The London banks are shaking / Suspicion is awaking' read the opening lines.[130] What the poems realize is a world without standards, or rather where the standard is confounded by an abiding sense that it is already a forgery. The collection is also a series of hilarious imitations of the work of well-known poets from the period, including Moore, Scott, Coleridge, and Wordsworth. Like Byron, Peacock connects paper and gold alike to writing, and the various forms of writing – poetry, news, and stamps – to each other. But the implication is that poetry is much *like* the kind of writing that emanates from the publishing houses every time there is a crisis of credit. In his parody of Wordsworth, 'A Mood of My Own Mind occurring during a gale of wind at midnight, while I was writing a paper on the currency, by the light of two mould candles, by W. W. esq. Distributor of Stamps', the poet himself is writing a pamphlet on paper money even though, the poem says, the whole issue 'perplexes' him. Wordsworth's duties as a representative of the taxation system – the bane of radical political economy – are further likened to the corruption that Bentham and others once leveled at the interested government parties. And everything is reduced finally to a subtle, musing, alcoholic fog.[131]

But the real object of Peacock's satire is not paper money but poetry. *Paper Money Lyrics* is a work of literary satire not economic debate. It contends that poetry could never really inspire economic reform because poets do not know anything practical about economics or money. Poets are *not* professionals but quacks. In the preface to *Paper Money Lyrics*, included when Peacock finally published the series in 1837, he recalls the familiar trope of the credit economy as a human body: the poems were composed 'during the prevalence of an influenza to which the beautiful fabric of paper credit is periodically subject; which is called commercial panic by citizens, financial crisis by politicians, and day of reckoning by the profane'.[132] Peacock lambasts not a financial system per se (about which he actually has very little to say) but the reaction of various uninformed groups (Peacock, we should remember, worked with James Mill at the East India Company) to the threat of monetary dissolution. As crises of credit can be compared to bodily illness, 'The *Lyrics*' can

> shadow out, in their order, the symptoms of the epidemic in its several stages; the infallible nostrums, remedial and preventive, proposed by every variety of that arch class of quacks, who call themselves political economists; the orders, counter-orders, and disorders, at the head of affairs, with respect to joint-stock banks, and the extinction of one-pound notes, inclusive of Scotland, and exclusive of Scotland; till the final patching up of the uncured malady by a series of false palliatives, which only nourished for another eruption the seeds of the original disease. The *tabes tacitis concepta medullis* has again blazed forth in new varieties of its primitive types – broken promises and bursting bubbles.[133]

Peacock is not satirizing political economy, but rather that class of quacks who call themselves political economists, i.e. everybody *but* the real economists. The upshot of this is that political economy is like proper medicine, empirical, a fact that in a preface to a collection of poems Peacock can present only negatively as missing from the quackery of citizens, politicians, and poets that he will satirize. There is little sense in this Preface or from the poems themselves that there is anything the poet or his readers can do to change the system. Scientific objectivity, presumed by the political economist, the medical practitioner, and the late-Romantic satirist prevents them all from proposing solutions. And there are no solutions to propose other than to let the market run its course.

Peacock clearly did not think much of the paper money system, of speculators and credit hounds. He was not alone. But there were just as many writers who wanted to revive a credit system based on honor rather than gold and who resented the machinations of the 'money men'. Thomas Hood's 1841 poem 'Miss Killmansegg and her Precious Leg', subtitled 'A Golden Legend' is a ripping yarn about a spoiled young woman who loses a leg when her horse 'banker' goes on a 'run' and she replaces the leg with one made of solid gold, making her the object of every speculator's eye. A prolific but penniless hack, Hood was castigating the mania for 'gold! and gold! and gold without end!' that by the early 1840s was the center of Britain's economic orthodoxy.[134] This was in many ways a reflection not simply of the public suspicions of that orthodoxy (which were largely warranted) but also of the sad dependency to which writers of poetry had been reduced.

In the later satires of Byron, Moore, and Peacock the confidence that Shelley hoped his audience would place in poetry falters. The idea that in the midst of absolutely relativity or contingency, as manifest by the ubiquity of a fraudulent paper money economy and a market for menial, imitative literature some distinctive notion of order or peace might emerge remains very strong. This feeling is accompanied by world-weariness about the role that poetry should play in the determination of economic values and establishment of political order. Thus, in the mid-nineteenth century poetry becomes more of a curiosity than a social force, a topic of intellectual debate and personal reflection rather than a principle of governance. That poets might and often do have something genuinely important to say about political and economic organization remained part of the aesthetics of the 1820s. But the poets' own anxieties about how far what they said could go and who, in the end, was listening prevented it from making much headway into the political realm.

5
Standard Novels

In March 1822, while visiting David Ricardo at his estate, Gatcomb Park, Maria Edgeworth saw Oliver Cromwell's head; 'not his picture', she wrote to her Aunt Margaret Ruxton, '– not his bust – nothing of stone or marble or plaister of Paris, but his real head, which is now in the possession of Mr. Ricardo's brother in law (Mr. Wilkinson)'. With macabre relish, Edgeworth related that it

> is the only head upon record which has after death been subject to the extremes of honor and infamy – It having been first embalmed and laid in satin state – Then dragged out of the coffin at the restoration – chopped from the body and stuck upon a pole before Westminster hall, where it stood twenty five years till one stormy night the pole broke and down fell the head at the centinel[']s [sic] feet who stumbled over it in the dark twice thinking it a stone, then cursed and picked it up and found it was a head. Its travels and adventures from the centinel through several hands would be too long to tell. It came in short into the Russell family and to one who was poor and in debt and who yet loved the head so dearly that he never would sell it to Coxe of the Museum till Coxe got him deep in his debt arrested and threw him into jail. Then and not till the last extremity he gave it up for liberty.[1]

While Wilkinson lectured ('compasses in hand'), with Ricardo and his wife holding the head by its broken pole, the question arose as to whether the head really was Cromwell's. Some of the company, having 'made proper allowances for want of flesh-muscles – eyes &c' agreed that the likeness was close; others did not or were repulsed with the whole encounter. Ricardo finally 'gave up too when a bit of cotton wool was dragged from the nostrils ('Oh I *cannot* stand the cotton wool') He delivered over the staff and went to the fire to comfort himself dragging up the skirt of his coat as men do in troubles great.'[2]

It is hard not to read Edgeworth's anecdote as an allegory for the standard. Emblazoned on coins and printed on paper banknotes, the head of a king is the customary guarantee of monetary value, the 'King's Standard'. But such icons never prevented kings and governments from overlooking the values that they were meant to guarantee, even as they used – or abused – their own money to increase their influence and power. To complicate matters more, Cromwell was not a king, only a 'protector' or, in later accounts an impostor, so the legitimacy of his coins was all the more questionable.[3] More important for me, though, are the observers' different attitudes. Ricardo's queasiness at the sight of the shrunken head, in all its corporeal nakedness, is especially intriguing. He was, after all, one of the architects of the gold standard. His and other political economists' inability to resolve the currency 'troubles' – distress, inflation, corruption, forgery – seems manifest in his embarrassed 'turning away'. Edgeworth, by contrast, was clearly enjoying herself. Cromwell's head provided her with an assortment of antiquarian details and narrative intrigues. She was delighted by the head's 'travels and adventures ... through several hands' and its continuous transformation from head to pole-top to stone to commodity to curiosity. She was cannily aware of the economic valences of the head and its story; she even associates it with the debt into which one of its owners, the unfortunate Russell, is plunged by the rapacious Coxe. But her point is not that the degraded head undermines monarchical legitimacy, economic order, or fiscal confidence; rather, it cultivates antiquarian interest and aesthetic enjoyment.

As not only a pioneer of the national tale and a formative influence on the more familiar Romantic novelists Jane Austen and Walter Scott, but also, with her father, an educator and economic experimentalist, Edgeworth was well placed to understand the vicissitudes of the British currency. Her own fiction, especially *The Absentee*, *Harrington*, and *Ormond*, often refer to banking and bank failures as well as to regional incongruity, anti-Semitism, and other aspects of the period's economic controversies.[4] Edgeworth was by no means the only novelist of the period to write about money in this way. Jane Austen's novels document the concerns of country people with prices and debt. Austen was familiar with the effects of fiscal mismanagement. During the post-war agricultural depression of 1816, her brother Henry, a partner in the successful country bank, Austen, Gray, and Vincent, declared bankruptcy after one of its agents failed to redeem several outstanding advances. His brother and uncle repaid a £30,000 surety that Henry had borrowed to assume the post of Receiver General for Oxfordshire. He suspended the allowance his sisters had received since their father died in 1809. Austen 'had been living for some years past at considerable expense, but not more than might become the head of a flourishing bank, and no blame of personal extravagance was ever imputed to him'.[5] We know from her letters that Austen was sorry for her brother's misfortunes: 'London is become a hateful place to him & he is always depressed by the idea of it.'[6] Nevertheless, the market determined Austen's fate and he accepted it. At the end of 1816, he was ordained into the Church of England and installed as curate at Chawton. Walter Scott too was plagued by financial embarrassments. Twice during his long career, first in 1813 and then, more seriously, in 1825 the publishing firms in which he held a personal stake were forced to declare bankruptcy after his partners were caught up in the investment fever of the early 1820s. Scott was relieved of having to sell his beloved estate Abbotsford by signing over the royalties to all future writing to his creditors.

Critics have long puzzled over what exactly these experiences tell us about their attitudes toward finance or political economy or what the novel might have contributed to the economic changes with which they were contemporary. Neither Austen nor Scott was a bourgeois apologist. Indeed, it is widely agreed that both Scott and Austen supported the broadly liberal agenda of the 'pseudo-gentry', the rentier class of landowners, professionals, and their families. But there is strong evidence, especially in their later works, that they understood the conflicts and contradictions attending the agrarian economy, and were wary of its simultaneous ties to global commerce and unnerving commitment to social stratification. Their witty and suggestive styles also cut chinks in the aristocratic armor of legitimacy even as their readers could escape, if only for a moment, from political, economic, and social difficulties through the elegantly formulated and always resolute marriage plots.[7] In keeping with the aims of this book, though, I want to nuance this dialectic by linking it to the debates over the standard of value. Austen and Scott were anti-bullionists, and there is a case to be made that the novels reflect an ideological allegiance to the paper money system. But they also understood, as Coleridge, Shelley, and Henry Austen did, that standards are as fluid, dynamic, and changeable as the values and stories that circulate around them. Our trust is largely a matter of avoidance or, possibly, enjoyment of the vicissitudes to which these standards are prone.

The novelists derived their sense of a dynamic standard from a discourse that was implicit in much of the economic debate surrounding them but which made a strong mark on the fiction of that era via writers like Maria Edgeworth: nationalism. Nationalist and monetary discourses intersect on the question of regional disparity. How the multiple currencies of a 'United' kingdom worked came to the fore on at least two occasions: in 1804, a parliamentary committee, including many of the men who would serve on the Bullion Committee in 1809–10, was formed to consider the viability of an independent Irish banking system under the terms of the suspension of cash payments. In 1826, in the wake of the first major financial crash since the resumption of cash payments, the British Parliament planned to incorporate Scotland, which at that time still had an independent 'free-banking' system, into the English gold standard. As it turned out, one of loudest protests against this move came from Walter Scott, who was at the time facing bankruptcy. Scott's and Austen's experiments with narrative form represent important instances of how writing about money could straddle the divide and negotiate the tension between local and, increasingly, modern modes of monetary exchange, which enshrined the regional differences within Britain, and a classical mode of economic, historical, and aesthetic discourse that sought to subordinate these differences, which they regarded as unruly, shallow, primitive, and potentially dangerous. Eventually both were absorbed into an idea of the standard fostering regional modernization and nationalist sentiment. Austen and Scott resisted even this mode of mediation and instead turned the debate over money and the national itself into the basis of a perplexed, and thus embarrassed literary form.

National currencies, national tales

Reading Austen against nationalist writing seems counterintuitive, if only because her novels are just so *English*. Yet, it is precisely that distinctively English quality that some critics have argued makes them utterly germane to the issue of national disparity in Britain.[8] Her characteristic irony decenters easy identification with ideological positions – and that extends to the economic tensions that to a great extent underlay the development of the national tale. For instance, *Pride and Prejudice* may be Austen's most paradigmatically conservative novel. Its plot is oriented directly around questions and conflicts of rank. The Bennetts represent the village-based pseudo-gentry, made prosperous by the easy availability of money and credit but at the same time unsettled through their participation in a larger, more fluid order represented by the various national and international institutions they are compelled to encounter: the city, the church, the aristocracy, the law, even the army. Marilyn Butler is right to see in Darcy, his country estate, his extensive library, his proud ancestral picture gallery, and the respect he earns from tenants and professionals alike, the perfect image of the enlightened gentleman, justified in the pressure he exerts against the global forces of speculation by the order and decorum that his local leadership produces.[9] Darcy exudes confidence, though it is a strict and somewhat untenable one in a world whose values have become fluid and dynamic. Lydia and Wickham, by contrast, represent the speculative wind of global expansion. Lydia is the name of the country where money was invented.[10] Wickham's entrapment of Georgiana Darcy, not to mention his lies to Elizabeth represent the seductive power of paper credit. Keeping the Wickhams in check requires acts of subterfuge on Lizzie's part and charity on Darcy's. They are bribed to keep their place; they thus provide an excuse for Darcy to maintain ideological counter-pressure on the forces of speculation and equality.

First drafted in late 1796 and early 1797 and tantalizingly entitled 'First Impressions', the plot of *Pride and Prejudice* seems, as Mary Poovey has recently argued, to 'gesture' to the suspension of cash payments in its dramatization of the tension between traditional and modern modes of standardization.[11] Poovey does not say outright that *Pride and Prejudice* is about the Bank Restriction Act. Rather, she argues that the novel misdirects its readers to follow referential leads and narrative intrigues, backwards and forwards through chapters, letters, indirect assumptions, and disappointed expectation. Austen's reader thus experiences the same sense of confusion that was present at the time of the suspension of cash payments and the war that precipitated it. Through her marriage plot, Austen dramatizes the way that such breaches of authorial contract could be adumbrated into a manageable form. 'Austen', Poovey writes, 'was able to incorporate these matters into a safe, because textual world of words, where they could be managed, translated into other terms, then simply dismissed'.[12] The goal was for literature to supplement the lack of a workable standard for paper credit by imagining a world in which there is one, namely the managerial prowess of Mr. Darcy and Elizabeth Bennett's intelligent and forgiving companionship. That Austen's 'mode of reading directed her readers repeatedly back to the text and *not* to the world outside helped cut the tie between this kind of literary text and the other prose genres that it otherwise so closely resembled while giving the literary experience a value that seemed exempt from market price'.[13] Such a reading implies that Austen's novel both did and did not speak to the economic controversies of its day. This is fair, but it is by no means unique to Austen, as Poovey herself suggests. What is more, the crisis of confidence staged in *Pride and Prejudice* was *already* a crucial generic marker of most fiction, including nationalist fiction published in Austen's day, and had been for a century or more. In as much as *Pride and Prejudice* refers to the problems attending the suspension of cash payments, I am suggesting, it does so in the context of a broader concern with Britain's 'mixed' national character.

To make this point, I want to compare *Pride and Prejudice* to Edgeworth's *The Absentee*. Published as part of the series *Tales of Fashionable Life* in 1812, the year before *Pride and Prejudice* was published, *The Absentee* is usually thought be a prime example of the national tale.[14] The two novels share certain key plot elements, though that parallel is made oblique by Edgeworth's frenetic and programmatic narrative method in contrast to Austen's more demure style. The first half of *The Absentee* revolves around the failure of an Irish noble family, headed by Lord Clonbury. Partly through the machinations of his misguided friend and adviser Terence O'Fay and partly through his unfortunate relationships with a merciless Jewish money-lender, Mordecai, Lord Clonbury is dangerously in debt, which Colambre calls his 'embarrassed circumstances'.[15] Colambre, and thus the narrative, move through London very much in the mode of an eighteenth-century tourist, though it is clear that his affections are nevertheless held by his mother's sensible but penniless Irish ward, Grace Nugent. After failing to fully settle his father's debts or alter his mother's pretensions Colambre travels in the second volume to Ireland to try and reestablish his family's ties to their long-neglected land and tenants. Disguised as a copper-mining engineer, Mr. Evans, Colambre meets his father's agent, Mr. Burke, who represents (by virtue of his namesake) the solution to the problem of value, social respect and good governance. Unfortunately, Burke is in charge only of the estate town. When he arrives at the family castle, Colambre encounters the scurrilous Garraghty brothers who have ruined the estate through their selfish manipulation of the local economy. The Garraghty brothers' rent day appears as a parody of the modern money market:

> The haggling for the price of gold; the time lost in disputing about the goodness of the notes, among some poor tenants, who could not read or write, and who were at the mercy of the man with the bag in his hand; the vexation, the useless haranguing of all who were

> obliged to submit ultimately – lord Colambre saw; and all this time he endured the smell of tobacco and whiskey, and the sound of various brogues, the din of men wrangling, brawling, threatening, whining, drawling, cajoling, cursing, and every variety of wretchedness.[16]

In submitting to the agents' mockery of the banking system, the Irish tenants, who cannot read their own notes, give up whatever distinctive national consciousness they might have. Heard as an assemblage of brogues and smells the tenants have no definitive national character anyway.

The cacophony of the scene leads Colambre to the novel's key question: 'is this Ireland?' Colambre's answer, uttered in a series of double negations, opens the way for the moral ambition of the text. 'No it is not Ireland. Let me not, like most of those who forsake their native country, traduce it. Let me not, even to my own mind, commit the injustice of taking a speck for a whole. What I have just seen is the picture only of that to which an Irish estate and Irish tenantry may be degraded in the absence of those whose duty and interest in it is to reside in Ireland, to uphold justice by example and authority; but who neglecting this duty, commit power to bad hands and bad hearts – abandon their tenantry to oppression and their property to ruin.'[17] Colambre feels he must replace 'not-Ireland' with a new version of itself. This not-not-Ireland will come into being when its absentee landlords and their benevolent presence are restored to the top of the social order. Yet, this is a restoration of something that never actually existed: Edgeworth's plan for benevolent landownership is a scheme, an ideal, based largely on her and her father's experiments with estate management. The metonymic movement of guineas and notes, intensified by the rough exchanges of dialects and brogues, is resolved by the invention of a lost culture under the auspices of the 'resident Irish proprietor'.[18]

Might not Austen's Wickham be read as a conventionally 'Irish' figure? He is brash and overconfident, a gambler and a manipulator, not to mention rather loose with the truth, like Edgeworth's loveable Larry or the rakish hanger-on Terrance O'Fay or the Garraghty brothers. Wickham is also a soldier, one of the conventional Anglo-Irish professions in eighteenth-century fiction and drama. Yet the more important parallels are generic. The twists, turns, indirections, and delays that Poovey traces in *Pride and Prejudice* match the odd, fractured combination of generic elements in *The Absentee*: travel writing, antiquarianism, post-Revolutionary diatribe, political economy, as well as the more familiar scandal sheets, disguises, intrigues, and marriage plots. Edgeworth and

Austen offer a surprisingly similar resolution to these paralleled political and generic emergencies: the imaginary figure of the presiding landowner, but one not rooted in aristocratic privilege but rather emerging from the new order of accommodation and practicality.

That new order is what historians mean by British nationalism. I say British nationalism to distinguish it from the more familiarly and culturally distinctive Irish and Scottish varieties, and to correlate it to a complex 'group' identity fostered in pro-British texts. British nationalism is characterized not by the transformation of a cultural identity into a sovereign state but, on the contrary, by the expansion of sovereignty into, or rather onto collected and subaltern communities. It is in this respect that British nationalism can be associated with British imperialism. Yet, British nationalism is less an exercise in domination than in the 'mutual accommodation' of various cultural identities into an imaginary whole, and this is what connects it to the rise of the novel.[19] As J. Paul Hunter and James Raven made clear some time ago, the novel developed in the early eighteenth century alongside the popular press as a way for publishers to profit from the new consumer culture and for the arbiters of that culture to delineate the forms of economic and social behavior appropriate to its, and their, well-being. If the new wealth was a sign of the new Britain, a point so general it does not even have to be made, then the new novel is *prima facie* a nationalist enterprise. Of course, as Ernest Gellner was only the first to notice, British nationalism did not emerge from the new market capitalism but largely, as Raven puts it, in 'response' to it, namely to fears that the political influence of large monopoly companies would erode Britain's traditionally mixed character and hierarchical society.[20] But the result of this response was not a curtailing of various signs of identity (national or otherwise) but their proliferation in local newspapers, tourist and travel guides, antiquarian profiles, paper money and coin collections. It was this massive outburst of media that, as Benedict Anderson famously claimed, helped to inculcate a new sense of 'empty time', an open and dynamic standard of diverse global experience.

Clifford Siskin notes further that a particular mode of writing appeared in the late eighteenth century that could delineate this common sense of diversity and mutual accommodation, what he calls novelism. The earlier novels of Samuel Richardson and Henry Fielding presumed that all 'good' writing was essentially imitative; they are 'guide books' for surviving the new world opened up by technologies of writing, including, we should add, paper credit.[21] In one of several prefaces appended to his *Pamela*, Richardson remarked that the book would provide a 'much-wanted Standard' not only for moral behavior but, more particularly, for the 'Kind of Writing' that *Pamela* was.[22] Richardson's labeling *Pamela* a standard was deliberate: it was 'an example of Purity' especially to the Romance writers of France, who 'shall have an opportunity to receive English Bullion in exchange for its own Dross, which have so long passed current among us' and the purveyors of 'pernicious *Novels*' which 'reduce our sterling substances to empty Shadow'.[23] For Richardson, a combination of sexual intrigue and moral upbraiding in domestic romance will produce a store of moral virtue and thus of literary value, one he based on a positive model of value in good coin. In spite of his dislike for *Pamela*, Fielding too was an imitator. His heroes, the travelers and adventurers who discover that they are 'really' gentlemen follow a pattern of recognition that is itself a product of imitation. Joseph Andrews and Tom Jones are their 'real' fathers' sons. The marriage plot, by this method, comes to signal the purpose of capitalist ventures: the invention of home.

The proliferation of novels in the second half of the eighteenth century entailed a falling off in the quality of the models that the novel could provide. At first, this proliferation was experimental: the 'it-narratives' and philosophical fictions of the 1750s and 60s, for instance, demonstrate a profound self-consciousness about the difficult relation between individual identity and the commodification and circulation of goods.[24] After 1774, the number of novels being published took off and the proliferation of new genres – travel stories, country-house fiction, the gothic, Jacobin and anti-Jacobin fiction – not to mention an abundance of women novelists created an ideological firestorm in which the old standard that Richardson and Fielding had imitated simply burned up. Released from its 'ancient' or 'intrinsic' models the amount of fiction being produced matched the number of ideological positions the genre represents and which individual works contain. As Robert Miles argues, the novel became 'philosophical romance' in which various schemes and plans for social and moral reform compete for discursive interest and investment and where the inequalities attending the new economy could be described and challenged.[25] In the wake of its proliferation, the novel changed from a genre of imitation to a genre of accommodation. Novelists and critics alike came to realize that the various perspectives that made up the nation had enlarged and the novel, flexible and voluble as it could be, could grow and adapt with it. Siskin suggests that the novel achieved the status of the preeminent genre of accommodation because the periodical essay, the earlier form to achieve that status, was losing its audience and splintering into various ideological sub-groups, a phenomenon that, as I argued in Chapter 2, is in part attributable to the rise of expertise.[26]

The novel's transformation into the 'standard' genre of nineteenth-century Britain was also borne out by its accommodation of various nationalist discourses: history and antiquarianism. As Katie Trumpener, Ian Duncan, Ina Ferris, and others have shown at length, the rise of the novel can be attributed as much to its accommodation of varying regional sympathies, especially in the wake of the Scottish and Irish rebellions of 1745 and 1798, as to its political flexibility.[27] These discourses also had a crucial stake in a simultaneous debate on regional currency. Contrary to popular contention, the Irish economy was quite progressive during the eighteenth century.[28] Economic growth in Ireland was largely due to its close commercial and monetary ties to Great Britain, ties that were in fact strongest during the period of Ireland's independence. Four times as many goods were exported from Ireland to Britain in 1780 than in 1700. Because Irish and Scots merchants had less contact with the continent, conducted very little currency trading, and were still predominantly agricultural, both countries had thriving local banking industries, the Bank of Ireland opening just after independence in 1783.[29] But because the communication networks in Ireland were basic, finance was inconsistent. Dublin was awash in banknotes by the middle of the century. In Belfast commerce was carried on only in specie.[30] The animosity intensified at periods when banking practices in Scotland and Ireland were seen to compromise English prosperity. During the Protestant Ascendancy, the monetary ties were stretched and, until the amalgamation of the Irish and English pounds, the two countries experienced several sudden and wide changes in their rate of exchange.

The way to resolve the exchange problem was for the Irish banking system to be absorbed into the English. The 1801 Act of Union contained two articles related directly to finance. While, according to article VI, Ireland would be responsible for its own revenues, according to article VII, it would also be responsible for a part of Britain's debt, 2/17ths to be precise. By 1804, Ireland's national debt has risen fourfold from 27 million to 107 million pounds – an increase rivaled only by the English. Once this absorption had been accomplished, it was possible for an argument about the recklessness and intransigence of the Irish banking system to be made – and it was explicitly in the 1804 Report on the Irish pound, a prelude to the *Bullion Report* and written by many of the same people including Horner and Thornton. As they would do, the 1804 committee claimed that excess issues at the Bank of Ireland had caused the depreciation; in other words, there had been a lack of restraint and control. And as was also the case in 1810, most of the witnesses interviewed by the committee had a different view. The 1798 Rebellion and a series of mediocre harvests had slowed down exports to Britain temporarily in 1798 and 1799; the Union had opened trade again and goods were flowing freely across the Irish Sea. The higher demand resulted in higher prices. Another factor was absenteeism: the lower value of the Irish pound meant that Irish landlords in England were receiving considerably less in rent. These views were widely discounted by the committee.

Where did the drive to absorb Irish finance come from? Obviously economic factors were at issue. The viability of Irish banking challenged the ubiquity of English finance, even in England. But a primary motivation for the advocates of a pan-British national currency was not just economic but discursive: it was based as much on ideals of order, decorum, and taste as it was on exchange rates. Writing in 1809, the unionist Member of the British Parliament Henry Parnell argued that the increase in Irish notes after 1797 was attributable partly to fears of invasion and rebellion – far more pressing in Ireland than England – but more directly to an increase in the price of food, and he cites Malthus as evidence of how this sudden demand could occur. It was the responsibility of the Bank to reduce the amount of notes being issued once the demand subsided. Its reluctance to do so, Parnell concluded, threw 'a very great obstacle in the way of returning cheapness'.[31] What is important about this is the way it connects to Enlightenment ideals of equilibrium and sufficiency, to limit and restraint. At all costs the system must be returned to its 'normal' state. But, the turn to paper in a time of anxiety, solving a potentially embarrassing situation with more embarrassment (or debt), demonstrates a crucially modern response to the Irish predicament.

It is in this respect that the decisions of the Irish pound committee are related to the developing tension between historians and antiquarianism. 'Antiquarians', Susan Manning writes, 'were the misers of historiography'.[32] For the doyens of the new human sciences, knowledge was only valuable if it was useful and that meant circulating, among a wide public audience. Like bankers and other financial experts, antiquarians were treated as purveyors of masses of mysterious information that was as harmful to the state as it was to the social status of its practitioners. In discovering among ancient dross practices of production, socialization, and exchange such as the use of money that, on one hand, were challenging principles of virtue and civility and, on the other, were evidently viable as practices, antiquarians were seen to justify a barbarianism that the Enlightenment sought to correct or dissipate. Irish and Scottish coinage was described by Enlightenment historians as inefficient, excessive, and dangerous in much the same way that paper money was described in the writers' own present, and most particularly in relation to those parts of Britain where paper was more common than metal, namely Scotland and Ireland. Like antiquarian texts, paper money produced connections, factions, and associations that for all their temporality and effectiveness could also be politically lethal. The solution was to 'antique' the Irish and Scottish banking systems, making their evident modernity appear primitive and ineffective and to replace that antiquarian modernity with a historical sensibility underlying the 'ancient standard of the realm'. The Society of Antiquarians, chartered in 1783 – the same year as the Bank of Ireland – appeared as a kind of secret society, the devotees of an arcane mystery religion. Many recent critics have traced the strong associations between the bad reputation of antiquarian pastimes and the low status of gothic fiction.

The problem with antiquarianism was that it was just too close to Enlightenment history, in the same way that during the bullion controversy financial expertise was slipping into the intellectual territory of political economy. As Barbara Benedict suggests, antiquarians were committed to the integrity of the individual case, be they objects or people and this sense of pleasurable variety and toleration strongly influenced the very empiricism that sought to refute its legitimacy.[33] On the basis of this split allegiance, Yoon Sun Lee divides the historical mindsets at the turn of the nineteenth century between 'patriotic historicism' which she associates with Burke's idea of a continuous national culture, and antiquarianism which made an important a break from the past:

> If the patriotic discourse of history constructed the nation as self-inheriting, continuously bequeathing institutions and national character to itself, antiquarian discourse and practice unobtrusively belied those assumptions: like the curiosity that greets it, the existence of the antiquarian object is contingent on processes of obsolescence and fragmentation as these afflict cultures, institutions, and nations. The possibility of antiquarian knowledge ... rests to a large extent on the prior division, erasure, and epistemological or material forfeiture of what may be construed as a nation's culture.[34]

This erasure signals the modernity of antiquarianism: rather than feel anxiety about market forces of division and replication, and thus rush to older notions of continuity, virtue, and culture to restrain them, antiquarians embraced those forces and converted them into the ground of their expertise. Antiquarianism was a marketplace in which opinions about trivial things, like the things themselves, increased in value far above the supposed 'real' value of labor or art. Like bankers and financers, antiquarians were experts in the field of manufacturing consensus through the circulation and discussion of texts, their own and their rivals. They eschewed the general, civilized discourses of moral philosophy and political economy and thus represented a threat to the social status of those intellectuals. Put another way, antiquarians were dangerously modern in precisely the way that Burke would describe the economy of the French: phantasmal, 'a traditional estate ... vaporized into worthlessness by an act of vandalism'.[35]

A further sign of the antiquarian's modernity, one connecting it further to the world of financial expertise, is its medium of exchange. Although the stock in trade of antiquarian conversation was objects like coins, pots, and paintings, its actual medium was paper. For the most part, antiquarians did not circulate coins and other collectibles. Their chief medium was the auction catalogue, a genre that served to challenge the logic of intrinsic value in two ways. First, a printer could easily place the coins on the block, cover them with ink, and then stamp them on paper.[36] Second, when a collection was sold, the auction houses sold lists of the individual coins as a way to advertise the sale and increase speculation. The auctioning off of the collections, with the individual value of each piece rising according to its buyer's predilection, defied standard assumptions about inheritance, property, and ownership. As Seamus Deane argues, the doubling of the field of historical progress between British and Scottish, English and Irish, British and French helped to entrench the idea (derived largely from Rousseau) of 'national character' as the determinant of economic success and social civility. Yet the point that needs to be made is that via serial publication and circulation, these distinct national characters were constantly being put in new lights, at one point ancient, at another modern, at another primitive.[37]

The process by which antiquarian curiosity was appropriated into the aesthetic that served as the foundation for economic standardization is evident as early as the seventeenth century when the study of ancient coins was already playing a prominent role in Irish antiquarian discourse. A good example of such a study is Sir James Ware's *History and Antiquities of Ireland*, first published in the 1650s and reprinted several times in the eighteenth century. It is 'uncertain', Ware conjectures, whether or not the Irish had a consistent coinage system before the first wave of English arrivals in the thirteenth century – though after that date 'it is certain that money was frequently Coin'd'.[38] It was the English who introduced proper minting techniques and standard denominations. Ware reproduces three 'primitive' coins dating, he thinks, from the middle of the twelfth century and compares them to coins from centuries after. The potential existence of coin, like the existence of a monarchy, legal system, and religion, proves the possibility that the Irish can be governed. The emphasis in Ware's historiography on the connection between coinage, governance, and monarchy indicates how that possibility should come about. Yet, typically, the uncertainty of native Irish money and with it the tendency of the Irish to prefer 'Combinations and Confederacies of Party' to a rational hierarchical rule serve to exoticize and marginalize Ireland.

This tendency is persistent in much eighteenth-century antiquarianism, especially that related to Scotland where fears of insurrection were more or less constant. Thus Thomas Snelling, in a book on early Scottish coins, writes about its medieval coinage: 'We find a great improvement in regard to the workmanship in the money here attributed to this king; the head, the cross, the letters are all better done, and the disposition of the whole more regular and uniform than before; and we shall venture a conjecture, that these improvements came from England.'[39] In his 1799 *History of the Union of England and Scotland*, Ebenezer Marshall noted '[t]he extreme poverty into which the Scottish kingdom had sunk, from the decay of trade', which in turn 'had caused a great scarcity of specie and had raised the foreign coin, that was current in it, above its real value. The English shilling was current among the Scots for thirteen pence, and the guinea, which, at the period of the Revolution, had passed for twenty-two shillings was now current for twenty-three shillings and eight pence Sterling. Ducatoons, dollars, and French crowns also contributed to form the currency in Scotland, and circulated at an encreased value.'[40] It was this 'deplorable condition of commerce among the Scots' that in Marshall's estimation prompted the Union.[41]

Many of the Irish travelogues that critics have identified as important influences on the national tale also examined Irish coinage. The paradigm instance is Arthur Young who embedded his own antiquarian expertise *into* texts whose ostensible purpose was to continue the work of cultivating political and national norms that the classicist opponents of antiquarianism had already begun. Edward Wakefield's *Account of Ireland, Statistical and Political* (1811) points to an uncomfortable combination of data and conjecture characteristic of tours of this period. In his 'Introductory Remarks', Wakefield explains that his purpose in undertaking the tour was to determine whether Ireland could sustain the kinds of land reforms that would make it an alternative source of agricultural staples.[42] Like Young, Wakefield felt that the agricultural productivity of the country could only be assessed through a full analysis of Irish culture and history. Ina Ferris has suggested that Wakefield's rather unnerved appreciation for the causes of the 1798 Rebellion were an important influence on the more discomforting aspects of the national tale.[43] The discussion of the Rebellion comes at the end of series of chapters on Irish history, including a long chapter on currency in which Wakefield compared the currencies of Ireland and England in different periods from the reign of Edward III to the middle of the eighteenth century. To make his comparisons legible, Wakefield produced a circular chart in which he positioned various units of account in circular orbits, hoping thereby to give some sense of how they might be compared temporally and qualitatively. At the centre of this constellation, Wakefield (or his printer) placed a large '1' in a distinctively bold type-face, resembling, in fact, the number on a printed banknote. This '1' is Wakefield's standard of value: the abstract unit of account against which all the other values represented in the diagram are presumably meant to be measured.

The quintessential example of the embedding of a metonymic antiquarian curiosity to an Enlightenment mandate is Roger Rudings' *Annals of the Coinage of Great Britain and its Dependencies*, first published in 1816.[44] The *Annals* is at heart a work of patient antiquarian description, yet it also carefully situates itself outside the closed world of antiquarian expertise (and thus of serialized diachronic knowledge) to interact with the intellectual field of political economy and monetary debate. In his original 1816 Preface, Rudings carefully distinguished his 'motives' from those of earlier antiquarians. Having listed and summarized many of the most important catalogues and surveys of British coins published since the sixteenth century, Rudings points out 'one radical error ... which runs through the whole of these ... although they are written upon an art the theory of which is unsettled, and the practical part of it confessedly defective, yet their tendency is to gratify curiosity only, without any attempt at the improvement of the theory, or the communication of practical knowledge'.[45] Rudings' motive was 'to show, from the experience of ages, the inadequacy of punishment, however severe, to prevent the commission of the crime of counterfeiting the money, whilst the temptation remains so powerful, and the execution of it so easy'.[46] In the closing sections of the introduction, Rudings suggests that the value of money will always depend on the forces of supply and demand and agrees with political economists that as useful a substitute as paper is, it will always require a fixed standard.

What made antiquarianism appear dangerous was not just its triviality or pedantry but its modernity, that is, the way it harnessed the media of print and paper to generate information that was self-consciously temporary and in flux. One does not have to look much further than the phrase 'ancient standard of the realm' as a popular by-word for the gold standard to see how important the cultivation of a classical sensibility was to the success to the economic programs of Horner, Brougham, and Ricardo. It was by being subordinated to the generalized aesthetic vision underlying Enlightenment's sense of the economy as a global whole that classical or 'patriotic' antiquarianism played a critical role in cultivating an idea of a *national* currency, not of Ireland or Scotland, but of Britain. This connection also has a specifically historical valence in the way the banking practices of Scotland and Ireland were being decried by the same commentators and in the same venues that were advocating for an aestheticized gold standard as the true sign of a fully heritable British cultural consciousness. The derogation of antiquarian paper was not really a matter of intellectual prestige, more a question of economic competition. In order for the idea of a British national character to function as the standard, British writers had to make it and its history the measure of those from Ireland and Scotland. This is also why in Ware, Wakefield, and others the 'primitive' Irish who in their murky past could not organize a proper currency are *in the present* so uncannily adaptive and resourceful. Their primitivism – or, in another sense, their national character – is the radical type of a dangerous modernity.

Like the antiquarians, Edgeworth in *The Absentee* cultivates a hybrid identity: modern and ancient, antiquarian and historical. Her national tale is thus a crucial genre of the crisis of confidence also apparent in the economic pamphlet literature, Christian economics, and much of the poetry of its time: refusing to accept the gold standard as the only possible solution to Britain's economic and social discomforts but not willing to accept that a standard cannot be found. In orchestrating a genre in which a variety of regional standards are displayed, Edgeworth's tale brings the difficulty of these conflicts directly to bear on the experience of reading. The novels of Austen and Scott turn that perplexity into the grounds for a new way of both generating and measuring cultural and political difference. They do so not by producing a new and robust form of confidence, but, in contrast, by making the novel the genre of embarrassment.

Empire and standardization: Austen's *Mansfield Park*

In *Bardic Nationalism*, Katie Trumpener contends that *Mansfield Park* might be thought of as Austen's English national tale. Its story was motivated by Austen's awareness of the economic and political controversies going on around her including the abolition of the slave trade, the campaign for which, Trumpener argues, is both politically and discursively related to the nationalist movements in Scotland and Ireland. Yet, for Trumpener, *Mansfield Park* illustrates a gradualist or accommodating stand characteristic of pan-British nationalism of the period, one that supported abolition but respected and to some extent endorsed the slower change that plantation owners and their customers alike demanded. This view was shared by, among others, Maria Edgeworth, whose story 'The Grateful Negro' Trumpener cites as a particular redolent example. But we also need to think about the colonial and nationalist subtexts of *Mansfield Park* in a slightly broader context, that of the standardization of the economy and the way literature and fiction in particular might contribute to or resist it.

As well as being Austen's most politically pessimistic novel, *Mansfield Park* is also her most explicitly allusive. As she was writing *Mansfield Park*, Austen seems to have been particularly aware of the proliferation of didactic works dealing with the subjects of financial stress and moral value as she was of gothic fiction and scandalous biographies.[47] Austen took a special interest in Hannah More.[48] A friend and associate of Henry Thornton, More was an advocate of evangelical economics; she believed that the advent of capitalism was profoundly beneficial to the progress of society. Its expansion required a standard that men and women living far apart could respect both as citizens of the same country and as participants in an emergent global economy. The model for this trust could not be, as it had been in the eighteenth century, the aristocratic landowner since commerce had grown beyond such local concerns, but rather God, who gave up his Son to assure the salvation of humankind and whose authority and benevolence are thereby inherent. More stressed financial acumen but also open charity: only the constant distribution of real wealth between strangers would maintain confidence. Women embodied the divine grace and moral self-consciousness at the domestic 'heart' of the British Empire.[49]

More outlined these principles in several popular works published between the 1790s and the 1810s including short fiction such as *Cheap Repository Tracts* and *Tom White*, and conduct manuals like *Strictures on the Modern System of Female Education* and *Christian Practical Piety*.[50] Among her most popular works was *Coelebs in Search of a Wife*, an idealized fiction celebrating the morality and charity of the intended wife Lucilla Stanley. In an early chapter Coelebs visits London and meets a host of young ladies of fortune who exemplify all that is damaging about fashionable life: selfishness, ignorance, and debt. Coelebs is taken by his London hosts, the generous and pious Sir John and Lady Belfield (whose name conjures the beauty of land) with another friend Lady Melbury (*Mal-bury* or 'bad town') to visit the house of a poor, sick family. The daughter of the family, named Fanny, makes flower arrangements, which Lady Melbury promises to buy. But when they arrive at the house, Lady Melbury reveals that she already owes the poor girl 700 pounds and offers to take more flowers on credit. Coelebs is outraged: 'I was particularly struck with the discrepancy of characters, all of which are yet included under the broad comprehensive appellation of *Christians* ... Not one who derided or even neglected its forms; and who in her own class would not have passed for religious. Yet how little of them adorned the profession she adopted! ... How superficial, or inconsistent, or mistaken, or hollow, or hypocritical, or self-deceiving, was that of all the others!' From these reflections, the novel produces its own standard of value: 'if we compare the copy with the model, the Christian with the Christianity, how little can we trace the resemblance! In what particular did their lives imitate the life of Him *who pleased not himself, who did the will of his father; who went about doing good?* How irreconcilable is their faith with the principles which He taught!'[51] What is important is not simply that felt Christianity is more genuine or honest than professed religion. What matters to More is that a person's consciousness of his or her sense of Christian truth is actually used to measure and thus correct that person's behavior. Virtue is a means to organize the relative worth of debts and speculations that both propel and endanger middle-class life.[52]

Many incidents in *Mansfield Park* point to More's influence.[53] When Henry Crawford blithely tells Fanny that her 'judgment' is his 'rule of right', she replies 'no! – do not say so. We have all a better guide in ourselves, if we would attend to it, than any other person can be.'[54] Edmund and Henry Crawford debate the problem of absenteeism, a concept that applied both to Anglican ministers who did not live in their parishes and to landlords who did not live on their estates, and which suggests that Austen knew the work of More's friend William Wilberforce whose *Practical View of the Prevailing System of Professed Christians* prompting parsons to participate actively and directly in the lives of their parishioners was reprinted in 1811.[55] Yet the standard of Christian principle is often questioned, even parodied in *Mansfield Park*. The opening chapter features lengthy conversations between Sir Thomas Bertram and his sister-in-law Mrs. Norris on the worldly and other-worldly benefits of the charitable plan of adopting Fanny Price, but the diction parrots the didactic speechifying of More's *Coelebs*. The episode at Sotherton chapel compares several manners of religious conviction. Austen could hardly be said to have embraced the cynical latitudinarianism of Mary Crawford: 'The obligation of attendance, the formality, the restraint, the length of time – altogether it is a formidable thing, and what nobody likes.'[56] Edmund concedes with Mary that church services are too long, but nevertheless contends that 'the influence of the place and of example may often rouse better feelings than are begun with'.[57] Yet Edmund's charitable compromise is undermined by Julia's irreligious suggestion that Maria and Mr. Rushworth should simply marry right there and then. The implication is that religious conviction has been replaced by other kinds of feeling – private, self-interested, even self-serving – though in a complex way those feelings themselves are inherent in the Anglicanism of Austen's day.[58]

Another scene in which Austen addresses the evangelical standard is the theatricals episode. It is usually read as a scene about representation and sincerity, the tension between Fanny's nature and Mansfield's culture. However, it is not really about the dangers of performing a play, but rather about the dangers of 'flow', both moral and economic. The aristocratic enthusiast Mr. Yates, whom Tom Bertram meets at the coastal resort town of Weymouth, is a confidence man full of fashionable 'schemes' and 'a love of the theatre so general, an itch for acting so strong ... that he could hardly out-talk the interest of his hearers. From the first casting of the parts to the epilogue, it was all bewitching, and there were few who did not wish to have been a party concerned or would have hesitated to try their skill.'[59] Fanny's declaration, 'Indeed, I cannot act' has as much to do with *action* as with *acting*. By refusing to *act* Fanny is refusing to *participate* in a venture that Austen links to the same fluid ineffability that she had formerly linked to Lydia and Wickham and which in this novel is associated with the slave trade. Fanny tries to maintain a position of moral authority *above* the activity that she witnesses and judges. By acting, Fanny would have to enter into an exchange network that she has been resisting all along but that Mrs. Norris, for one, would like her to join: 'I am quite ashamed of you, Fanny, to make such a difficulty of obliging your cousins in a trifle of this sort.'[60] To be obligated in this way would enmesh her in the expanding network of enthusiasms, improvements, and speculations. Even before she agrees to 'act' Fanny participates in the preparations for the rehearsals, mending the curtains and assisting the other players, including Edmund and Mary Crawford, with their lines. This is a further indication of Fanny's moral rather than familial authority. As in More, it is the persistence or confidence in individual moral sincerity that maintains credit in the midst a global, speculative economy. But once Sir Thomas returns and work on the play ceases, Fanny does not have to act: her moral authority has been usurped by that of the father whose absence – both actual and moral – marks the driving crisis of the novel. The conflict between Fanny and Sir Thomas over her marriage to Henry Crawford marks the tension between the traditional standards of power and democratic, evangelical standards of moral duty and self-affirmation.

This conflict plays into our sense of Austen's attitude toward slavery. Given her skepticism about More, Austen might well have felt some uneasiness about More's friend and fellow abolitionist, Thomas Clarkson, whose *History of the Abolition of the Slave Trade* Austen read sometime after its publication in 1808.[61] Austen's reading of Clarkson has been interpreted several times as an indication of her own anti-slavery sentiments.[62] Clarkson's book documented the decision of the abolitionists *not* to pursue the cause of emancipation outright for fear of alienating the commercial interest – to whom they were temperamentally allied anyway – or potentially supportive politicians who, following the loss of the American colonies, otherwise felt that the liberation of the West Indian slave populations would threaten British interests.[63] Like More, Edgeworth, and other writers of 'grateful negro' stories and poems, Clarkson believed that the end of the slave trade would make plantation owners take better care of their slaves and give the slaves themselves some cause to respect those owners and hope for future emancipation. Clarkson expanded the eighteenth-century standard of responsible landownership into the imperial sphere as a corrective to the purely commercial arguments being used by many West India merchants against the abolitionist position.

Austen's interest in the vicissitudes of imperial commerce is further suggested by her perusal of two other authors that she mentions in her letters along with Clarkson: Claudius Buchanan and Sir Charles Pasley. These works share a concern with social order in an era of changing commercial fortunes and imperial expansion.[64] In his *Essay on the Military Policy and Institutions of the British Empire*, Pasley urged that the best way for Britain to retain economic power was to maintain both an open trade policy (modeled on Smith's *Wealth of Nations*) and a permanent standing army akin to that of ancient Rome.[65] Buchanan, whose fame as the leader of the movement for the evangelical reform of both the East India Company and the subcontinent itself culminated in the publication of his *Christian Researches in Asia*, similarly presumed against the prevailing Orientalist view that the economic success of the Empire could be assured only through its complete Anglicization.[66] What is most remarkable about these texts is their confidence, both in the sheer bravado of their rhetoric and the global scope of their ambitions.

Remarking in a letter that she had initially 'protested against' Pasley's *Essay*, Austen nevertheless found it 'delightfully written and highly entertaining. I am as much in love with the author as ever I was with Clarkson or Buchanan.'[67] This is usually taken to confirm Austen's agreement with the content of these books: but, as with More, Austen was more invested in the way the books are written than in what they say or recommend.[68] Austen's investment in *writing* signals a different idea of where the standard of value comes from: not in the confidence that More, Clarkson, Buchanan, or Pasley offer but rather the circulation of paper. Austen simply does not know what to make of the imperial economy and its reliance on the limitless spread of the very medium, paper, that it also in its political economy seeks to control or abandon.[69]

The episode that bears most directly on these conversations about the imperial standard concerns the gold cross that Fanny's brother William Price gives to her when he visits Mansfield. The cross is a significant object: it represents not only the sacrifice of Christ and the symbolic value of gold was supposed to have, but also the global economy of trade, speculation, and imperial incursion. The cross tantalizes us with the prospect of a standard of value through which to judge the characters. Austen makes no mention *at all* of the possible value the cross might have as either a Christian symbol or as a piece of gold. It is, in this scene, exclusively a commodity, except insofar as it is a source of potential embarrassment for Fanny. Fanny's 'anxious considerations' increase when she visits Mary Crawford, who offers her a necklace.[70] Feeling 'obliged to yield' and 'longing to know which might be the least valuable', Fanny ultimately 'determined in her choice at least, by fancying there was one necklace more frequently placed before her eyes than the rest'. Mary stresses the unimportance of the obligation Fanny puts herself under in selecting 'what Miss Crawford least wished to keep', even teasing her with the possibility that it is a ruse to get her to oblige herself to Henry, who had bought the chosen necklace for Mary in the first place.[71]

The difficulties increase further when Edmund offers Fanny another chain and then on hearing that she has already been given one by the Crawfords, refuses to let her wear it. 'For one night, Fanny, for only one night, if it *be* a sacrifice; I am sure you will, upon consideration, make that sacrifice rather than give pain to one who has been so studious of your comfort. Miss Crawford's attentions to you have been – not more than you were justly entitled to – I am the last person to think that *could be*, but they have been invariable; and to be returning them with what must have something the air of ingratitude, though I know it could never have the *meaning*, is not in your nature.'[72] Fanny must see herself as part of the status economy that both Henry Crawford and Sir Thomas insist that she acknowledges and in which she is herself an object of exchange. In the end, Fanny wears all three gifts: 'She had, to oblige Edmund, resolved to wear it; but it was too large for the purpose. His, therefore, must be worn; and having, with delightful feelings, joined the chain and the cross – those memorials of the two most beloved of her heart, those dearest tokens so formed for each other by everything real and imaginary – and put them round her neck, and seen and felt how full of William and Edmund they were, she was able, without an effort, to resolve on wearing Miss Crawford's necklace too.'[73]

But this compromise, which puts Fanny in the midst of the status network of the two families, has already been compromised in turn by Fanny's investment in Edmund's letter:

> She had all the heroism of principle, and was determined to do her duty; but having also many of the feelings of youth and nature, let her not be much wondered at, if, after making all these good resolutions on the side of self-government, she seized the scrap of paper on which Edmund had begun writing to her, as a treasure beyond all her hopes, and reading with the tenderest emotion these words, 'My very dear Fanny, you must do me the favour to accept' locked it up with the chain, as the dearest part of the gift. It was the only thing approaching to a letter which she had ever received from him; she might never receive another; it was impossible that she ever should receive another so perfectly gratifying in the occasion and the style. Two lines more prized had never fallen from the pen of the most distinguished author – never more completely blessed the

> researches of the fondest biographer. The enthusiasm of a woman's love is even beyond the biographer's. To her, the handwriting itself, independent of anything it may convey, is a blessedness. Never were such characters cut by any other human being as Edmund's commonest handwriting gave! This specimen, written in haste as it was, had not a fault; and there was a felicity in the flow of the first four words, in the arrangement of 'My very dear Fanny', which she could have looked at for ever.[74]

In equating 'the scrap of paper' with a 'treasure', Austen brings out the aura of value that surrounds paper money, a form that has value by being endorsed and signed. Yet, Fanny's admiration for it as a material piece of writing also draws attention to its status as an object, or a curiosity, that exceeds the value system outlined in its content. Something about this letter points to the margins of the closed economy of debt and obligation and toward the residual values such a closed system seeks to deny. That Fanny takes the letter as 'the dearest part of the gift' also suggests the extent to which she elevates this 'text' above the nexus of obligations that it ostensibly signifies. There is a pertinent irony in the way Fanny treats the 'handwriting itself, independent of anything it may convey' not just as a gift but as a 'blessedness'. As at Sotherton, Fanny is seeking 'holiness' in icons and representations. She discovers in Edmund's handwriting 'felicity', and indeed, the performative act of giving that this letter constitutes is more felicitous than Edmund expects. The narrative depicts Fanny's embrace of the letter as a moment of profound feeling enmeshed in duties, associations, and convictions.[75]

Fanny's incorporation into the literary network of the Bertram household is illustrated further by her fondness for Sir Thomas' accounts of his West Indian adventures: 'I love to hear my uncle talk of the West Indies' she says to Edmund not long after Sir Thomas' return, 'I could listen to him for an hour together. It entertains me more than many other things have done – but then', she adds, 'I am unlike other people I dare say'.[76] This is a critical distinction. Fanny admits here that she is *not* mortified by the fact that their family comforts are products of slave labor. Others in the family clearly are reluctant to know about this – or more likely just indifferent, as Fanny herself senses: 'there was such a dead silence! And while my cousins were sitting by without speaking a word, or seeming at all interested in the subject, I did not like – I thought it would appear as if I wanted to set myself off at their expense, by shewing a curiosity and pleasure in his information which he must wish his own daughters to feel.'[77] What Fanny wants to subdue here is her excitement: she is, in a sense, embarrassed by her own reactions in the face of her cousins' apparent indifference, or their awkward self-consciousness about what, exactly, they do know about the plantation. Yet, Sir Thomas' tales also entertain. 'Sir Thomas Bertram's Adventures in Antigua' is an unwritten book of self-justification within *Mansfield Park*.

Treating Sir Thomas' account of himself as a kind of narrative equates it to the salacious (scandalous, Mary Crawford calls it) story, set of course in London, of Maria Rushworth's wild and hopeless affair with Henry Crawford which is itself the sequel to (or second part of) Tom Bertram's illness (incurred by gambling and loose living), and Mary Crawford's attempt to win back Edmund's good graces. Occupying four of the last five chapters of *Mansfield Park*, much of this story is relayed to Fanny by other people in the form of letters and one long interview between Fanny and Edmund. Indeed, in this semi-epistolary state, *Mansfield Park* seems to revert into the kind of novel that *Pride and Prejudice* also was, that is, an eighteenth-century novel in which scandals and tangles are rectified by the imposition of an implied system of management, the standard of honor. Austen intertwines accounts of Tom's illness and Maria's indiscretions with the diction of metropolitan scandal *and* of financial controversy: Tom's illness is 'alarming', 'distressing', 'grieved', 'evil', the suggestion being that narrative fantasy will ultimately prove a balm to social and economic ills.[78]

Fanny's father confirms the affair when he reads about it in a London tabloid. These stories of illness and scandal are a source of profound embarrassment, 'the influence of London [was] very much at war with all respectable attachments'; when Mr. Price reports the incident to her she exclaims, 'it cannot be true – it must mean some other people'.[79] But the realization that Maria's scandal *is* true produces in Fanny a new kind of response:

> She spoke with the instinctive wish of delaying shame, she spoke with a resolution which sprung from despair, for she spoke which what she did not, could not believe herself. It had been the shock of conviction as she read. The truth rushed on her; and how she could have spoken at all, how she could even have breathed – was afterwards matter of wonder to herself ... The horror of a mind like Fanny's, as it received the conviction of such guilt, and began to take in some part of the misery that must ensue, can hardly be described. At first it was a sort of stupefaction; but every moment was

> quickening her perception of the horrible evil. She could not doubt, she dared not indulge a hope of the paragraph being false.[80]

Austen's indirect style encompasses the journalistic language employed by Lady Bertram and Mary Crawford, heightening the confusion Fanny feels between her sense of shame and her understanding of truth. Fanny must 'delay' her shame and speak so that her moral conscience does not disrupt the social order. The affair is not her fault, and yet she feels keenly its disruptive effects. Mary also betrays a palpable sense of embarrassment, as Edmund later reports: 'She was astonished, exceedingly astonished – more than astonished. I saw her change countenance. She turned extremely red. I imagined I saw a mixture of many feelings – a great though short struggle – half a wish of yielding to truth half a sense of shame – but habit, habit carried it. She would have laughed if she could.'[81] Edmund experiences a shock similar to Fanny's even when, after the fact, he relates his encounter with Mary to Fanny: 'Edmund was so much affected, that Fanny, watching him with silent, but most tender concern, was almost sorry that the subject had been entered on at all' – though not altogether regretful that a truth has been exposed. Austen does not treat these reactions as one and the same: they register, in fact, very different kinds of standards. With her recourse to 'habit', Mary Crawford recalls the studied confidence of Burney and Hume. Edmund and Fanny are, by contrast, embarrassingly sincere: 'The heart must be open and everything told.'[82]

Speaking the embarrassing truth entails something other than a fixed standard. It allows the standards that fill the market of ideas to speak for themselves, through regions and colonies, without resolution and without assurance. As such it is a perfectly suitable standard for a culture that, as Britain had become in the nineteenth century, was utterly commercialized even as it largely retained its old aristocratic structures of vertical power and local attachment. For many historians, in fact, it is this archaism that allowed the British commercial system to be as successful as it was. But Austen's fiction also shows us that, in the wake of the crisis of value and the introduction of the gold standard – victories for a different kind of leveling, bourgeois confidence – Britain's archaic social structure had to represent itself in a new, more self-conscious manner, one that hid the embarrassing truth of its own indebtedness. But this is less an act of suppression than it is of hiding in plain sight. 'Let other pens dwell on guilt and misery', Austen's narrator declares in the last chapter, 'I quit such odious subjects as soon as I can, impatient to restore to everybody, not greatly in fault themselves, to tolerable comfort, and to have done with all the rest'.[83] And this is I think exactly to the point. In expressing her own embarrassment at the end of her novel – no one is at fault, there is no guilt, everyone just has to go on tolerably well – Austen is articulating a new kind of standard.

Scott, speculation, and the crisis of 1825

In 1815, Walter Scott reviewed Austen's *Emma* in the *Quarterly Review*. Along with Richard Whately's review of *Persuasion* and *Mansfield Park* which appeared a few months later, Scott's is widely credited with being the first review of Austen to recognize in her novels not only something new but something truly ordinary, in the sense of realistic as well as regulated. But Scott and Whately – who was a protégé of Edward Copleston and who would later become the Drummond Professor of Political Economy at Oxford – also understood that Austen's ordinariness was largely a product of her engagement with a wide range of discourses, including religion, the gothic, and political economy. At the end of *Emma*, Scott wryly observed, 'the facile affections of Harriet Smith are transferred, like a bank bill in need of indorsation, to her former suitor, the honest farmer'.[84] To thus situate affection, honesty, and bank bills in one sentence might seem disjunctive – and they are – but as all of Austen's later novels suggest, it is this not-quite consistent blending of moral, philosophical, and economic discourses, and especially those related to money and value, that signals her achievement as a novelist, and, to recall Siskin, the triumph of novelism.[85]

In his own historical romances, Scott also conceived of these seemingly opposing forces – emotion, finance, and truth – as operating in simultaneously unified and disjunctive manner. But while Austen's polite 'Englishness' belies the ideological tensions within her stories, Scott's awkward conjunctions of ideological positions and nationalist perspectives betray more starkly than in Austen the conflicts that the standard novel set out to resolve. In the tradition of the national tale, the Waverley novels used the historical mystique of a Scottish cultural tradition to manufacture a myth of spectacular heroism to ground both the threat and the banality of Britain's speculative commerce. Following Burke, Ferguson, and other 'conservative' thinkers, Scott put monarchy at the center of a pan-British *bildung* to guarantee national unity and economic purpose. The spectacle of the British monarchy was the standard – both literally and figuratively speaking – for its speculative finance and trade economy. I use the word 'speculative' here in two senses: (1) as a synonym for 'visual' in the sense that the hero or monarch who guarantees an investment tends to be visible or at least represented in highly iconographic terms; (2) to connote a sense of futurity or wishfulness, thereby acknowledging that the ventures being guaranteed by the hero or monarch are conjectural investments in a possible future. If these two uses of the term seem contradictory, they are, and most especially as they are used by Scott. Thus, to take a familiar example, in *Waverley* the idea of a reclaimed Stuart monarchy is embodied in the noble figure of Prince Charles, though his gambling and foolhardiness are also indications of the 'speculative' nature of the Jacobite campaign. Scott's monarchs are not absolutists. Bonnie Prince Charlie, Richard the Lionheart, and Charles II, among other of Scott's monarchs, are fallible and sympathetic, charismatic, but often highly imaginative and, indeed, speculative. They often find themselves in situations where their authority is in doubt and their identities insecure. But, in the context of Scott's historical romances, these qualities lend them the sheen of realism. Monarchy is seen in Scott to be something imaginary and, indeed, fictional but nevertheless symbolically vital to the unity of the nation. Scott's brilliant fictionalizations of the monarch as someone that understands the doubts and hesitations of his people, and falls into the same errors and doubts, make its ghostly presence the symbolic earmark of a lost but eminently valued historical tradition, one both ironic and redemptive.[86]

Scott did not believe that gold would ensure the stability of finance any more than he believed that commerce could thrive without a strong state. *The Antiquary*, which Scott was writing during the Corn Law debates and published just prior to the introduction of the gold standard, features two money plots. The first is resolved when the German 'illuminatus' Dousterswivel, who has convinced Sir Arthur Wardour that a treasure is buried beneath his chapel is exposed as a fraud by the novel's hero, Lovel, and the local itinerant, Edie Ochiltree. The second plot ends when Lovel reveals himself to be the lost son of the melancholy Earl of Glenallan. Both fortunes are restored by papers confirming the speculations of the novel's titular antiquary, Jonathan Oldbuck, whose own belief in ancient communal ideals are revealed to be flights of historical fancy.[87] Of course, *The Antiquary* is also about antiquarians; as such it engages in the problematic of antiquarian modernity, the way that the expert writing of antiquarians produces relations between objects, including coins, giving them value that in an economy of standardized equivalence they will not have. This excess is paradigmatic of the Waverley novels generally: they create a national history that produces real sentiments that return in the form of interpretations that the novels themselves cannot entirely accommodate.[88]

But in the later phase of Scott's career, the tension between nationalism and commerce that Scott had in 1816 managed to bridge fell apart. In 1825, Scott was confronted with the possibility that the 'speculative' national and political identity he had constructed for Scotland in his historical fictions and had linked in several of them with Scotland's vibrant paper money system – *The Antiquary, Rob Roy, The Fortunes of Nigel* – would be lost in an ocean of debts and obligations under which both he and the nation found themselves. In the wake of the 1825 crisis, Parliament charged the Scottish financial system, one of the most extensive in Europe, with insolvency and impracticability. The solution to the crash, which included the reformation of the Scottish system, was not simply the institutionalization of a fixed standard of value – that had actually existed in England for a decade already – but rather the centralization or, in the language of the time, consolidation of British finance under the auspices of a central but largely invisible authority: the Bank of England. What is important about these reforms is that this central authority had no symbolic or visual presence: with the introduction of branch and deposit banking and by offering many, small alternatives for investment, the Bank of England assumed a new authority by diversifying itself and its services into myriad new exchange forms. In this way, the Bank succeeded where the London Corresponding Society and the *Political Register* had failed in loosening the government's grip on economic decisions, only this was not in the service of social reform but rather of financial (and profitable) centralization.[89]

In several works published in the years during and following his own financial collapse, including his most direct and sustained contribution to the debates about money, authority, and standardization *The Letters of Malachi Malagrowther,* Scott would attempt to revive rhetorically a spectacular standard of value. Scott defended the Scottish banks on the essentially nationalist grounds that a 'diversity' of financial institutions will better serve the mixed British economy than either an abstract principle of 'uniformity' or 'innovation'.[90] His ground for such a claim was essentially nationalistic. 'For God's sake', Scott declared, 'let us remain as Nature made us, Englishmen, Irishmen, and Scotchmen, with something like the impress of our several countries upon each! We could not become better subjects ... if we all resembled each other like so many smooth shillings!'[91] Via such contentions, the attempt to bring the gold standard to Scotland is thus easily interpreted as an act of rank imperialism and its failure a triumph of the Scottish anti-colonial spirit; as Silvana Colella points out, 'the banks present a specifically Scottish alternative to the English search for uniformity ... Diversity rather than uniformity is, in fact, the distinguishing feature of the Scottish monetary system.'[92] Beyond national autonomy, though, Scott also committed himself to a *speculative* system based on local trust or 'confidence' as opposed to a consolidated system based on diversified, mathematical equivalence.

Because its relatively small population and rugged geography prevented the easy transport of metallic currencies, Scotland had little in the way of metallic reserves, relying instead on locally issued paper credit. This credit was kept afloat by private diligence and public accountability. To English charges that Scottish banks were financially suspect because they did not rely on reserves of precious metals, Scott answered that the security of the Scottish banking system is based on a form of public accountability, 'the watchful superintendence of the whole profession being extended to the strength and weakness of the general system at each particular point; or, in other words, to the management of each individual Company'.[93] The mechanism of this security is publication: 'every Bank throughout Scotland is obliged to submit its circulation, twice a-week in Edinburgh, to the inspection of the Argus-eyed tribunal'.[94] The Scottish banking system is a 'republic' and 'the public have, in this manner, the best possible guarantee against rash and ill-concocted speculations, from those who are not only best informed on the subject, but, being most interested in examining each new project of the kind, are least likely to be betrayed intro a rash confidence, and have the power of preventing a doubtful undertaking at the very outset'.[95] Scott modeled his idea of the 'republic' of Scottish finance on the Enlightenment republic of letters. The English 'seized with a jealous tenacious, wrangling, overbearing humour' intended to undermine Enlightenment principles, Scottish of course, which had brought Britain its economic power in the first place. 'We cease at once to be the Northern Athenians ... we have become the caterpillars of the island instead of its pillars'.[96] In letter three, Scott invents an English rival, Christopher Chrysal, who defends the English system on a decidedly irrational love for gold. This is why Scott can give Scottish banking the somewhat paradoxical epithet of 'practical system'.

The association of Scottish bankers and 'the Northern Athenians' points to the origins of nineteenth-century political economy in the Glasgow Enlightenment, and most especially with Adam Smith. But though it certainly owes a debt to Smith, by way of Burke and to a lesser extent Gibbon, the political economy that influenced Scott most directly is not that of Ricardo and McCulloch, but a conservative economics that looked to the country estate rather than the trading house for its guarantees against 'rashness'. As discussed in Chapter 2, agriculturalists like Sir John Sinclair argued that the benevolent state, modeled on the manor, should control the economy paternalistically. The guarantee of control was the managerial acumen and moral fiber of the benevolent landowner. Other conservatives were prepared to accept Ricardo's practical account of how the market economy worked, though they refuted his claim that capitalism was the only possible basis for the idea of economic or, more to the point, social value. Scott sympathized with these conservative views: the true standard of value lay in the symbolic order of the country estate. But his admiration for the practical 'republic' and 'tribunals' of Scottish finance also led Scott toward a more affective, even violent defense. Several times in the letters, Scott hints that the Scots might take up arms to defend their financial liberty, such as the moment when he alludes to the magically numbered '45' Scottish Members of Parliament or refers to the government as 'the enemy'. Initially, Scott claims that the 'body politic' in Scotland is healthy and thus is in no need of 'physic' as the English quack economists seem to think. By the third letter, that same body is being encouraged to lift the blazon for the 'auld cause'. Scott's respondents, including John Wilson Croker, writing in the character of 'Edward Bradwardine' disparagingly pointed out the allusions to cudgels and regiments and the lost 45. Respondents were also quick to point out that suspension of cash payments and the credit system it endorsed were instituted and maintained largely for the symbolic purpose of fighting a patriotic war. In *Familiar Epistles* Daniel Dreadnaught denounced Scott's argument on precisely these anti-Jacobite grounds. 'I abominate the system', he proclaimed, 'which has heaped countless injuries on my country, for the navigation of a river with which she had nothing to do; for the restoration of an old man, about whose concerns we ought to have been regardless, and for the possession of a barren rock!'[97]

In a letter to Croker written after the Malagrowther skirmish, Scott explained what this rhetoric was meant to accomplish. 'Scotland, completely liberalized', Scott wrote,

> will be the most dangerous neighbour to England that she has been since 1639. There is yet time to make a stand, for there is yet a great deal of good and genuine feeling in the country. But if you *unscotch* us you will find us damned mischievous Englishmen. The restless and yet laborious and constantly watchful character of the people, their

> desire for speculation in politics or any thing else, only restrained by some proud feelings about their own country, now become antiquated and which late measure will tend much to destroy, will make them, under a wrong direction, the most formidable revolutionists who ever took the field of innovation.[98]

Scott's used of the term 'antiquated' is critical here.[99] As Manning observes, late eighteenth-century antiquarians' 'investment in the immediate pleasures of the particular, without investigation or sublimation of that pleasure, made them vulnerable, in the cultural currency of the eighteenth century not only of incivility but of "enthusiasm", defined as [the] incapacity to link things with thoughts'.[100] In a similar way, the 'speculative' but 'watchful character' of the Scots – the very character that makes their paper credit work – would become an object of antiquarian 'investment' or Jacobite nostalgia once outlawed by English policy. Within Scott's argument on behalf of the confident 'republic' of Scottish banking, then, there lies a fiercer, almost overwrought attachment to the symbolic value of Scottish banks as *Scottish*, a commitment with the potential to undermine the confidence, trust, and social stability of the Scottish economy that Scott suggested was its national character.

The Letters of Malachi Malagrowther represent Scott's attempt to revive an economy of speculation, in the sense of both the unbacked credit system it defends and the spectacular or iconic confidence that it rhetorically conveys, in the face of its loss to the faceless powers of 'innovation' and centralized diversification. Many of the fictional and historical works that Scott wrote in the years following the publication of the *Letters* project that same hoped-for revival. *Woodstock*, for instance, which Scott began in autumn 1825 and published in May 1826, concerns Charles II's escape from the Battle of Woodstock just prior to his flight to France by way of the 'Royal Oak' in which it is said he hid. In Scott's novelization, the Oak is on the estate of Sir Henry Everard, whose family is divided between Royalist and Parliamentarian sympathies and much of the novel concerns Charles' various attempts to hide from Cromwell and his proselytizing minions and convince the Everard family of his virtue. He succeeds, and the closing tableau of the novel, set on the day of his Coronation in 1660, might be seen as a testament to Scott's belief in the power of enlightened monarchy – or at least his hope in its possible revival.

But by the time he began *Chronicles of the Canongate*, in mid-1826, much of this renewed confidence had receded to be replaced by a profound embarrassment. Not a novel per se but a compendium of linked stories, *Chronicles* moved away from the hopefulness of *Woodstock* and the other romances and toward a darker, more fragmented sense of the end of speculative confidence in the face of financial diversification. The frame narrative, which is about Chrystal Croftangry, the last in a line of Scottish landowners who, having squandered the family fortunes, returns to Edinburgh to set up as an antiques dealer, is in itself a quite fully realized statement of Scott's misgivings about the possibility of national or Romantic revival. There is a similar pattern of deliberate misreading in the three stories that make up the *Chronicles* all of which point to the failure of the speculative economy that Scott had tried to resurrect. The violent consequences of 'antiquing' Scott warned of in his letter to Croker is the basic theme of the first two stories. 'The Highland Widow' is the story of Elspeth, wife of the Highland outlaw Hamish McTavish, killed while garrisoned by the English after Culloden, and her son, also Hamish, who refuses to become an outlaw like his father and joins a Scottish regiment to fight in America. When Hamish visits his mother before he is due to depart, she drugs him. When his troop arrives to reclaim his after he has exceeded his furlough, Hamish shoots the sergeant, is taken prisoner, court-martialed, and shot. Elspeth pledges her loyalty to the Stuart cause and flees into the wilderness becoming the literal embodiment of 'antiquated' feelings. But she also represents the need to make a symbolic or speculative understanding of life, including money, meaningful at a time when such efforts are overshadowed by modern exchange practices. In a memorable scene, Hamish sends his mother a five-guinea coin, the proceeds from his enlistment in the Highland regiment; she 'remained gazing on the money as if the impress of the coin could have conveyed information how it was procured'.[101] Re-employing the metaphor of impression that, in the first Malagrowther letter, Scott had used to define both the national feeling behind the distinct cohesiveness of Scottish banking and its grounding in Scottish empirical philosophy, Scott has Elspeth deliberately fail to read the coin and misunderstand its now strictly economic function. For Scott, coins, like the monarchs whose faces are imprinted on them, have both symbolic value and financial value as guarantees of the vitality of the nation. But to Elspeth, whose whole world is appreciable *only* as a series of meaningful icons, the systemic 'meaning' of coins as instruments of fluid exchange makes no sense.

'The Two Drovers' is a complex tale about a Highland cattleman, Robin Oig, and his sometime English friend, also a cowman, Harry Wakefield. Having made their way to Cumberland, Oig and Wakefield unfortunately negotiate respectively with the squire and the bailiff for the same pasture. When the two arrive at the local alehouse, Wakefield is egged on by his fellow Englishman to challenge Oig, who initially refuses to fight, but then when provoked, stabs Wakefield with his dirk, which he had been keeping in trust for a lowland drover. Again, feelings and sensations become focused on an object which then becomes the means of a proto-revolutionary murder. The crisis at the heart of the 'Two Drovers' is the substitution of Oig's economy of trust and honor with an economy of omnipresent though invisible reason. The presiding judge at Oig's trial offers this general assessment of what *should have* happened:

> The first object of civilization is to place the general protection of the law, especially administered, in the room of the wild justice, which every man cut and carved for himself, according to the length of his sword and the strength of his arm. The law says to the subjects, with a voice only inferior to that of the Deity, 'Vengeance is mine'. The instant there is time for passion to cool, and reason to interpose, an injured party must become aware, that the law assumes the exclusive cognizance of the right and wrong betwixt the parties, and opposes her inviolable buckler to every attempt of the private party to right itself.[102]

Scott sensed that law can also become the 'buckler' of retribution. This is a clear case of what Foucault called a disciplinary process: a law-abiding 'subject' is created out of an external injunction to suppress certain feelings of desire or self-identification. Through education people are taught to respect civility. But if they transgress that civility the law 'antiquates' into its archaic violent form. The relationship between law and subject also changes from one based on mutual respect to one based on affective responses and overt domination. The danger of any symbolic system, no matter how rational or unifying it may be, is that it has the potential to become violent, especially for the sake of its coherence.

Similar complexities surround Richard Middlemas, the ambitious antihero of 'The Surgeon's Daughter'. The longest of the three tales, really a novella in its own right, 'The Surgeon's Daughter' tells the story of Menie Gray, daughter of the Selkirk doctor, Gideon Gray, and the rivals for her hand, the doctor's two students, Adam Hartley and Richard Middlemas, the latter the ward of Dr. Gray. Famous for its setting in colonial India (a setting in which not one but *two* colonial British armies operate, the regulars and the East India Company's, the latter to which both Middlemas and General Tresham/Witherington belong), most of the story focuses on the circumstances and consequences of Middlemas' birth. His parents, we eventually learn, are the eloping General, then only a captain, who is also both a Jacobite and a Catholic, and the daughter of a wealthy Portugese-Jewish merchant who pays Middlemas' adopted Highland guardian, Dr. Gray, for his upkeep without any regard or fondness. Middlemas' claim in early-adolescence that he is a 'free-born Englishman' is ironic not only because he is in conventional terms anything but, but also because his lineage acts to demonstrate just how fetishistic such national designations are becoming in an increasingly global economy.

Scott's financial metaphors focus on the interplay between the economics of exchange and the affective power of persuasion and love. The scene in which Middlemas confronts his parents is a parody of Shakespearean scenes of familial recognition that were a commonplace in many novels, including Scott's own. But in this case, instead of 'seeing' his parents as the fulfillment of his ambition to discover his 'true' identity, Middlemas abjects them: 'O, my more than father … how much greater a debt do I owe to you than to the unnatural parents, who brought me into this world by their sin, and deserted me through their cruelty!'[103] This leads to complete confusion: Zilia dies after bashing out a discordant lament on the harpsichord while the General forces his son to 'look upon [his] parents who [he] hast so much envied – whom thou hast so often cursed. Look at that pale emaciated form, a figure of wax, rather than flesh and blood – that is thy mother – that is, the unhappy Zilia de Moncada, to whom thy birth was the source of shame and misery, and to whom thy ill-omened presence hath now brought death itself.'[104] He then rages into a fury and threatens to kill his other children. The General's, Zilia's, and Middlemas' self-understandings are revealed in this moment not to be ratified by a hidden bond, but rather by their individual miscomprehension of their systematic existences. Once set into contention by the exposure of this system, the organization breaks down.

The tragedy is that the standard of value that might underlie the characters' attempts to vindicate themselves before the others or serve as a possible point of comparison between them has been replaced by a new standard of systemic inevitability, much as the symbolic standards trusted by Oig are replaced at the end of the story by the 'buckler' of the law. Not even Hartley and his wife Menie Grey can withstand the 'agitation' and 'shock' of the events of their story: Hartley dies of a colonial disease two years later and Menie refuses to marry probably in memory of Hartley but also in her continual irrational devotion to Richard. Once again affection undermines security. This is not to say that the novella does not *suppose* a standard, that is, of fetishistic glamor of wealth and adventure such as is presented to Richard Middlemas by his credulous Nurse and Tom Hilary. But at the same time, it also presents to us the way in which these fantasies circulate as, in a word, systems and by extension, empires. As Tara Ghoshal Wallace observes, it is 'such insistence on the reality of imperial fantasies that constructs the imperial identity'.[105] The trouble is, it is not the imperial fantasy that wins, but rather the ebb and flow of a diversified global capitalism.

Yet, I would also venture to suggest that 'The Surgeon's Daughter' provides a different kind of standard to *both* the 'fantasy' of glory that Scott associated with empire *and* the systemic intransigence of finance. In a strange scene, Hartley and Menie are on their way into the interior of India when they come upon the near-lifeless body of Sadhu Sing and hear the story of how his bride was taken from him on their wedding day by a tiger. Via Hartley, the narrator, makes the rather facile analogy between this story and 'the probable fate of [Menie] almost within the grasp of a more formidable tiger than that whose skeleton lay beside Sadhu Sing', the Indian Prince for whom Middlemas fought and whose wedding is disrupted by a tiger attack.[106] Scott was aware that a comparison between these two marriages is *possible*: at the creek in the jungle, 'the travellers stopped to drink, and to refresh themselves and their horses; and it was near this spot that Hartley saw a sight which forced him to compare the subject which engrossed his own thoughts, with the distress that had afflicted another'. The narrative projects a frame of reference that will be able to bring the two 'systems' of the story – the British and the Indian – into a hybrid construction. They are not the same, as the narrative makes clear, for Menie's fate is *not* that of Sing's bride, any more than Scottish farms cultivated by free credit (as Scott describes in the *Letters of Malachi Malagrowther*) are the same as the 'impenetrable thicket' that the plain has become once war has 'suspended the labours of industry'.[107] The end of the tale offers not a speculative vision of imperial or financial unity that might regulate or oppose the flow of finance, but rather an opportunity to view both the failure of speculation and the consolidation of capital flow as parts of a constellated object of a critical and comparative judgment, to see them, that is, *as* the 'thicket' that they really are once the 'labors' and 'industry' of narrative are over.

In this way, *Chronicles of the Canongate* provides a standard of comparison through which various cultures can be measured against each other – Britain and India, Scotland and England, the Highlands and India – which is apparent, in a way that the consolidated standard of financial diversification is *not*, in the tensions and contradictions of literary form. This is not the same thing as saying that Scott invents an imperial ideology, for there is no specific imperial agenda associated with the standard of comparison as such. The novel neither represents a standard (on the contrary all its speculative, monarchical figures are either absent, corrupt, or destroyed) nor embodies a particular economic system (as the *Letters* had done). Rather, the consolidated text is an effect of the continual comparisons between different economic and cultural systems, manifest in the antiquarian tendencies of Croftangry and in the process of reading that he and other collectors in the frame narrative exemplify. By contrast to his polemical writings, Scott's fiction allows us to recognize the conflicts and unevenness of the economic field by staging their de-consolidation. It is by virtue of such embarrassments that the Romantic novel comprehended capitalism's entrepreneurial spirit.

Conclusion: A Romantic Economy

In this book, I have been documenting the contributions of Romantic authors to debates about money and standardization. For the most part, the purveyors of the literary arts were undecided about whether the standard should be something static and universal or something malleable and governable. How then is it possible that this thing we call Romanticism could also *be* the standard? The answer is that it was no more the standard than gold was. Rather, much of the literature of this period was committed to the idea that a standard was possible and necessary in an era of relativity and choice, though it expressed that commitment more by describing what the standard was *not* rather than explaining what it was. But once the perplexities of the economic debates of the Romantic period had overwhelmed the general sense of confidence advocated in Enlightenment economics, the debate could be at least quelled or tamed by the notion that consumers could choose to believe in something that would help them to measure or model other forms of value. Like Christianity or, as Coleridge contended, *as* Christianity, literary knowledge did not have to be in play in order to be the standard. It merely had to stand as a reminder or point of agreement that could quell controversies and disputes. It was a way, to paraphrase Ricardo, to avoid the embarrassment of not having a standard.

The next step would be to track how nineteenth-century literature continued to intersect with gold standard economics as, over the course of 50 or so years, it became a fundamental principle in British policy and discourse and, in 1874, the international measure of global trade. To a certain extent, this work has already begun. Victorianists Gordon Bigelow, Reginia Gagnier, Amanda Anderson, Lauren Goodlad, and Deanna Kreisel, to name a few, have argued convincingly that the British state was not the all-encompassing, panoptical overlord that an earlier generation of new-historicists insisted it was, but rather that it was decidedly 'liberal', that is, far more open to individual choice and difference than in early generations and utterly conscious of the exploitation and inequality that this liberalism, unfortunately, also enabled. To conclude, I want to make a case for interpreting Victorian liberalism as, at least formatively, a continuation of the standardizing project that I associate with Romanticism. The central figure here is John Stuart Mill, who, while no Romantic, might well be thought of as one of the first Romanticists. Thanks to the *Autobiography*, everyone knows that Mill was raised by his father on a rich diet of Benthamite utilitarianism with huge portions of Ricardo's economics and converted at age 19 to Romantic bliss after imbibing the more selective pleasures of Wordsworth and Coleridge. Mill did not abandon the objectivist streak that he had learned from his father and his mentors, and as one of the most influential economists of the century he helped to make the gold standard, which he thoroughly endorsed, a linchpin of economic discourse and policy. Also like Ricardo, Mill acknowledged that gold itself had no magical standardizing properties. But over the course of his career Mill tried to reconcile the seemingly irreconcilable opposition between Romanticism and Ricardianism by making literature a standard for the individualized, industrial economy that was also held together by gold. For Mill, literature and gold were not allegorically related, but, in keeping with his Coleridgean predilections, manifestations of the same symbolic system.

My initial point of reference for examining this trend in Mill's thought will be neither his political economy nor his Romantic aesthetics. I begin instead with his comments on a literary form that he made clear could *not* stand as the standard, though this is the very form that most palpably combined the two discourses that Mill sought to reconcile. In the autumn of 1833, Mill reviewed *A Tale of the Tyne*, the twenty-first installment of Harriet Martineau's 25-volume collection, *Illustrations of Political Economy*. Conceived in the aftermath of her father's bankruptcy in 1826 and inspired in part by James Mill's 1827 *Elements of Political Economy* (the textbook for which John Stuart's adolescent notes on Ricardo had provided the basis), Martineau's collection was a handbook of economic principles – the division of labor, the theories of value and population, the elements of money and banking, and so on – with each principle fictionalized into a didactic tale.[1] Though long held as one of several 'popularizations' of Ricardian economics to appear in the 1820s and 30s, the *Illustrations* has recently been credited by literary scholars as bearing a critique of economic reductionism by way of a championing of narrative sympathy.[2] The reading of Martineau as a literary critic of economics has been rendered more urgent by the uncovering of the many reviews of *Illustrations* by prominent literary men such as Josiah Conder, George Poulet-Scrope, and Edward Bulwer-Lytton, who sought to exclude the *Illustrations* from the ranks of both political economy *and* literary fiction.[3] Like his fellow reviewers Mill was uneasy with the way Martineau combined science and literature. 'All the truths of her science', he wrote, 'do not equally admit of being illustrated by a succession of interesting incidents, and she has sometimes, instead of working the principle into the body of her tale, found herself thrown upon the last resource of foisting it in under cover of scientific conversations between her principle characters.' But, in contrast to those critics who found this mixture ideologically problematic, Mill sympathized with what he believed were Martineau's political intentions. Martineau's subject, the practice of impressing young men into the military against their will, 'was eminently susceptible of striking illustration and powerful enforcement through the medium of a fictitious history'.[4] Martineau's hero 'is but a type of the countless multitudes of real living men, who have been immolated, body and soul, like him, and died the living death which he so powerfully describes'. *Tale of the Tyne* allowed Mill to reflect on the irony that while press gangs were routinely denounced in Parliament, slavery and exploitation were not: 'Miss Martineau', he suggested, 'should send a copy of this tale to each of his Majesty's Ministers'.[5]

In his review of the final installment of the *Illustrations*, published the following year in *The Monthly Repository*, Mill distinguished the didactic and political intent that he had praised Martineau for from the 'science' of political economy. The final volume was a 'compendium' of the principles each tale had illustrated, something Mill generally approved, with one important caveat. A 'science', he wrote, 'is a connected *body* of truth; the *entire* philosophy of some distinctly definable portion of the field of nature: and when it is taught as Science, that is, with a view to the perfection of speculative knowledge rather than to the readiness of practical application, the teacher aims at making such a selection of its truths, and at presenting them in such an order, as will best exhibit the connectedness of the whole'.[6] But this 'was not the task which Miss Martineau set before herself ... Her object was, not to exhibit the science as a whole, but to illustrate such parts of it as lead directly to important practical results.'[7] For Mill, Martineau was first and foremost a didactic writer. Her aim was to explicate the social and moral problems that attend economic policies and to agitate for political reform. It was not to resolve or even explicate the actual laws on which those policies were based. In a letter to Carlyle, Mill praised Martineau for her opposition to the faith most people put in a division of labor in which working-class men and women are forced into servitude. Mill looked forward to the time when that system should 'expire', a point he would make again in his *Principles of Political Economy* and *On Liberty*.[8] Yet, this didacticism disqualified Martineau from being a literary writer. In Mill's view, Martineau saw the moral problems attending the economy and she sought and then offered reasonable solutions to those problems. She illustrated, for the sake of reader, what the economy looks like under the practical difficulties in which it is involved and compares these, by way of narrative development, to what an economy should look like with right and trust standards so applied. What Mill sought in both literature and political economy was not confidence, but embarrassment, the perplexities that arise in the economic state, the opportunity for critical dissent and reflection, and the struggle for truth rather than the application of principle.

During the same period in which he wrote these reviews, Mill wrote two of his best-known essays: 'Thoughts on Poetry and its Varieties' and 'On the Definition of Political Economy; and on the Method of Investigation Proper to it'.[9] It would be easy to use these essays to establish the disciplinary divide between 'poetry' and 'political economy' as an element of Mill's thought – a divide that corresponds to the one Mill lays out in 'Coleridge' and 'Bentham' six years later. But there is an important similarity in these essays, namely the distinction they both make between 'nature' and 'art', the former of which is expressible by science *and* poetry and the latter of which is the domain of 'illustrations'. Mill begins 'On the Definition of Political Economy' by defining an old idea of political economy as a 'collection' of empirically observed phenomena. 'Like the wall of a city', Mill notes in a famous metaphor, the older method 'has usually been erected, not to be a receptacle for such edifices as might afterwards spring up, but to circumscribe an aggregation already in existence'. Under this Lockean methodology, there were no preexisting categories through which associated empirical observations could be organized. 'Without any intentional classification, the facts classed themselves. They became associated in the mind, according to their general and obvious resemblances; and the aggregates thus formed, having to be frequently spoken of as aggregates, came to be denoted by a common name. Any body of truths which had thus acquired a collective denomination was called a *science*.'[10] The 'walls' we construct through theoretical knowledge do not shape our observations; they merely define a set of associations. This procedure 'confounds the essentially distinct, though closely connected, ideas of *science* and *art* ... The one deals in facts, the other in precepts. Science is a collection of *truths*; art a body of *rules*, or directions for conduct. The language of science is, This is, or, This is not; This does, or does not, happen. The language of art is, Do this; Avoid that. Science takes cognizance of a *phenomenon*, and endeavours to discover its *law*; art proposes to itself an *end*, and looks out for sneaks to effect it.'[11] Laws define how economic behaviors work regardless of practical benefits. Ends, by contrast, imply that a method of distributing knowledge has a practical purpose.

For this confusion Mill blames the genre he calls illustration: 'The definition most generally received among instructed persons, and laid down in the commencement of most of the professed treatises on the subject, is to the following effect: – That Political Economy informs us of the laws which regulate the production, distribution, and consumption of wealth. To this definition is frequently appended a familiar illustration.'[12] Although Mill does not attribute the illustrative method directly to Martineau, he does associate it with household management:

> Political Economy, it is said, is to the state, what domestic economy is to the family ... Undoubtedly the beneficial result, the great practical *application* of Political Economy, would be to accomplish for a nation something like what the most perfect domestic economy accomplishes for a single household. But supposing this purpose realised, there would be the same difference between the rules by which it might be effected, and Political Economy, which there is between the art of gunnery and the theory of projectiles, or between the rules of mathematical land-surveying and the science of trigonometry.[13]

It is interesting that Mill would equate in his metaphors running a household, firing a gun, and surveying land: all of these 'practical' matters can be accomplished by anyone working in the 'field' as it were, be they housekeepers, soldiers, or surveyors, under the auspices of a 'state', be it a family, a government, or a business. Mill's point was not that illustrations or applications are unmanly activities. His point is that science should be distinct from practice. Political economy, 'the theory of projectiles', and 'the science of trigonometry' imply a degree of mathematical understanding with no application but the further development of theory.

In the rest of 'Definition', Mill defended the distinctive use of scientific processes of observation and abstraction. Political economy should channel inductive observations of human behaviors not into policies or application but rather into new principles of human consciousness, what he called 'the laws of the human mind'.[14] With this realization, Mill admitted that economic theory is deductive. Theoretical abstractions of the kind promoted by economists are 'only true under certain suppositions, in which none but general causes – causes common to the *whole class* of cases under consideration – are taken into account'.[15] At the same time, these deductions are useful because they help to establish what Mill called 'tendencies' of human nature around which inductive claims can be assessed. The difference between science and art has to do with the effect of exceptions on general claims. In art, 'the exception does not run by insensible degrees into the rule, like what are called exceptions in science. In a question of practice it frequently happens that a certain thing is either fit to be done, or fit to be altogether abstained from, there being no medium. If, in the majority of cases, it is fit to be done, that is made the rule.' Accordingly, if a certain event or practice does not fit the rule, 'the rule is now done with, and dismissed; a new train of ideas is introduced, between which and those involved in the rule there is a broad line of demarcation; as broad and *trenchant* as the difference between Ay and No'.[16] For Mill, a total change in the system cannot be tolerated in science because it would threaten the edifice of human nature that science must explain. The science of political economy as Mill formulates it tries to uncover the root causes of economic behaviors, causes that theory may not have recognized before. It works on the premise that exceptions established in theory can change that theory radically with each new discovery, but the basic tendencies of human nature will not be entirely abandoned.

A work like Martineau's *Illustrations* thus has no place in Mill's scientific establishment. Science demands that its general claims be tested and improved. But the exceptions that might accrue from these tests cannot be said to undermine the whole system of laws and principles on which the science rests. This is what distinguishes the scientific method from that of the illustration in which, Mill argues, either the rule is merely applied to a practice or the exception undermines the entire system of rules. For Mill, the development of scientific truths can never cease, which is why the application of these truths by means of illustrations for moral ends is on one hand politically powerful and on the other theoretically irrelevant. Science as Mill conceives it is a speculative, imaginative endeavor. It requires not simply a means to generalize about the present but also a sense of futurity that hinges on our incapacity to fully generalize.[17]

The gold standard was an important example of Mill's 'speculative knowledge'. In 1833, Mill wrote two reviews in which he considered the bullion controversy and related monetary matters directly. One of these, 'The Currency Juggle', was a review of evidence presented by Thomas Attwood during yet another committee meeting, this time to renew the Charter of the Bank of England.[18] Attwood was an industrialist, but he was also the founder of the Birmingham Union, a proto-chartist movement that had been campaigning for workers' rights since the 1810s. His brother Matthias was an important banker in his own right, and a future Director of the Bank of England. Both advocated a state-controlled paper money economy. The creation of money by a centralized, national bank would inspire industry by ensuring that there would always be enough capital available to meet the demands of industry and wages. As Mill remarked, views like this had already been widely disparaged, by William Cobbett and others, as an easy way for 'fraudulent debtors' to get past the law, since under such forced depreciation schemes their shillings owed would only be worth sixpence. As well, the bullion controversy, and especially, the 'writings of Mr. Henry Thornton, Lord King, Mr. Ricardo, Mr. Huskisson, Mr. Blake, etc. and the Report of the Bullion Committee' had already disseminated the principle of the gold standard.[19] But, Mill also observed that Attwood's whole argument is based precisely on the quantity theory – that money will fall in value as its quantity increases – that had been espoused by Hume and Smith and cited by the above scholars against the financial experts in 1810.[20] Why is it impossible for the Bank to adjust the value of the currency rather than rely on a commodity like gold?

The answer, for Mill, was that the standard had little to do with paper and gold at all. Any argument that relies on the presumption of quick solutions, such as the 'rash speculations' of men of 'practical experience' like Attwood, is doomed to misunderstand the larger truths at stake in it. In Attwood's reckoning, the crash of 1825 – the same one that ruined Scott and Martineau – would have been avoided if the government had issued enough currency to create full employment. Mill countered that there was just enough employment in 1825 to meet to demands of capital growth; as the 1833 committee explained to Attwood, the same effects as an increase in money would have been met by lowering prices which, had economic conditions been more favorable (and less speculative), would have eventually readjusted the employment balance. To attempt to regulate the economy by adjusting the amount of currency in circulation is a mere pipe dream: 'At the bottom of the fundholder's pocket, Mr. Attwood expects to find the philosopher's stone. As great a man as Mr. Attwood, the King of Brobdingnag, declared it to be his creed, that the man who calls into existence two blades of grass where only one grew before, deserves better of his country than the whole tribe of statesmen and warriors.'[21]

Mill concluded his review by observing that 'it is only for want of discussion that these schemes find any favourers among sincere men'. This idea of discussion is an important one for Mill, and I think it is crucial that it comes up here in an essay on money and the standard. In *On Liberty*, as David Kaufmann has shown in a brilliant chapter on Mill and Austen, 'discussion' is 'the only means of supplementing knowledge and opinion. It serves as the crucible of wisdom.'[22] But already in the early 1830s, Mill made a similar case in 'Thoughts on Poetry and its Varieties'. Central to Mill's liberal aesthetic is the notion that poetry, one of the 'higher arts', conveys what are fundamental human truths that provide, a 'unity of feeling ... the harmonizing principle which a central idea is to minds of another class, and supplying the coherency and consistency which would else have been wanting'.[23] Just as he precluded Martineau from political economy, and money from distribution on the grounds that they play no part in determining human tendencies, so fiction cannot really count as 'truth' in the way poetry can:

> The truth of poetry is to paint the human soul truly: the truth of fiction is to give a true picture of life. The two kinds of knowledge are different, and come by different ways, come mostly to different persons. Great poets are often proverbially ignorant of life. What they know has come by observation of themselves; they have found within them one highly delicate and sensitive specimen of human nature, on which the laws of emotion are written in large characters, such as can be read off without much study. Other knowledge of mankind, such as comes to men of the world by outward experience, is not indispensable to them as poets: but to the novelist such knowledge is all in all; he has to describe outward things, not the inward man; actions and events, not feelings; and it will not do for him to be numbered among those who, as Madame Roland said of Brissot, know man but not men.[24]

Fiction is an illustration of outward life. It is 'other knowledge ... not indispensable'. It can, as it does in Austen and Scott, reflect frustrations with 'outward things' but it cannot exemplify the general character of inner life by its own self-exemplification.

Mill's Romanticism was neither abstract nor specialized. He reviewed De Quincey's *Logic of Political Economy* just as he was starting work on his own *Principles of Political Economy*, published in 1848, noting that the *Logic* would be especially interesting to 'that limited class' who 'feel an intellectual necessity for the co-ordination of ... detached opinions ... and to the deeper principles which ought to be at the foundation of all'.[25] Mill treated the *Logic* as a commentary on Ricardo, one which rather than merely supplying illustrations of individual principles clarifies the more fundamental 'roots of its truths'. Mill praised De Quincey for drawing significant distinctions between particular terms and concepts 'to see very exactly in which respect some received mode of expressing a scientific principle misses the mark'.[26] But Mill was particularly delighted by the liveliness with which De Quincey illustrated Ricardo's theory of value, dialogues between imagined buyers and sellers, the account of people buying music boxes on steamboats in Lake Superior, the comparison between race horses and hunters, the story of Charles II's rhinoceros: 'what pleasant reading' De Quincey 'can make of a dry scientific discussion'. These are not illustrations meant to teach readers how to apply economic principles but examples through which they can discuss those principles' theoretical import. It is in that respect that Mill finds the *Logic* 'useful'.[27] Readers who *are* interested in thinking through the theory of value on a 'scientific' basis can employ a literary turn of mind to appreciate its 'subtleties'.

That Mill also appreciated De Quincey's ability to clarify the distinctions between vicarious and technical knowledge is a telling indication of the fundamental duality in Mill's intellectual ambitions. Distinction with and alongside pleasure: this is the aesthetic at stake in Mill's reflections on value. For what Mill found in De Quincey was not the literature of power as such but rather the literature of knowledge *about* power. Mill had already produced his own version of the distinction between the literatures of power and knowledge in 'Thoughts on Poetry and its Varieties' when he distinguished the 'poetry of culture', represented by Wordsworth, from the 'poetic temperament', represented by Shelley. Mill associated Wordsworth's poetics with 'choice' and 'distribution' and Shelley's with 'production': for Mill to use economic terminology to think about the varieties of poetics speaks volumes about the intersection of these two discourses in his thought.

The same duality inspired the essays on 'Bentham' and 'Coleridge'. Mill asserted in the latter essay that 'it is impossible to speak of Coleridge ... without reverting to Bentham'. The two thinkers probably held each other in contempt, but they are tied, Mill suggests, by the fact that they both insisted on 'the necessity of a philosophy' to govern the progress of social affairs. Like German idealism, Coleridge's philosophy was based on a relentless critique of Enlightenment rationalism and the privileging of mechanical necessity. But this did not make Coleridge a subjectivist. On the contrary, his thought (like Kant's) was marked by complex and obscure metaphysical tendencies precisely because it was reacting against the simplicity that pervades, in the idealist perspective, mechanistic thinking. In the midst of that reaction, Coleridge was at the same time devoted to an understanding of truth, in all its complexity, refusing religious and moral injunctions as superficial dogma. Like Bentham, whom Mill also noted was opposed to jingoistic reductions, Coleridge appreciated that human behavior was difficulty and that such difficulties had to be embraced as part of the idea of the human. Mill insisted that both poetry and political economy would attract the 'limited' intellectual 'class', to those, that is, tasked with the responsibility of understanding and disseminating the principles and the ambiguities of modern life – to those, that is, who comprehend the standard.[28]

Mill did not conceive of the standard as the knowledge that civilized people already have or that is consistent for all time. Rather a standard is the knowledge people come to appreciate through continuous discussion and reform. The site of that continuous reformation is literature – but not, importantly, just any literature, only that which is itself attuned to the 'long view' of constant revaluation that is at stake in the process of standardization itself, in short, Romanticism. Mill's Romantic economics is certainly ideological in a precise sense: its encompassing of the variability and potentiality of human passion is constrained within certain generic limits and presumptions of national identity and social feeling. The ideology it presents is a liberal one. Mill did not simply want to make people aware of the moral side of economic life. Rather he sought to cultivate a sense of the standard that would entrench values of individual self-reflection and aesthetic appreciation and thus provide a supplement to the indivisible but largely indiscernible value of gold. In this respect, then, Mill rescued poetry from its period of political decline after Shelley precisely by de-politicizing it, by making it the metaphorical equivalent of a natural property (the value of gold) and the center of a humane discipline (literature).

Fiction, by contrast, he left to the realm of illustration: pictures of human life that can, unfortunately, tend in the direction of rash speculation, imaginative flights of fancy of the kind satirized by Swift and Pope in the early eighteenth century and which still filled the pages of poems and pamphlets in Mill's time, as it does the blogosphere today.

But what this proves above all is that Mill was also wrong. In 'Thoughts on Poetry', Mill refused to grant fiction the status of literature. But at that same time, as Mill reviewed Martineau, the novel had already begun to achieve a standard value rivaling that of poetry. Witness the success of Scott's magnum opus and of *Bentley's Standard Novels* that, among other things, republished all of Austen's works for the first time since the 1810s, and they have never been out of print since.[29] What is more, the novel achieved its standard form not, as in Mill's conception of poetry, by revealing the mysterious properties of life that politics and science forget, but rather by engaging directly in the political, economic, and moral questions of its day. Mill's own writing is, by the same token, a kind of illustration, a picture of the world at his time and invoking its ideas and standards that is just as liable to fall into perplexity and confusion as any other – and that is exactly what Mill insists should happen in order for the standard to remain free. The standard must be fluid and dynamic, a myth of origin that also encompasses avenues of change.

Notes

1 Realms of Gold

1. John Maynard Keynes, 'Social Consequences of Changes in the Value of Money', *Essays in Persuasion*. 1923. *Collected Writings of John Maynard Keynes* Vol. 9 (Cambridge: Cambridge University Press, 1978), 62.
2. The 'social meaning of money' has received a good deal of analysis from historians and sociologists. See especially Geoffrey Ingham, 'On the Underdevelopment of the "Sociology of Money"', *Acta Sociologica* 41 (1998): 3–18; and Deborah Valenze, *The Social Life of Money in the English Past* (Cambridge: Cambridge University Press, 2006).
3. On the history of the gold standard and the rise of the British national currency see especially Eric Helleiner, *The Making of National Money: Territorial Currencies in Historical Perspective* (Ithaca: Cornell University Press, 2003), 19–121; Emily Gilbert and Eric Helleiner, eds., *Nation-States and Money: The Past, Present, and Future of National Currencies* (London: Routledge, 1999); and John F. Chown, *A History of Money from AD 800* (London: Routledge, 1994), 67–73, 232–45. For the literary importance of the Victorian 'culture of honesty' see John Kucich, *Repression in Victorian Fiction: Charlotte Brontë, George Eliot, and Charles Dickens* (Berkeley: University of California Press, 1987).
4. Larry Neal, 'The Financial Crisis of 1825 and the Restructuring of the British Financial System', *Federal Reserve Bank of St. Louis Review* 80 (May/June 1998): 53–76; and some corrections in Michael D. Bordo, 'Commentary', *Federal Reserve Bank of St. Louis Review* 81 (1998): 77–82.
5. On the response to the gold standard and its limitations see Karl Polanyi, *The Great Transformation* (Boston: Beacon, 1944) and Barry Eichengreen, *Globalizing Capital: A History of the International Monetary System* (Princeton: Princeton University Press, 1996). Gordon Bigelow contends that the gold standard may have been partly responsible for the Irish potato famine. See *Fiction, Famine, and the Rise of Economics in Victorian Britain and Ireland* (Cambridge: Cambridge University Press, 2003), 80–5.
6. Matthew Rowlinson, *Real Money and Romanticism* (Cambridge: Cambridge University Press, 2010), 33–56. Rowlinson's attention to regional differences in the use of money in this chapter is, I think, the most important part of what is the only book yet published to focus exclusively on the connection between money and Romanticism. Rowlinson's account of the overt 'allegorical' reading of the way Scott, Keats, and Dickens theorized the persistent complexity of money, its 'curiosity' as an object, and its resistance to forms of generalization is compatible with my own – though Rowlinson discusses neither the bullion controversy nor the introduction of the gold standard in any detail.
7. On the 'traumatic' prevalence of forgery in nineteenth-century fiction, see Sarah Malton, *Forgery in Nineteenth-Century Literature and Culture: Fictions of Finance from Dickens to Wilde* (Basingstoke: Palgrave Macmillan, 2009).

8. To see how diverse monetary opinion in the Victorian era was, consult Mary Poovey, ed., *The Financial System in Nineteenth-Century Britain* (Oxford: Oxford University Press, 2003).
9. Keynes' theory of money is based on the idea that states use it primarily to manage and distribute their taxation revenues, such as through military expansion. The use of money for private exchange practices is a residual effect of government policy. This view has found some favor with economic historians who argue for the pervasive influence of the state on the financial and commercial revolutions in eighteenth-century Britain.
10. Keynes, 'Social Consequences', 65, 63.
11. I borrow the term 'regulative ideal' from Amanda Anderson who uses it to describe the concept of 'objectivity' as outlined by Lorraine Daston and Peter Gallison: 'the notion of a regulative ideal usefully displaces stark assertions that objectivity is a deluded and false enterprise, insofar as it allows for the self-reflective aspiration to an ideal that is known to be ultimately unattainable'. 'Epistemological Liberalism', *Victorian Studies* 50 (2008): 658–65.
12. The most important book to make this claim, in its aesthetic context, is Barbara Hernstein Smith, *Contingencies of Value: Alternative Perspectives for Critical Theory* (Cambridge, MA: Harvard University Press, 1988). In moral philosophy, the best-known argument for moral relativism is John L. Mackie, *Ethics: Inventing Right and Wrong* (Harmondsworth: Penguin, 1977), who calls himself an 'empiricist' but whose work is close to the positivist tradition of Ayer and Stevenson. For an insightful critique of Mackie see Julia Annas, 'Moral Knowledge as Practical Knowledge', *Social Philosophy and Policy* 18 (2001): 236–56.
13. Charles Taylor, *Modern Social Imaginaries* (Durham: Duke University Press, 2004), 12. Taylor puts the origin of the modern social imaginary in the economic changes of the late seventeenth century, the so-called financial revolution, and especially in the philosophy of John Locke. In Chapter 2 I will argue that a traditional social order lingered well into the eighteenth century and that the 'modern' standard did not come into being until the beginning of the nineteenth.
14. The *OED* tells us that the origin of the English word 'standard' is 'somewhat obscure'. It originally had nothing to do with weights and measures, a meaning that only emerged in the fifteenth century. First used in the twelfth, the standard was 'a banner or flag ... the king's standard being the point of reunion of the army, and the center from which commands are issued'. The word has an 'etymological association' with the Latin *standere*, 'to stand'; standards and flags are prominent vertically and can be said to 'stand in' for the king, general, or other leader as a way to corral or cheer the troops. But the Latin root of 'standard' is actually '*extendere*, to stretch out'.
15. On the idea of intrinsic value in mercantilism see Andrea Finkelstein, *Harmony and the Balance: An Intellectual History of Seventeenth-Century English Economic Thought* (Ann Arbor: University of Michigan Press, 2000), 41–4, 88; Mary Poovey, *A History of the Modern Fact* (Chicago: University of Chicago Press, 1998), 66–91; Jonathan Gil Harris, *Sick Economies: Drama, Mercantilism, and Disease in Shakespeare's England* (Philadelphia: University of Pennsylvania Press, 2004), 6; Carl Wennerlind, 'Credit-Money as the Philosopher's Stone: Alchemy and the Coinage Problem in Seventeenth-Century England',

in *Oeconomics in the Age of Newton*, ed. Margarate Schabas and Neil De Marchi, *History of Political Economy*, Supplement 35 (2003): 238–9.

16. John Bender and David E. Wellbery, 'Rhetoricality: On the Modernist Return of Rhetoric', in *The Ends of Rhetoric: History, Theory, Practice*, ed. John Bender and David E. Wellbery (Stanford: Stanford University Press, 1990), 25.
17. The royal proclamations affecting the coinage can be found in Paul L. Hughes and James Francis Larkin, eds., *Tudor Royal Proclamations* (New Haven: Yale University Press, 1964–9).
18. On the history of the Royal Mint and its challenges see Sir John Craig, *The Mint: A History of the London Mint from A.D. 287 to 1948* (Cambridge: Cambridge University Press, 1953); Christopher Edgar Chaliss, ed., *A New History of the Royal Mint* (Cambridge: Cambridge University Press, 1992); J. D. Gould, *The Great Debasement: Currency and the Economy in Mid-Tudor England* (Oxford: Clarendon Press, 1970); and Thomas Sargeant and François R. Velde, *The Big Problem of Small Change* (Princeton: Princeton University Press, 2002).
19. The literature on these changes is extensive. Apart from P. G. M. Dickson's *The Financial Revolution: A Study of the Development of Public Credit, 1688–1756* (Basingstoke: Macmillan, 1967; Aldershot: Gregg Revivals, 1993), see Joyce Appelby, 'Locke, Liberalism, and the Natural Law of Money', *Past and Present* 71 (1976): 43–69; and *Economic Thought and Ideology in Seventeenth-Century England* (Princeton: Princeton University Press, 1978); John Brewer, *Sinews of Power: War, Money, and the English State: 1688–1783* (New York: Knopf, 1989); George Caffentzis, *Clipped Coins, Abused Words, and Civil Government: John Locke's Philosophy of Money* (New York: 1989); Larry Neal, *The Rise of Financial Capitalism: International Capital Markets in the Age of Reason* (Cambridge: Cambridge University Press, 1990).
20. Isaac Newton, *Representation Third to the Right Honourable the Lords Commissioners of His Majesty's Revenue*, in J. R. McCulloch, *A Collection of Scarce and Valuable Tracts on Money* (London, 1856), 274–9.
21. On bodily metaphors in eighteenth-century conversations about financial 'schemes' and 'speculations' see Peter de Bolla, *The Discourse of the Sublime: Readings in History, Aesthetics, and the Subject* (Oxford: Blackwell, 1989), 103–41; Catherine Ingrassia, *Authorship, Commerce, and Gender in Early Eighteenth-Century England* (Cambridge: Cambridge University Press, 1998), 17–39; and Robert Mitchell, *Sympathy and the State in the Romantic Era: Systems, State Finance, and the Shadows of Futurity* (London: Routledge, 2007).
22. On bills of exchange see Ian Baucom, *Specters of the Atlantic: Finance Capital, Slavery, and the Philosophy of History* (Durham: Duke University Press, 2006), 44; and Rowlinson, *Real Money and Romanticism*, 37–8.
23. On the 'mediocrity' of the Liverpool Administration, see Richard Brown, *Church and State in Modern Britain, 1700–1850* (London: Routledge, 1991), 170–201.
24. Boyd Hilton, *Corn, Cash, and Commerce: The Economic Policies of the Tory Governments* (Oxford: Oxford University Press, 1977), 26–7.
25. Thomas De Quincey, 'Resumption of Cash Payments by the Bank of England', *Westmoreland Gazette*, February 6, 1819, in *Works of De Quincey*, vol. 1, ed. Grevel Lindop (London: Pickering & Chatto, 2000–3), 337.

26. E. P. Thompson, *The Making of the English Working Class* (New York: Pantheon, 1963), 314–49.
27. Paul Delaney, *Literature, Money, and the Market from Trollope to Amis* (Basingstoke: Palgrave Macmillan, 2002). Delaney argues that the post-Romantic culture of 'rentiers' typified by writers like Shelley and Austen demonstrates the persistence of aristocratic ideals, most importantly their faith in the intrinsic value of land, into modernity. See also Frances O'Gorman, ed., *Victorian Literature and Finance* (Oxford: Oxford University Press, 2007); and Deanna Kreisel, *Economic Woman: Demand, Gender, and Narrative Closure in Eliot and Hardy* (Toronto: University of Toronto Press, 2011).
28. Cleanth Brooks, 'Irony as a Principle of Structure', in David Richter, ed., *The Critical Tradition: Classic Texts and Contemporary Trends*, 3rd edn. (Boston: Bedford/St. Martin's Press, 2007), 799.
29. The crisis of representation in language has of course translated into post-structural interpretations of money. See especially Jacques Derrida, *Given Time I: Counterfeit Money*, trans. Peggy Kamuf (Chicago: University of Chicago Press, 1994). For an excellent reading of post-structuralism's *compliance* with the tenets of contemporary economic doctrine see Michael Tratner, 'Derrida's Debt to Milton Friedman', *New Literary History* 34 (2003): 791–806.
30. See J. G. A. Pocock, *The Machiavellian Moment: Florentine Political Thought and the Atlantic Republican Tradition* (Princeton: Princeton University Press, 1975, repr. 2003), 413–506; and 'The Mobility of Property and the Rise of Eighteenth-Century Sociology', in *Virtue, Commerce, and History: Essays on Political Thought and History, Chiefly in the Eighteenth Century* (Cambridge: Cambridge University Press, 1985).
31. Liz Bellamy, *Commerce, Morality, and the Eighteenth-Century* Novel (Cambridge: Cambridge University Press, 1998); Patrick Brantlinger, *Fictions of State: Culture and Credit in Great Britain, 1694–1994* (Ithaca, NY: Cornell University Press, 1996); Catherine Gallagher, *Nobody's Story: The Vanishing Acts of Women Writers in the Marketplace, 1670–1820* (Berkeley and Los Angeles: University of California Press, 1994); Deirdre Shauna Lynch, *The Economy of Character: Novels, Market Culture, and the Business of Inner Meaning* (Chicago: University of Chicago Press, 1998); Sandra Sherman, *Finance and Fiction in the Eighteenth Century: Accounting for Defoe* (Cambridge: Cambridge University Press, 1996).
32. Lynch, *The Economy of Character*, 76.
33. Mary Poovey, *Genres of the Credit Economy: Mediating Value in Eighteenth- and Nineteenth-Century Britain* (Chicago: University of Chicago Press, 2008). Poovey stresses the 'difficulty' of the economic debates of the early nineteenth century and surrounding the cash suspension though she is somewhat too hasty in generalizing the various contributions of Francis Horner, Henry Thornton, and David Ricardo as representative of an 'economic establishment' and contrasting them to the political activism of William Cobbett and Richard Bray.
34. Poovey, *Genres*, 286.
35. Poovey, *Genres*, 371.
36. James Chandler, *England in 1819: The Politics of Literary Culture and the Case of Romantic Historicism* (Chicago: University of Chicago Press, 1998), esp. 166–74. Robert Miles offers an excellent account of these tensions in the recent critical reception of Jane Austen in 'New Historicism, New Austen,

New Romanticism', in *Romanticism, History, Historicism: Essays on an Orthodoxy*, ed. Damien Walford Davies (London: Routledge, 2009), 182–203.

37. Mark Osteen and Martha Woodmansee, 'Taking Account of the New Economic Criticism: An Historical Introduction', in *The New Economic Criticism*, ed. Osteen and Woodmansee (London: Routledge, 1999), 3–50.
38. Andrew Elfenbein, *Romanticism and the Rise of English* (Stanford: Stanford University Press, 2009); Ian Hunter, *Culture and Government: The Emergence of Literary Education* (Basingstoke: Macmillan, 1988); Robert Crawford, *Devolving English Literature* (Oxford: Clarendon Press, 1992).
39. Elfenbein, *Romanticism and the Rise of English*, 15.
40. Quoted in Carl Wennerlind, 'Money Talks, But What is it Saying? Semiotics of Money and Social Control', *Journal of Economic Issues* 35 (2001): 557–74 (560). See also Alan W. Dyer, 'Making Semiotic Sense of Money as a Medium of Exchange', *Journal of Economic Issues* 23 (1989): 503–10.
41. Margot C. Finn, *The Character of Credit: Personal Debt in English Culture, 1740–1914* (Cambridge: Cambridge University Press, 2003); Craig Muldrew, *The Economy of Obligation: The Culture of Credit and Social Relations in Early Modern England* (Basingstoke: Macmillan, 1998); 'Hard Food for Midas: Cash and its Social Value in Early Modern England', *Past and Present* 170 (2001): 78–120; 'Interpreting the Market: The Ethics of Credit and Community Relations in Early Modern England', *Social History* 18 (1993): 163–8; Valenze, *Social Life of Money*.
42. William St. Clair, *The Reading Nation in the Romantic Period* (Cambridge: Cambridge University Press, 2007); Clifford Siskin, *The Work of Writing: Literature and Social Change in Britain, 1700–1830* (Baltimore: Johns Hopkins University Press, 1999), 11, 109–12; Raymond Williams, 'Means of Communication as Means of Production', in *Problems in Materialism and Culture: Selected Essays* (London: New Left Books, 1980), 50–63; John Feather, *A History of British Publishing* (London: Routledge, 1988).
43. Marcus Wood, *Radical Satire and Print Culture, 1790–1832* (Oxford: Clarendon Press, 1994), 55. See also Kevin Gilmartin, *Print Politics: The Press and Radical Opposition in Early Nineteenth-Century England* (Cambridge: Cambridge University Press, 1996) and Paul Keen, *The Crisis of Literature in the 1790s Print Culture and the Public Sphere* (Cambridge: Cambridge University Press, 1999).
44. Brewer, *Sinews of Power*, 221–49.
45. Siskin, *Work of Writing*, 140–52; Jon Klancher, *The Making of English Reading Audiences, 1790–1832* (Madison: University of Wisconsin Press, 1987).
46. 'This ideal of authenticity becomes crucial owing to a development that occurs after Rousseau ... that each of us has an original way of being human: each person has his or her own "measure".' Charles Taylor, 'The Politics of Recognition', in *Multiculturalism: Examining the Politics of Recognition*, ed. Amy Gutman (Princeton: Princeton University Press, 1994), 25–74 (30).
47. Phillip Connell, *Romanticism, Economics, and the Question of 'Culture'* (Oxford: Oxford University Press, 2001); Catherine Gallagher, *The Body Electric: Life, Death, and Sensation in Political Economy and the Victorian Novel* (Princeton: Princeton University Press, 2006); Maureen McLane, *Romanticism and the Human Sciences: Poetry, Population, and the Discourse of the Species* (Cambridge: Cambridge University Press, 2000).
48. The fundamentals are laid out in Brian Massumi, *Parables for the Virtual: Movement, Affect, Sensation* (Durham: Duke University Press, 2002) and

Eve Kosofsky Sedgwick, *Touching Feeling: Affect, Pedagogy, Performance* (Durham: Duke University Press, 2003).

49. Andrea Henderson, *Romanticism and the Painful Pleasures of Modern Life* (Cambridge: Cambridge University Press, 2008).
50. Ian Baucom, *Specters of the Atlantic: Finance Capital, Slavery, and the Philosophy of History* (Durham: Duke University Press, 2006).
51. Robert Mitchell, *Sympathy and the State in the Romantic Era: Systems, State Finance, and the Shadows of Futurity* (London: Routledge, 2007).
52. Henry Thornton, *An Enquiry into the Nature and Effects of the Paper Credit of Great Britain* (London: Hatchard, 1802), 13.
53. Thornton, *Paper Credit*, 13.
54. Sir James Steuart, *An Inquiry into the Principles of Political Economy* (1767), ed. Andrew. S. Skinner, Noboru Kobayashi, and Hiroshi Mizuta (London: Pickering & Chatto, 1998). See especially Book III, 'Of Money and Coin' and Book IV, 'Of Credits and Debts'.
55. Thornton, *Paper Credit*, 14.
56. The American theorist Sinnae Ngai calls confidence 'the tone of capitalism', by which she means both the general disposition or mood that capitalist activity requires to sustain itself and the point of access for critical reflections on capitalism's forms of 'ideological communication'. See *Ugly Feelings* (Cambridge, MA: Harvard University Press, 2009), 62.
57. Goffman's book on the way people manage affects for the sake of self-presentation is *The Presentation of Self in Everyday Life* (New York: Anchor, 1959). But his theory of embarrassment, which in fact complicates his general view, was outlined three years earlier in 'Embarrassment and Social Organization', *American Journal of Sociology* 62 (1956): 264–71. See also W. Crozier, ed., *Shyness and Embarrassment: Perspectives from Social Psychology* (Cambridge: Cambridge University Press, 1990).
58. Eve Kosofsky Sedgwick and Adam Frank, 'Shame in the Cybernetic Fold: Reading Silvan Tomkins', in *Shame and Its Sisters: A Silvan Tomkins Reader*, ed. Sedgwick and Frank (Durham: Duke University Press, 1995), 1–28 (22). Tomkins' notes on Shame are included in the same volume under the heading 'Shame–Humiliation and Contempt–Disgust', 133–78.
59. 'The speculative temporality of affect', Mitchell writes, is 'fundamentally opposed to the speculative temporality of finance'. I disagree: finance capital is a by-product of rational processes of equivalence and exchange, but money, including state money, is in no way distinguishable from affective processes. See Mitchell, *Sympathy and the State*, 20–1.
60. Martha Nussbaum, *Upheavals of Thought: The Intelligence of Emotions* (Cambridge: Cambridge University Press, 2003), 22.
61. Charles Taylor describes 'human flourishing' as the condition and the goal of 'a purely self-sufficient humanism', a belief system that really only existed in certain intellectual conceptions from the late seventeenth to the late eighteenth centuries. For Taylor, Nussbaum's emotional confidence in the valued objects or memories that enable her to 'flourish' would be the mark of a 'disciplinary' self of the kind advanced by Locke. The modern self, by contrast, has for Taylor more belief-options than self-sufficient flourishing, including religion. See *A Secular Age* (Cambridge, MA: Harvard University Press, 2007), 17–18.

62. Charles Altieri, *The Particulars of Rapture: An Aesthetics of Emotion* (Ithaca: Cornell University Press, 2003), 154, 166.
63. Altieri, *The Particulars of Rapture*, 156.
64. Thomas Pfau, *Romantic Moods: Paranoia, Trauma, and Melancholy, 1790–1840* (Stanford: Stanford University Press, 2005), 31.
65. Rei Terada makes this point about post-structuralism in *Feeling in Theory: Emotion After the Death of the Subject* (Cambridge, MA: Harvard University Press, 2001).
66. Anthony Giddens, *The Consequences of Modernity* (Stanford: Stanford University Press, 1990), 38.
67. Giddens, *The Consequences of Modernity*, 38–9.
68. Giddens, *The Consequences of Modernity*, 41.
69. Giddens, *The Consequences of Modernity*, 41.
70. On the scientific elements of Ricardo's political economy see Margaret Schabas, *The Natural Origins of Economics* (Chicago: University of Chicago Press, 2005), 112–19. Schabas takes issue with the mainstream of economic historians who, while accepting that Ricardo learned a great deal from Bentham and the utilitarians, his thought was primarily deductive and geometric rather than inductive and quantitative.
71. According to Claudia Klaver, *A/Moral Economics: Classical Political Economy and Cultural Authority in Nineteenth-Century England* (Columbus: Ohio State University Press, 2002), 19.
72. David Ricardo, *The Principles of Political Economy and Taxation*, in *The Works and Correspondence of David Ricardo*, ed. Piero Sraffa (Cambridge: Cambridge University Press, 1951–73), 1. 12.
73. Letter to James Mill, September 5, 1823, *Works* 9. 387.
74. Ricardo, *Works* 1. 45
75. Ricardo, *Works* 1. 46.
76. See 'The Work of Art in the Age of Mechanical Reproduction', in *Illuminations*, ed. Hannah Arendt (New York: Schocken, 1968), 236.
77. In *Keats and Embarrassment* (Oxford: Clarendon Press, 1984), Christopher Ricks argued that embarrassment played a crucial role in the developing character of the English middle class in the nineteenth century. A brilliant set of close-readings, Ricks' book is also an important, and overlooked, contribution to the study of poetic affect.
78. 'An Epistle to Allen Lord Bathurst', in *Alexander Pope: The Major Works*, ed. Pat Rogers (Oxford: Oxford University Press, 1993), 257, ll. 127–32.
79. Pope, 'To Bathurst', 253, ll. 39–40.
80. Terry Eagleton, *The Ideology of the Aesthetic* (Oxford: Basil Blackwell, 1990), 38.
81. Colin Nicholson, *Writing and the Rise of Finance: Capital Satires of the Early Eighteenth Century* (Cambridge: Cambridge University Press, 1994), 30.
82. Eagleton, *Ideology*, 54.
83. Peter de Bolla, *The Discourse of the Sublime: Readings in History, Aesthetics, and the Subject* (Oxford: Basil Blackwell, 1989).
84. G. Gabrielle Starr, 'Ethics, Meaning, and the Work of Beauty', *Eighteenth-Century Studies* 35 (2002): 361–78.
85. David Hume, *Essays Moral, Political, and Literary*, ed. Eugene F. Miller (Indianapolis: Liberty, 1986).
86. Adam Smith, *An Inquiry into the Nature and Causes of the Wealth of Nations*, ed. R. H. Campbell and A. S. Skinner (Oxford: Clarendon Press, 1976), 53–64.

87. Smith, *Wealth of Nations*, 321.
88. Dugald Stewart, 'The Life and Writings of Adam Smith', in Volume 11 of *The Collected Writings of Dugald Stewart*, ed. William Hamilton (Edinburgh: Constable, 1854–60), 62–3.
89. The first price currents and 'exchange rate currents' documenting the relative prices of European currencies were published in Antwerp in the 1540s and migrated to Amsterdam in the seventeenth century. See John J. McCusker, 'The Demise of Distance: The Business Press and the Origins of the Information Revolution in the Early Modern Atlantic World', *American Historical Review* 110 (2005): 295–321 (300).
90. See Daniel A. Rabuzzi, 'Eighteenth-Century Commercial Mentalities as Reflected and Projected in Business Handbooks', *Eighteenth-Century Studies* 29 (2005): 169–89.
91. See Gillian Russell, '"Faro's Daughters": Female Gamesters, Politics, and the Discourse of Finance in 1790s Britain', *Eighteenth-Century Studies* 33 (2000): 481–504.
92. See *The European Magazine and London Review* 45 (1804): 172; and 50 (1806): 426. The misquotation of Pope may have been channeled through Joel Barlow's *The Vision of Columbus* (London, 1787), which also conjoined 'realms' with 'gold'.
93. John Keats, *Complete Poems*, ed. Jack Stillinger (Cambridge, MA: Harvard University Press, 1978), 34.
94. The gold of the first line has been thought by some critics to refer to the gold leaf that more important, and thus more expensive books in Keats' time were inlaid with on their covers. Carl L. Johnson, 'The Realms of Gold', *Keats–Shelley Journal* 9 (1960): 6–10.
95. The expedition was foiled by the colonists' belief that they could sell wigs, combs, bonnets, and of course bibles to the Native population. Both Cortez and Balboa found sources of new wealth, primarily gold, in the Aztec and Peruvian empires. Charles Rzepka notes the extensive commentary on Latin American affairs in *The Examiner* in '"Cortez: Or Balboa, Or Somebody Like That": Form, Fact, and Forgetting in Keats's "Chapman's Homer" Sonnet', *Keats–Shelley Journal* 51 (2002): 35–75 (53–4).
96. Cited in Rzepka, '"Cortez: Or Balboa, Or Somebody Like That"', 39–40.
97. Lewis M. Schwartz, 'Keats' Critical Reception in Newspapers of his Day', *Keats–Shelley Journal* 21–2 (1972–3): 37–52.

2 The Bullion Controversy

1. William Pitt, *The Bullion Controversy: A Serio-Comic Satiric Poem* (London: Longman, 1811), 1.
2. Today, the term 'bullion controversy' often encompasses all monetary debates from the 1790s to the 1830s. I am using it to refer primarily to debates about money that preceded the 1816 coinage reform. The debates that followed this date tend to assume the theoretical if not practical necessity of the gold standard. See David Laidler, 'The Bullion Controversy', in *The New Palgrave Dictionary of Economics*, ed. John Eatwell, Murray Milgate, and Peter Newman (Basingstoke: Palgrave Macmillan, 1987), 289–94.

3. The name William Pitt does seem to have been his own, though there is no mention of the coincidence of it with that of the two Prime Ministers in the poem.
4. Robert Southey, *Letters from England* (New York, 1808), 113.
5. John Wilson, 'Political Economy: Essay II', *Blackwood's Edinburgh Magazine* 16 (1824): 40.
6. Edwin Cannan, *The Paper Pound of 1797–1821: A Reprint of the Bullion Report* (London: P. S. King, 1919).
7. Frank Fetter, *Development of British Monetary Orthodoxy, 1797–1875* (Cambridge, MA: Harvard University Press, 1965), preface.
8. Fetter, *Orthodoxy*, 105–6, 230–3.
9. Fetter, *Orthodoxy*, preface.
10. Fetter, *Orthodoxy*, 283.
11. For a sociological perspective see John W. Houghton, *Culture and Currency: Cultural Bias in Monetary Theory and Policy* (Boulder, CO: Westview, 1991); Mary Poovey briefly reviews the bullion controversy in *Genres of the Credit Economy*, 175–81.
12. Samuel Weber, *Mass Mediarus: Form, Technics, Media* (Stanford: Stanford University Press, 1996), 7.
13. William B. Warner, *Licensing Entertainment: The Elevation of Novel Reading in Britain, 1684–1750* (Berkeley: University of California Press, 1998), 177–9.
14. On media interaction, or remediation, see Jay David Bolter and Richard Grusin, eds., *Remediation: Understanding New Media* (Cambridge: MIT Press, 2001).
15. I borrow the term 'media consciousness' from Kevis Goodman, *Georgic Modernity and British Romanticism: Poetry and the Mediation of History* (Cambridge: Cambridge University Press, 2004).
16. For descriptions of the general euphoria in Britain about its global victories in 1759, see Kathleen Wilson, *The Sense of the People: Politics, Culture, and Imperialism in England 1715–1785* (Cambridge: Cambridge University Press, 1995), 197–8.
17. H. V. Bowen, 'British Conceptions of Global Empire 1756–83' *Journal of Imperial and Commonwealth History* 26 (1998): 1–27.
18. My account of this is based on Giovanni Arrighi's *The Long Twentieth Century: Money, Power, and the Origin of Our Times* (London: Verso, 1994), 159–72.
19. The public sphere is not, then, a singular entity but a site of 'cultural and ideological contest or negotiation among a variety of publics'. George Eley, 'Nations, Publics, and Political Cultures: Placing Habermas in the Nineteenth Century', in *Habermas and the Public Sphere*, ed. C. Calhoun (Cambridge: MIT Press, 1992), 289–339 (290).
20. Stephen Turner, 'What is the Problem with Experts?' *Social Studies of Science* 31 (2001): 123–49 (125). At its most paranoid, the sense that liberal democracy is controlled by 'mandarins' who stand above rational exchange and determine its ideological trajectories and disciplinary procedures leads to the conclusion that liberalism itself, not to mention the public sphere from which it emerged, cannot be said in the final analysis to exist. This view is most explicitly stated by Stanley Fish in *There's No Such Thing as Free Speech, and It's a Good Thing* (New York: Oxford University Press, 1994) though it is more eloquently, and influentially, articulated by Michel Foucault in *Discipline and Punish: The Birth of the Prison*, trans. Alan Sheridan

(New York: Vintage, 1979). For a selected survey of these views see Turner, 'What is the Problem with Experts?' 124–9.

21. Harry Collins and Robert Evans, *Rethinking Expertise* (Chicago: University of Chicago Press, 2007), 18.
22. Collins and Evans, *Rethinking Expertise*, 24.
23. Collins and Evans, *Rethinking Expertise*, 31. See also Evan Selinger and Robert Crease, eds., *The Philosophy of Expertise* (New York: Columbia University Press, 2006).
24. As J. A. Downie describes it, what distinguishes the pamphlet is a combination of a 'polemical objective', including its awareness of the prejudices of readers confounded by ongoing debates, and its ability to transform that sense of discomfort into coherent ideals, to 'give shape' to 'shapeless anxieties'. See 'Public Opinion and the Political Pamphlet', in *The Cambridge History of English Literature 1660–1780*, ed. John Richetti (Cambridge: Cambridge University Press, 2005), 549–71 (551). See also James Mulvihill, *Upstart Talents: Rhetoric and the Career of Reason in English Romantic Discourse, 1790–1820* (Newark: University of Delaware Press, 2004).
25. For a fuller discussion of Burke's remarks on the loan see Dermot Ryan, '"A New Description of Empire": Edmund Burke and the Regicide Republic of Letters', *Eighteenth-Century Studies* 44 (2010): 1–19 (12–13). For the complexities and contradictions of Burke's economic views generally see J. G. A. Pocock, 'The Political Economy of Burke's Analysis of the French Revolution', in *Virtue, Commerce, and History*, 197; and Tom Furniss, *Edmund Burke's Aesthetic Ideology: Language, Gender, and Political Economy in Revolution* (Cambridge: Cambridge University Press, 1993).
26. William Morgan, *Additional Facts Addressed to the Serious Attention of the People of Great Britain, Respecting the Expenses of the War and the State of the National Debt* (Debrett, 1796), 48–9.
27. Samuel Taylor Coleridge, *The Watchman* No. II (Wednesday, March 9, 1796), in *The Collected Works of Samuel Taylor Coleridge*, vol. 2, ed. L. Patton (Princeton: Princeton University Press, 1970), 56–66.
28. Thomas Paine, *Dissertation on Government, the Affairs of the Bank, and Paper Money* (Philadelphia, 1786).
29. Reissues were still being produced through the first half of the nineteenth century, making it perhaps the most popular work of monetary thought in the century, seconded by Locke's *Further Considerations*.
30. Thomas Paine, *The Decline and Fall of the English System of Finance* (Paris, 1796), 2.
31. Paine, *Decline and Fall*, 11.
32. Paine, *Decline and Fall*, 3.
33. Daniel Wakefield, *A Letter to Thomas Paine, in reply to his Decline and Fall of the English System of Finance* (London, 1796), 4.
34. Wakefield, *A Letter to Thomas Paine*, 6.
35. Wakefield, *A Letter to Thomas Paine*, 4–5.
36. George Chalmers, *Strictures on a Pamphlet Written by Thomas Paine* (London, 1796), 2.
37. Joseph Smith, *An Examination of Mr. Paine's Decline and Fall of the English System of Finance in a letter to a Friend* (London, 1796).
38. *Parliamentary History of England, From the Earliest Period to the Year 1803*, 36 vols. (London: T. C. Hansard, 1806–18), 3. 324.

39. *Parliamentary History*, 3. 336.
40. *Parliamentary History*, 3. 343.
41. Andreas Michael Andreades, *History of the Bank of England, 1640–1903* (London: Frank Cass, 1909), 200; cited in Mark Schoenfield, *British Periodicals and Romantic Identity: The 'Literary Lower Empire'* (Basingstoke: Palgrave Macmillan, 2009), 59.
42. On Gilray's and other caricaturists' depiction of the Bank Restriction Act, see Ian Heywood, 'Paper Promises: Restriction, Caricature, and the Ghost of Gold', in *Romanticism, Forgery, and the Credit Crisis*, special issue of *Romantic Praxis* (2012).
43. Alexander Campbell, *The Guinea Note, A Poem by Timothy Twig, Esquire* (Edinburgh: A. Leslie, 1797), 2.
44. Campbell, *Guinea Note*, 4.
45. Walter Boyd, *Letter to the Right Honourable William Pitt: On the Influence of the Stoppage of Issues in Specie at the Bank of England: on the Prices of Provisions and other Commodities* (London: Wright, 1801), 3.
46. Boyd, *Letter to Pitt*, 24.
47. Anon., *Brief Observations on a Late Letter Addressed to the Right Hon. W. Pitt by Walter Boyd, Esq. on the Stoppages of Issue in Specie by the Bank of England* (London: Debrett, 1801), 5.
48. See P. J. Cain and A. G. Hopkins, 'Gentlemanly Capitalism and British Expansion Overseas: I. The Old Colonial System 1688–1850', *Economic History Review* 39 (1986): 501–25.
49. Sir Francis Baring, *Observations on the Publication of Walter Boyd* (London: Debrett, 1801). It is telling, though, that both of Baring's replies to Boyd as well as the anonymous *Brief Observations* were published by Debrett, who at the time was the chief publisher of Tory speeches and, beginning in 1802, of Debrett's *Baronetage*, the chief register of aristocratic prestige and accomplishment.
50. Boyd, *Letter to Pitt*, 7; Baring, *Observations*, 14–15.
51. *The Monthly Magazine or British Register* XI (1801): 573. Frend's pamphlet is *The Effect of Paper Money on the Price of Provisions; or the Point in Dispute between Mr. Boyd and Sir Francis Baring, examined, the Bank Paper-Money Proved to be an Adequate Cause for the High Price of Provisions*. Thomas Surr, *Refutation of Certain Misrepresentations Relative To The Nature And Influence Of Bank Notes: And Of The Stoppage Of Issues In Specie, At The Bank Of England, Upon The Prices Of Provisions, As Stated In The Pamphlets Of Walter Boyd, Esq. and Mr. William Frend* (London: Hurst, 1801).
52. *The New Annual Register, or General Repository of History, Politics, and Literature for the Year 1801* (London: Robinson, 1802).
53. The annual register, one of the dominant encyclopaedic genres of the eighteenth century, was intended to enable its readers to understand all of the knowledge possible at their contemporary moment under the auspices of its own chronological sequencing. A historical sensibility, he suggests, is one that encompasses everything according to its observed present. See Chandler, *England in 1819*, 123–4.
54. Charles Jenkinson, *A Treatise on the Coins of the Realm: In a Letter to the King* (London: J. J. W. Birch and Je. R. Grenfell, 1880), 352–3; cited in Rowlinson, *Real Money and Romanticism*, 48.
55. On 'mixing' as a precondition for the emergence of Romanticism, see Clifford Siskin, *The Historicity of Romantic Discourse* (Oxford: Oxford University Press, 1988).

56. It is also possible that Horner and his fellow Whigs took the high price of gold as an opportunity to undermine Tory fiscal policy and grip on power. See Kenneth Bourne and William Banks Taylor, eds., *The Horner Papers: Selections from the Letters and Miscellaneous Writings of Francis Horner MP, 1795–1817* (Edinburgh: Edinburgh University Press, 1994), 570.
57. *Report Together With the Minutes of Evidence and Accounts from the Select Committee on the High Price of Gold Bullion* (London: Johnson, 1810).
58. Letter to Murray, June 26, 1810, in *The Horner Papers*, ed. Bourne and Taylor, 643.
59. Cited in Biancamaria Fontana, *Rethinking the Politics of Consumer Society: The Edinburgh Review, 1802–1832* (Cambridge: Cambridge University Press, 1985), 123.
60. Just how complex Cruikshank's argument appears is already evinced by his full title: *Observations on Money, as the Medium of Commerce Shewing* [sic] *the Present Circulating Medium of this Country to be Defective in Those Requisites which a Medium of Commerce Ought to Possess, and Pointing Out in What Manner the Defect May be Remedied; and Also The Real Effect that a Greater or Less Quantity of Circulating Medium has on the Country: Together with Remarks on the Present State of the Nation: to which are subjoined a few practical inferences* (London: Richardson, 1811).
61. Simon Cock, *An Examination of the Report of the Bullion Committee: Shewing* [sic] *That the Present High Price of Bullion, Together with the Scarcity of Gold Coin, and Also the Low Rate of the Foreign Exchanges, Are Not Attributable to the Issue of Bank Paper; and Explaining What Are the True Causes by Which These Effects Have Been Produced* (London, 1810), iii.
62. Sir James Steuart, *Principles of Banks and Banking as Coin and Paper with the Consequences of Any Excessive Issue on the National Currency, Course of Exchange, Price of Provisions, Commodities, and Fixed Incomes* (London: J. Davies, 1810).
63. *Morning Chronicle*, September 21, 1810. The speech was later published in pamphlet form as *The Speech of Randall Jackson, Esq. delivered at the General Court of the Bank of England, held on the 20th of September, 1810, respecting the Report of the Bullion Committee of the House of Commons; with Notes on the Subject of that Report* (London: Richardson, 1810).
64. David Ricardo, 'Letter to the *Morning Chronicle on Randle Jackson's "Bank Speech"*', *Morning Chronicle* (September 24, 1810), in *Minor Papers on the Currency Question 1809–23*, ed. Jacob Hollander (Baltimore: Johns Hopkins University Press, 1932), 79–80.
65. William Huskisson, *The Question Concerning the Depreciation of Our Currency Stated and Examined* (London: Murray, 1810), iii.
66. Huskisson, *Depreciation*, 2–3.
67. See Nathan Sussman, 'William Huskisson and the Bullion Controversy, 1810', *European Journal of the History of Economic Thought* 4 (1997): 237–57.
68. See for instance Peter Carey, *A Letter to William Huskisson, M.P. On His Late Publication* (London: Richardson, 1811).
69. John Hill, A*n Inquiry into the Causes of the Present High Price of Gold Bullion in England and Its Connection with the State of Foreign Exchanges, with Observations on the Report of the Bullion Committee: In a Series of Letters Addressed to Thomas Thompson, Esq. M.P., One of the Members of the Bullion Committee* (London: Longman 1810), 86.

70. Sir John Sinclair, *Political Maxims Regarding Coin and Paper Currency* (Edinburgh, 1810); *Observations on the Report of the Bullion Committee* (London: Bulmer, 1810); *Remarks on a Pamphlet Entitled 'The Question &c'* (London, 1811); *The Speech of the Right Honourable Sir John Sinclair, Bart, On the Subject of the Report in the House of Commons on Wednesday, the 15th of May, 1811* (London: B. McMillan, 1811).
71. Sinclair, *Remarks*, 16.
72. William Kingsman, *Letter to the Right Honourable Sir John Sinclair, Bart. (author of the History of the Revenue, and other fugitive pieces) on the subject of his remarks on Mr. Huskisson's pamphlet*, 2nd edn. (London: J. Ridgway, 1811), 23.
73. Kingsman, *Letter*, 23.
74. [George Canning and George Ellis], 'Sir John Sinclair's Remarks', *Quarterly Review* 5 (1811): 120–38.
75. [George Ellis], 'Huskisson, on the Depreciation of Currency', *Quarterly Review* 4 (1810): 453.
76. My account of Lowe is drawn from Benjamin Christie Nangle, *The Monthly Review Second Series, 1790–1815: Index of Contributors and Articles* (Oxford: Clarendon Press, 1955), 38–39.
77. [Joseph Lowe], 'Ricardo, Grenfell, Mushet, Sir P. Francis, and others on the Depreciation of Banknotes', *Monthly Review* 63 (1810): 182.
78. [Joseph Lowe], 'Monthly Catalogue: Politics', *Monthly Review* 63 (1810): 435.
79. [Joseph Lowe], 'Huskisson on the Depreciation of Our Currency', *Monthly Review* 63 (1810): 413.
80. [Joseph Lowe], 'Blake's *Observations on the State of the Exchange*', *Monthly Review* 64 (1811): 1.
81. [Joseph Lowe], 'Ricardo, Grenfell, Mushet, Sir P. Francis, and others on the Depreciation of Banknotes', *Monthly Review* 63 (1810): 180.
82. [Joseph Lowe], 'Sir John Sinclair's *Observation on the Report of the Bullion Committee*', *Monthly Review* 63 (1810): 288.
83. [Joseph Lowe], 'On the Report of the Bullion Committee', *Monthly Review* 63 (1810): 464.
84. 'On the Bullion Report and Mr. Huskisson's Pamphlet', *The Times* (December 4, 1810): 3. See also I. W. P., 'On the Price of Bullion and Circulation of Paper', *The Times* (October 19, 1810): 2; A Constant Reader, 'Bullion Report', *The Times* (October 25, 1810): 3.
85. Brougham, Horner, and Jeffrey were members of the Speculative Society, 'the most famous of the University clubs', where young men honed their rhetorical skill on current affairs. See Leslie Hunter, *The Scottish Education System* (Oxford: Pergamon, 1968), 209–12; J. V. Smith, 'Reflections on the Popular Enlightenment of Early Nineteenth-Century Scotland', in Walter M. Huens and Hamish M. Paterson, eds., *Scottish Culture and Scottish Education, 1800–1900* (Edinburgh: John Donald, 1983), 28–30.
86. Klancher, *English Reading Audiences*, 69–71.
87. Jerome Christensen, 'The Dark Romanticism of the *Edinburgh Review*', in *Romanticism at the End of History* (Baltimore: Johns Hopkins University Press, 2000), 107–28; Ian Duncan, 'Edinburgh, Capital of the Nineteenth Century', in *Romantic Metropolis: The Urban Scene of British Culture, 1780–1840*, ed. James

Chandler and Kevin Gilmartin (Cambridge: Cambridge University Press, 2005), 45–64 (62–4); Schoenfield, *British Periodicals and Romantic Identity*, 49–78.

88. Henry Thornton, *An Enquiry into the Nature and Effects of the Paper Credit of Great Britain* (London: Hatchard, 1802).
89. See Antoin E. Murphy, 'Paper Credit and the Multi-Personae Mr. Henry Thornton', *European Journal of the History of Economic Thought* 10 (2003): 429–53 (431–2); S. Meacham, *Henry Thornton of Clapham, 1760–1815* (Cambridge, MA: Harvard University Press, 1964); E. M. Forster, *Marianne Thornton* (London: A. Deutsch, 2000), Ch. 1.
90. Thornton, *Enquiry*, 75.
91. Thornton, *Enquiry*, 111.
92. For summaries of Thornton's position see F. A. von Hayek, 'Introduction' to *An Enquiry into the Nature and Effects of the Paper Credit of Great Britain* (London: George Allen & Unwin, 1939), 11–65; D. A. Reisman, 'Henry Thornton and Classical Monetary Economics', *Oxford Economic Papers* New Series 23 (1971): 70–89.
93. Francis Horner, 'Thornton on the Paper Credit of Great Britain', *Edinburgh Review* 1 (1802): 172–201 (188).
94. Horner, 'Thornton on Paper Credit', 189–90.
95. Horner, 'Thornton on Paper Credit', 190.
96. Horner, 'Thornton on Paper Credit', 173–4, 198.
97. Horner, 'Thornton on Paper Credit', 174.
98. Horner, 'Lord King's *Thoughts on the Restriction of Payments*', *Edinburgh Review* 3 (1804): 402–21 (403).
99. Horner, 'Lord King's *Thoughts*', 420–1.
100. Horner, 'Thornton on Paper Credit', 172.
101. Horner, 'Thornton on Paper Credit', 173.
102. Horner, 'Thornton on Paper Credit', 189.
103. Horner, 'Thornton on Paper Credit', 189.
104. Writing in 1855, Walter Bagehot remarked that this unconcern for details was the signature of the early reviewers' gentlemanly style. See 'The First Edinburgh Reviewers', *National Review* (1855), in *The Collected Works of Walter Bagehot: The Literary Essays Volume 1*, ed. Norman St. John-Stevas (Cambridge, MA: Harvard University Press, 1965), 309–41 (312–13).
105. Horner, 'Thornton on Paper Credit', 196.
106. Horner, 'Thornton on Paper Credit', 196.
107. [James Mill], 'Smith on Money and Exchange', *Edinburgh Review* 7 (1808), 35.
108. Mill, 'Smith on Money', 38.
109. Thomas Smith, *The Bullion Question Impartially Discussed in an Address to the Editors of the* Edinburgh Review (London, 1812), 2.
110. Smith, *The Bullion Question*, 3–4.
111. Smith, *The Bullion Question*, 33.
112. David Ricardo, *The High Price of Bullion* (London: Murray, 1810), 55.
113. Ricardo, *High Price of Bullion*, 55.
114. This is not to say that Ricardo's theoretical confidence was natural or jejune. From about 1800 on, Ricardo was an avid reader of Locke, Hume, Smith, and Thornton. See *Minor Papers*.
115. Ricardo, *High Price of Bullion*, 55.
116. Ricardo, *High Price of Bullion*, 55.

117. Ricardo, *High Price of Bullion*, 56.
118. Ricardo, *High Price of Bullion*, 99.
119. Tomas Robert Malthus, *Works of Thomas Robert Malthus, Volume 2: An Essay on the Principle of Population*, ed. E. A. Wrigley and David Souden (London: Pickering, 1986), 16.
120. Thomas Robert Malthus, 'Depreciation of Paper Currency', *Edinburgh Review* 17 (1811): 339–72, in *Works of Thomas Robert Malthus, Volume 7: Essays on Political Economy*, ed. E. A. Wrigley and David Souden (London: Pickering, 1986), 55, 39.
121. Malthus, 'Depreciation of Paper Currency', 42.
122. Malthus, 'Depreciation of Paper Currency', 26–7.
123. [Francis Jeffrey], 'Madame de Stael, De La Littérature', *Edinburgh Review* 21 (1813): 1–50. See Fontana, *Rethinking the Politics of Consumer Society*, 173–5; and Connell, *Romanticism, Economics*, 95–6.
124. Joseph Hume, *Thoughts on the New Coinage with Reflections on Money and Coins and a New System of Coins and Weights on a Simple and Uniform Principle* (London: Stockdale, 1816), 26. On Hume see Ronald K. Hutch and Paul R. Ziegler, *Joseph Hume: The People's MP* (Philadelphia: American Philosophical Society, 1986).
125. David Ricardo, *Proposal for an Economical and Secure Currency* (London, 1816) in *The Works and Correspondence of David Ricardo*, vol. 4, ed. Piero Sraffa and M. H. Dobb (Cambridge: Cambridge University Press, 1951–73), 43–142.
126. J. R. McCulloch, 'Economical and Secure Currency', *Edinburgh Review* 21 (1818): 54–79. McCulloch's first article, 'Ricardo's Political Economy', *Edinburgh Review* 20 (1818): 59–87, was a summary of the *Principles* that remained a foundation of Ricardian economics for a generation. For more on McCulloch and the 'popularization' of Ricardo see S. G. Checkland, 'The Propagation of Ricardian Economics in England', *Economica* 16 (1949): 40–52; Fontana, *Rethinking the Politics of Commercial Society*, 75–78; Poovey, *History of the Modern Fact*, 295–8; and Klaver, *A/Moral Economics*, 31–52.
127. Thomas Smith, *A Reply to Mr. Ricardo's Proposals for an Economical and Secure Currency* (London, 1816), 6. See also *Letter to the Right Honourable the Earl of Liverpool on the Proposed New Coinage* (London, 1816), where Smith outlines similar reasons for not implementing a gold standard.
128. [J. G. Lockhart], 'Ricardo and the *Edinburgh Review*', *Blackwood's Edinburgh Magazine* (October 1818): 58–62 (59).
129. Lockhart, 'Ricardo and the *Edinburgh Review*', 59.

3 The Idea of Paper Money

1. Samuel Taylor Coleridge, *Lectures on the History of Philosophy, 1818–19*, ed. J. R. de J. Jackson, vol. 8 of *The Collected Works of Samuel Taylor Coleridge*, 400–1.
2. *On the Constitution of Church and State*, ed. John Barrell, vol. 10 of *The Collected Works of Samuel Taylor Coleridge*, 12.
3. Coleridge, letter to William Mudford, February 9, 1819, in *Collected Letters of Samuel Taylor Coleridge*, ed. E. L. Griggs (Oxford: Clarendon Press, 1956–71), 4.920; cited in Boyd Hilton, *The Age of Atonement: The Influence of Evangelicalism on Social and Economic Thought, 1795–1865* (Oxford: Clarendon Press, 1988), 128.

4. Phil Connell has clarified the continuity between Coleridge's earlier writing on money and credit, in which he urged that the national debt sustained national confidence, and the later concept of the national Church. Other critics have subsequently contended that the relationship is more distinctive than continuous: the sustaining power of the national debt produces a counter-discipline of literary, symbolic comprehension.
5. My take on Coleridge's idealism, which I do not develop at length here, is informed mainly by Paul Hamilton, *Coleridge and German Philosophy: A Poet in the Land of Logic* (London: Continuum, 2007).
6. For a popular (and somewhat hyperbolic) view of the secularization of Scottish thought in the eighteenth century see Arthur Herman, *How the Scots Invented the Modern World: The True Story of How Western Europe's Poorest Nation Created Our World and Everything in It* (New York: Crown, 2001). But the fact is that religion is rarely discussed in scholarly studies of eighteenth-century economics. In Margaret Schabas and Carl Wennerlind's recent collection *David Hume's Political Economy* (London: Routledge, 2008), the index entry on 'religion' refers to three passages, the longest of which is a discussion by George Caffentzis of Hume's dismissive treatment of 'artificial fictions, art, religion, and myth'.
7. See Andrea Finkelstein, *Harmony and the Balance: An Intellectual History of Seventeenth-Century English Economic Thought* (Ann Arbor: University of Michigan Press, 2000).
8. Cited in Robert Hole, *Pulpits, Politics, and Public Order in England, 1760–1832* (Cambridge: Cambridge University Press, 1989), 15.
9. On the tensions between the empiricism and authority see *inter alia* Pocock, *The Machiavellian Moment* and Michael McKeon, *The Origin of the English Novel, 1600–1740* (Baltimore: Johns Hopkins University Press, 1987).
10. Joseph Priestley, *Lectures on History and General Policy* (London: Johnson, 1788), 305.
11. Priestley, *Lectures*, 413.
12. As Daniel White shows in *Early Romanticism and Religious Dissent* (Cambridge: Cambridge University Press, 2006), Priestley's and other dissenters' claims for the independence of the individual under the law were products of an intellectual culture that prided itself on dissent and disagreement both against the status quo and within itself. Through the exercise of reason, the mind would come to see the fundamental purpose of existence as being commensurate with a general standard of empirical truth.
13. Richard Price, *A Review of the Principal Questions of Morals*, ed. D. D. Raphael (Oxford: Clarendon Press, 1984), 156.
14. Richard Price, *Observations on the proper method of keeping the Accounts, and determining from year to year the state of the Society for Equitable Assurances on Lives & Survivorships* (London, 1774).
15. Richard Price, 'Of the Security of a Virtuous Course', in *Sermons by Richard Price and Joseph Priestley* (London, 1830), 7. Price's and Priestley's sermons were frequently published in the late eighteenth and nineteenth centuries.
16. Taylor, *Secular Age*, 178.
17. Hole, *Pulpits, Politics, and Public Order*, 83–94.
18. Bentham had already published several pamphlets on money during the early years of the suspension. In *Proposal for the Circulation of a New Species of*

Paper Currency (London, 1795), Bentham described a series of mechanisms, including a government monopoly and anti-forgery precautions that he believed would stabilize the value of money while still allowing for the commercial benefits of an expanded issue of banknotes. In *Paper Mischief Exposed* (London, 1800), Bentham argued that the paper credit crisis was the fault of over-eager country bankers. *The True Alarm* was drafted in 1801 and Bentham contemplated publishing it in 1810 at the height of the bullion debates but was told not to by Ricardo and James Mill.

19. Jeremy Bentham, *Collected Works of Jeremy Bentham: Correspondence, Volume 9, January 1817 to June 1820*, ed. Steven Conway (Oxford: Oxford University Press, 1993), 42.
20. Bentham, *Correspondence, Volume 9*, 49.
21. Hilton, *Age of Atonement*. See especially pp. 125–30 for Hilton's take on the bullion controversy.
22. A. M. C. Waterman notes the Christian economists 'freed political economy from attachment to any particular religious or political creed, making it equally accessible to all so that all would submit to its discipline. And by safeguarding the integrity of each, it validated the ideological alliance of political economy and Christian Theology.' *Revolution, Economics, and Religion: Christian Political Economy, 1798–1833* (Cambridge: Cambridge University Press, 1991), 11.
23. My reading of Malthus on demand, and as a theorist of culture, comes from Christopher Herbert, *Culture and Anomie: Ethnographic Imagination in the Nineteenth Century* (Chicago: University of Chicago Press, 1991), 74–149.
24. Malthus, *The Works of Thomas Malthus, Volume 7: Essays on Political Economy*, 101–2.
25. It was in that capacity that Copleston corresponded with Coleridge, not on spiritual or intellectual matters but rather over concern at the 'intemperance' of Hartley Coleridge, who had taken a fellowship. Though primarily a religious thinker – he is sometimes credited with founding the Noetic School of rational theology – Copleston made a name for himself in 1811 by publishing a spirited defense of the university system against the calumnies of the *Edinburgh Review*.
26. Salim Rashid, 'Edward Copleston, Robert Peel, and Cash Payments', *History of Political Economy* 15 (1983): 249–59.
27. Edward Copleston, *A Letter to the Right Honourable Sir Robert Peel, MP for the University of Oxford, on the Pernicious Effects of a Variable Standard of Value: especially as it Regards the Condition of the Lower Orders and the Poor Laws* (Oxford: Murray, 1819), 4, 10–11.
28. Edward Copleston, 'State of the Currency', *Quarterly Review* 27 (1822): 239.
29. Copleston, 'State of the Currency', 243.
30. Waterman, *Revolution, Economics, and Religion*, 227.
31. Thomas Chalmers, *Christian and Civic Economy of Large Towns* (Glasgow, 1821), 9–10. On Chalmers' promotion of 'self help' see Lauren Goodlad, *Victorian Literature and the Victorian State: Character and Governance in a Liberal Society* (Baltimore: Johns Hopkins University Press, 2003), 39–48 and Poovey, *Genres*, 238–9.
32. Hilton, *Age of Atonement*, 127.
33. *The Letters of Charles and Mary Lamb*, vol. 3 (London: Taylor & Francis, 1978), 68.

34. See Zachery Leader, 'Coleridge and the Uses of Journalism', in *Grub Street and the Ivory Tower: Literary Journalism and Literary Scholarship from Fielding to the Internet*, ed. Jeremy Treglown and Bridget Bennett (Oxford: Clarendon Press, 1998), 22–40; Angela Esterhammer, 'Coleridge in the Newspapers, Periodicals, and Annuals', in *The Oxford Handbook to Samuel Taylor Coleridge*, ed. Frederick Burwick (Oxford: Oxford University Press, 2009), 165–84; Deidre Coleman, 'The Journalist', in *The Cambridge Companion to Coleridge*, ed. Lucy Newlyn (Cambridge: Cambridge University Press, 2002), 126–41.
35. Gilmartin, *Print Politics*, 2.
36. Gilmartin, *Print Politics*, 168.
37. As Poovey notes in *Genres*, 189–90, in spite of trenchant materialism, Cobbett relied on a notion of collective imagination to promote his model of economic enfranchisement.
38. William Cobbett, *Paper Against Gold and Glory Against Prosperity: Or, An Account of the Rise, Progress, Extent, and Present State of the Funds and of the Paper-money of Great Britain; and Also of the Situation of that Country as to Its Debt and Other Expenses; Its Navigation, Commerce, and Manufactures; Its Taxes, Population, and Paupers; Drawn from Authentic Documents, and Brought Down to the End of the Year 1814* (London: J. Macreery, 1815), 15.
39. Leonora Mattras, *William Cobbett: The Politics of Style* (Cambridge: Cambridge University Press, 1995), 157–82.
40. Cobbett, *Paper Against Gold*, 149–50.
41. See John W. Osborne, 'Cobbett's Anti-Semitism', *The Historian* 47 (1984): 86–92. Cobbett held similarly contradictory views on women whom he idealized as the innocent bearers of domestic comfort and encouraged as participants in his democratic revolution. See Tim Fulford, *Romantic Masculinities: Gender, Politics, and Poetics in the Writings of Burke, Coleridge, Cobbett, Wordsworth, De Quincey, and Hazlitt* (Basingstoke: Palgrave Macmillan, 1999), 163–9.
42. Samuel Taylor Coleridge, *The Friend*, ed. Barbara Rooke, vol. 4 of *The Collected Works of Samuel Taylor Coleridge* (London: Routledge, 1969), I.16.
43. Coleridge, *The Friend*, I.21.
44. In making this case, I am contradicting to some extent Kevin Gilmartin's argument in *Writing Against Revolution: Literary Conservatism in Britain 1790–1832* (Cambridge: Cambridge University Press, 2007), 207–52, that Coleridge's distrust of journalism's democratic appeal is a sign of his ideological conservatism. Coleridge was unquestionably conservative, and Gilmartin's comparison of his views with Southey's makes a compelling case, but there is nothing simplistic or uniform about this position or about its ideological nature. As Mark Canuel argues, 'universalizing gestures in *The Friend* are accompanied by refusals of universalization'. *The Friend* 'affirms its own authority not by forming consensus but by refusing it'. See 'Coleridge's Polemic Divinity', *English Literary History* 68 (2001): 929–63 (936). See also Forest Pyle, *The Ideology of Imagination: Subject and Society in the Discourse of Romanticism* (Stanford: Stanford University Press, 1995).
45. Connell outlines the contexts for this essay in *Romanticism, Economics*, 149–55. In his 1807 pamphlet *Britain Independent of Commerce*, published on the heels of the Napoleonic blockade, the physiocrat and naturalist William Spence argued that since British wealth came from agriculture, the country did not need to trade with Europe; tax revenues were a useful way to redirect

the wealth of landowners away from luxury and toward national sustenance. In *Commerce Defended*, James Mill accused Spence of naïve patriotism, warmongering, and a complete ignorance of the fundamental principles of both trade and taxation. In a surprising turn, Cobbett defended the arch-conservative Spence, claiming against Mill that Spence's anti-commercial support for the tax was radical in spirit if not in intent.

46. Coleridge, *The Friend*, II.159.
47. Coleridge, *The Friend*, II.160.
48. Coleridge, *The Friend*, I.232–3.
49. 'On Vulgar Errors' was reprinted almost right away in extracts by Coleridge's editor Daniel Stuart in both *The Courier* and *The Morning Post*. See *The Friend* II. 494. Stuart wrote to Coleridge: 'No 12 is a most brilliant one. I shall make a long extract from it in the Courier and another in the Morning Post.'
50. Coleridge 'The Bullion Controversy I', in *Essays on His Own Times*, volume 7 of *The Collected Works of Samuel Taylor Coleridge*, 2.229.
51. Coleridge, *Essays on His Own Times*, 2.251.
52. Coleridge, *Essays on His Own Times*, 2.125.
53. Coleridge, *Essays on His Own Times*, 2.132.
54. Coleridge, *Essays on His Own Times*, 2.235.
55. Coleridge, *Essays on His Own Times*, 2.132–3.
56. Samuel Taylor Coleridge, *Notebooks of Samuel Taylor Coleridge*, vol. 3, ed. Kathleen Coburn (London: Routledge & Kegan Paul, 1957), 4102.
57. Much later Coleridge seems to have changed his mind and become one of many writers to endorse the Corn Laws as a bastion of British economic strength. 'Those who argue that England may safely depend upon a supply of foreign corn', Coleridge remarked in the spring of 1834, 'if it grow none or an insufficient quantity of its own, forget that they are subjugating the necessities of life to the mere luxuries or comforts of society'. And then six weeks later: 'It may be admitted that the great principles of commerce require the interchange of commodities to be free; but commerce, which is barter, has no proper range beyond luxuries or conveniences; – it is properly the complement to the full existence and development of a state. But how can it be shown that the principles applicable to an interchange or conveniences or luxuries apply also to an interchange or necessaries? No state can be such properly, which is not self-subsistent at least; for no state that is not so, is essentially independent. The nation that cannot even exist without the commodity of another nation is the perfect slave of that other nation.' Transcribed by Coleridge's nephew, these comments likely reflect Henry Nelson Coleridge's more definitive Tory mentality, especially after the passing of the Reform Bill threatened more aristocratic privileges than the high price of corn. For the relations between Coleridge's conservative politics and mysticism, see Nigel Leask, *The Politics of Imagination in Coleridge's Critical Thought* (Basingstoke: Macmillan, 1988).
58. Coleridge, *Letters*, 4.549.
59. For Coleridge's notes on Fichte see Samuel Taylor Coleridge, *Marginalia*, ed. George Walley, H. J. Jackson, and J. R. de J. Jackson, *The Collected Works of Samuel Taylor Coleridge*, vol. 12 (Princeton: Princeton University Press, 1999), 2.616–22. On his claims that the commerce of a nation should be entirely at the disposal of the state, Coleridge noted that 'Fichte would have made a more pernicious

& despotic Tyrant than Caligula.' On German monetarism see Richard T. Gray, 'Hypersign, Hypermoney, Hypermarket: Adam Muller's Theory of Money and Romantic Semiotics', *New Literary History* 31 (2000): 293–314 and 'Economic Romanticism: Monetary Nationalism in Johann Gottlieb Fichte and Adam Muller', *Eighteenth-Century Studies* 36 (2003): 535–57.

60. For more on the political background to the *Statesman's Manual* see Daniel Fried, 'The Politics of the Coleridgean Symbol', *Studies in English Literature, 1500–1900* 46 (2006): 763–79.
61. Samuel Taylor Coleridge, *Lay Sermons*, ed. R. J. White, vol. 6 of *The Collected Works of Samuel Taylor Coleridge* (Princeton: Princeton University Press, 1972), 5.
62. Coleridge, *Lay Sermons*, 8.
63. Coleridge, *Lay Sermons*, 223.
64. Coleridge, *Lay Sermons*, 212.
65. Coleridge, *Lay Sermons*, 216–17.
66. Coleridge, *Lay Sermons*, 223.
67. Coleridge, *Lay Sermons*, 229.
68. Coleridge, *Lay Sermons*, 217.
69. See Charles Taylor's definition of secularism: 'faith, even for the staunchest believer, is one human possibility among others', *Secular Age*, 3.
70. Coleridge, *Lay Sermons*, 15.
71. Coleridge, *Lay Sermons*, 20
72. Coleridge, *Lay Sermons*, 18. Coleridge had derived the notion of the copula and of relational possibility from Schelling, who argued that the decision that something 'is' is an act of reason not merely of sense. Yet, as an act of reason, the perception of being also avoids any firm commitment to identity as that decision can be changed according to the condition of the object's being.
73. Coleridge, *Lay Sermons*, 20–1.
74. On Berkeley's political economy see T. W. Hutchison, 'Berkeley's Querist and its Place in the Economic Thought of the Eighteenth Century', *British Journal for the Philosophy of Science* 4 (1953): 52–77; Frank Petrella, 'George Berkeley's Theory of Economic Policy and Classical Economic Liberalism', *Southern Economic Journal* 32 (1966): 275–84.
75. Cited in *The Friend*, I.242.
76. Coleridge, *The Friend*, I.243.
77. Coleridge, *The Friend*, I.233–34.
78. Coleridge, *The Friend*, I.229–30.
79. Ian Balfour, channeling Paul de Man, goes so far as to suggest that there is no such thing as a symbol as Coleridge conceives it, except as the desired end of its metonymic chain. See *The Rhetoric of Romantic Prophecy* (Stanford: Stanford University Press, 2002), 250–86. For the theological background to the metonymic underpinnings of the symbol, see Nicholas Halmi, *The Genealogy of the Romantic Symbol* (Oxford: Oxford University Press, 2007).
80. Coleridge, *Lay Sermons*, 29
81. Coleridge, *Lay Sermons*, 28.
82. Coleridge, *Lay Sermons*, 29. For more on Coleridge and the relationality of the symbol, see Halmi, *Genealogy*, 121–32 and David Aram Kaiser, *Romanticism, Aestheticism, and Nationalism* (Cambridge: Cambridge University Press, 1999), 30–6.

83. Coleridge, *Marginalia*, 5: 687.
84. The Taylor brothers wrote more than 50 pamphlets and one didactic poem entitled *Money for the Million*. See John Taylor, *Money for the Million, or Straw for the Tale of Bricks* (London: Tailant and Allen, 1857).
85. Heather Jackson, *Romantic Readers: The Evidence of Marginalia* (New Haven: Yale University Press, 2005), 256.
86. Samuel Taylor Coleridge, *On the Constitution of Church and State*, ed. John Barrell. *The Collected Works of Samuel Taylor Coleridge*, vol. 10 (Princeton: Princeton University Press, 1972), 12.
87. William Hazlitt, 'Mr. Coleridge's Lay Sermon', *The Examiner* (September 8, 1816), repr. in *Political Essays, with Sketches of Public Characters* (London: Hone, 1819), 117–18. For a full discussion of the circumstances surrounding Hazlitt's review, see Robert Keith Lapp, *Contest for Cultural Authority: Hazlitt, Coleridge, and the Distresses of the Regency* (Detroit: Wayne State University Press, 1999), 49–66.
88. Hazlitt, 'Mr. Coleridge's Lay Sermon', 118
89. Hazlitt, 'Mr. Coleridge's Lay Sermon', 119.
90. Hazlitt, 'Mr. Coleridge's Lay Sermon', 120.
91. Hazlitt, 'The Speeches of Brougham and Western', *Political Essays*, 105.
92. William Hazlitt, *Essay on the Principles of Human Action* (London, 1805), 25.
93. Jacques Khalip argues that Hazlitt rejects the 'cost-benefit analysis' inherent in utilitarianism in order to redefine 'subjectivity' as 'a network of interlacing temporal strands which do not so much materialize personhood as fantasize it into being' rendering subjects essentially interchangeable – a condition that Hazlitt's occasional essays also expose. 'Virtual Conduct: Disinterested Agency in Hazlitt and Keats', *English Literary History* 73 (2006): 885–912 (890).
94. Hazlitt, 'On the Want of Money', in *Table Talk: Opinions on Books, Men, and Things* (New York: Wiley and Putnam, 1845), 9.
95. Hazlitt, 'On the Want of Money', 10.
96. See Frederick Burwick, 'De Quincey on Coleridge', in *Coleridge's Afterlives*, ed. James Vigus and Jane Wright (Basingstoke: Palgrave Macmillan, 2008), 36–53; Daniel Sanjiv Roberts, *Revisionary Gleam: De Quincey, Coleridge, and the High Romantic Argument* (Liverpool: Liverpool University Press, 2000).
97. Thomas De Quincey, 'Papers on the Bank of England [I] Introduction', in *The Works of Thomas De Quincey, Volume 20: Prefaces &c. to the Collected Editions, Published Addenda, Marginalia, Manuscript Adenda, Undatable Manuscripts*, ed. Frederick Burwick et al. (London: Pickering & Chatto, 2003), 152.
98. Thomas De Quincey, 'Resumption of Cash Payments by the Bank of England', *Works of Thomas De Quincey, Volume 1: Writings 1799–1820*, ed. Barry Symonds (London: Pickering & Chatto, 2000), 338.
99. De Quincey, 'Paper of the Bank of England IV', in *Works* 20, 191.
100. De Quincey, 'Ricardo and Adam Smith', in *The Collected Writings of Thomas De Quincey*, ed. David Masson (Edinburgh, 1890), 9:115.
101. 'Ricardo and Adam Smith', 9:117.
102. Margaret Russett, *De Quincey's Romanticism: Canonical Minority and the Forms of Transmission* (Cambridge: Cambridge University Press, 1997).
103. De Quincey, 'Ricardo and Adam Smith', 9:117.
104. Josephine McDonagh, 'Debt and Desire: De Quincey and the Psychology of Economics', *Wordsworth Circle* 25 (1994): 86–89. Gordon Bigelow, *Fiction,*

Famine, and the Rise of Economics in Victorian Britain and Ireland (Cambridge: Cambridge University Press, 2003), 100–3.

105. Henry Nelson Coleridge, Preface to 'Table Talk' (1835), in *Table Talk and Omniana of Samuel Taylor Coleridge*, ed. Thomas Ashe (London: Bell, 1884), 11.
106. H. Coleridge, Preface to 'Table Talk', 13.
107. See Alan Vardy, 'Her Father's "Remains": Sara Coleridge's Edition of *Essays on His Own Times*', in *Nervous Reactions: Victorian Recollections of Romanticism*, ed. Joel Faflak and Julia Wright (Albany: SUNY Press, 2004), 207–27. On growth as a fundamental tenet of the 'historicity' of Romanticism, see Siskin, *Historicity of Romantic Discourse*.
108. Derwent Coleridge, 'Preface' to Samuel Taylor Coleridge, *The Lay Sermons* (London: Moxon, 1852), vi.
109. *Samuel Taylor Coleridge: The Critical Heritage Volume 2: 1834–1900*, ed. J. R. de. J. Jackson (London: Routledge, 1991), 131.
110. *Coleridge: The Critical Heritage*, 131.
111. Richard Cronin, *Romantic Victorians: English Literature, 1824–1840* (Basingstoke: Palgrave Macmillan, 2007), 149.
112. On Sterling's theology see Anthony John Harding, *Coleridge and the Inspired Word* (Montreal: McGill-Queen's University Press, 1985), 113–37.
113. Hilton, *Age of Atonement*, 48.
114. Cronin, *Romantic Victorians*, 148.
115. *Athenaeum* 1828, 218. Cited in Cronin, *Romantic Victorians*, 148.

4 Monetary Forgery and Romantic Poetics

1. Phillip Handler, 'The Limits of Discretion: Forgery and the Jury at the Old Bailey 1818–21', in *'The Dearest Birthright of the People of England': The Jury in the History of the Common Law*, ed. John W. Cairns and Grant McLeod (Oxford and Portland, OR: Hart, 2002), 155–72 (156).
2. Carl Wennerlind, 'The Death Penalty as Monetary Policy: The Practice and Punishment of Monetary Crime, 1690–1830', *History of Political Economy* 36 (2004): 129–59.
3. Randall McGowan, 'From Pillory to Gallows: The Punishment of Forgery in the Age of the Financial Revolution', *Past and Present* 165 (1999): 107–40 (112–13).
4. Johnson wrote several letters defending Dodd and attempting to defer his execution. See James Boswell, *Life of Johnson*, ed. George Birkbeck Hill (New York: Harper, 1891), 3.158–68.
5. William Dodd, *The Convict's Address to his Unhappy Brethren* (London, 1777), 26.
6. Dodd, *Convict's Address*, 9.
7. Boswell, *Life of Johnson*, 3.189.
8. William Dodd, *Thoughts in Prison: in Five Parts. To Which Are Added, His Last Prayers, Written in the Night Before His Death and Other Miscellaneous Pieces* (London, 1777). See Christina Lupton, *Knowing Books: Consciousness of Mediation in Eighteenth-Century Britain* (Philadelphia: University of Pennsylvania Press, 2012), 101–10.
9. Andrew Motion, *Wainwight the Poisoner* (London: Faber, 2001).

10. On literary forgery in the Romantic period see Paul Baines, *The House of Forgery in Eighteenth-Century Britain* (Aldershot: Ashgate, 1999); Nick Groom, *The Forger's Shadow: How Forgery Changed the Course of Literature* (London: Picador, 2002); Tillar Mazzeo, *Plagiarism and Literary Property in the Romantic Period* (Philadelphia: University of Pennsylvania Press, 2007); and Margaret Russett, *Fictions and Fakes: Forging Romantic Authenticity, 1760–1845* (Cambridge: Cambridge University Press, 2006).
11. Records of the correspondence between the Bank, their solicitors, and those in the prisons and hulks can be found in the Bank of England Archive Freshfield Files Section 25.
12. Fetter, *Monetary Orthodoxy*, 72.
13. Virginia Hewitt and J. M. Keyworth, *As Good as Gold: 300 Years of British Bank Note Design* (London: British Museum Publications, 1994), 67–81.
14. Virginia Hewitt, 'Applegarth's Answers: Anti-forgery Note Designs for the Bank of England, 1818–1821', in *Proceedings of the XIth International Numismatic Congress Organized for the 150th Anniversary of the Société Royale de Numismatique de Belgique*, September 8–13, 1991, Brussels, ed. Tony Hackins and Ghislaine Moucharte, Vol. 4 (Louvain-la-Neuve: International Numismatic Commission, 1991), 222.
15. Hewitt and Keyworth, *As Good As Gold*, 65.
16. Henry Brougham, 'Increase of Forgeries', *Edinburgh Review*, 28 (1818): 203–15 (205).
17. Brougham, 'Increase of Forgeries', 208.
18. Brougham, 'Increase of Forgeries', 212.
19. *Rotten-Rag, Manufactory!!! The Threadneedle-Street Catechism*, 7th edn. (London: Fairburn, 1818), 3.
20. *Rotten-Rag, Manufactory!!!*, 7–8.
21. T. J. Wooler, *Black Dwarf* (London, 19 January 1819): 20.
22. Handler, 'Limits of Discretion', 161.
23. William Hone, *John Wilke's Catechism* THAT IS TO SAY, *An Instruction, to be learned of every Person before he be brought to be confirmed a Placeman or Pensioner by the Minister* (London, 1817), 7–8.
24. Marcus Wood includes Hone's corrected manuscript for the *Catechism* in *Radical Satire*, 272–90.
25. On Hone and other radicals' debunking of prosecutions see Gilmartin, *Print Politics* and Victoria Myers, 'Blasphemy Trials and *The Cenci*: Parody as Performative', in *Spheres of Action: Speech and Performance in Romantic Culture*, ed. Alexander Dick and Angela Esterhammer (Toronto: University of Toronto Press, 2009), 100–23.
26. Cited in V. A. C. Gatrell, *The Hanging Tree: Execution and the English People, 1770–1868* (Oxford: Oxford University Press, 1994), 187–8. See also Jeffrey N. Cox, *Politics and Poetics in the Cockney School: Keats, Shelley, Hunt and their Circle* (Cambridge: Cambridge University Press, 1998), 203.
27. For the Christian undercurrents of Hone's satire see Hole, *Pulpits, Politics*, 214–28.
28. 'Parlimentary Proceeding', *The Examiner* 110 (February 4, 1810), 66.
29. See for instance, 'Forged Bank Notes', *The Examiner* 291 (July 25, 1813), 477–8; 'Bank Notes', *The Examiner* 561 (September 27, 1818), 620–1.
30. *The Examiner* 528 (February 8, 1818), 92–3.
31. 'Report on Bank-Note Forgery', *The Examiner* 581 (February 14, 1819), 107.
32. 'Report on Bank-Note Forgery', *The Examiner* 581 (February 14, 1819), 108.

33. Kenneth Neil Cameron, 'Shelley, Cobbett, and the National Debt', *Journal of English and Germanic Philology* 42 (1943): 197–209. See also Brantlinger, *Fictions of State*, 116–17; Jerrold Hogle, *Shelley's Process: Radical Transference and the Development of His Major Works* (Oxford: Oxford University Press, 1988), 236; Connell, *Romanticism, Economics*, 227.
34. Percy Shelley, 'A Philosophical View of Reform', in *The Complete Works of Percy Bysshe Shelley*, ed. Roger Inpen and Walter E. Peck (New York: Gordian, 1965), 7: 26.
35. *Shelley's Poetry and Prose*, ed. Donald A Reiman and Neil Freistat (New York: Norton, 2002), 44.
36. Shelley, *Complete Works*, 10: 20. Claire Clairemont was reading Cobbett while living with the Shelleys in the springs of 1819 and 1820. See Cameron, 'Shelley, Cobbett', 199.
37. Cited in Cox, *Poetry and Politics*, 203.
38. For a full reading of the play as a reflection on the equivocations between truth and falsehood evident in the forgery trials see Linda Brigham, 'Count Cenci's Abysmal Credit', *Texas Studies in Language and Literature* 38 (1996): 340–58.
39. *Shelley's Poetry and Prose*, 317, ll. 37.
40. Shelley, *Complete Works* 8: 158.
41. Shelley, *Complete Works*, 10: 120.
42. Terrence Allan Hoagwood, *Skepticism and Ideology: Shelley's Political Prose and its Philosophical Context from Bacon to Marx* (Iowa City: University of Iowa Press, 1988), 189.
43. Cox, *Politics and Poetics*, 208.
44. Jerrold Hogle, 'Shelley and the Conditions of Meaning', in *Evaluating Shelley*, ed. Timothy Clark and Jerrold E. Hogle (Edinburgh: University of Edinburgh Press, 1996), 48–74 (65–6).
45. See Finn, *Character of Credit*.
46. Hogle, 'Shelley and the Condition of Meaning', 67.
47. *Shelley's Poetry and Prose*, 318, ll. 75–6, 81–2.
48. *Shelley's Poetry and Prose*, 321, ll. 176–83.
49. Steven Jones, *Shelley's Satire: Violence, Exhortation, and Authority* (DeKalb: Northern Illinois University Press, 1994), 119.
50. *Shelley's Poetry and Prose*, 322, ll. 217–21.
51. *Shelley's Poetry and Prose*, 322, ll. 223–4.
52. *Shelley's Poetry and Prose*, 322, l. 226.
53. For *The Mask of Anarchy* as a dramatic work, see Cox, *Poetry and Politics*, 143–4.
54. *Shelley's Poetry and Prose*, 322–3, ll. 230–42.
55. *Shelley's Poetry and Prose*, 323, ll. 246–57.
56. *Shelley's Poetry and Prose*, 323, ll. 250–2.
57. *Shelley's Poetry and Prose*, 321, ll. 188–95.
58. *Shelley's Poetry and Prose*, 324, ll. 297–8.
59. Shelley, *Complete Works*, 7: 49.
60. Shelley, *Complete Works*, 7: 49 (emphasis added).
61. Shelley, *Complete Works*, 7: 49 (emphasis added).
62. Shelley, *Complete Works*, 7: 338.
63. Shelley, *Complete Works*, 7: 10.
64. Shelley, *Complete Works*, 7: 12.
65. Shelley, *Complete Works*, 7: 20.

66. Shelley, *Complete Works*, 7: 10. Connell has linked this passage with others in Shelley's *oeuvre* demonstrating his admiration for Jeremy Bentham and William Godwin over and above Malthus. See *Economics, Romanticism*, 217–23. That Shelley would align himself in the 'View' with philosophical radicalism – a movement that also includes Ricardo – suggests again that his reflections on forgery in the *Mask* belong to the broader context of economic and political critique that I have already outlined. Shelley's views on economic reason and monetary standardization in the 'View' and *The Mask of Anarchy* are not precisely the same as those proposed by Bentham or Ricardo. Shelley's antagonism toward political economists – including Bentham – would become clear in the *Defence of Poetry*, which also contains many passages from the unpublished 'View'.
67. *Shelley's Poetry and Prose*, 202.
68. *Shelley's Poetry and Prose*, 201.
69. *Shelley's Poetry and Prose*, 134.
70. *Shelley's Poetry and Prose*, 134–5.
71. *Shelley's Poetry and Prose*, 135.
72. *Shelley's Poetry and Prose*, 135.
73. *Shelley's Poetry and Prose*, 135.
74. On Haydon, see Finn, *Character of Credit*, 67–76.
75. *Shelley's Poetry and Prose*, 240.
76. *Shelley's Poetry and Prose*, 239.
77. *Shelley's Poetry and Prose*, 235, 2.1.13–19.
78. *Shelley's Poetry and Prose*, 259, 3.3.5–6.
79. *Shelley's Poetry and Prose*, 265, 3.4.54–9. On the lyricism of *Prometheus Unbound*, see Maureen McLane, *Romanticism and the Human Sciences* (Cambridge: Cambridge University Press, 2000), 152–6.
80. *Shelley's Poetry and Prose*, 313, ll. 196–210.
81. I am largely in agreement with Robert Mitchell's reading of Shelley's poetics as forging a 'utopian' alternative to banking and its economy. See *Sympathy and the State*, 169. Yet, I am less optimistic than he is about the potential for Romantic poetry – even Shelley's – to disentangle itself from the credit economy it lampoons and decries.
82. See Chandler, 'The Pope Controversy: Romantic Poetics and the English Canon', *Critical Inquiry* 10 (1984): 481–509 (482–5).
83. Connell has reminded us of Peacock's extensive connections among the circle of philosophical radicals including Bentham and around which Shelley had earlier associated himself. See *Romanticism, Economics, and the Question of Culture*, 210–33. Robert Mitchell has noted further the way Peacock entwined the language of the radicals' critique of the paper money system, the same rhetoric that Shelley had employed in the 'Philosophical View', to attack poetry. 'Peacock presented the poets as the original of the financial speculator ... poetry began as a mechanism that allowed kings to extend their prestige and "credit".' See *Sympathy and the State*, 196.
84. Stephanie Kuduk Weiner, *Republican Politics and English Poetry, 1789–1874* (New York: Palgrave Macmillan, 2005), 35–65.
85. Cited in Kuduk Weiner, *Republican Politics*, 39.
86. *Shelley's Poetry and Prose*, 503.

87. Thomas Love Peacock, 'The Four Ages of Poetry', in *The Works of Thomas Love Peacock* (London: Richard Bentley, 1875), 3.325.
88. See St. Clair, *Reading Nation*, 319–22.
89. *Shelley's Poetry and Prose*, 500.
90. William Hazlitt in *Shelley: The Critical Heritage*, ed. James E. Barcus (London: Routledge, 1975), 335.
91. 'Remarks on Shelley's *Adonais*', in *Shelley: The Critical Heritage*, ed. Barcus, 301.
92. Robert Kaufman, 'Negatively Capable Dialectics: Keats, Vendler, Adorno, and the Theory of the Avant-Garde', *Critical Inquiry* 27 (2001): 354–84 (382, 368–9).
93. *The Letters of John Keats 1814–1821*, ed. Hyder Edward Rollins (Cambridge, MA: Harvard University Press, 1958), 2.322.
94. Cox, *Poetry and Politics*, 190–4.
95. Keats, *Complete Poems*, ed. Stillinger, 83, ll. 777–80.
96. Keats, *Letters*, ed. Rollins, 1.219.
97. The circumstances surrounding Keats' financial difficulties are documented at length in Robert Gittings, *The Keats Inheritance* (London: Heinemann, 1964).
98. For economic readings of the 1819 romances see Cox, *Poetics and Politics*, 187–226; Marjorie Levinson, *Keats's Life of Allegory: The Origins of a Style* (Oxford: Blackwell, 1988), 255–9; Kurt Heinzelman, 'Self-Interest and the Politics of Composition in Keats's Isabella', *English Literary History* 55 (1988): 159–93; Porsha Fermanis, 'Isabella, Lamia, and Merry Old England', *Essays in Criticism* 56 (2006): 139–62; Rowlinson, *Real Money and Romanticism*, 100–55.
99. On the Ode's hyper- and thus anti-referentiality see Ian Jack, *Keats and the Mirror of Art* (Oxford: Clarendon Press, 1967), 214–24; Theresa M. Kelley, 'Keats, Ekphrasis, and History', in *Keats and History*, ed. Nicholas Roe (Cambridge: Cambridge University Press, 1995), 212–37.
100. Cox, *Poetry and Politics*, 151.
101. For Benjamin's take on film and its openness to dialectical analysis (akin to Freud) see 'The Work of Art in the Age of Mechanical Reproduction', in *Illuminations*, trans. Harry Zohn, ed. Hannah Arendt (New York: Schocken, 1968), 235–6.
102. Cox, *Poetry and Politics*, 149. Grant Scott discusses the *Annals'* importance in (and Keats' contributions to) ongoing debates about the 'truthfulness' of the Elgin Marbles. See 'Beautiful Ruins: The Elgin Marbles Sonnet in its Historical and Generic Contexts', *Keats–Shelley Journal* 39 (1990): 123–50.
103. See 'Preface' to *Annals of the Fine Arts* 3 (1818): iii–viii.
104. Keats, *Complete Poems*, 252, ll. 176–8.
105. Keats, *Complete Poems*, 252, ll. 186–9.
106. Keats, *Complete Poems*, 254, ll. 277–81.
107. Keats, *Complete Poems*, 266–7, ll. 28, 63.
108. Keats, *Complete Poems*, 268, ll. 111–12.
109. Tilottama Rajan, 'Keats, Poetry, and "The Absence of Work"', *Modern Philology* 95 (1998): 334–51 (342).
110. K. K. Ruthven, 'Keats and "Dea Moneta"', *Studies in Romanticism* 15 (1976): 445–59. Keats' financial difficulties are explained at length by Robert Gittings in *The Keats Inheritance*.
111. Keats, *Complete Poems*, 362–3, ll. 61–80.
112. Ruthven, 'Keats and "Dea Moneta"', 458.

113. Lord Byron, *Letters and Journals*, ed. Leslie Marchand (London: Belknap, 1976), 8.12.
114. Lord Byron, *Don Juan*, in *The Complete Poetical Works*, ed. Jerome J. McGann (Oxford: Clarendon Press, 1986), vol. 5, 495, ll. 4–7.
115. Byron, *Don Juan*, 495, ll. 14–15.
116. Byron, *Don Juan*, 496, ll. 25–32.
117. Byron, *Don Juan*, 496, ll. 37–40.
118. Byron, *Don Juan*, 496, ll. 57, 60.
119. Byron, *Don Juan*, 501, ll. 160.
120. Byron, *Don Juan*, 501, ll. 161–8.
121. Byron, *Don Juan*, 498, ll. 106–8.
122. Lord Byron, *The Age of Bronze*, in *The Complete Poetical Works*, ed. McGann, vol. 6, 17, l. 537.
123. Byron, *The Age of Bronze*, 19, ll. 578–81.
124. Byron, *The Age of Bronze*, 20, l. 627.
125. Byron, *The Age of Bronze*, 19, l. 598.
126. Jerome Christensen, *Lord Byron's Strength: Romantic Writing and Commercial Society* (Baltimore: Johns Hopkins University Press, 1995). Byron's defense of Pope in the controversies surrounding his 'morality' is a good indication of how Byron understands 'strength' not entirely as a bodily virtue (as power) but also as an intellectual and indeed textual quality. It is strength that keeps an imitation from being merely a copy. See Chandler, 'The Pope Controversy'.
127. See Tom Mole, *Byron's Romantic Celebrity: Industrial Culture and the Hermeneutics of Intimacy* (Basingstoke: Palgrave Macmillan, 2007).
128. Thomas Moore, *Odes Upon Corn, Cash, and Catholics, and Other Matters, Selected from the Columns of the Times Journal* (London: Longman, 1828), 4–6. On the title page appeared the logo: 'None but little minds fear little books.'
129. John Sutherland, 'The British Book Trade and the Crash of 1826', *The Library* 9 (1987): 148–61.
130. Peacock, *Paper Money Lyrics*, in *The Works of Thomas Love Peacock*, vol. 3.222.
131. Peacock, *Paper Money Lyrics*, 3.231.
132. Peacock, *Paper Money Lyrics*, 3.221.
133. Peacock, *Paper Money Lyrics*, 3.221–2.
134. *Complete Poetical Works of Thomas Hood* (London: G. P. Putnam, 1878), 233.

5 Standard Novels

1. Maria Edgeworth, *Letters from England 1813–1844*, ed. Christina Colvin (Oxford: Clarendon Press, 1971), 364–5. According to Ricardo's biographer, David Weatherall, the head was genuine, its provenance finally established in 1934. *David Ricardo: A Biography* (Boston: Martinus Nijhoff, 1976), 122 n4.
2. Edgeworth, *Letters from England*, 366.
3. That coins bearing Cromwell's image did pass current, even after the Restoration, raises further questions about the legitimacy of the 'ancient' standard of the realm minted by the Stuarts and Hanoverians and defended by politicians and economists alike in the early nineteenth century. Coins bearing Cromwell's image were issued during the Interregnum as part of an effort to persuade him to take the crown. What is more, many of these coins

circulated as money *after* the Restoration when Cromwell was being pilloried (literally) as a traitor.

4. On Edgeworth and banking see Gallagher, *Nobody's Story* and Mark Canuel, *Religion, Toleration, and British Writing, 1790–1830* (Cambridge: Cambridge University Press, 2002).
5. Richard A. Austen-Leigh, *Austen Papers, 1704–1856* (Spottiswode: Ballantyne, 1942), 211.
6. *Jane Austen's Letters to Her Sister Cassandra and Others*, ed. R. W. Chapman (Oxford: Clarendon Press, 1932), 489.
7. For a review of this 'Romantic' turn in Austen studies see Miles, 'New Historicism, New Austen, New Romanticism'.
8. For a nuanced and complex reading of Austen's relation to the national tale by way of their common 'gothic' form, see Miranda Burgess, *British Fiction and the Production of Social Order, 1740–1820* (Cambridge: Cambridge University Press, 2000), 150–85.
9. Marylin Butler, *Jane Austen and the War of Ideas* (Oxford: Clarendon Press, 1974).
10. For a reading of the Lydian myth and its relation to economic theory see Marc Shell, *The Economy of Literature* (Baltimore: Johns Hopkins University Press, 1978), 11–62.
11. Poovey calls Austen's experiment a 'gestural aesthetic'. See *Genres*, 357–72 passim.
12. Poovey, *Genres*, 371.
13. Poovey, *Genres*, 372.
14. Developed primarily in Ireland, largely in response to the catastrophe of the 1798 Rebellion, and latterly in Scotland, the national tale combined elements of domestic novels, romance, travel-writing, and antiquarianism to assert if not the compatibility of modern forms of value (represented by English landownership and contractual law) and archaic traditions (represented by Gaelic and Highland culture) then possibly their not-quite peaceful co-existence in cosmopolitan Britain. The tenuousness is important. What marks the national tale generically is the way it fails to convert Britain's various cultural and regional identities into a comprehensive national unit. The novels of Sydney Owenson are usually thought to define the paradigm of the national tale; her marriage plots convey both the desirability of union and its inevitable tensions. See for instance, Mary Jean Corbett, *Allegories of Union in Irish and English Writing, 1790–1870: Politics, History, and the Family from Edgeworth to Arnold* (Cambridge: Cambridge University Press, 2000); Ina Ferris, *The Romantic National Tale and the Question of Ireland* (Cambridge: Cambridge University Press, 2007); Katie Trumpener, *Bardic Nationalism: The Romantic Novel and the British Empire* (Princeton: Princeton University Press, 1997).
15. Maria Edgeworth, *The Absentee*, ed. W. J. McCormack and Kim Walker (Oxford: Oxford University Press, 1988), 135.
16. Edgeworth, *The Abesentee*, 161–2.
17. Edgeworth, *The Abesentee*, 162.
18. Edgeworth, *The Absentee*, 261.
19. Siskin, *Work of Writing*, 181.
20. Ernest Gellner, *Nations and Nationalism*, ed. R. I. Moore (Oxford: Basil Blackwell, 1983), 2.

21. Siskin, *Work of Writing*, 182–3.
22. Samuel Richardson, *Pamela*, ed. Thomas Keymer and Alice Wakely (Oxford: Oxford University Press, 2001), 5.
23. Richardson, *Pamela*, 8. For the relation between Richardson's novelistic discourse and the emerging systems of political economy see Burgess, *British Fiction*, 25–72.
24. On the economic valences of it-narratives, see the essays collected in Mark Blackwell, ed., *The Secret Life of Things: Animals, Objects, and It-Narratives in Eighteenth-Century England* (Cranbury: Bucknell University Press, 2007).
25. Robert Miles, 'What is a Romantic Novel?' *Novel: A Forum on Fiction* 34 (2001): 180–201.
26. Siskin, *Work of Writing*, 186.
27. See texts cited above, note 14 on Irish context. For the novel's relation to Scottish nationalism around and after the 1745 Jacobite rebellion, see Ian Duncan, *Scott's Shadow: The Novel in Romantic Edinburgh* (Princeton: Princeton University Press, 2007) and Leith Davis, *Acts of Union: Scotland and the Literary Negotiation of the British Nation 1707–1830* (Stanford: Stanford University Press, 1998).
28. My account of the Bank of Ireland and the Irish Pound Report comes from L. M. Cullen, 'The Irish Economy in the Eighteenth Century', in *The Formation of the Bank of Ireland*, ed. L. M. Cullen (Cork: Mercier, 1969), 9–21; Cormac O Grada, 'Reassessing the Irish Pound Report of 1804', *Bulletin of Economic Research* 43 (1991): 5–19; G. E. Boyle and P. T. Geary, 'The Irish Currency Report of 1804', *Central Bank and Financial Services Authority of Ireland Quarterly Bulletin* (2004): 107–24.
29. For the details of the establishment of the Bank of Ireland, see T. K. Whitaker, 'Origins and Consolidation, 1783–1826', in *Bicentenary Essays: Bank of Ireland 1783–1983*, ed. F. S. L. Lyons (London: Gill and Macmillan, 1983), 11–29.
30. This was one of the complaints levied against the Irish banking system by Lord Peter King in *Thoughts on the Restriction of Specie at the Banks of England and Ireland* (London, 1803). See Boyle and Geary, 'The Irish Currency Report of 1804', 114.
31. Henry Parnell, *The Principles of Currency and Exchange* (London, 1809), 72.
32. Susan Manning, 'Antiquarianism, the Scottish Science and Man, and the Emergence of Modern Disciplinarity', in *Scotland and the Borders of Romanticism*, ed. Leith Davis, Ian Duncan, and Janet Sorenson (Cambridge: Cambridge University Press, 2004), 57–76 (63).
33. See Barbara Benedict, *Curiosity: A Cultural History of Early Modern Inquiry* (Chicago: University of Chicago Press, 2002). In *The Rise of English Nationalism: A Cultural History, 1740–1830* (Basingstoke: Macmillan, 1987), 111–14, Gerald Newman argues that the rise and spread of antiquarian societies contributed to the development of the modern nationalism in Britain.
34. Yoon Sun Lee, 'A Divided Inheritance: Scott's Antiquarian Novel and the British Nation', *English Literary History* 64 (1997): 537–67 (539).
35. Seamus Deane, *Strange Country: Modernity and Nationhood in Irish Writing Since 1790* (Oxford: Clarendon Press, 1997), 21.
36. Thomas Snelling, a London coin dealer who became one of the leading numismatists of the century, published several collections of 'plates' all with extensive commentary.

37. On serialization in nationalist formation see Benedict Anderson, 'Nationalism, Identity, and the World-in-Motion: On the Logics of Seriality', in *Cosmopolitics: Thinking and Feeling Beyond the Nation*, ed. Bruce Robbins and Pheng Cheah (Minneapolis: University of Minnesota Press, 1998), 117–33.
38. Sir James Ware, *The History and Antiquities of Ireland* (Dublin, 1705), 71.
39. Thomas Snelling, *A View of the Silver Coin and Coinage of Scotland* (Edinburgh, 1774), 5.
40. Ebenzer Marshall, *A History of the Union of Scotland and England Stating the Circumstances Which Brought that Event Forward to a Conclusion and the Advantages Resulting From it To the Scots* (Edinburgh, 1799), 213–14.
41. Modern historians have agreed, though economic factors remain somewhat supplementary to broader arguments about national identity. For a review of the ongoing debates, see Christopher A. Whately, *Scottish Society, 1707–1830: Beyond Jacobitism, Towards Industrialization* (Manchester: Manchester University Press, 2000), 48–52, 87.
42. Edward Wakefield, *Account of Ireland, Statistical and Political* (London: Longman, 1811), vi.
43. Ferris, *Romantic National Tale*, 21.
44. Reprinted in 1819 and significantly expanded in 1840, Rudings' *Annals* is still used as a key guide to the history of British coinage and is still highly regarded as a reference tool among coin collectors.
45. Roger Rudings, *Annals of the Coinage of Great Britain and Its Dependencies*, 3rd edn. (London: Hearne, 1840), xiv.
46. Rudings, *Annals*, xiv.
47. Lee Erickson, 'The Economy of Novel Reading: Jane Austen and the Circulating Library', in *The Economy of Literary Form* (Baltimore: Johns Hopkins University Press, 1996), 125–41.
48. For Austen's comments on More see *Jane Austen's Letters to her Sister*, 256, 410. See also Peter Garside and Elizabeth McDonald, 'Evangelicalism and *Mansfield Park*', *Trivium* 10 (1975): 34–50; David Monaghan, '*Mansfield Park* and Evangelicalism: A Reassessment', *Nineteenth-Century Fiction* 3 (1978): 215–30; Mary Waldron, 'The Frailties of Fanny: *Mansfield Park* and the Evangelical Movement', *Eighteenth-Century Fiction* 6 (1994): 259–81.
49. A. Mellor, *Mothers of the Nation: Women's Political Writing in England, 1780–1832* (Bloomington: Indiana University Press, 1996), 32–4. See also T. Haskell, 'Capitalism and the Origins of the Humanitarian Sensibility', parts 1 and 2, in *The Antislavery Debate: Capitalism and Abolitionism as a Problem in Historical Interpretation*, ed. T. Bender (Berkeley: University of California Press, 1992), 107–60.
50. Hannah More, *Strictures on the Modern System of Female Education with A View of the Principles and Conduct Prevalent Among Women of Rank and Fortune* (London: Cadell, 1799) and *Practical Piety, or, The Influence of the Religion of the Heart on the Conduct of Modern Life* (London: Cadell, 1811).
51. Hannah More, *Coelebs in Search of a Wife: Comprehending Observations of Domestic Habits and Manners, Religion and Morals* (London: Cadell, 1809), 191–2.
52. Though hardly a Jacobin – on the contrary – More was nevertheless the object of some critical circumspection in the loyalist press, notably the *Anti-Jacobin Review*, which took her to task for promulgating charity on such a wide and abstract canvas. Charity was best administered within the confines

of the estate where it could also form the basis for a respect for the benevolence of a hierarchical order. See Anne Stott, *Hannah More: The First Victorian* (Oxford: Oxford University Press, 2003), 243.

53. For a comparison of Hannah More's narrative strategies and Austen's narrative persona see Emily Rena-Dozier, 'Hannah More and the Invention of Narrative Authority', *English Literary History* 71 (2004): 209–27.
54. Jane Austen, *Mansfield Park*, ed. John Wiltshire, in *The Cambridge Edition of the Works of Jane Austen* (Cambridge: Cambridge University Press, 2005), 478.
55. On absenteeism in *Mansfield Park* in both its religious and economic connotations see Gabrielle D. V. White, *Jane Austen in the Context of Abolition: 'A fling at the slave trade'* (Basingstoke: Palgrave Macmillan, 2006), 22–7.
56. Austen, *Mansfield Park*, 101.
57. Austen, *Mansfield Park*, 101–2.
58. See Colin Jager, '*Mansfield Park* and the End of Natural Theology', *Modern Language Quarterly* 63 (2002): 31–63.
59. Austen, *Mansfield Park*, 86.
60. Austen, *Mansfield Park*, 172.
61. Thomas Clarkson, *History of the Progress and Accomplishment of the Abolition of the Slave Trade* (Philadelphia: Parke, 1808).
62. Responding to Edward Said's claim in *Culture and Imperialism* (New York: Vintage, 1994) that *Mansfield Park* demonstrates Austen's tacit complicity with the slavery-based transatlantic capitalism of her time, most critics have argued instead that Austen was in *Mansfield Park* registering a moral critique of slavery; see for instance You-Me Park and Rajeswari Sunder Rajan, eds., *The Postcolonial Jane Austen* (New York: Routledge, 2004).
63. George E. Boulukos, 'The Politics of Silence: *Mansfield Park* and the Amelioration of Slavery', *Novel: A Forum on Fiction* 39 (2006): 361–83. See also Richard Allen, 'The British Nation and the Colonies: *Mansfield Park*', in *Literature and Nation: Britain and India, 1800–1900*, ed. Richard Allen and Harish Trivedi (New York: Routledge, 2000), 43–54 and Christopher Leslie Brown, *Moral Capital: Foundations of British Abolitionism* (Chapel Hill: University of North Carolina Press, 2006).
64. William Galperin, *The Historical Austen* (Philadelphia: University of Pennsylvania Press, 2003), 161–6.
65. C. W. Pasley, *Essay on the Military Policy and Institutions of the British Empire* (London: Edmund Lloyd, 1811).
66. Claudius Buchanan, *Christian Researches in Asia with Notices of the Translation of the Scriptures* (New York, 1812). For context see Karen Chancey, 'The Star in the East: The Controversy over Christian Missions to India, 1805–1813', *Historian* 60 (1998): 507–23.
67. Austen, *Letters to her Sister*, 292.
68. Tim Fulford, 'Sighing for a Solider: Austen and Military Pride and Prejudice', *Nineteenth-Century Literature* 57 (2002): 153–78.
69. For the power of paper to produce its own standards and systems as well as the concomitant intersection between 'bank-paper' and 'book-paper' see Kevin McLaughlin, *Paperwork: Fiction and Mass Mediacy in the Paper Age* (Philadelpia: University of Pennsylvania Press, 2005).
70. Austen, *Mansfield Park*, 296.
71. Austen, *Mansfield Park*, 300.

72. Austen, *Mansfield Park*, 306.
73. Austen, *Mansfield Park*, 314.
74. Austen, *Mansfield Park*, 307–8.
75. In 'To Eat the Bread of Paraphrase: The Professionalization of Sermon Writing', a paper delivered at the 2008 ASECS conference, Christina Lupton suggested this episode exemplifies how eighteenth-century readers made handwriting the sign of an authentic self. See also her *Knowing Books*.
76. Austen, *Mansfield Park*, 230.
77. Austen, *Mansfield Park*, 231.
78. Austen, *Mansfield Park*, 494–5.
79. Austen, *Mansfield Park*, 501, 509.
80. Austen, *Mansfield Park*, 510.
81. Austen, *Mansfield Park*, 531.
82. Austen, *Mansfield Park*, 529, 524.
83. Austen, *Mansfield Park*, 553.
84. [Sir Walter Scott,] review of Jane Austen, *Emma*, *Quarterly Review* 14 (1815) cited in B. C. Southam, ed., *The Critical Heritage: Jane Austen, Volume 1, 1811–1870* (London: Taylor & Francis, 2005), 70.
85. On political economy in *Emma* see Robert Miles, 'A Fall in the Price of Bread: Speculation and the Real in *Emma*', *Novel* 37 (2003–4): 66–85 and Beth Foakes Tobin, 'The Moral and Political Economy of Property in Austen's *Emma*', *Eighteenth-Century Fiction* 2 (1990): 229–54.
86. For the economic valences of the Waverley Novels see Burgess, *British Fiction*; Ian Duncan, *Scott's Shadow: The Novel in Romantic Edinburgh* (Princeton: Princeton University Press, 2007); Evan Gottlieb, '"To Be at Once Another and the Same": Walter Scott and the End(s) of Sympathetic Britishness', *Studies in Romanticism* (2004): 187–208; Katherine Sutherland, 'Fictional Economies: Adam Smith, Walter Scott and the Nineteenth-Century Novel', *English Literary History* 54 (1987): 97–127.
87. Silvana Colella, 'Monetary Patriotism: *The Letters of Malachi Malagrowther, The Antiquary*, and the Currency Question', *Nineteenth Century Studies* 17 (2003): 53–71; and Lee, 'A Divided Inheritance'.
88. For a full analysis of *The Antiquary* as a novel about the 'curiosity' of the money form, see Rowlinson, *Real Money and Romanticism*, 55–99.
89. My account of the 1825 financial panic is drawn largely from Larry Neal, 'The Financial Crisis of 1825 and the Restructuring of the British Financial System', *Federal Reserve Bank of St. Louis Review* (May/June 1998): 53–76 with some corrections from Michael Bordo, 'Commentary', *Federal Reserve Bank of St. Louis Review* (1998): 77–82.
90. The historian N. T. Phillipson observed in 1968 that the *Letters of Malachi Malagrowther*, which Scott wrote to protest the incursion of centralizing English financial policy on the Scottish 'free banking system', exemplify the general resentment Scottish rural people and Edinburgh elites alike felt toward London's various attempts to integrate the bureaucracies of Scotland and England between 1780 and 1830, though ultimately, Phillipson concluded, like many such campaigns Scott's letters did little more than express an 'ideology of noisy inaction'. See 'Nationalism and Ideology', in *Government and Nationalism in Scotland: An Enquiry by Members of the University of Edinburgh*, ed. J. N. Wolfe (Edinburgh: Edinburgh

University Press, 1969), 186. Caroline McCracken-Flesher in *Possible Scotlands: Walter Scott and the Story of Tomorrow* (Oxford: Oxford University Press, 2005) documents the wide support that Scott's letters received, even from those like Henry Dundas Lord Melville who had originally approved of Parliament's motion. Scott turned to his readers' sense of their own 'otherness' to recharge Scottish nationalism with a new progressive sense of its own difference within a changing British union. Those few scholars who have examined these works in relation to his financial troubles have tended to do so with an eye still trained firmly on the problem of Scottish national identity.

91. Walter Scott, *Letters of Malachi Malagrowther on the Currency*, in *Miscellaneous Prose Works of Sir Walter Scott*, ed. Robert Cadell (Edinburgh: Cadell, 1836), 373.
92. Colella, 'Monetary Patriotism', 58.
93. Scott, *Malachi Malagrowther*, 336.
94. Scott, *Malachi Malagrowther*, 337.
95. Scott, *Malachi Malagrowther*, 337.
96. Scott, *Malachi Malagrowther*, 361.
97. Daniel Dreadnaught, *Familiar Epistles, Letter the First: Addressed to Malachi Malagrowther, Esq.* (London: Griffiths, 1826), 11.
98. John Wilson Croker. *The Croker Papers: The Writings and Correspondence of the Late John Wilson Croker*, ed. Louis J. Jennings (London: Murray, 1884), 3: 318.
99. The *OED* attributes this use of the term 'antiquate' to two sources, an *Edinburgh Review* article of 1821 and a letter from Scott to Lockhart, 1823.
100. Manning, 'Antiquarianism', 63.
101. Walter Scott, *Chronicles of the Canongate*, ed. Claire Lamont (Edinburgh: Edinburgh University Press, 2000), 82.
102. Scott, *Chronicles*, 146.
103. Scott, *Chronicles*, 231.
104. Scott, *Chronicles*, 232.
105. Tara Ghoshal Wallace, 'The Elephant's Foot and the British Mouth: Walter Scott on Imperial Rhetoric', *European Romantic Review* 13 (2002): 311–24 (322).
106. Scott, *Chronicles*, 271.
107. Scott, *Chronicles*, 270.

Conclusion: A Romantic Economy

1. Martineau was also a member of the Society for the Diffusion of Useful Knowledge, which paid for a second series of *Illustrations* in 1836. See Alan Richardson, *Literature, Education, and Romanticism: Reading as a Social Practice, 1789–1832* (Cambridge: Cambridge University Press, 1994), 217–33 and Shelagh Hunter, *Harriet Martineau: The Poetics of Moralism* (Aldershot: Scolar, 1995), 7–59. For Martineau's reading of James Mill see Brian Cooper and Marguerite S. Murphy, 'The Death of the Author at the Birth of Social Science: The Cases of Harriet Martineau and Adolphe Quetelet', *Studies in the History and Philosophy of Science* 31 (2000): 1–36 (6).
2. On Martineau as a popularizer of Ricardo see Robert Blaug, *Ricardian Economics: A Historical Study* (Westport, CT: Greenwood, 1973), 130. Literary studies of the *Illustrations* include Catherine Gallagher, *The Industrial*

Reformation of English Fiction: Social Discourse and Narrative Form, 1832–1867 (Chicago University of Chicago Press, 1985); Elaine Freedgood, 'Banishing Panic: Harriet Martineau and the Popularization of Political Economy', *Victorian Studies* 38 (1995): 33–53; Klaver, *A/Moral Economics*, 53–78.

3. Josiah Conder, '*Illustrations of Political Economy*', *Eclectic Review* 8 (1832): 44–72; William Empson, 'Mrs. Marcet-Miss Martineau', *Edinburgh Review* 57 (1833): 1–39; Edward Bulwer-Lytton, 'On Moral Fictions: Miss Martineau's Illustrations of Political Economy', *New Monthly Magazine* 10 (1833): 146–51; George Poulet Scrope, 'Miss Martineau's Monthly Novels', *Quarterly Review* 49 (1833): 136–52. See also Lisa Scholl, *Translation, Authorship, and the Victorian Professional Woman: Charlotte Brontë, Harriet Martineau, and George Eliot* (Farnham: Ashgate, 2011), 106–8.
4. John Stuart Mill, 'A Tale of the Tyne', *Examiner* (1833): 677–8 (677).
5. Mill, 'A Tale of the Tyne', 677.
6. John Stuart Mill, 'On Miss Martineau's Summary of Political Economy', *The Monthly Repository* 8 (1834): 318–22.
7. Mill, 'On Miss Martineau's Summary', 319.
8. John Stuart Mill, *The Earlier Letters of John Stuart Mill, 1812–1848*, in *The Collected Works of John Stuart Mill, Volume XIII, Letters*, ed. Francis E. Minelea (Toronto: University of Toronto Press, 1963), 152.
9. Mill began the essay in 1831, the year *Illustrations of Political Economy* began to appear, completed it in 1833, and published it in the *London and Westminster Review* in 1836. John Stuart Mill, 'On the Definition of Political Economy and the Method of Investigation Proper to it', in *Essays on Some Unsettled Questions of Political Economy* (London: Parker, 1844), 86–116.
10. Mill, 'Definition', 86.
11. Mill, 'Definition', 88–9.
12. Mill, 'Definition', 89.
13. Mill, 'Definition', 89–90.
14. Mill, 'Definition', 93.
15. Mill, 'Definition', 104.
16. Mill, 'Definition', 114.
17. On the way Mill 'denaturalizes' political economy see Margaret Schabas, 'John Stuart Mill and the Concepts of Nature', *Dialogue* 34 (1995): 447–65.
18. 'The Currency Juggle', *Tait's Edinburgh Magazine* (1833): 461–7, repr. in *The Collected Works of John Stuart Mill, Volume IV, Essays on Economics and Society Part 1*, ed. John M. Robson (Toronto: University of Toronto Press, 1967), 181–92.
19. Mill, 'Currency Juggle', 188.
20. Mill, 'Currency Juggle', 186.
21. Mill, 'Currency Juggle', 186.
22. David Kaufmann, *The Business of Common Life: Novels and Classical Economics Between Revolution and Reform* (Baltimore: Johns Hopkins University Press, 1995), 158.
23. John Stuart Mill, 'Thoughts on Poetry and its Varieties', in *Dissertations and Discussions, Political, Philosophical, and Historical* (London: Longman, 1867), 63–94. 'The Currency Juggle' was also republished in this volume.
24. Mill, 'Thoughts on Poetry', 67–8.
25. Mill, 'De Quincey's Logic of Political Economy', in *The Collected Works of John Stuart Mill, Volume IV, Essays on Economics and Society Part I*, 393.

26. Mill, 'De Quincey's Logic of Political Economy', 395.
27. Mill, 'De Quincey's Logic of Political Economy', 401.
28. John Stuart Mill, 'Coleridge', in *The Collected Works of John Stuart Mill, Volume X, Essays on Ethics, Religion, and Society*, ed. John M. Robson, Introduction by F. E. L. Priestley (Toronto: University of Toronto Press, 1985).
29. On *Bentley's Standard Novels* see St. Clair, *Reading Nation*, 361–4.

Bibliography

A Constant Reader. 'Bullion Report', *The Times* (October 25, 1810): 3.

Allen, Richard. 'The British Nation and the Colonies: *Mansfield Park*', in *Literature and Nation: Britain and India 1800–1900*, ed. Richard Allen and Harish Trivedi. New York: Routledge, 2000, 43–54.

Altieri, Charles. *The Particulars of Rapture: An Aesthetics of Emotion*. Ithaca: Cornell University Press, 2003.

Anderson, Amanda. 'Epistemological Liberalism', *Victorian Studies* 50 (2008): 658–65.

Anderson, Benedict. *Imagined Communities: Reflections on the Origins and Spread of Nationalism*, rev. edn. London: Verso, 1991.

—— 'Nationalism, Identity, and the World-in-Motion: On the Logics of Serality', in *Cosmopolitics: Thinking and Feeling Beyond the Nation*, ed. Bruce Robbins and Pheng Cheah. Minneapolis: University of Minnesota Press, 1998, 117–33.

Anderson, William. *The Iniquity of Banking*. London, 1797.

Andreades, Andreas Michael. *History of the Bank of England, 1640–1903*. London: Frank Cass, 1909.

Annas, Julia. 'Moral Knowledge as Practical Knowledge', *Social Philosophy and Policy* 18 (2001): 236–56.

Anonymous. *Brief Observations on a Late Letter Addressed to the Right Hon. W. Pitt by Walter Boyd, Esq. on the Stoppages of Issue in Specie by the Bank of England*. London: Debrett, 1801.

Appelby, Joyce. 'Locke, Liberalism, and the Natural Law of Money', *Past and Present* 71 (1976): 43–69.

—— *Economic Thought and Ideology in Seventeenth-Century England*. Princeton: Princeton University Press, 1978.

Aram Kaiser, David. *Romanticism, Aestheticism, and Nationalism*. Cambridge: Cambridge University Press, 1999.

Armstrong, Nancy. *Desire and Domestic Fiction: A Political History of the Novel*. Oxford: Oxford University Press, 1987.

—— *How Novels Think: The Limits of Individualism from 1719–1900*. New York: Columbia University Press, 2005.

Arrighi, Giovanni. *The Long Twentieth Century: Money, Power, and the Origin of Our Times*. London: Verso, 1994.

Austen, Jane. *Jane Austen's Letters to her Sister Cassandra and Others*, ed. R. W. Chapman. Oxford: Clarendon Press, 1932.

—— *Mansfield Park*, ed. John Wiltshire, in *The Cambridge Edition of the Works of Jane Austen*. Cambridge: Cambridge University Press, 2005.

—— *Pride and Prejudice*, ed. Pat Rogers, in *The Cambridge Edition of the Works of Jane Austen*. Cambridge: Cambridge University Press, 2006.

Austen-Leigh, Richard A. *Austen Papers, 1704–1856*. Spottiswode: Ballantyne, 1942.

Bagehot, Walter. 'The First Edinburgh Reviewers', *National Review* (1855), in *The Collected Works of Walter Bagehot: The Literary Essays Volume 1*, ed. Norman St. John-Stevas. Cambridge, MA: Harvard University Press, 1965, 309–41.

Baines, Paul. *The House of Forgery in Eighteenth-Century Britain*. Aldershot: Ashgate, 1999.

Balfour, Ian. *The Rhetoric of Romantic Prophecy*. Stanford: Stanford University Press, 2002.

Barcus, James E. ed. *Shelley: The Critical Heritage*. London: Routledge, 1975.

Baring, Sir Francis. *Observations on the Publication of Walter Boyd, M.P.* London: Debrett, 1801.

Barlow, Joel. *The Vision of Columbus*. London, 1787.

Batailles, Georges. *The Accursed Share, Volume 1: Consumption*, trans. Robert Hurley. New York: Zone Books, 1991.

Baucom, Ian. *Specters of the Atlantic: Finance Capital, Slavery, and the Philosophy of History*. Durham: Duke University Press, 2006.

Baudrillard, Jean. 'The Structural Law and Value and the Order of the Simulacra', trans. Charles Levin, in *The Structural Allegory: Reconstitutive Encounters with the New French Thought*, ed. John Fekete. Minneapolis: University of Minnesota Press, 1984, 54–73.

Bellamy, Liz. *Commerce, Morality, and the Eighteenth-Century Novel*. Cambridge: Cambridge University Press, 1998.

Bellanger, Terry. 'Publishers and Writers in Eighteenth-Century England', in *Books and Their Readers in Eighteenth-Century England*, ed. Isabel Rivers. New York: St. Martin's Press, 1982, 1–26.

Bender, John and David E. Wellbery. 'Rhetoricality: On the Modernist Return of Rhetoric', in *The Ends of Rhetoric: History, Theory, Practice*, ed. John Bender and David E. Wellbery. Stanford: Stanford University Press, 1990, 3–39.

Benedict, Barbara. *Curiosity: A Cultural History of Early Modern Inquiry*. Chicago: University of Chicago Press, 2002.

Benjamin, Walter. 'The Work of Art in the Age of Mechanical Reproduction', in *Illuminations*, trans. Harry Zohn, ed. Hannah Arendt. New York: Schocken, 1968, 217–52.

Bentham, Jeremy. *Proposal for the Circulation of a New Species of Paper Currency*. London, 1795.

—— *Paper Mischief Exposed*. London, 1801.

—— *Collected Works of Jeremy Bentham: Correspondence, Volume 9, January 1817 to June 1820*, ed. Steven Conway. Oxford: Oxford University Press, 1993.

Bigelow, Gordon. *Fiction, Famine, and the Rise of Economics in Victorian Britain and Ireland*. Cambridge: Cambridge University Press, 2003.

Blackwell, Mark, ed. *The Secret Life of Things: Animals, Objects, and It-Narratives in Eighteenth-Century England*. Cranbury: Bucknell University Press, 2007.

Blake, William. *Observations on the Principles Which Regulate the Course of Exchange; and on the Present Depreciated State of the Currency*. London, 1810.

Blaug, Robert. *Ricardian Economics: A Historical Study*. Westport, CT: Greenwood, 1973.

Bolter, Jay David and Richard Grusin, eds. *Remediation: Understanding New Media*. Cambridge, MA: MIT Press, 2001.

Bordo, Michael D. 'Commentary', *Federal Reserve Bank of St. Louis Review* (1998): 77–82.

—— *The Gold Standard and Related Regimes*. Cambridge: Cambridge University Press, 1999.

Bosanquet, Charles. *Practical Observations on the Report of the Bullion-Committee*, 2nd corr., with a supplement edn. London: Richardson, 1810.

Boswell, James. *Life of Johnson*, ed. George Birkbeck Hill. New York: Harper, 1891.

Boulukos, George E. 'The Politics of Silence: *Mansfield Park* and the Amelioration of Slavery', *Novel: A Forum on Fiction* 39 (2006): 361–83.

Bourdieu, Pierre. *The Field of Cultural Production*, ed. Randal Johnson. New York: Columbia University Press, 1993.

Bourne, Kenneth and William Banks Taylor, eds. *The Horner Papers: Selections from the Letters and Miscellaneous Writings of Francis Horner MP, 1795–1817*. Edinburgh: Edinburgh University Press, 1994.

Bowen, H. V. 'The Bank of England During the Long Eighteenth Century, 1694–1820', in *The Bank of England: Money, Power, and Influence 1694–1994*, ed. Richard Roberts and David Kynaston. Oxford: Clarendon Press, 1995, 3–20.

—— 'British Conceptions of Global Empire 1756-83' *Journal of Imperial and Commonwealth History* 26 (1998): 1–27.

Boyd, Walter. *A Letter to the Right Honourable William Pitt: On the Influence of the Stoppage of Issues in Specie at the Bank of England: on the Prices of Provisions and other Commodities*. London: Wright, 1801.

Boyle, G. E. and P. T. Geary. 'The Irish Currency Report of 1804', *Central Bank and Financial Services Authority of Ireland Quarterly Bulletin* (2004): 107–24.

Brantlinger, Patrick. *Fictions of State: Culture and Credit in Britain, 1694–1994*. Ithaca: Cornell University Press, 1996.

Brewer, John. *The Sinews of Power: War, Money, and the English State, 1688–1783*. New York: Knopf, 1989.

Brigham, Linda. 'Count Cenci's Abysmal Credit', *Texas Studies in Language and Literature* 38 (1996): 340–58.

Brooks, Cleanth. 'Irony as a Principle of Structure', in David Richter, ed., *The Critical Tradition: Classic Texts and Contemporary Trends*, 3rd edn. Boston: Bedford/St. Martin's Press, 2007, 799–807.

Brougham, Henry. 'Bowles' Reflections at the Conclusion of the War', *Edinburgh Review* 1 (1802): 94–8.

—— 'Increase of Forgeries', *Edinburgh Review* 28 (1818): 203–14.

Brown, Christopher Leslie. *Moral Capital: Foundations of British Abolitionism*. Chapel Hill: University of North Carolina Press, 2006.

Brown, Richard. *Church and State in Modern Britain, 1700–1850*. London: Routledge, 1991.

Buchanan, Claudius. *Christian Researches in Asia with Notices of the Translation of the Scriptures*. New York, 1812.

Bulwer-Lytton, Edward. 'On Moral Fictions: Miss Martineau's Illustrations of Political Economy', *New Monthly Magazine* 10 (1833): 146–51.

Burgess, Miranda. *British Fiction and the Production of Social Order, 1740–1820*. Cambridge: Cambridge University Press, 2000.

Burke, Edmund. *Reflections on the Late Revolution in France*, ed. Conor Cruise O'Brien. Harmondsworth: Penguin, 1969.

Burwick, Frederick. 'De Quincey on Coleridge', in James Vigus and Jane Wright, eds., *Coleridge's Afterlives*. Basingstoke: Palgrave Macmillan, 2008, 36–53.

Butler, Marilyn. *Jane Austen and the War of Ideas*. Oxford: Clarendon Press, 1974.

Byron, George Gordon, Lord. *Letters and Journals*, ed. Leslie Marchand. London: Belknap, 1976.

—— *The Complete Poetical Works*, ed. Jerome J. McGann. Oxford: Clarendon Press Press, 1986.

Caffentzis, Constantine George. *Clipped Coins, Abused Words, and Civil Government: John Locke's Philosophy of Money*. New York: Autonomedia, 1989.

Cain, P. J. and A. G. Hopkins. 'Gentlemanly Capitalism and British Expansion Overseas: I. The Old Colonial System 1688–1850', *Economic History Review* 39 (1986): 501–25.

Cameron, Kenneth Neil. 'Shelley, Cobbett, and the National Debt', *Journal of English and Germanic Philology* 42 (1943): 197–209.

Campbell, Alexander. *The Guinea Note, A Poem by Timothy Twig, Esquire.* Edinburgh: A. Leslie, 1797.

Cannan, Edwin. *The Paper Pound of 1797–1821: A Reprint of the Bullion Report.* London: P. S. King, 1919.

[Canning, George and George Ellis]. 'Sir John Sinclair's Remarks', *Quarterly Review* 5 (1811): 120–38.

Canuel, Mark. 'Coleridge's Polemic Divinity', *English Literary History* 68 (2001): 929–63.

—— *Religion, Toleration, and British Writing, 1790–1830*. Cambridge: Cambridge University Press, 2002.

Carey, Peter. *A Letter to William Huskisson, M.P. On His Late Publication*. London: Richardson, 1811.

Carrier, James G. *Gifts and Commodities: Exchange and Western Capitalism Since 1700*. London: Routledge, 1995.

Chaliss, Christopher Edgar, ed. *A New History of the Royal Mint*. Cambridge: Cambridge University Press, 1992.

Chalmers, George. *Strictures on a Pamphlet Written by Thomas Paine*. London, 1796.

Chalmers, Thomas. *Christian and Civic Economy of Large Towns*. Glasgow, 1821.

Chancey, Karen. 'The Star in the East: The Controversy over Christian Missions to India, 1805–1813', *Historian* 60 (1998): 507–23.

Chandler, James. 'The Pope Controversy: Romantic Poetics and the English Canon', *Critical Inquiry* 10 (1984): 481–509.

—— *England in 1819: The Politics of Literary Culture and the Case of Romantic Historicism*. Chicago: University of Chicago Press, 1998.

Checkland, S. G. 'The Propagation of Ricardian Economics in England', *Economica* 16 (1949): 40–52.

Chown, John F. *A History of Money from AD 800*. London: Routledge, 1994.

Christensen, Jerome. *Lord Byron's Strength: Romantic Writing and Commercial Society*. Baltimore: Johns Hopkins University Press, 1995.

—— 'The Dark Romanticism of the *Edinburgh Review*', in *Romanticism at the End of History*. Baltimore: Johns Hopkins University Press, 2000, 107–28.

Clarkson, Thomas. *History of the Progress and Accomplishment of the Abolition of the Slave Trade*. Philadelphia: Parke, 1808.

Clive, John. *Scotch Reviewers: The* Edinburgh Review, *1802–1815*. London: Faber, 1957.

Cobbett, William. *Paper Against Gold and Glory Against Prosperity: Or, An Account of the Rise, Progress, Extent, and Present State of the Funds and of the Paper-money of Great Britain; and Also of the Situation of that Country as to Its Debt and Other Expenses; Its Navigation, Commerce, and Manufactures; Its Taxes, Population, and Paupers; Drawn from Authentic Documents, and Brought Down to the End of the Year 1814*. London: J. Macreery, 1815.

Cock, Simon. *An Examination of the Report of the Bullion Committee: Shewing [Sic] That the Present High Price of Bullion, Together with the Scarcity of Gold Coin, and Also the Low Rate of the Foreign Exchanges, Are Not Attributable to the Issue of Bank Paper; and Explaining What Are the True Causes by Which These Effects Have Been Produced*. London, 1810.

Colella, Silvana. 'Monetary Patriotism: *The Letters of Malachi Malagrowther, The Antiquary*, and the Currency Question', *Nineteenth-Century Studies* (2003): 53–71.

Coleman, Deidre. 'The Journalist', in *The Cambridge Companion to Coleridge*, ed. Lucy Newlyn. Cambridge: Cambridge University Press, 2002, 126–41.

Coleridge, Samuel Taylor. *Collected Letters of Samuel Taylor Coleridge*, ed. E. L. Griggs Oxford: Clarendon Press, 1956–71.

—— *Notebooks of Samuel Taylor Coleridge*, ed. Kathleen Coburn. London: Routledge & Kegan Paul, 1957–2002.

—— *The Collected Works of Samuel Taylor Coleridge*. Princeton: Princeton University Press, 1969–2009.

—— *The Friend*, ed. Barbara Rooke, vol. 4 of *The Collected Works of Samuel Taylor Coleridge*. London: Routledge, 1969.

—— *Samuel Taylor Coleridge: The Critical Heritage, Volume 2: 1834–1900*, ed. J. R. de. J. Jackson. London: Routledge, 1991.

Colley, Linda. *Britons: Forging the Nation, 1707–1837*. New Haven: Yale University Press, 1992.

Collins, Harry and Robert Evans. *Rethinking Expertise*. Chicago: University of Chicago Press, 2007.

Conder, Josiah. '*Illustrations of Political Economy*', *Eclectic Review* 8 (1832): 44–72.

Connell, Philip. *Romanticism, Economics, and the Question of 'Culture'*. Oxford: Oxford University Press, 2001.

Cooper, Brian and Marguerite S. Murphy. 'The Death of the Author at the Birth of Social Science: The Cases of Harriet Martineau and Adolphe Quetelet', *Studies in the History and Philosophy of Science* 31 (2000): 1–36.

Copeland, Edward. 'The Austens and the Elliots: A Consumer's Guide to *Persuasion*', in *Jane Austen's Business: Her World and Her Profession*, ed. Juliet McMaster and Bruce Stovel. Basingstoke: Macmillan, 1996, 136–53.

—— *Women Writing About Money: Women's Fiction in England 1790–1820*. Cambridge: Cambridge University Press, 2004.

Copleston, Edward. *A Letter to the Right Honourable Sir Robert Peel, MP for the University of Oxford, on the Pernicious Effects of a Variable Standard of Value: especially as it Regards the Condition of the Lower Orders and the Poor Laws*. Oxford: Murray, 1819.

—— 'State of the Currency', *Quarterly Review* 27 (1822): 239–67.

Corbett, Mary Jean. *Allegories of Union in Irish and English Writing, 1790–1870: Politics, History, and the Family from Edgeworth to Arnold*. Cambridge: Cambridge University Press, 2000.

Cox, Jeffrey N. *Poetry and Politics in the Cockney School: Keats, Shelley, Hunt and their Circle*. Cambridge: Cambridge University Press, 1998.

Craig, Sir John. *Newton at the Mint*. Cambridge: Cambridge University Press, 1946.

—— *The Mint: A History of the London Mint from A.D. 287 to 1948*. Cambridge: Cambridge University Press, 1953.

Crawford, Robert. *Devolving English Literature*. Oxford: Clarendon Press, 1992.

Croker, John Wilson. *The Croker Papers: The Writings and Correspondence of the Late John Wilson Croker*, ed. Louis J Jennings. London: Murray, 1884.

Cronin, Richard. *Romantic Victorians: English Literature, 1824–1840*. Basingstoke: Palgrave Macmillan, 2007.

Crowley, Tony. *Standard English and the Politics of Language*, 2nd edn. Basingstoke: Palgrave Macmillan, 2003.

Crozier, W., ed. *Shyness and Embarrassment: Perspectives from Social Psychology*. Cambridge: Cambridge University Press, 1990.

Cruikshank, James. *Observations on Money, as the Medium of Commerce Shewing [sic] the Present Circulating Medium of this Country to be Defective in Those Requisites which a Medium of Commerce Ought to Possess, and Pointing Out in What Manner the Defect May be Remedied; and Also The Real Effect that a Greater or Less Quantity of Circulating Medium has on the Country: Together with Remarks on the Present State of the Nation: to which are subjoined a few practical inferences*. London: Richardson, 1811.

Cullen, L. M. 'The Irish Economy in the Eighteenth Century', in *The Formation of the Bank of Ireland*, ed. L. M. Cullen. Cork: Mercier, 1969, 9–21.

Daston, Lorraine and Peter Gallison. 'Epistemological Liberalism', *Victorian Studies* 50 (2008): 658–65.

Davis, Leith. *Acts of Union: Scotland and the Literary Negotiation of the British Nation 1707–1830*. Stanford: Stanford University Press, 1998.

de Bolla, Peter. *The Discourse of the Sublime: Readings in History, Aesthetics, and the Subject*. Oxford: Basil Blackwell, 1989.

De Quincey, Thomas. *The Collected Writings of Thomas De Quincey*, ed. David Masson. Edinburgh, 1890.

—— *The Works of Thomas De Quincey*, ed. Grevel Lindop. 21 vols. London: Pickering & Chatto, 2000–3.

Deane, Seamus. *Strange Country: Modernity and Nationhood in Irish Writing Since 1790*. Oxford: Clarendon Press, 1997.

Delaney, Paul. *Literature, Money, and the Market from Trollope to Amis*. Basingstoke: Palgrave Macmillan, 2002.

Derrida, Jacques. *Given Time I: Counterfeit Money*, trans. Peggy Kamuf. Chicago: University of Chicago Press, 1994.

Dick, Alexander. '"The Ghost of Gold": Forgery Trials and the Standard of Value in Shelley's Mask of Anarchy', *European Romantic Review* (2007): 381–400.

Dickson, P. G. M. *The Financial Revolution: A Study of the Development of Public Credit, 1688–1756*. Basingstoke: Macmillan, 1967; Aldershot: Gregg Revivals, 1993.

Dodd, Nigel. *The Sociology of Money: Economics, Reason, and Contemporary Society*. Cambridge: Polity Press, 1994.

Dodd, William. *The Convict's Address to his Unhappy Brethren*. London, 1777.

—— *Thoughts in Prison: in Five Parts. To Which Are Added, His Last Prayers, Written in the Night Before His Death and Other Miscellaneous Pieces*. London, 1777.

Downie, A. J. 'Public Opinion and the Political Pamphlet', in *The Cambridge History of English Literature 1660–1780*, ed. John Richetti, Cambridge: Cambridge University Press, 2005, 549–71.

Dreadnaught, Daniel. *Familiar Epistles, Letter the First: Addressed to Malachi Malagrowther, Esq*. London: Griffiths, 1826.

Duncan, Ian. 'Edinburgh, Capital of the Nineteenth Century', in *Romantic Metropolis: The Urban Scene of British Culture, 1780–1840*, ed. James Chandler and Kevin Gilmartin. Cambridge: Cambridge University Press, 2005, 45–64.

—— *Modern Romance and Transformations of the Novel: The Gothic, Scott, Dickens*. Cambridge: Cambridge University Press, 2005.

—— *Scott's Shadow: The Novel in Romantic Edinburgh*. Princeton: Princeton University Press, 2007.

Dyer, Alan W. 'Making Semiotic Sense of Money as a Medium of Exchange', *Journal of Economic Issues* 23 (1989): 503–10.

Eagleton, Terry. *The Ideology of the Aesthetic*. Oxford: Basil Blackwell, 1990.

Easton, Fraser. 'The Political Economy of *Mansfield Park*: Fanny Price and the Atlantic Working Class', *Textual Practice* 12 (1998): 459–88.

Eatwell, J., M. Milgate, and P. Newman, eds. *The New Palgrave Dictionary of Economics*. Basingstoke: Macmillan, 1987.

Edgeworth, Maria. *Letters from England, 1813–1844*, ed. Christina Colvin. Oxford: Clarendon Press, 1971.

—— *The Absentee*, ed. W. J. McCormack and Kim Walker. Oxford: Oxford University Press, 1988.

Eichengreen, Barry. *Globalizing Capital: A History of the International Monetary System*. Princeton: Princeton University Press, 1996.

Eley, George. 'Nations, Publics, and Political Cultures: Placing Habermas in the Nineteenth Century', in *Habermas and the Public Sphere*, ed. C. Calhoun. Cambridge, MA: MIT Press, 1992, 289–339.

Elfenbein, Andrew. *Romanticism and the Rise of English*. Stanford: Stanford University Press, 2009.

Elgie, Robert and Helen Thompson. *The Politics of Central Banks*. London: Routledge, 1998.

Eliot, Simon. '1825–1826: Years of Crisis?' in *The Edinburgh History of the Book in Scotland Vol. 3, Industry and Ambition 1800–1880*, ed. Bill Bell. Edinburgh: Edinburgh University Press, 2007, 91–5.

[Ellis, George]. 'Huskisson, on the Depreciation of Currency', *Quarterly Review* 4 (1810).

[Empson, William]. 'Mrs. Marcet-Miss Martineau', *Edinburgh Review* 115 (1833): 1–39.

Engell, James. 'Wealth and Words: Pope's *Epistle to Bathurst*', *Modern Philology* 85 (1988): 433–46.

Erickson, Lee. *The Economy of Literary Form*. Baltimore: Johns Hopkins University Press, 1996.

Esterhammer, Angela. 'Coleridge in the Newspapers, Periodicals, and Annuals', in *The Oxford Handbook to Samuel Taylor Coleridge*, ed. Frederick Burwick. Oxford: Oxford University Press, 2009, 165–84.

Feather, John. *A History of British Publishing*. London: Routledge, 1988.

Ferguson, Niall. *The Ascent of Money: A Financial History of the World*. New York: Penguin, 2008.

Fermanis, Porsha. 'Isabella, Lamia, and Merry Old England', *Essays in Criticism* 56 (2006): 139–62.

Ferris, Ina. *The Romantic National Tale and the Question of Ireland*. Cambridge: Cambridge University Press, 2007.

Fetter, Frank W. *Development of British Monetary Orthodoxy, 1797–1875*. Cambridge, MA: Harvard University Press, 1965.

Finkelstein, Andrea. *Harmony and the Balance: An Intellectual History of Seventeenth-Century English Economic Thought*. Ann Arbor: University of Michigan Press, 2000.

Finn, Margot C. *The Character of Credit: Personal Debt in English Culture, 1740–1914*. Cambridge: Cambridge University Press, 2003.

Fish, Stanley. *There's No Such Thing as Free Speech, and It's a Good Thing*. New York: Oxford University Press, 1994.

Fonblanque, John de Grenier. *Doubts as to the Expediency of Adopting the Recommendation of the Bullion Committee*. London: Chapple, 1810.

Fontana, Biancamaria. *Rethinking the Politics of Commercial Society: The Edinburgh Review, 1802–1832*. Cambridge: Cambridge University Press, 1985.

Forster, E. M. *Marianne Thornton*. London: A. Deutsch, 2000.

Foucault, Michel. *Discipline and Punish: The Birth of the Prison*, trans. Alan Sheridan. New York: Vintage, 1979.

Freedgood, Elaine. 'Banishing Panic: Harriet Martineau and the Popularization of Political Economy', *Victorian Studies* 38 (1995): 33–53.

Fried, Daniel. 'The Politics of the Coleridgean Symbol', *Studies in English Literature, 1500–1900* 46 (2006): 763–79.

Fulford, Tim. *Romantic Masculinities: Gender, Politics, and Poetics in the Writings of Burke, Coleridge, Cobbett, Wordsworth, De Quincey, and Hazlitt*. Basingstoke: Palgrave Macmillan, 1999.

—— 'Apocalyptic Economics and Prophetic Politics: Radical and Romantic Responses to Malthus and Burke', *Studies in Romanticism* 40 (2001): 345–68.

—— 'Sighing for a Solider: Austen and Military Pride and Prejudice', *Nineteenth-Century Literature* 57 (2002): 153–78.

Furniss, Tom. *Edmund Burke's Aesthetic Ideology: Language, Gender, and Political Economy in Revolution*. Cambridge: Cambridge University Press, 1993.

Gallagher, Catherine. *The Industrial Reformation of English Fiction: Social Discourse and Narrative Form, 1832–1867*. Chicago: University of Chicago Press, 1985.

—— *Nobody's Story: The Vanishing Acts of Women in the Marketplace, 1670–1820*. Berkeley: University of California Press, 1994.

—— *The Body Electric: Life, Death, and Sensation in Political Economy and the Victorian Novel*. Princeton: Princeton University Press, 2006.

Galperin, William. *The Historical Austen*. Philadelphia: University of Pennsylvania Press, 2003.

Garside, Peter and Elizabeth McDonald. 'Evangelicalism and *Mansfield Park*', *Trivium* 10 (1975): 34–50.

Gatrell, V. A. C. *The Hanging Tree: Execution and the English People, 1770–1868*. Oxford: Oxford University Press, 1994.

Gellner, Ernest T. *Nations and Nationalism*, ed. R. I. Moore. Oxford: Basil Blackwell, 1983.

Giddens, Anthony. *The Consequences of Modernity*. Stanford: Stanford University Press, 1990.

Gil Harris, Jonathan. *Sick Economies: Drama, Mercantilism, and Disease in Shakespeare's England*. Philadelphia: University of Pennsylvania Press, 2004.

Gilbert, Emily and Eric Helleiner, eds. *Nation-States and Money: The Past, Present, and Future of National Currencies*. London: Routledge, 1999.

Gilmartin, Kevin. *Print Politics: The Press and Radical Opposition in Early-Nineteenth Century England*. Cambridge: Cambridge University Press, 1996.

—— *Writing Against Revolution: Literary Conservatism in Britain, 1790–1832*. Cambridge: Cambridge University Press, 2007.

Gittings, Robert. *The Keats Inheritance*. London: Heinemann, 1964.

Giuseppi, John. *The Bank of England: A History from its Foundations in 1694*. London: Evans, 1966.

Goffman, Erving. 'Embarrassment and Social Organization', *American Journal of Sociology* 62 (1956): 264–71.

—— *The Presentation of Self in Everyday Life*. New York: Anchor, 1959.
Goodlad, Lauren. *Victorian Literature and the Victorian State: Character and Governance in a Liberal Society*. Baltimore: Johns Hopkins University Press, 2003.
Goodman, Kevis. *Georgic Modernity and British Romanticism: Poetry and the Mediation of History*. Cambridge: Cambridge University Press, 2004.
Gottlieb, Evan. '"To Be at Once Another and the Same': Walter Scott and the End(s) of Sympathetic Britishness', *Studies in Romanticism* 43 (2004): 187–208.
Gould, J. D. *The Great Debasement: Currency and the Economy in Mid-Tudor England*. Oxford: Clarendon Press, 1970.
Goux, Jean-Joseph. *Symbolic Economics After Marx and Freud*. Ithaca: Cornell University Press, 1990.
Gray, Richard T. 'Hypersign, Hypermoney, Hypermarket: Adam Muller's Theory of Money and Romantic Semiotics', *New Literary History* 31 (2000): 293–314.
—— 'Economic Romanticism: Monetary Nationalism in Johann Gottlieb Fichte and Adam Muller', *Eighteenth-Century Studies* 36 (2003): 535–57.
Great Britain. Parliament. House of Commons Select Committee on the High Price of Gold Bullion. *Report, Together with Minutes of Evidence, and Accounts, from the Select Committee on the High Price of Gold Bullion*. London: Ridgway, 1810.
Grenfell, John. *A Defence of Bank Notes against the Opinions Which Have Been Published in the Morning Chronicle, Cobbett's Register, and a Recent Pamphlet, Entitled the High Price of Bullion, a Proof of the Depreciation of Bank Notes, with Observations on the Balance of Trade and the Course of Exchange*. London: Richardson, 1810.
Groom, Nick. *The Forger's Shadow: How Forgery Changed the Course of Literature*. London: Picador, 2002.
Guillory, John. *Cultural Capital: The Problem of Literary Canon Formation*. Chicago: University of Chicago Press, 1995.
Habermas, Jürgen. *The Structural Transformation of the Public Sphere: An Inquiry into the Category of Bourgeois Society*, trans. Thomas Burger and Frederick Lawrence. Cambridge, MA: MIT Press, 1991.
Halmi, Nicholas. *The Genealogy of the Romantic Symbol*. Oxford: Oxford University Press, 2007.
Hamilton, Paul. 'Romantic Economies and the Sublimation of Money', *Wordsworth Circle* 26 (1995): 79–81.
—— *Coleridge and German Philosophy: A Poet in the Land of Logic*. London: Continuum, 2007.
Handler, Philip. 'The Limits of Discretion: Forgery and the Jury at the Old Bailey 1818–21', in *'The Dearest Birthright of the People of England': The Jury in the History of the Common Law*, ed. John W. Cairns and Grant McLeod. Oxford and Portland, OR: Hart, 2002, 155–72.
Harding, Anthony John. *Coleridge and the Inspired Word*. Montreal: McGill-Queen's University Press, 1985.
Haskell, T. 'Capitalism and the Origins of the Humanitarian Sensibility', parts 1 and 2, in *The Antislavery Debate: Capitalism and Abolitionism as a Problem in Historical Interpretation*, ed. T. Bender. Berkeley: University of California Press, 1992, 107–60.
Havelock, Eric A. *The Muse Learns to Write: Reflections on Orality and Literacy from Antiquity to the Present*. New Haven: Yale University Press, 1986.
Hayek, F. A. von. 'Introduction' to Henry Thornton, *An Enquiry into the Nature and Effects of the Paper Credit of Great Britain*. London: Allen & Unwin, 1939, 11–65.

Hazlitt, William. *Essay on the Principles of Human Action*. London, 1805.
—— *Political Essays, with Sketches of Public Characters*. London: Hone, 1819.
—— *Table Talk: Opinions on Books, Men, and Things*. New York: Wiley and Putnam, 1845.
Heinzelman, Kurt. 'Self-Interest and the Politics of Composition in Keats's Isabella', *English Literary History* 55 (1988): 159–93.
Helleiner, Eric. *The Making of National Money: Territorial Currencies in Historical Perspective*. Ithaca: Cornell University Press, 2003.
Henderson, Andrea. *Romanticism and the Painful Pleasures of Modern Life*. Cambridge: Cambridge University Press, 2008.
Henkin, David M. 'Promiscuous Circulation: the Case of Paper Money', in *City Reading: Written Words and Public Spaces in Antebellum New York*. New York: Columbia University Press, 1998, 137–65.
Herbert, Christopher. *Culture and Anomie: Ethnographic Imagination in the Nineteenth Century*. Chicago: University of Chicago Press, 1991.
Herman, Arthur. *How the Scots Invented the Modern World: The True Story of How Western Europe's Poorest Nation Created Our World and Everything in It*. New York: Crown, 2001.
Hewitt, Virginia. 'Applegarth's Answers: Anti-forgery Note Designs for the Bank of England, 1818–1821', in *Proceedings of the XIth International Numismatic Congress Organized for the 150th Anniversary of the Société Royale de Numismatique de Belgique, Brussels, September 8th–13th, 1991*. Vol. IV, ed. Tony Hackins and Ghislaine Moucharte. Louvain-la-Neuve: International Numismatic Commission, 1993, 219–27.
Hewitt, Virginia and J. M. Keyworth. *As Good as Gold: 300 Years of British Bank Note Design*. London: British Museum Publications, 1994.
Heywood, Ian. 'Paper Promises: Restriction, Caricature, and the Ghost of Gold', *Romanticism, Forgery, and the Credit Crisis. Romantic Praxis*. Special Issue (2012).
Hill, John. *An Inquiry into the Causes of the Present High Price of Gold Bullion in England and Its Connection with the State of Foreign Exchanges, with Observations on the Report of the Bullion Committee: In a Series of Letters Addressed to Thomas Thompson, Esq. M.P., One of the Members of the Bullion Committee*. London: Longman, 1810.
Hilton, Boyd. *Corn, Cash, and Commerce: The Economic Policies of the Tory Government, 1815–30*. Oxford: Oxford University Press, 1977.
—— *The Age of Atonement: The Influence of Evangelicalism on Social and Economic Thought, 1795–1865*. Oxford: Clarendon Press, 1988.
Hirschman, Albert O. *The Passions and the Interests: Political Arguments for Capitalism Before its Triumph*, repr. Princeton: Princeton University Press, 1997.
Hoagwood, Terence Allan. *Skepticism and Ideology: Shelley's Political Prose and its Philosophical Context from Bacon to Marx*. Iowa City: University of Iowa Press, 1988.
Hogle, Jerrold. *Shelley's Process: Radical Transference and the Development of His Major Works*. Oxford: Oxford University Press, 1988.
—— 'Shelley and the Conditions of Meaning', in *Evaluating Shelley*, ed. Timothy Clark and Jerrold E. Hogle. Edinburgh: Edinburgh University Press, 1996, 48–74.
Hole, Robert. *Pulpits, Politics, and Public Order in England, 1760–1832*. Cambridge: Cambridge University Press, 1989.
Hone, William. *John Wilke's Catechism* THAT IS TO SAY, *An Instruction, to be learned of every Person before he be brought to be confirmed a Placeman or Pensioner by the Minister*. London, 1817.

Hood, Thomas. *Complete Poetical Works of Thomas Hood*. London: G. P. Putnam, 1878.

Horner, Francis. 'Thornton on the Paper Credit of Great Britain', *Edinburgh Review* 1 (1802): 172–201.

—— 'Lord King's Thoughts on the Restriction of Payments in Specie at the Banks of England and Ireland', *Edinburgh Review* 4 (1803): 402–21.

—— *The Horner Papers: Selections from the Letters of Miscellaneous Writings of Francis Horner MP, 1795–1817*, ed. Kenneth Bourne and William Banks Taylor. Edinburgh: Edinburgh University Press, 1994.

Horwitz, Steven. 'Monetary Exchange as an Extra-Linguistic Social Communication Process', in *Individuals, Institutions, and Interpretations: Hermeneutics Applied to Economics*, ed. David L. Prychitko. Aldershot: Avebury, 1995, 154–75.

Houghton, John W. *Culture and Currency: Cultural Bias in Monetary Theory and Policy*. Boulder, CO: Westview, 1991.

Hughes, Paul L. and James Francis Larkin, eds. *Tudor Royal Proclamations*. New Haven: Yale University Press, 1964–9.

Hume, David. *Essays Moral, Political, and Literary*, ed. Eugene F. Miller. Indianapolis: Liberty, 1986.

Hume, Joseph. *Thoughts on the New Coinage with Reflections on Money and Coins and a New System of Coins and Weights on a Simple and Uniform Principle*. London: Stockdale, 1816.

Hunt, Leigh, ed. *The Examiner*. London: J. Hunt, 1808–21.

—— *Selected Writings of Leigh Hunt. Volume 2: Periodical Essays, 1815–1824*, ed. Greg Kucich and Jeffrey N. Cox. London: Pickering & Chatto, 2003.

Hunter, Ian. *Culture and Government: The Emergence of Literary Education*. Basingstoke: Macmillan, 1988.

Hunter, J. Paul. *Before Novels: The Cultural Contexts of Eighteenth-Century English Fiction*. New York: Norton, 1990.

Hunter, Leslie. *The Scottish Education System*. Oxford: Pergamon, 1968.

Hunter, Shelagh. *Harriet Martineau: The Poetics of Moralism*. Aldershot: Scolar, 1995.

Huskisson, William. *The Question Concerning the Depreciation of Our Currency Stated and Examined*. London: Murray, 1810.

Hutch, Ronald K. and Paul R. Ziegler, eds. *Joseph Hume: The People's MP*. Philadelphia: American Philosophical Society, 1986.

Hutchison, T. W. 'Berkeley's Querist and its Place in the Economic Thought of the Eighteenth Century', *British Journal for the Philosophy of Science* 4 (1953): 52–77.

Ingham, Geoffrey. 'On the Underdevelopment of the "Sociology of Money"', *Acta Sociologica* 41 (1998): 3–18.

Ingrassia, Catherine. *Authorship, Commerce, and Gender in Early Eighteenth-Century England*. Cambridge: Cambridge University Press, 1998.

Jack, Ian. *Keats and the Mirror of Art*. Oxford: Clarendon Press, 1967.

Jackson, Heather. *Romantic Readers: The Evidence of Marginalia*. New Haven: Yale University Press, 2005.

Jackson, Randall. *The Speech of Randall Jackson, Esq. delivered at the General Court of the Bank of England, held on the 20th of September, 1810, respecting the Report of the Bullion Committee of the House of Commons; with Notes on the Subject of that Report*. London: Richardson, 1810.

Jager, Colin. '*Mansfield Park* and the End of Natural Theology', *Modern Language Quarterly* 63 (2002): 31–63.

Jeffrey, Francis. 'Mournier, de l'Influence des Philosophes, Francs-Maçons, et Illuminées, sur la Revolution de France', *Edinburgh Review* 1 (1802): 1–18.

—— 'Madame de Stael, De La Littérature', *Edinburgh Review* 21 (1813): 1–50.

Jenkinson, Charles. *A Treatise on the Coins of the Realm: In a Letter to the King*. 1805. Repr. London: J. J. W. Birch and Je. R. Grenfell, 1880.

Johnson, Carl L. 'The Realms of Gold', *Keats–Shelley Journal* 9 (1960): 6–10.

Johnson, Samuel. *The Adventurer and the Idler*, in *The Works of Samuel Johnson in Nine Volumes*. Vol. 4. Oxford: Talboy and Wheeler, 1825.

Jones, Steven. *Shelley's Satire: Violence, Exhortation, and Authority*. DeKalb: Northern Illinois University Press, 1994.

Kaufman, Robert. 'Negatively Capable Dialectics: Keats, Vendler, Adorno, and the Theory of the Avant-Garde', *Critical Inquiry* 27 (2001): 354–84.

—— 'Shelley's Defense of Adorno', *English Literary History* 63 (1996): 707–33.

Kaufmann, David. *The Business of Common Life: Novels and Classical Economics Between Revolution and Reform*. Baltimore: Johns Hopkins University Press, 1995.

Keach, William. 'Shelley and the Revolutionary Left', in *Evaluating Shelley*, ed. Timothy Clark and Jerrold E. Hogle. Edinburgh: Edinburgh University Press, 1996, 75–90.

Keats, John. *The Letters of John Keats*, ed. Hyder Edward Rollins, 2 vols. Cambridge, MA: Harvard University Press, 1958.

—— *The Complete Poems*, ed. John Barnard. London: Penguin, 1973.

—— *Complete Poems*, ed. Jack Stillinger. Cambridge, MA: Harvard University Press, 1978.

Keen, Paul. *The Crisis of Literature in the 1790s Print Culture and the Public Sphere*. Cambridge: Cambridge University Press, 1999.

Kelley, Theresa M. 'Keats, Ekphrasis, and History', in *Keats and History*, ed. Nicholas Roe. Cambridge: Cambridge University Press, 1995, 212–37.

Kelly, Gary. 'Jane Austen's Real Business: The Novel, Literature, and Cultural Capital', in *Jane Austen's Business: Her World and Her Profession*, ed. Juliet McMaster and Bruce Stovel. Basingstoke: Macmillan, 1996, 154–67.

Keynes, John Maynard. 'Social Consequences of Changes in the Value of Money', in *Essays in Persuasion*. 1923. *Collected Writings of John Maynard Keynes*, Vol. 9. Cambridge: Cambridge University Press, 1978.

Khalip, Jacques. 'Virtual Conduct: Disinterested Agency in Hazlitt and Keats', *English Literary History* 73 (2006): 885–912.

King, Lord Peter. *Thoughts on the Restriction of Specie at the Banks of England and Ireland*. London, 1803.

Kingsman, William. *A Letter to the Right Honourable Sir John Sinclair, Bart. (Author of the History of the Revenue, and Other Fugitive Pieces,) on the Subject of His Remarks on Mr. Huskisson's Pamphlet*, 2nd edn. London: J. Ridgway, 1811.

Kittler, Friedrich. *Discourse Networks, 1800/1900*, trans. Michael Metteer, with Chris Cullens. Foreword by David Wellbery. Stanford: Stanford University Press, 1990.

Klancher, Jon P. *The Making of English Reading Audiences, 1790–1832*. Madison: University of Wisconsin Press, 1987.

Klaver, Claudia. *A/Moral Economics: Classical Political Economy and Cultural Authority in Nineteenth-Century England*. Columbus: Ohio State University Press, 2002.

Koster, John Theodore. *Short Statement, of the Trade in Gold Bullion; Shewing the True Causes of the General Scarcity and Consequent High Price of That Precious Metal; Also, Demonstrating That the Notes of the Bank of England Are Not Depreciated*. 2nd enlarged edn. Liverpool: T. Cadell and W. Davies, 1811.

Kreisel, Deanna. *Economic Woman: Demand, Gender, and Narrative Closure in Eliot and Hardy*. Toronto: University of Toronto Press, 2011.

Kucich, John. *Repression in Victorian Fiction: Charlotte Brontë, George Eliot, and Charles Dickens*. Berkeley: University of California Press, 1987.

Kuduk Weiner, Stephanie. *Republican Politics and English Poetry, 1789–1874*. New York: Palgrave Macmillan, 2005.

Kynaston, David. 'The Bank of England and the Government', in *The Bank of England: Money, Power, and Influence, 1694–1994*, ed. Richard Roberts and David Kynaston. Oxford: Clarendon Press, 1995, 19–55.

Laidler, David. 'The Bullion Controversy', in *The New Palgrave Dictionary of Economics*, ed. John Eatwell, Murray Milgate, and Peter Newman. Basingstoke: Palgrave Macmillan, 1987, 289–94.

Lamb, Charles and Mary. *The Letters of Charles and Mary Lamb*. London: Taylor & Francis, 1978.

Lapp, Robert Keith. *Contest for Cultural Authority: Hazlitt, Coleridge, and the Distresses of the Regency*. Detroit: Wayne State University Press, 1999.

Lauderdale, James Maitland. *The Depreciation of the Paper Currency of Great Britain Proved*. London and Edinburgh: Printed for Longman Hurst Rees Orme and Brown; Constable and Co., 1812.

Leader, Zachery. 'Coleridge and the Uses of Journalism', in *Grub Street and the Ivory Tower: Literary Journalism and Literary Scholarship from Fielding to the Internet*, ed. Jeremy Treglown and Bridget Bennett. Oxford: Clarendon Press, 1998, 22–40.

Leask, Nigel. *The Politics of Imagination in Coleridge's Critical Thought*. Basingstoke: Macmillan, 1988.

Lee, Yoon Sun, 'A Divided Inheritance: Scott's Antiquarian Novel and the British Nation', *English Literary History* 64 (1997): 537–67.

Levinson, Marjorie. *Keats's Life of Allegory*. Oxford: Basil Blackwell, 1988.

Locke, John. *Further Considerations Concerning Raising The Value Of Money; Wherein Mr. Lowndes's Arguments For It In His Late Report Concerning An Essay For The Amendment Of The Silver Coins, Are Particularly Examined*, in *Locke on Money*, ed. P. H. Kelly. Oxford: Clarendon Press, 1991.

Lockhart, John Gibson. 'Ricardo and the Edinburgh Review', *Blackwood's Edinburgh Magazine* (October 1818): 58–62. Reprinted in *David Ricardo: Critical Responses*, ed. Terry Peach. London: Routledge, 2003, 99–106.

[Lowe, Joseph]. 'Huskisson on the Depreciation of Our Currency', *Monthly Review* 63 (1810): 413.

—— 'Monthly Catalogue: Politics', *Monthly Review* 63 (1810): 435.

—— 'On the Bullion Report and Mr. Huskisson's Pamphlet', *The Times* (December 4, 1810): 3.

—— 'On the Report of the Bullion Committee', *Monthly Review* 63 (1810): 464.

—— 'Ricardo, Grenfell, Mushet, Sir P. Francis, and others on the Depreciation of Banknotes', *Monthly Review* 63 (1810): 182.

—— 'Sir John Sinclair's *Observation on the Report of the Bullion Committee*', *Monthly Review* 63 (1810): 288.

—— 'Blake's *Observations on the State of the Exchange*', *Monthly Review* 64 (1811): 1.

Lupton, Christina. *Knowing Books: Consciousness of Mediation in Eighteenth-Century Britain*. Philadelphia: University of Pennsylvania Press, 2012.

Lynch, Deirdre Shauna. *The Economy of Character: Novels, Market Culture, and the Business of Inner Meaning*. Chicago: University of Chicago Press, 1998.

Lyons, F. S. L., ed. *Bicentenary Essays: Bank of Ireland, 1783–1983*. London: Gill and Macmillan, 1983.

Mackie, John L. *Ethics: Inventing Right and Wrong*. Harmondsworth: Penguin, 1977.

Malthus, Thomas Robert. *The Works of Thomas Robert Malthus, Volume 2: An Essay on the Principle of Population*, ed. E. A. Wrigley and David Souden. London: Pickering, 1986.

—— *The Works of Thomas Robert Malthus, Volume 7: Essays on Political Economy*, ed. E. A. Wrigley and David Souden. London: Pickering, 1986.

Malton, Sarah. *Forgery in Nineteenth-Century Literature and Culture: Fictions of Finance from Dickens to Wilde*. Basingstoke: Palgrave Macmillan, 2009.

Manning, Susan. 'Antiquarianism, the Scottish Science and Man, and the Emergence of Modern Disciplinarity', in *Scotland and the Borders of Romanticism*, ed. Leith Davis, Ian Duncan, and Janet Sorenson. Cambridge: Cambridge University Press, 2004, 57–76.

Marshall, Ebenezer. *A History of the Union of Scotland and England Stating the Circumstances Which Brought that Event Forward to a Conclusion and the Advantages Resulting From it To the Scots*. Edinburgh, 1799.

Massumi, Brian. *Parables for the Virtual: Movement, Affect, Sensation*. Durham: Duke University Press, 2002.

Mattras, Leonora. *William Cobbett: The Politics of Style*. Cambridge: Cambridge University Press, 1995.

Mazzeo, Tillar. *Plagiarism and Literary Property in the Romantic Period*. Philadelphia: University of Pennsylvania Press, 2007.

McCormick, Ted. 'Alchemy in the Political Arithmetic of Sir William Petty', *Studies in the History and Philosophy of Science* 37 (2006): 290–307.

McCracken-Flesher, Caroline. *Possible Scotlands: Walter Scott and the Story of Tomorrow*. Oxford: Oxford University Press, 2005.

McCulloch, J. R. 'Ricardo's Political Economy', *Edinburgh Review* 20 (1818): 59–87.

—— 'Economical and Secure Currency', *Edinburgh Review* 21 (1818): 54–79.

—— *A Collection of Scarce and Valuable Tracts on Money*. London, 1856.

—— *A Collection of Scarce and Valuable Tracts and Other Publications on Paper Money and Banking*. London, 1857.

McCusker, John J. 'The Demise of Distance: the Business Press and the Origins of the Information Revolution in the Early Modern Atlantic World', *American Historical Review* 110 (2005): 295–321.

McDonagh, Josephine. 'Debt and Desire: De Quincey and the Psychology of Economics', *Wordsworth Circle* 25 (1994): 86–89.

McGowan, Randall. 'From Pillory to Gallows: The Punishment of Forgery in the Age of the Financial Revolution', *Past and Present* 165 (1999): 107–40.

McKendrick, Neil, John Brewer, and J. H. Plumb. *The Birth of Consumer Society: The Commercialization of Eighteenth-Century England*. Bloomington: Indiana University Press, 1982.

McKeon, Michael. *The Origin of the English Novel, 1600–1740*. Baltimore: Johns Hopkins University Press, 1987.

McLane, Maureen. *Romanticism and the Human Sciences: Poetry, Population, and the Discourse of the Species*. Cambridge: Cambridge University Press, 2000.

McLaughlin, Kevin. *Paperwork: Fiction and Mass Mediacy in the Paper Age*. Philadelphia: University of Pennsylvania Press, 2005.

McLuhan, Marshall and Quentin Fiore. *The Medium is the Massage: An Inventory of Effects*. New York: Gingko, 2001.

Meacham, S. *Henry Thornton of Clapham, 1760–1815*. Cambridge, MA: Harvard University Press, 1964.

Mellor, Anne. *Mothers of the Nation: Women's Political Writing in England, 1780–1830*. Bloomington: Indiana University Press, 2000.

Mercator. *Considerations on the Present State of Bank Notes, Specie, and Bullion; in a Series of Letters Addressed to the Right Honorable [Sic]— In Two Parts*. London: Printed for the Author, and sold by David Arnot; John Lake; Sherwood and Co.; And all other Booksellers, 1811.

Miles, Robert. 'What is a Romantic Novel?' *Novel: A Forum on Fiction* 34 (2001): 180–201.

—— 'A Fall in the Price of Bread: Speculation and the Real in *Emma*', *Novel* 37 (2003–4): 66–85.

—— *Romantic Misfits*. Basingstoke: Palgrave Macmillan, 2008.

—— 'New Historicism, New Austen, New Romanticism', in *Romanticism, History, Historicism: Essays on an Orthodoxy*, ed. Damian Walford Davies. London: Routledge, 2009, 182–202.

Mill, James. 'Smith on Money and Exchange', *Edinburgh Review* 7 (1808).

Mill, John Stuart. 'A Tale of the Tyne', *Examiner* (1833): 677–8.

—— 'On Miss Martineau's Summary of Political Economy', *The Monthly Repository* 8 (1834): 318–22.

—— 'On the Definition of Political Economy and the Method of Investigation Proper to it', *London and Westminster Review* (1836).

—— *Essays on Some Unsettled Questions of Political Economy*. London: Parker, 1844, 86–116.

—— *Dissertations and Discussions, Political, Philosophical, and Historical*. London: Longman, 1867.

—— *The Collected Works of John Stuart Mill*, ed. John M. Robson. Toronto: University of Toronto Press, 1963–71.

Miller, D. A. *The Novel and the Police*. Berkeley: University of California Press, 1988.

Mitchell, Robert. *Sympathy and the State in the Romantic Era: Systems, State Finance, and the Shadows of Futurity*. London: Routledge, 2007.

Mole, Tom. *Byron's Romantic Celebrity: Industrial Culture and the Hermeneutics of Intimacy*. Basingstoke: Palgrave Macmillan, 2007.

Monaghan, David. '*Mansfield Park* and Evangelicalism: A Reassessment', *Nineteenth-Century Fiction* 3 (1978): 215–30.

Moore, Thomas. *Odes Upon Corn, Cash, and Catholics, and Other Matters, Selected from the Columns of the Times Journal*. London: Longman, 1828

More, Hannah. *Strictures on the Modern System of Female Education with A View of the Principles and Conduct Prevalent Among Women of Rank and Fortune*. London: Cadell, 1799.

—— *Coelebs in Search of a Wife: Comprehending Observations of Domestic Habits and Manners, Religion and Morals*. London: Cadell, 1809.

—— *Practical Piety, or, The Influence of the Religion of the Heart on the Conduct of Modern Life*. London: Cadell, 1811.

Morgan, E. V. 'Some Aspects of the Bank Restriction Period, 1797–1821', *Economic History* 3 (1939): 205–21.

Morgan, William. *Additional Facts Addressed to the Serious Attention of the People of Great Britain, Respecting the Expenses of the War and the State of the National Debt*. Debrett, 1796.

Motion, Andrew. *Wainwright the Poisoner*. London: Faber, 2001.

Mulcaire, Terry. 'Public Credit; or The Feminization of Virtue in the Marketplace', *PMLA* 114 (1999): 1029–42.

Muldrew, Craig. 'Interpreting the Market: The Ethics of Credit and Community Relations in Early Modern England', *Social History* 18 (1993): 163–8.

—— *The Economy of Obligation: The Culture of Credit and Social Relations in Early Modern England*. Basingstoke: Macmillan, 1998.

—— 'Hard Food for Midas: Cash and its Social Value in Early Modern England', *Past and Present* 170 (2001): 78–120.

Mulvihill, James. *Upstart Talents: Rhetoric and the Career of Reason in English Romantic Discourse, 1790–1820*. Newark: University of Delaware Press, 2004.

Murphy, Antoin E. 'Paper Credit and the Multi-Personae Mr. Henry Thornton', *European Journal of the History of Economic Thought* 10 (2003): 429–53.

Myers, Victoria. 'Blasphemy Trials and *The Cenci*: Parody as Performative', in *Spheres of Action: Speech and Performance in Romantic Culture*, ed. Alexander Dick and Angela Esterhammer. Toronto: University of Toronto Press, 2009, 100–23.

Nangle, Benjamin Christie. *The Monthly Review Second Series, 1790–1815: Index of Contributors and Articles*. Oxford: Clarendon Press, 1955.

Neal, Larry. *The Rise of Financial Capitalism: International Capital Markets in the Age of Reason*. Cambridge: Cambridge University Press, 1990.

—— 'The Financial Crisis of 1825 and the Restructuring of the British Financial System', *Federal Reserve Bank of St. Louis Review* (May/June 1998): 53–76.

New Annual Register, or General Repository of History, Politics, and Literature for the Year 1801. London: Robinson, 1802.

Newman, Gerald. *The Rise of English Nationalism: A Cultural History, 1740–1830*. Basingstoke: Macmillan, 1987.

Ngai, Sinnae. *Ugly Feelings*. Cambridge, MA: Harvard University Press, 2009.

Nicholson, Colin. *Writing and the Rise of Finance: Capital Satires of the Early Eighteenth Century*. Cambridge: Cambridge University Press, 1994.

Nussbaum, Martha. *Upheavals of Thought: The Intelligence of Emotions*. Cambridge: Cambridge University Press, 2003.

O'Gorman, Frances, ed. *Victorian Literature and Finance* Oxford: Oxford University Press, 2007.

O Grada, Cormac. 'Reassessing the Irish Pound Report of 1804', *Bulletin of Economic Research* 43 (1991): 5–19.

Osborne, John W. 'Cobbett's Anti-Semitism', *The Historian* 47 (1984): 86–92.

Osteen, Mark and Martha Woodmansee. 'Taking Account of the New Economic Criticism: An Historical Introduction', in *The New Economic Criticism*, ed. Osteen and Woodmansee. London: Routledge, 1999, 3–50.

P., I. W. 'On the Price of Bullion and Circulation of Paper', *The Times* (October 19, 1810): 2.

Paine, Thomas. *Dissertation on Government, the Affairs of the Bank, and Paper Money*. Philadelphia, 1786.

—— *The Decline and Fall of the English System of Finance*. Paris, 1796.

Park, You-Me and Rajeswari Sunder Rajan, eds. *The Postcolonial Jane Austen*. New York: Routledge, 2004.

Parliamentary History of England, From the Earliest Period to the Year 1803, 36 vols. London: T. C. Hansard, 1806–18.

Parnell, Henry. *The Principles of Currency and Exchange*. London, 1809.

Parsons, Wayne. *The Power of the Financial Press: Journalism and Economic Opinion in Britain and America*. New Brunswick: Rutgers University Press, 1989.

Pasley, C. W. *Essay on the Military Policy and Institutions of the British Empire*. London: Edmund Lloyd, 1811.

Peacock, Thomas Love. *The Works of Thomas Love Peacock*. London: Richard Bentley, 1875.

Perkin, Harold. *The Origins of Modern English Society, 1780–1880*. London: Routledge, 1969.

Petrella, Frank. 'George Berkeley's Theory of Economic Policy and Classical Economic Liberalism', *Southern Economic Journal* 32 (1966): 275–84.

Pfau, Thomas. *Romantic Moods: Paranoia, Trauma, and Melancholy, 1790–1840*. Stanford: Stanford University Press, 2005.

Phillipson, N. T. 'Nationalism and Ideology', in *Government and Nationalism in Scotland: An Enquiry by Members of the University of Edinburgh*, ed. J. N. Wolfe. Edinburgh: Edinburgh University Press, 1969.

Pitt, William. *The Bullion Debate: A Serio-Comic Satiric Poem*. London: Longman, 1811.

Pocock, J. G. A. *The Machiavellian Moment: Florentine Political Thought and the Atlantic Republican Tradition*. Princeton: Princeton University Press, 1975.

—— *Virtue, Commerce, and History: Essays on Political Thought and History, Chiefly in the Eighteenth Century*. Cambridge: Cambridge University Press, 1985.

Polanyi, Karl. *The Great Transformation: The Political and Economic Origins of Our Time*. Boston: Beacon, 1944.

Poovey, Mary. *A History of the Modern Fact: Problems of Knowledge in the Sciences of Wealth and Society*. Chicago: University of Chicago Press, 1998.

—— 'Writing about Finance in Victorian England: Disclosure and Secrecy in the Culture of Investment', *Victorian Studies* 45 (2002): 17–41.

—— ed. *The Financial System in Nineteenth-Century Britain*. Oxford: Oxford University Press, 2003.

—— *Genres of the Credit Economy: Mediating Value in Eighteenth- and Nineteenth-Century Britain*. Chicago: University of Chicago Press, 2008.

Pope, Alexander. *The Major Works*, ed. Pat Rogers. Oxford: Oxford University Press, 1993.

Pottinger, George. *Heirs of the Enlightenment: Edinburgh Reviewers and Writers, 1800–1830*. Edinburgh: Scottish Academic Press, 1992.

'Preface' to *Annals of the Fine Arts* 3 (1818): iii–viii.

Price, Richard. *Observations on the proper method of keeping the Accounts, and determining from year to year the state of the Society for Equitable Assurances on Lives & Survivorships*. London, 1774.

—— 'Of the Security of a Virtuous Course', in *Sermons by Richard Price and Joseph Priestley*. London, 1830.

—— *A Review of the Principal Questions of Morals*, ed. D. D. Raphael. Oxford: Clarendon Press, 1984.

Priestley, Joseph. *Lectures on History and General Policy*. London: Johnson, 1788.

Pyle, Forest. *The Ideology of Imagination: Subject and Society in the Discourse of Romanticism*. Stanford: Stanford University Press, 1995.

Rabuzzi, Daniel A. 'Eighteenth-Century Commercial Mentalities as Reflected and Projected in Business Handbooks', *Eighteenth-Century Studies* 29 (2005): 169–89.

Radzinowicz, Leon. *A History of English Criminal Law and Its Administration from 1750*, Vol. 1. London: Stevens and Sons, 1948.

Rajan, Tilottama. 'Keats, Poetry, and "The Absence of Work"', *Modern Philology* 95 (1998): 334–51.

Rashid, Salim. 'Edward Copleston, Robert Peel, and Cash Payments', *History of Political Economy* 15 (1983): 249–59.

—— 'Political Economy as Moral Philosophy: Dugald Stewart of Edinburgh', *Australian Economic Papers* 26 (1987): 145–56.

Raven, James. *Judging New Wealth: Popular Publishing and Responses to Commerce in England, 1750–1800*. Oxford: Clarendon Press, 1992.

Redish, Angela. 'The Evolution of the Gold Standard in England', *Journal of Economic History* 50 (1990): 789–805.

Reisman, D. A. 'Henry Thornton and Classical Monetary Economics', *Oxford Economic Papers* New Series 23 (1971): 70–89.

Rena-Dozier, Emily. 'Hannah More and the Invention of Narrative Authority', *English Literary History* 71 (2004): 209–27.

Report Together With the Minutes of Evidence and Accounts from the Select Committee on the High Prince of Gold Bullion. London: Johnson, 1810.

Ricardo, David. *The High Price of Bullion a Proof of the Depreciation of Bank Notes*. London: Murray, 1810.

—— *Observations on Some Passages in an Article in the Edinburgh Review on the Depreciation of Paper Currency: Also Suggestions for Securing to the Public a Currency as Invariable as Gold, with a Very Moderate Supply of That Metal: Being the Appendix to the Fourth Edition of 'the High Price of Bullion,' &C*. London; Edinburgh; Dublin: Printed for J. Murray; William Blackwood; M. N. Mahon, 1811.

—— *Reply to Mr. Bosanquet's Practical Observations on the Report of the Bullion Committee*. London; Edinburgh; and Dublin: Printed for J. Murray; William Blackwood; and M. N. Mahon, 1811.

—— 'Letter to the *Morning Chronicle on Randle Jackson's "Bank Speech"*', *Morning Chronicle* (Sept. 24, 1810), in *Minor Papers on the Currency Question 1809–23*, ed. Jacob Hollander. Baltimore: Johns Hopkins University Press, 1932, 79–80.

—— *The Works and Correspondence of David Ricardo*, ed. Piero Sraffa. Cambridge: Cambridge University Press, 1951–73.

Richardson, Alan. *Literature, Education, and Romanticism: Reading as Social Practice, 1780–1832*. Cambridge: Cambridge University Press, 1996.

Richardson, Samuel. *Pamela*, ed. Thomas Keymer and Alice Wakely. Oxford: Oxford University Press, 2001.

Ricks, Christopher. *Keats and Embarrassment*. Oxford: Clarendon Press, 1984.

Rogers, Deborah. 'The Commercialization of Eighteenth-Century English Literature', *Clio* 18 (1989): 171–8.

Rose, Mark. 'The Author as Proprietor: *Donaldson v. Becket* and the Genealogy of Modern Authorship', *Representations* 23 (1988): 51–85.

Ross, Trevor. 'Copyright and the Invention of Tradition', *Eighteenth-Century Studies* 26 (1992): 1–28.

Rotten-Rag Manufactory!!! The Threadneedle-Street Catechism; or, Bank-Bubble Exposed: Appointed By No-Directors, To be Read in All Public and Private Houses

Throughout the United Kingdom, for the Instruction of John Bull and Family in the History and Mystery of Bank Notes, 7th edn. London: Fairburn, 1818.

Rowlinson, Matthew. *Real Money and Romanticism*. Cambridge: Cambridge University Press, 2010.

Rudings, Roger. *Annals of the Coinage of Great Britain and Its Dependencies*, 3rd edn. London: Hearne, 1840.

Russell, Gillian. '"Faro's Daughters": Female Gamesters, Politics, and the Discourse of Finance in 1790s Britain', *Eighteenth-Century Studies* 33 (2000): 481–504.

Russett, Margaret. *De Quincey's Romanticism: Canonical Minority and the Forms of Transmission*. Cambridge: Cambridge University Press, 1997.

—— *Fictions and Fakes: Forging Romantic Authenticity, 1760–1845*. Cambridge: Cambridge University Press, 2006.

Ruthven, K. K. 'Keats and "Dea Moneta"', *Studies in Romanticism* 15 (1976): 445–59.

—— *Faking It*. Cambridge: Cambridge University Press, 2001.

Ryan, Dermot. '"A New Description of Empire": Edmund Burke and the Regicide Republic of Letters', *Eighteenth-Century Studies* 44 (2010): 1–19.

Rzepka, Charles. '"Cortez: Or Balboa, Or Somebody Like That": Form, Fact, and Forgetting in Keats's "Chapman's Homer" Sonnet', *Keats–Shelley Journal* 51 (2002): 35–75.

Said, Edward. *Culture and Imperialism*. New York: Vintage, 1994.

Sanjiv Roberts, Daniel. *Revisionary Gleam: De Quincey, Coleridge, and the High Romantic Argument*. Liverpool: Liverpool University Press, 2000.

Sargeant, Thomas and François R. Velde. *The Big Problem of Small Change*. Princeton: Princeton University Press, 2002.

Schabas, Margaret. 'John Stuart Mill and the Concepts of Nature', *Dialogue* 34 (1995): 447–65.

—— *The Natural Origins of Economics*. Chicago: University of Chicago Press, 2005.

Schabas, Margaret and Carl Wennderlind, eds. *David Hume's Political Economy*. London: Routledge, 2006.

Schoenfield, Mark. *British Periodicals and Romantic Identity: The 'Literary Lower Empire'*. Basingstoke: Palgrave Macmillan, 2009.

Scholl, Lisa. *Translation, Authorship, and the Victorian Professional Woman: Charlotte Brontë, Harriet Martineau, and George Eliot*. Farnham: Ashgate, 2011.

Schudson, Michael. 'Embarrassment and Erving Goffman's Idea of Human Nature', *Theory and Society* 13 (1984): 633–48.

Schwartz, Lewis M. 'Keats' Critical Reception in Newspapers of his Day', *Keats–Shelley Journal* 21–2 (1972–3): 37–52.

Scott, Grant F. 'Beautiful Ruins: The Elgin Marbles Sonnet in its Historical and Generic Contexts', *Keats–Shelley Journal* 39 (1990): 123–50.

Scott, Walter. *Letters of Malachi Malagrowther on the Currency. Miscellaneous Prose Works of Sir Walter Scott*, ed. Robert Cadell. Edinburgh: Cadell, 1836.

—— *The Edinburgh Edition of the Waverley Novels*, ed. David Hewitt. Edinburgh: Edinburgh University Press, 1993–2012.

[Scrope, George Poulet]. 'Miss Martineau's Monthly Novels', *Quarterly Review* 49 (1833): 136–52.

Sedgwick, Eve Kosofsky. *Touching Feeling: Affect, Pedagogy, Performance*. Durham: Duke University Press, 2003.

Sedgwick, Eve Kosofsky and Adam Frank, *Shame and Its Sisters: A Silvan Tomkins Reader*. Durham: Duke University Press, 1995.

Seglin, George. 'Steam, Hot Air, and Small Change: Matthew Boulton and the Reform of Britain's Coinage', *Economic History Review* 56 (2003): 478–509.

Selinger, Evan. 'Expertise and Public Ignorance', *Critical Review* 15 (2003): 375–86.

Selinger, Evan and Robert Crease, eds. *The Philosophy of Expertise*. New York: Columbia University Press, 2006.

Shell, Marc. *The Economy of Literature*. Baltimore: Johns Hopkins University Press, 1978.

Shelley, Percy. *The Complete Works of Percy Bysshe Shelley*, ed. Roger Ingpen and Walter E. Peck. New York: Gordian, 1965.

—— *Shelley's Poetry and Prose*, ed. Donald H. Reiman and Sharon B. Powers. New York: Norton, 2002.

Sherman, Sandra. *Finance and Fictionality in the Early Eighteenth Century: Accounting for Defoe*. Cambridge: Cambridge University Press, 1996.

Siberling, N. J. 'Financial and Monetary Policy of Great Britain during the Napoleonic Wars', *The Quarterly Journal of Economics* 38 (1924): 214–33; 397–439.

Simmel, Georg. *The Philosophy of Money*, ed. David Frisby, trans. Tom Bottomore and David Frisby. London: Routledge, 1990.

Sinclair, John. *Observations on the Report of the Bullion Committee*. London: Bulmer, 1810.

—— *Political Maxims Regarding Coin and Paper Currency*. Edinburgh, 1810.

—— *The Speech of the Right Honourable Sir John Sinclair, Bart. On the Subject of the Bullion Report in the House of Commons, on Wednesday, the 15th of May, 1811*. London: B. McMillan, 1811.

Siskin, Clifford. *The Historicity of Romantic Discourse*. Oxford: Oxford University Press, 1988.

—— *The Work of Writing: Literature and Social Change in Britain, 1700–1830*. Baltimore: Johns Hopkins University Press, 1999.

Smith, Adam. *An Inquiry into the Nature and Causes of the Wealth of Nations*, ed. R. H. Campbell and A. S. Skinner. Oxford: Clarendon Press, 1976.

Smith, Barbara Hernstein. *Contingencies of Value: Alternative Perspectives for Critical Theory*. Cambridge, MA: Harvard University Press, 1988.

Smith, Joseph. *An Examination of Mr. Paine's Decline and Fall of the English System of Finance in a letter to a Friend*. London, 1796.

Smith, J. V. 'Reflections on the Popular Enlightenment of Early Nineteenth-Century Scotland', in *Scottish Culture and Scottish Education 1800–1900*, ed. Walter M. Huens and Hamish M. Paterson. Edinburgh: John Donald, 1983.

Smith, Thomas. *The Bullion Question Impartially Discussed in an Address to the Editors of the* Edinburgh Review. London, 1812.

—— *Letter to the Right Honourable the Earl of Liverpool on the Proposed New Coinage*. London, 1816.

—— *A Reply to Mr. Ricardo's Proposals for an Economical and Secure Currency*. London, 1816.

Snelling, Thomas. *A View of the Silver Coin and Coinage of Scotland*. Edinburgh, 1774.

Southam, B. C., ed. *The Critical Heritage: Jane Austen, Volume 1, 1811–1870*. London: Taylor & Francis, 2005.

Southey, Robert. *Letters from England*. New York, 1808.

St. Clair, William. *The Reading Nation in the Romantic Period*. Cambridge: Cambridge University Press, 2007.

Stafford, Fiona. 'The *Edinburgh Review* and the Representation of Scotland', in *British Romanticism and the* Edinburgh Review: *Bicentenary Essays*, ed. Massimiliano Demata and Duncan Wu. Basingstoke: Palgrave Macmillan, 2002, 33–57.

Starr, G. Gabrielle. 'Ethics, Meaning, and the Work of Beauty', *Eighteenth-Century Studies* 35 (2002): 361–78.

Steuart, Sir James. *Principles of Banks and Banking as Coin and Paper with the Consequences of Any Excessive Issue on the National Currency, Course of Exchange, Price of Provisions, Commodities, and Fixed Incomes*. London: J. Davies, 1810.

—— *An Inquiry into the Principles of Political Economy* (1767), ed. Andrew S. Skinner, Noboru Kobayashi, and Hiroshi Mizuta. London: Pickering & Chatto, 1998.

Stewart, Dugald. *Collected Writings of Dugald Stewart*, ed. William Hamilton. Edinburgh: Constable, 1854–60.

Stewart, Susan. *Crimes of Writing: Problems in the Containment of Representation*. Durham: Duke University Press, 1994.

Stott, Anne. *Hannah More: The First Victorian*. Oxford: Oxford University Press, 2003.

Sussman, Nathan. 'William Huskisson and the Bullion Controversy, 1810', *European Journal of the History of Economic Thought* 4 (1997): 237–57.

Sutherland, John. 'The British Book Trade and the Crash of 1826', *The Library* 9 (1987): 148–61.

Sutherland, Katherine. 'Fictional Economies: Adam Smith, Walter Scott and the Nineteenth-Century Novel', *English Literary History* 54 (1987): 97–127.

Taylor, Charles. 'The Politics of Recognition', in *Multiculturalism: Examining the Politics of Recognition*, ed. Amy Gutman. Princeton: Princeton University Press, 1994, 25–74.

—— *Modern Social Imaginaries*. Durham: Duke University Press, 2004.

—— *A Secular Age*. Cambridge, MA: Harvard University Press, 2007.

Taylor, John. *Money for the Million, or Straw for the Tale of Bricks*. London: Tailant and Allen, 1857.

Terada, Rei. *Feeling in Theory: Emotion After the Death of the Subject*. Cambridge, MA: Harvard University Press, 2001.

Thompson, E. P. *The Making of the English Working Class*. New York: Pantheon, 1963.

Thornton, Henry. *An Enquiry into the Nature and Effects of the Paper Credit of Great Britain*. London: Hatchard, 1802.

Tobin, Beth Foakes. 'The Moral and Political Economy of Property in Austen's *Emma*', *Eighteenth-Century Fiction* 2 (1990): 229–54.

Tratner, Michael. 'Derrida's Debt to Milton Friedman', *New Literary History* 34 (2003): 791–806.

Trotter, Coutts. *The Principles of Currency and Exchanges Applied to the Report from the Select Committee of the House of Commons, Appointed to Inquire into the High Price of Gold Bullion, &C. &C.* London, 1810.

Trumpener, Katie. *Bardic Nationalism: The Romantic Novel and the British Empire*. Princeton: Princeton University Press, 1997.

Turner, Stephen. 'What is the Problem with Experts?' *Social Studies of Science* 31 (2001): 123–49.

Valenze, Deborah. *The Social Life of Money in the English Past*. Cambridge: Cambridge University Press, 2006.

Vardy, Alan. 'Her Father's "Remains": Sara Coleridge's Edition of *Essays on His Own Times*', in *Nervous Reactions: Victorian Recollections of Romanticism*, ed. Joel Faflak and Julia Wright. Albany: SUNY Press, 2004, 207–27.

Wakefield, Daniel. *A Letter to Thomas Paine, in reply to his Decline and Fall of the English System of Finance*. London, 1796.

Wakefield, Edward. *Account of Ireland, Statistical and Political*. London: Longman, 1811.

Waldron, Mary. 'The Frailties of Fanny: *Mansfield Park* and the Evangelical Movement', *Eighteenth Century Fiction* 6 (1994): 259–81.

Wallace, Tara Ghoshal. 'The Elephant's Foot and the British Mouth: Walter Scott on Imperial Rhetoric', *European Romantic Review* 13 (2002): 311–24.

Walters, Gwyn. 'The Booksellers in 1759 and 1774: The Battle for Literary Property', *Library* 29 (1974): 287–315.

Ware, Sir James. *The History and Antiquities of Ireland*. Dublin, 1705.

Warner, William B. *Licensing Entertainment: The Elevation of Novel Reading in Britain, 1684–1750*. Berkeley: University of California Press, 1998.

Waterman, A. M. C. *Revolution, Economics, and Religion: Christian Political Economy, 1798–1833*. Cambridge: Cambridge University Press, 1991.

Weatherall, David. *David Ricardo: A Biography*. Boston: Martinus Nijhoff, 1976.

Weber, Samuel. *Mass Mediarus: Form, Technics, Media*. Stanford: Stanford University Press, 1996.

Wennerlind, Carl. 'Money Talks, but What is it Saying? Semiotics of Money and Social Control', *Journal of Economic Issues* 35 (2001): 557–74.

—— 'Credit-Money as the Philosopher's Stone: Alchemy and the Coinage Problem in Seventeenth-Century England', in *Oeconomics in the Age of Newton*, ed. Margarate Schabas and Neil De Marchi. *History of Political Economy* 35 (2003): 235–62.

—— 'The Death Penalty as Monetary Policy: The Practice and Punishment of Monetary Crime, 1690–1830', *History of Political Economy* 36 (2004): 129–59.

Wharton, Richard. *Remarks on the Jacobinical Tendency of the Edinburgh Review*. London, 1809.

Whately, Christopher A. *Scottish Society, 1707–1830: Beyond Jacobitism, Towards Industrialization*. Manchester: Manchester University Press, 2000.

Whitaker, T. K. 'Origins and Consolidation, 1783–1826', in *Bicentenary Essays: Bank of Ireland 1783–1983*, ed. F. S. L. Lyons. London: Gill and Macmillan, 1983, 11–29.

White, Daniel. *Early Romanticism and Religious Dissent*. Cambridge: Cambridge University Press, 2006.

White, Gabrielle D. V. *Jane Austen in the Context of Abolition: 'A fling at the slave trade'*. Basingstoke: Palgrave Macmillan, 2006.

Williams, Raymond. 'Means of Communication as Means of Production', in *Problems in Materialism and Culture: Selected Essays*. London: New Left Books, 1980, 50–63.

Wilson, John. 'Political Economy: Essay II', *Blackwood's Edinburgh Magazine* 16 (1824): 34–45.

Wilson, Kathleen. *The Sense of the People: Politics, Culture, and Imperialism in England 1715–1785*. Cambridge: Cambridge University Press, 1995.

Winch, Donald. *Riches and Poverty: An Intellectual History of Political Economy in Britain, 1750–1834*. Cambridge: Cambridge University Press, 1996.

Wood, Marcus. *Radical Satire and Print Culture, 1790–1832*. Oxford: Clarendon Press, 1994.

Woodmansee, Martha. 'The Genius and the Copyright: Economic and Legal Conditions for the Emergence of "the Author"', *Eighteenth-Century Studies* 17 (1984): 425–48.

Wooler, T. J. *Black Dwarf*. London, 1817–24.

Zelizer, Viviana. *The Social Meaning of Money: Pin Money, Paychecks, Poor Relief, & Other Currencies*. New York: Basic Books, 1994.

Index

CPSIA information can be obtained at www.ICGtesting.com
Printed in the USA
LVOW13*1730190314

378094LV00012B/311/P

9 781137 292919